Evaluation Thesaurus

Fourth Edition

"The rules of the game: learn everything, read everything,
inquire into everything... "

From "Reflections on the composition of *Memoirs of Hadrian*" by Marguerite Yourcenar (the first woman elected to join 'the immortals' of the French Academy, in 1981)

Evaluation Thesaurus

Fourth Edition

Michael Scriven

SAGE PUBLICATIONS
The International Professional Publishers
Newbury Park   London   New Delhi

For information address:

 SAGE Publications, Inc.
2455 Teller Road
Newbury Park, California 91320

SAGE Publications Ltd.
6 Bonhill Street
London EC2A 4PU
United Kingdom

SAGE Publications India Pvt. Ltd.
M-32 Market
Greater Kailash I
New Delhi 110 048 India

Printed in the United States of America

Library of Congress Cataloging-in-Publication Data

Scriven, Michael.
 Evaluation thesaurus / Michael Scriven. — 4th ed.
   p.   cm.
 ISBN 0-8039-4363-6 (c). — ISBN 0-8039-4364-4 (p)
 1. Evaluation — Dictionaries. I. Title.
AZ191.S37   1991
025.4'9 — dc20   91-9264
                                                    CIP

92 93 94 10 9 8 7 6 5 4 3

Sage Production Editor: Susan McElroy

CONTENTS

PREFACE

OBJECTIVES

This is a book about evaluation in the everyday sense in which it refers to the process of determining the merit, worth, or value of things—or to the result of that process. The field of evaluation includes many substantial and well-recognized subareas such as product evaluation, personnel evaluation, program evaluation, policy evaluation, proposal and performance evaluation—the latter includes, for example, the evaluation of student work on tests, of soloists at concerts, and of athletic performances. Efforts to make one or another of these fields more systematic, objective, and explicit have gone on for a long time—at least three thousand years—but recently one of the subareas has become the focus of a great increase of effort at development, and considerable success.

That area is program evaluation. It entered a new era in the late 1960s, and has since become a widely accepted field of research and investigation. The most obvious *cause* of this boom in the United States—parallel developments were occurring in Canada, Sweden, and West Germany—was the decision by Congress to fund some very large educational programs, programs for which it mandated and funded evaluation. The most obvious *effects* were the emergence of a self-conscious new field and a substantial cadre of practitioners. One aim of this book is to serve as a guidebook to that new field—to its wide range of terminology, models, techniques, and positions—and as a source for some practical checklists, ideas, and procedures which are not available elsewhere. However, the guidebook function is not restricted to program evaluation; the book contains substantial although by no means comprehensive coverage of the concepts and terminology of the other fields of evaluation already mentioned, and of other areas where evaluation is used such as the crafts and physical disciplines.

The book has a second function. The new field of program evaluation soon bloomed with creative ideas about what was referred to as 'the nature of evaluation'—in fact, it was just program evaluation—and enlightening models of its practice and nature. But none of these, not even the sum of these, provided a sound concept of a new *discipline* by contrast with a new *field of research*. The models and the discussions of them share serious limitations and serious flaws. An attempt is made here to explain these problems, to solve them, and to integrate the solutions into a radically different conception of evaluation. The introductory essay that follows this preface is devoted to providing a general sense of the premises and procedures of this view of evaluation.

NOTES

Format: The fourth edition of the *Evaluation Thesaurus* (*ET4*) is intended to serve as a text–cum–reference–guide to evaluation, treated from the point of view described above. It developed from a 1977 pamphlet with the same title, and the dictionary definition of the term "thesaurus", rather than Roget's interpretation of it, still applies to this much larger, very different, and now completely rewritten work: "a book containing a store of words or information about a particular field or set of concepts" (*Webster III*); "a treasury or storehouse of knowledge" (*Oxford English Dictionary*); "any dictionary, encyclopedia, or comprehensive reference book" (*Random House Dictionary*, 2nd Edition unabridged). Some may feel that a few entries are too partisan to include in a reference work, but the intent is to provide a reference to evaluation as seen from a particular point of view, and that necessarily means criticism of other views. If the partisanship seems to disqualify the book as a reference, one might view it as a very short text (the introductory essay "The Nature of Evaluation") with a very long annotated glossary. This format is of course unconventional for texts—and there are good reasons for the usual format—but there are some trade-off advantages to the format used here. It is very difficult to find a good logical order in which to approach evaluation—a massively multidisciplinary subject—without wading through a great deal of water too deep for many readers and too shallow for many others. With *ET4*, readers can make their own selection of branches to follow, in terms of difficulty and interest, and skip past the rest. Linear subjects do best with linear texts; evaluation may tolerate a branching approach.

The format does have one of the advantages of browsing library shelves—while looking for one item, others catch one's eye and sometimes prove interesting. And for some people, the bite-size chunking by entries has attractions by comparison with the sometimes very long chapters of a standard text. It may even qualify as bedtime reading for sleepy scholars. If that seems too close to dreaming, riffle the pages and see if you can resist stopping to check on a couple of items. You *could* resist the temptation? Clearly not an inquiring mind.

Alternatives: We already have at least four encyclopedias in three fields of evaluation, anthologies, many texts in the conventional format, and many works providing glossaries. But for some readers, the larger compendia contain more than they want or wish to purchase while the texts contain too little; their glossaries are quite brief. All are restricted to program evaluation or educational evaluation, whereas this covers, albeit briefly, many other areas—and many hundreds of topics within program evaluation that the others do not mention. Finally, neither the references nor the glossaries attempt an overview, whereas this effort is woven around an overview. Each approach has its advantages and disadvantages.

Uses: Although this book is intended to be read by professionals in many fields for personal and professional interest, and by the well-educated general reader, there are several ways in which it can be used for instructional purposes. It can serve as a supplementary text for instructors who wish to use a more conventional primary text with *ET4* as background or wish to develop basic topics in their own way and provide tailored strings of references in *ET4* for other topics. Or one can use it as a primary text, providing the students with a customized sequence of topics to cover, and supplementing this approach with worked examples or another text. Two thousand of my doctoral students have used *ET3* in this way by starting with the Key Evaluation Checklist entry and following the branches from it, then doing the same with some other major threads such as personnel evaluation. Despite the fact that this kind of combination text and reference work is unfamiliar and involves substantial compromises, their anonymous ratings have been higher than when using a conventional text by the same author.

Errors: A book with the range of this one cannot add 110,000 words without adding errors, and the original 60,000, although rewritten for this edition, probably still have their own quota. The publisher has a record of supporting regular revisions if they achieve any significant sales—and perhaps the existence of four editions will speak for the author's interest in improvement. The author would be most appreciative of corrections, additions, and other suggestions; because he also does the typesetting, identification of typos is appreciated. Please mail them to him at P.O. Box 69, Point Reyes, CA94956 or fax to (415) 663-1913.

<u>Bookdisks:</u> Between editions, the book is steadily revised in electronic form. That format—referred to here as a "bookdisk"—has drawbacks compared to hardcopy, but provides some advantages that should be taken into account when evaluating it. (i) Bookdisks are much *faster* to search than by using standard indexes[1]; (ii) they are much *easier* to search—typing three letters and the Return key beats lengthy bouts of two-way page-turning (and does not require touch-typing skills); (iii) the search is *more reliable* than all but the very best current scholarly indexing[2]; (iv) the document itself is *more up to date* than the last printed version (this advantage increases quickly with time); (v) one can *instantly change the layout and font*—its family, style or size—to one the reader prefers[3]; (vi) with a small accessory, the document can jump modalities and *read itself out loud*, providing an instant book for the sight-impaired reader (who can also initiate the search without touch-typing skills); (vii) only in this form can one *find all references* to a word in a thesaurus—for example, to a name, reference or year—since thesauri like this are 'indexed' by topics only; (viii) one can *cut and paste passages* into other documents, for detailed annotation, discussion, and quotation; (ix) the *storage space* required for a library of bookdisks is about 3% of that required for books[4]; (x) we have already reached the point where the space occupied by a small computer that

---

[1] For example, the best word processor for dealing with long documents (Nisus) will find an occurrence of any term or phrase in the 170,000 words in this work in about a second, without preindexing. Even Microsoft Word only takes an average of 12 seconds (maximum of 25 seconds), which is notably faster than finding an index entry and then finding a referenced page, and adds up if you are following a string of references. (To achieve these speeds with Word, you need to put the program and file into memory, and you need at least a 25MHz computer using a 386DX or 68030 processor with 5MB of RAM and a fast cache.)

[2] It will find every occurrence of a term, although it will miss references that are semantically appropriate when they do not provide syntactic clues—but so will most professional indexers. Those who prefer a printed index can have a good word processor automatically prepare one to their specifications.

[3] This option, plus the use of well-designed black type on paper-white screens at VGA resolutions or better (480 x 640 pixels on a 10" diagonal screen) virtually eliminates the erstwhile strain of reading books on a computer screen.

[4] The volume of a bookdisk is almost exactly 1.66 cubic inches (approximately 3.5" square by 1/8" thick), and this book is about 50 cubic inches, so the ratio is 30:1 in this case, but it will sometimes be more and sometimes less, since the disk has a fixed size while that of the book is variable.

will read bookdisks onto a letter-size screen, plus two bookdisks, is less than the space required by two standard size books—beyond two books, the *weight savings* increase rapidly—a matter of interest to the traveler, student, and commuter; (xi) the fast-spreading use of magnetic cards and laserdisks for storage, instead of magnetic disks, will multiply the space savings for media by a factor of 100 immediately, 500 with DVI compression.

Two remaining problems with the bookdisk, now that booksized display devices are becoming available, are copy protection—the reason the *Encyclopedia Britannica* is not yet on disk—and choice of electronic format. The author and publisher of *ET4* will be trying some experiments in this area, certainly for more recent Macintosh and MS-DOS computers whose floppy drives will handle a disk with a megabyte of uncompressed data, later perhaps for magnetic card reading micros. Interested readers can contact the author to find out about such arrangements. These 'inter-editions', on disk only, will normally be updated every six months[5], and are expected to incorporate or append some notes on new issues, references to significant new books and articles, responses to reviews of and suggestions about *ET4*[6], lists of major changes incorporated in the current version of the main text, graphics to illustrate points (something planned for *ET5*), perhaps some teaching materials such as outlines.

Inclusions: Criteria for including a topic were as follows: either the topic was an essential element in some view of or procedure for evaluation, *or* it was requested by participants in evaluation workshops, courses, or client conferences[7]; *and* a useful short account seemed feasible. Some caveats follow. (i) There is more current slang and jargon in here than would usually be recognized by a respectable scholarly publication—but they are exactly what give newcomers the most trouble. (And besides, though some of the slang is unlovely, some of it embodies the poetry and imaginativeness of a new field far better than more pedestrian and technical prose.) (ii) There's not much on

---

[5] Orders sent out between the six-month intervals may contain the changes made to that date, but if so, no effort will be made to update everything to that date. Intereditions will be numbered in the style used by software, so the next ones will be 4.1, 4.2, etc. Two drawbacks: they will have to be copy-protected, and they will not have had the benefit of professional proofreading. They will be formatted for screen reading rather than for hardcopy printing, but that is easily changed to suit your taste.

[6] Perhaps including excerpts from correspondence, with permission of course.

[7] There are a few exceptions—for example, cases where the author thought the entry might be entertaining.

the solid statistics and measurement material because that's very well covered elsewhere, but there is a little, because participants in some inservice workshops for managers have limited or long-gone statistical background and find a few basic definitions helpful[8]. (iii) There's a good deal about the federal/state contract process because that's the way much of evaluation is funded, and because its jargon is especially pervasive and mysterious. (There's also a good deal on the work of evaluation consultants, for those in the game or considering it; it's a perspective on the field, too.) (iv) Some references are given— but only a few key ones, because too many just leave the reader's problem of selection unanswered; these are expressed in a readable rather than a pedantic bibiliographic format (but always adequately for search procedures). The scholar will usually find further references in the few given: that was one consideration for their selection— another was ease of location. (Where no author's name is given, the present author is responsible.) Acronyms and abbreviations, besides a few that deserve more than translation, are in a supplement to reduce clutter; they cover earlier usages in particular because it is those that mystify the delver into the older literature. There is a small amount of overlap in entries, to avoid paper-chases.

Acknowledgments: The University of San Francisco and the Pacific Graduate School of Psychology deserve special mention in a listing of indebtedness, for their support of two incarnations of the Evaluation Institute where some of the development for this sequence of volumes was done: Allen Calvin was instrumental in both arrangements. Special thanks, too, to Dan Stufflebeam, head of the Evaluation Center at Western Michigan University; as director of the federal R&D Center for Research on Educational Accountability and Teacher Evaluation (CREATE), he provided substantial support for the work involved in the new edition. CREATE is funded by the U.S. Department of Education's Office of Educational Research and Improvement and Dan Stufflebeam, who has contributed much to the discipline of evaluation, has also contributed much to improving my thinking about it.

In 1971–1972 the U.S. Office of Education (represented by John Egermeier) was kind enough to fund the development of a training program—to which I gave the then novel title of "Qualitative Educational Evaluation"—at the University of California at Berkeley, and from that emerged the glossary from which this work grew. Two

---

[8] For such individuals, so common in evaluation workshops, an excellent text is available that contains no formulas at all, but takes the reader to the point of understanding advanced statistics: *Statistics: A Spectator Sport* by Richard Jaeger (2nd edition, Sage, 1990.)

contracts with Region IX of HEW, to assist in building staff evaluation capability, led me from giving workshops to developing materials that could be more widely distributed, more detailed, and more easily used for later reference than the usual seminar notes. My students, colleagues, and assistants in those courses and workshops—especially Jane Roth and Howard Levine—as well as in others at Berkeley, Nova, the Universities of San Francisco and Western Australia, AERA, Capitol, Western Michigan's Evaluation Center and at other distant campuses, have been the source of many improvements in defining and refining the concepts in this exploding and explosive field—and so have many friends and clients. To all of these, many thanks.

The current edition became rather more than the simple revision originally planned, as the five thousand extra words to update a pocket reference guide became a hundred and five thousand to support a reconceptualization. This massive expansion made life difficult for the publisher, and special thanks are due to Deborah Laughton, my editor at Sage, for her editorial suggestions as well as the amiability with which she handled such an unruly project. Thanks, too, to Susan McElroy who managed the production side, and Maria Bergstad who did the proofreading—they were equally good-humored and efficient under trying circumstances. When an albatross hatches from a chicken's egg, one can't help worrying whether the bird will soar for seventy years or soon hang around someone's neck; but they never showed the strain. Well, *hardly* ever.

On the home front, there was considerable negative environmental impact on spouse and secretary from many months of refusal to deal with almost anything else in order to get this project finished. Before it was done, the lava flow of incoming paper had burst from the bounds of my study into the dining room and taken over the floor, the chairs, half of the view, and most of the dining table. The complaints from correspondents who failed to appreciate the chance for their missives to be part of a major archaeological dig also posed a severe diplomatic challenge. Grateful thanks to Mary Anne Warren for not letting the extra burden interfere with twenty years of much appreciated encouragement on the home front, and to Deborah Murray who kept the office running—and kept smiling.

Inverness, California
July, 1991

INTRODUCTION:
THE NATURE OF EVALUATION

1. Overview: Evaluation is the process of determining the merit, worth and value of things, and evaluations are the products of that process. Treating evaluation as an area of applied social science—the usual approach today—requires that one either constrict the meaning of evaluation to an absurd extent, or that one expand the domain of the social sciences to an absurd extent. Instead, evaluation is here treated as a key analytical process in all disciplined intellectual and practical endeavors. It is said to be one of the most powerful and versatile of the 'transdisciplines'—tool disciplines such as logic, design, and statistics—that apply across broad ranges of the human investigative and creative effort while maintaining the autonomy of a discipline in their own right. It is argued that only by taking this transdisciplinary view is it possible to avoid several dead-ends and serious mistakes that have bedeviled the new developments in program evaluation since their appearance—and have done the same to the field of policy studies that emerged about a decade later, and to some other fields of earlier vintage such as personnel evaluation, performance evaluation (including student testing), and product evaluation.

The transdisciplinary view[9] attempts to develop solutions to these difficulties by undertaking two tasks. The first involves extending the

---

[9] This concept, like most of those referred to in the introductory essay, has an entry in the body of the thesaurus that provides somewhat more detail. It would have been confusing to footnote all such forward references, but a considerable effort was made to provide entries for any term that might seem to need further elaboration.

floorplan of evaluation to its legal limits so that it embraces all the application areas—and improving its internal communications. The second involves digging its foundations more deeply. The boundaries are defined by following the dictionary instead of redefining the term to include just one area of applied evaluation—the current practice—which means overlooking or dismissing the other applications. From this broader point of view about evaluation, program evaluation—for example—is seen as simply one applied field in a general discipline of evaluation, one which is trying to solve many of the same problems that other applications have already solved. While program evaluation is an area that uses many investigative techniques from the social sciences, it also uses—or should use—many from other disciplines (such as law, logic, and ethics), from other areas of applied evaluation (such as personnel and product evaluation), and from the developments in the foundations of evaluation—loosely speaking, 'evaluation theory'. Those developments are particularly aimed to assist each applied field with the problem that is now their Achilles heel—the problem of achieving the usual standards of validity for their evaluative conclusions.

The use of the transdisciplinary view to assist existing fields of applied evaluation is one of three reasons for introducing and developing it. The second aim is to provide resources for the improvement of evaluation techniques and reports within traditional areas that are not fields of applied evaluation. In the usual academic disciplines, for example, it should lead to rethinking a range of activities from research design and proposal refereeing to reviews of research literature and papers submitted to journals—as well as field-specific areas like literary criticism and teacher training. In other disciplines—for example, gymnastics, craftwork, diving, and dance—it should affect the procedures for judging performances and training regimens, for purposes of self-improvement and creativity as well as in competitions.

The third aim, and the most important one, is to generate a radical alteration in attitude toward the process and nature of evaluation itself. At the general level, it is hoped that the arguments here destroy the intellectual foundations of the doctrine of value-free science, and hence open the doors to improving evaluation in and with the help of science. It is widely believed in intellectual circles outside science that the value-free doctrine is already dead. Its demise is usually ascribed to the recognition of two facts: that scientists' personal values play an important role in affecting their choice of field and of explanatory models and that science has substantial social consequences. These banal observations have never been denied by anyone before or since the invention of the value-free doctrine and are completely irrelevant

2

to it. The value-free doctrine is a much more serious challenge, and stands in the way of any claim to establish a discipline of evaluation. It is therefore an early item on the agenda here.

At a more specific level, the hope is to induce a much higher degree and quality of evaluation in all professionals when they go about their work as teachers, researchers, or practitioners, not least in their commitment to and in the quality of their self-evaluation (referred to here as 'the professional imperative'). For the future, the hope is that this approach will liberate evaluation from the strong chains that still bind it, so that work on it as a discipline in its own right will accelerate, and will produce a substantial range of benefits to thought and practice.

2. Discipline vs. practice: Evaluation is a new discipline but an ancient practice. The earliest craft workers of which we have a record, the stone–chippers, left a track record of gradually improving quality of materials and design, at single sites and across the millenia— evaluation's signature in stone. There is no craft without evaluation, and in some crafts the evaluation activity has reached considerable heights. In the heyday of Japanese sword–making, for example, sword evaluation became a hereditary profession whose most distinguished practitioners signed the tang of the great blades next to the sword-smith's signature—the Good Housekeeping Seal for the samurai. But evaluation is not just part of technology.

The systematic practice of personnel and program evaluation goes back to the dynasties in China and the Egyptian empires. But evaluation is not just a subfield of management.

The evaluation of performances is the backbone of any physical discipline, from t'ai chi to shooting, drill, dancing, or diving. But evaluation is not home-based in the instincts of judges, instructors or training manuals—or even in education as a whole, where every one of us leaves our most extensive evaluation trail.

3. Scientific aspects of evaluation: The most obvious location for a discipline of evaluation is the sciences. Indeed, there is a point to talking about 'scientific evaluation' by contrast with unsystematic or subjective evaluation; and a point to talking about 'the science of evaluation' by contrast with its practice, meaning by that phrase to include the explicit study of the principles and practice that is missing from all the previous examples. But evaluation is not just a science, emerging as so many other sciences have, from the practice and wisdom of artisans and technologists, of healers and rulers.

Evaluation is like a science in that it involves the production of knowledge rather than of art, anecdotes, or artefacts—for example, knowledge about the relative merit of different ways to teach or study, or to change health care practice, or to use catalysts in

3

accelerating the action of growth hormones. This is one of the most precious kinds of knowledge and it is not restricted to applied knowledge. Science itself is only distinguishable from pseudoscience by means of evaluation—by evaluation of the quality of evidence, research designs, instruments, interpretations, and so on—evaluation *within* science. In recent years, moreover, much of the most significant work in evaluation has been done under the aegis of applied social science. But that is not its residence. Indeed full-scale evaluation is still, officially, an illegal immigrant in this country—although, as we will see, one of its poor relations has a visa. Evaluation is no more a citizen of the sciences than is mathematics—although no less.

4. The ubiquity of evaluation: The process of disciplined evaluation permeates all areas of thought and practice, evading primary location in any one. It is found in scholarly book reviews, in engineering's quality control procedures, in the Socratic dialogs, in serious social and moral criticism, in mathematics, and in the opinions handed down by appellate courts. This intellectual process of evaluation is one that technology and science share with all other disciplines, with the crafts, and with rational thought in general. It is the process whose duty is the systematic and objective determination of merit, worth, or value. Without such a process, there is no way to distinguish the worthwhile from the worthless.

This process is not a simple one. In the usual taxonomy of cognitive processes it is listed as the most sophisticated of all, and its logic is complex enough to have evaded satisfactory analysis for two millenia. Yet it is not so complex that it could not have been analyzed before this, were it not for a special handicap that has been placed on such studies. To understand the nature and origins of that handicap, we need to look at the nature of evaluation in more detail.

5. The nature of evaluation: Evaluation is not the mere accumulation and summarizing of data that is clearly relevant for decision making, although there are still evaluation theorists who take that to be its definition. In the management context, that task is the now highly developed and largely computerized responsibility of MIS, management information systems[10]. In all contexts, gathering and analyzing the

---

[10] Even the addition to MIS of the computerized analytic tools referred to as DSS, decision support systems, does not begin to provide a framework for *evaluation*, although it helps with the data component of it. See "Transferring Decision Support Concepts to Evaluation", by Sauter and Mandell in *Evaluation and Program Planning*, v. 13, no. 4, (Fall 1990). DSS tools still lack many that are required for evaluation, such as nonmoney cost analysis. Of course, the usual quite sophisticated tools of cost analysis, such as time dis-

4

data that is needed for decision making—difficult though that often is[11]—comprises only one of the two key components in evaluation; absent the other component, and absent a procedure for combining them, we simply lack anything that qualifies as an evaluation . *Consumer Reports* does not just test products and report the test scores; it (i) *rates or ranks* by (ii) *merit or cost-effectiveness*.

To get to that kind of conclusion requires an input of something besides data, in the usual sense of that term. The second element is required to get to conclusions about merit or net benefits, and it consists of evaluative premises or standards. Even if you wanted to say that this other element simply comprises further factual claims, so that there is no other needed input besides data, you would have to introduce some novel methods of data-reduction in order to generate evaluative conclusions when this second kind of data is included—as well as some novel procedures for determining which of these claims and standards are valid. The distinctive aspect of evaluation would then become the these new processes. Thus it is at best extremely misleading to define evaluation as the provision of useful information, as if it were like the usual process of providing useful information. One might as well define research or investigative journalism or for that matter mathematics, as the presentation of information. To the extent that this can be said at all, it fails to provide the crucial distinguishing characteristics which we expect from a useful definition.

A more straightforward approach is just to say that evaluation has two arms, only one of which is engaged in data-gathering. The other arm collects, clarifies, and verifies relevant values and standards. Even in the simplest cases, where we are doing product evaluation to select something purely for our own use—so the 'relevant values' are largely our own preferences—these values are subject to override because of legal, ethical, or environmental considerations. And even in these simplest cases, there are many logical and scientific tasks involved in clarifying the values side of evaluation, which include identifying and removing (i) inconsistencies in individual sets of values, (ii) misunderstandings and misrepresentations of values, and (iii) false factual assumptions underlying them; (iv) distinguishing

---

counting of costs and the provision of lifetime as well as purchase costs, are also essential parts of any DSS to be used for evaluative purposes—along with half a dozen other types of investigatory apparatus.

[11] Apart from the usual problems of discovery and tabulation, a useful MIS database may require ongoing automatic verification of data by cross-checking it against incoming data, and assigning continually updated confidence levels to it.

between wants and needs; and dealing with the problems of (v) ensuring that we have identified *all* relevant dimensions of merit, (vi) finding appropriate measures for them (by contrast with naming the abstract qualities that we know we want); (vii) weighting these dimensions in some way that accurately reflects our intentions; and (viii) validating any standards we locate.

Even with its two arms in place, evaluation needs a head to coordinate them, and that requires not only deciding on the instructions that have to be given to the arms so that they bring in the right package of elements—the evaluation design problem[12]—but it also requires solving the problem of how to combine what the arms deliver in some justified and systematic way—the synthesis problem. In the evaluation of laptop computers, for example, where a hundred and eighty criteria are relevant, each important to a significant group of users, the combinatorial procedure is extremely critical. Analysis of the usual way of integrating performance data by using numerical weights shows it to be fallacious, even with a tenth this many dimensions.

These selection and synthesis problems are hard enough to lead *Consumer Reports* into serious mistakes in product evaluation, and important enough to make it extraordinary that there is only a handful of discussions of them in the research literature. When we move to typical problems in program evaluation, where we have to deal with the conflicting interests of many parties playing different roles in supporting or using a complex program, the situation worsens. In personnel evaluation, too, where ethical issues become even more important, we increasingly find that the assembly of data—even the selection of data-types for assembly—is only the tip of the evaluation iceberg.

To further complicate the field, much of the best evaluation does not use—and could not usefully use—any of the tools that have been developed to handle the problems just mentioned[13]. When—for ex-

---

[12] Determining which facts are relevant and which standards are appropriate is often very hard. Only highly routinised evaluation involves dealing with facts and standards that have been predetermined as "the right stuff and all the right stuff". In particular, one almost always requires (i) data about all entities that are seriously competitive with the one being evaluated (a selection procedure for which there is no algorithm); (ii) data about the state of the art and (iii) the state of upcoming art in the field being evaluated; (iv) data identifying *all* significantly impacted groups; and (v) data about *all* significantly relevant standards.

[13] Or at most uses them at the neural processing level rather than in any explicit way.

ample—practicing physicists are evaluating proposals for more research on heavy neutrinos, or the Supreme Court is assessing the merits of a new line of argument for prohibiting abortion, they are not likely to be materially assisted by evaluation designs and instruments from the fields of program, personnel, or product evaluation. One might suppose that in such cases only experts in the field would have anything to contribute. In fact, indispensable though the expert contributions are, the evaluator also has a useful perspective on the actual and potential validity of such discussions. Some relevant considerations include (i) the issues of bias and conflict of interest, well analyzed in the legal literature, but not well applied to decision making by the Supreme Court or to scientific review; (ii) the use of procedures like the 'calibration' of human judges, the 'blinding' of referees, and the balancing of panels; (iii) the validation of commonly used criteria for estimating expertise; (iv) the relative merits of four alternative procedures for combining the ratings of different experts, especially multiple-cutoff vs. compensatory approaches; (v) studies of cases where later precedent reverses court decisions—or later evidence refutes panel decisions—to get an estimate of the validity of panel judgments in this field; (vi) procedures for evaluating the metatheories underlying the specialists' evaluations, something that involves significant skills in addition to subject matter expertise.

Evaluation is not only a long step beyond data-gathering, but a long way from the expression of taste or the production of essentially subjective 'value-judgments', as the common caricatures would have it. In fact, expressions of taste or preference, although they sometimes provide a small part of the input data, are often sharply and correctly *contrasted* with evaluative conclusions—for example, we normally and rightly distinguish between our liking for teachers and our estimate of their merit as good teachers. As for the notion that evaluation is essentially subjective in some way that science is not, there is little in science that is more objective than the evaluation of student performance on a well-constructed mathematics test, or the recognition of failure in an attempt at a flyaway double from the high bar. Provably valid evaluation by skilled observers is common enough, and similar enough to scientific observation and classification, to be immune to jibes about subjectivity.

There remains a grain of truth to the idea that evaluation is simply a useful variety of data-reduction—evaluation does reduce a large volume of information about various matters to a tiny kernel, sometimes exactly what we need. In an extended sense of "data", there can hardly be a more powerful example of data-reduction than the compression of a year's worth of detailed observation and testing of a student into the laconic grade on a transcript. This is reminiscent of, although far more complicated than, the data-reduction effectuated by descriptive statistics, when, for example, a dataset with thousands of elements is described by one or two measures such as the mean and the standard deviation. And the reasons for the reduction are the same. The pragmatist does not want to wade through piles of raw performance data, partly because life isn't long enough, and partly because one can easily miss the main implications of the data when doing so. These points are the same whether the data refers to census figures or the durability of stainless steel cutlery or digital watches. What one wants to hear about is the bottom line—the big picture, the overall significance, the trends or the winners. It's easier to verify the reliability of the statistician or evaluator than to do the analysis oneself. Evaluation, like statistics, is a life raft in the sea of information sludge—for the consumer.

But the evaluator, in order to provide a valid conclusion for the consumer to use, has to know how to get to the bottom line, and that cannot be done by the data-reduction procedures of descriptive statistics. It has to be done in the particular way that evaluation reduces facts and values to evaluative conclusions. The hard questions remain: what facts, what values, how reduced, how valid, how credible?

6. Attitudes to evaluation: The credibility of evaluations brings in psychological factors that go beyond rational estimation. Many people think that the use of evaluation as a data reduction process—summarizing a year's work into a grade, for example—is a kind of crime. In some circumstances, indeed, such a radically reductive kind of evaluation would be completely inappropriate—circumstances that demand a much richer and fuller evaluative account, as, for example, when the need is to help the student or a counselor plan changes of program or study approach. But in other circumstances and for other purposes, such as selection for admission to advanced courses, jobs or graduate school, there is probably no better general approach than the letter grade, to judge from decades of extended experimentation with alternatives.

On the other hand, for someone sceptical about evaluation on logical-philosophical grounds, the concept of data reduction is legitimate enough in itself; the fallacy lies in the extension of it to cover reduction of data about values as well as facts about performance. But the sceptic can only be sceptical on abstract grounds; practical life cannot proceed without evaluation, nor can intellectual life, nor can the moral life, and they are not built on sand. The real question is how to do evaluation well, not how to avoid it. Yet the wish to avoid it is very deep, albeit very confused. "Judge not that ye be not judged" is

8

an ancient saying, and the fact that it is essentially self-refuting has not prevented it reemerging in the form "There is no legitimate place in science for value-judgments", the equally self-refuting doctrine of value-free science[14]. This schizophrenic combination of resistance to evaluation with continued use of it in the resisters' own lives creates a distinctive twist to the discipline. What makes it unique is the pervasiveness of this affective dimension. It has another side, of course, because the quest for quality is as much a part of the human condition as dislike for messengers that sometimes bring bad news.

Although evaluation often does a great deal of good—it leads to saved money and lives, and to improvements in the quality of life, products, pride, and performance—it is rarely possible to do it without cost or at least risk to someone. If you rate a Honda motorcycle best and buy one, Yamaha suffers; if you select one applicant for a job, another misses out; even if all you improve is your personal best time for the 10 km walk, others are bypassed and may feel worse. It is true that there are many occasions when even the choice of a statistic—the legal blood-alcohol level, for example, or the housing density that leads to incorporation of property into a township—leads to major adverse consequences for many individuals. But this is almost always—rather than occasionally—true of evaluation, and for those who wish to avoid hurting others, or to avoid the risk of hurt to themselves, the attraction of blackballing evaluation from membership in the club of intellectually respectable activities has proven overwhelming.

7. The paradoxical status of evaluation: If the arguments here are sound, the importance and range of evaluation form a strange contrast with the refusal of any academic discipline to treat the subject of evaluation seriously until the last third of the twentieth century[15].

---

[14] The defense that this is a claim about science, rather than within it, fails—so it is argued below—because disciplines cannot divorce themselves from their metatheories. Although practicing scientists love to dismiss philosophy of science as idle chatter compared to real science, every time a new paradigm begins to shake things up the best of them jump straight into metatheoretical discussion, much of it straight philosophy of science, and much of it making elementary mistakes. In the twentieth century, relativity theory, quantum mechanics, cosmology, and robotics have followed the long road from the earliest days of science on which the Greek atomists, the Galileans, the Darwinians and the Freudians have left their footsteps. That road is built on epistemological foundations one can ignore only until the inevitable earthquake.

[15] Philosophy is an important exception. Ethics is a special case of evaluation—the evaluation of acts, attitudes, the principles governing them, and the justification of such principles, all of this *from a certain point of view*. Ethics has

Even now, there is little tendency to award it any significant status in the pantheon of inquiry.

• Although it is listed in the Bloom taxonomy of educational objectives as the highest of six levels of cognitive function, evaluation is not a topic in any of the standard school or college subjects.

• Evaluation is the only intellectual skill required in every branch of science, but it is not included in any of the lists of intellectual skills said to make up scientific method, found at the beginning of every major school science text and science curriculum project.

• Evaluation is the process whereby every student in college gets there and remains there, but its legitimacy is denied in most social science courses by the very instructors who give those evaluations and will defend them with evidence and good reasoning.

The status of evaluation in the twentieth century represents one of the most striking paradoxes in the history of thought: An essential—and perhaps the most important—ingredient in all intellectual and practical activity has been explicitly banned or implicitly excluded from discussion or acknowledgment in most of its natural territory.

The psychological, social, and political reasons, as well as the intellectual ones, for this bizarre situation—for this 'intellectual treason of the intellectuals'—are discussed in the pages of the present work. Its cost to intellectual life and social progress has been enormous, as scholars deliberately avoided direct approaches to the problems of their society. If the status of evaluation as an 'untouchable' subject is to be radically changed, there must be a direct attack on the myths responsible for this paradox, and also there must also be works that set out the elements of an alternative view of evaluation, a view of it as perhaps the most important and pervasive process of which the human mind is capable.

Developing such a view requires backing up the techniques of

---

a longer history of theory than any other area of evaluation, but its focus is quite limited and the theories have always been highly controversial, so it has had little effect on other areas of evaluation. Attempts have also been made within philosophy to develop a general study of valuing (axiology) and a formal logic of evaluation—deontic logic. The logic failed for the same reasons that have handicapped most attempt to apply formal logic. In recent years, however, applied ethics has developed considerable autonomy and some substantial local skills for dealing with an important range of problems notably in medical ethics and business ethics.

evaluation with a core of methodological and conceptual discussion that applies across the crafts and disciplines. The first of these discussions have now been going on in several fields for a quarter of a century, and they have been fertile enough to legitimate treating these fields as deserving respect in their own right. But the discussions do not yet reach deep enough or connect well enough to make any of the fields—or all of them together—into a discipline.

8. From practice to methodology to discipline: The first step beyond the basic practice of evaluation—something present in every field—is probably the step to the formulation of scoring or judging guides (rubrics) to govern that practice. These begin to identify rules that are to govern (prescriptive) evaluation. They may well have developed first in the area of performance evaluation, perhaps by the time of the Chinese civil service examinations, or earlier in the evaluation of competitions between warriors or athletes, although we have no direct evidence of this. Such rules are still extremely limited in scope. One might suppose that they were next elaborated, following the lines along which we know that logic developed, to include guidelines in which common errors or difficulties were described. Here we begin to formulate the practical methodology of evaluation, for very limited cases of prescriptive evaluation. It is still a long step—in time and logic—from that point to discussions of the methodology of program evaluation, where we are laying down principles for general evaluative *investigation and analysis*—for example, principles about the proper use of experimental or quasi-experimental designs in program evaluation, or principles about the proper use of cost-benefit analysis in program evaluation. That step was made much easier by the emergence of discussions of methodology in a hundred other areas across a thousand years. With it, we took a long step toward developing a discipline—but there was still a long way to go.

Methodology is the study of investigative or practical procedures, aimed at improving practice—and the methods resulting from that study; to a lesser extent it is concerned with improving our understanding of practice. Now, discussions about 'the methodology of evaluation' presuppose some sense of the emergence and dimensions of a new field and precipitate discussion of its nature. In evaluation, however, most methodology has only been developed within the confines of the subfield of program evaluation, which leaves us far short of a general discipline[16]. Just as statistics is not merely biostatistics, so evaluation is more than one of its applied fields. To get to a true discipline of evaluation, at least two further steps must be taken. On the

---

[16] Multiattribute utility analysis is a recent exception.

11

one hand, the restricted conception has to be extended to include not only the other fields devoted to evaluation—fields such as product and personnel evaluation, policy studies, and quality assurance—but also to include major uses of evaluation within fields with other names, the academic and nonacademic disciplines. And these members of the evaluation community must be related, put in touch, and studied for what they can contribute to the common cause.

On the other hand, and more important, we must take a longer step, a step beyond discussions of methodology toward a discussion of such topics as (i) the proposals just made for defining the boundaries and contents of evaluation; (ii) the differences between this territory and others (is this essentially a science, a humanity, an art, a craft, or something else?); (iii) the connections between this territory and others; (iv) reasons why certain methods work or fail in this territory (metamethodology); (v) arguments for any proposed general logic of evaluation, and about its limitations; (vi) the kinds of data and theories that are appropriate[17]; (vii) social, psychological, historical, anthropological, and political theories about its nature and travails (including multidisciplinary work on intercountry differences[18]); and (viii) the directions it should move. The term used here for most of this third-level discussion is *metatheory*[19].

---

[17] An excellent example of the argument about appropriate data is provided by the discussion in the history of psychology of the Wundtian reliance on introspection. A classic example of argument about types of theory comes from particle theory—the debate about the acceptability of nondeterministic theories.

[18] Some of this is now being done by the Working Group on Policy and Program Evaluation of the IIAS; see **Utilization** in the thesaurus.

[19] The term "metatheory" is now widely used for this, but there is some overlap with what is called "the philosophy of X", although both terms convey a misleading impression of a highly explicit body of knowledge. Where there is an existing subject referred to as 'the philosophy of X', as in the case of the philosophy of history or the philosophy of science, it only partly overlaps metatheory. The differences provide some slight justification for the widespread distaste among academicians for 'philosophy of' subjects; in part, however, one soon finds out that the distaste is for something few of them can do well or understand but need when paradigm clashes occur. The differences include some or all of the following: (i) Although some aspects of the metatheory are dealt with in the philosophy of science (or history, etc.), many others are not and the selection is often made on the grounds of philosophical interest, rather than importance for the discipline under discussion; (ii) the topics selected are often discussed in the recondite vocabulary and framework of philosophy; (iii) those discussions are often not well-informed about the reali-

12

In the case of evaluation, it is reasonable to expect the metatheory to provide an account of evaluation that will distinguish it from measurement, observation, and nonevaluative description; it should be able to explain and cope with the attacks on and arguments for the idea of evaluation as a discipline and for various attempts to pass off substitutes such as information summaries; and it should be able to suggest and justify fruitful lines for research and development. Absent the metatheory, we only have a group of fields of practice and research differentiated by subject matter, some discussions of methodology in each field—and a little more. The little more is part of a metatheory for part of evaluation—that is, we have *some* models for *program* evaluation.

9. The Country of the Mind: To convey the situation now and as it is projected, it may help to use an analogy. One can think of the disciplines—sociology or chemistry, for example—as *estates* clustered in *counties* that correspond to the major subdivisions of knowledge such as the physical sciences, engineering, the crafts, or the humanities. The main house on each estate, like the Great Houses of plantation days, is both a habitation and the center of a substantial industry[20]. In the Country of the Mind, while some houses are Great Houses, some are much more modest dwellings, the homes of semiautonomous fields or areas of work rather than of an autonomous discipline. The houses on an estate have a ground floor representing applied work, a floor above that which is devoted to developing instruments, methods, and

---

ties of practice; (iv) they are not primarily aimed at improving practice; and (v) they rarely include serious work on implicit commitments. The greater part of the *influence* of the metatheory comes from the discussions among, role-modeling by, or the thinking of practitioners. This is not to say that the practitioners' discussions are of higher quality than those of the philosophers, or even to say that they are of high quality; and it is certainly not to say that the practitioners' discussion is not affected by the philosophers' discussion, even if this is not acknowledged. In the metatheoretical debates over the Copenhagen interpretation of quantum theory and the interpretation of special relativity the quality of the practitioners' discussion was outstanding, but the discussions of explanation or causation in history and the social sciences are quite primitive—as also, according to the claim here, are those dealing with evaluation throughout the disciplines.

[20] The feudal connotations are intentional; academia is a country of fiefdoms, to a greater extent than it should be—as exploited research assistants and would-be interdisciplinarians are well aware. At least, the estates are run by an Executive Committee rather than a hereditary noble, even if the Committees often include too many senescent pundits squabbling over privileges.

techniques, and a top floor where the theoretical work is done. Up in the attic, out of sight for most of the time, is the den of metatheory: the plans, titles, and records concerning the house and grounds. These include the sketches by the original owners and those requesting later modifications, the actual building plans, the list of subcontractors, the landscape architect's plans and notes, the illustrated essay on the house from *Architectural Review* (and some others that were less favorable), the electrical and phone circuit plans, the locations of emergency services, maps of the region, the help available from nearby estates, and so on.

Sometimes there's someone working up there; most of the time, there isn't. But when certain kinds of trouble strike, we rush to the attic. Now the metatheory isn't just the work done in the attic, though the records of it are all there. The architect's plans of a building are not just marks on paper: The metatheory is embodied in the way the building was built and the way the grounds were laid out. Almost no one bothers with such matters until they need to expand the house or estate, or change its shape or use or appearance. Then we start looking for and arguing about the plans—and even about the architectural style, the paradigm. The metatheory affects almost everything that goes on in the house, in the sense of providing limits to it, providing the internal access to it via stairs and elevators, and giving it an appearance, from facade to floor plan.

In this allegory, the *interdisciplinary subjects* are estates located where one or more regions overlap, built as a joint project. *Multidisciplinary approaches* are recognized by noticing that some suites on the methodology floor are virtual duplicates of those to be found in other mansions. And the *transdisciplines* are the utilities—electricity, water, gas, sewers, telephone, data lines or microwave systems, cable or satellite television, radio, roads, and public transportation. Not all the estates use all of these—and some generate their own versions—but each utility provides service to many estates.

Now the telephone utility, for example, isn't just the phone line; it's a business in its own right. Somewhere in the countryside there's a Great House for the telephone company. On its ground floor are the public phone booths for those without a phone at home, the accounting department, and the service staff dealing with customer problems—although of course the main service provided is to be found in the other houses of the region serviced. The next floor up has engineers designing and improving transmission line grids, and the top floor naturally houses a branch of the Bell Labs, a full-scale research effort, much of it pure research.

Suppose that we take the telephone utility to represent the transdiscipline of statistics. The main service that statistics provides is to be found in its use in the houses on distant estates such as the House of Demography; but back at the House of Statistics, the three floors are fully occupied by, in ascending order, (i) the statistical consulting service, (ii) those developing new *general* statistical tools, and (iii) those working on probability theory and other foundational notions[21]. There's still an attic, with maps of the region and plans of all the houses served, transcripts of the great debates between Bayesians and Fisherians, the architect's plan—and of course the building that incorporates these plans—so there's a metatheory of the transdiscipline just as for other disciplines. In the transdisciplines, the door to the attic from the theory floor is usually open, because there is considerable traffic between those floors.

Transdisciplines are different from the regular disciplines in that they have two kinds of applications, one category of them being located out in the houses on other estates, involved in the everyday mainline work there, on every floor of the house, while the others have graduated to the status of semiautonomous applications with their own houses on the grounds of the transdiscipline's headquarters. Still fields of study rather than disciplines in their own right, these houses may be adjacent to the grounds of another estate (as Biostatistics, for example, is near the Biology estate; or as Personnel Evaluation is located near the Management and the Organizational Psychology properties). New customers requiring practical assistance will come through the door of the main house for service or go to one of the associated application houses if they see one of them as providing service in the area of their needs. Incidentally, the House of Statistics uses other utilities besides the one it supplies; and of course it is located in the County of Mathematics.

How does one identify transdisciplines[22]? The widespread use of evaluative reasoning does not of itself imply that there should be a discipline of evaluation; not all intellectual tools with great horizontal range generate associated disciplines. The logic of explanation, for example, is used across most disciplines, is an important subarea in the philosophy of science, and a key part of the philosophy of mind and other subjects. But explanation theory, unlike statistics and evaluation,

---

[21] Note that both the first and second floor are involved with both general and particular problems—the pure/applied distinction is not the general/-particular distinction.

[22] Other transdisciplines include parts or all of information theory, ethics, communications and presentations (including data visualization), applications software, hermeneutics (in its original sense), and decision analysis.

does not generate substantial applied areas as do the transdisciplines. Their applications are often so complex and essential that special courses are given on them in areas other than the host area—statistics for the psychology graduate student, program evaluation for the educational administrator, policy analysis for those in or aiming at government service, medical ethics for nurses, and/orquality assurance for engineers. Explanation falls short in *application depth*; and so do many branches of mathematics that have significant uses here and there across the disciplines, such as vector calculus or number theory. There could hardly be four encyclopedias on even the most widely discussed application of explanation theory, say for explanation in history. They are probably best treated as part of the home subject—philosophy or mathematics, in these two examples. Explanation theory is at most just a small house on the Philosophy estate, between the Philosophy of History house and the Philosophy of Science house, or perhaps just a shared wing that stretches between them. But what about Philosophy itself—surely its applications across the disciplines are substantial enough; should it be called a transdiscipline?

A subject like Philosophy or Economics is remarkably versatile, in that there is an philosophical aspect or an economic perspective on a wide range of subject matter (including evaluation); the same can be said, even more strongly, of physics and of psychology. But these subjects are mainline subjects, primary disciplines, the creators of findings about the world, by contrast with the transdisciplines like measurement or statistics that deal with investigative tools and formal or abstract objects. Thus, although many of the primary disciplines do provide substantial tools and knowledge to other fields and disciplines, in this way matching the transdisciplines, their essential nature is to be found elsewhere. They trade in something more concrete than a utility service.

In the Country of the Mind, the Physics estate—like Philosophy or Economics—can be thought of as holding shares in other estates as well as in a number of houses on its own estate. In the case of Physics, it owns shares in the Electronics estate, and in houses such as Surface Physics. Some of these other estates have spun off from Physics (although Astronomy, for example, came earlier). Physics still straddles a hub from which roads lead out to them, and ships supplies to all of them and to other estates—in return for which Physics receives some goods as well as credit with its primary funding source, the government. Similarly, Economics can be thought of as providing supplies or services to a range of subjects—sometimes even spinning off and co-owning interdisciplines like Economic History—and the same can be said, in general terms, about psychology and philosophy.

16

The primary disciplines have long provided important supplies and services to each other; doing that is not the sole province of transdisciplines. There can be no intellectual activity without primary disciplines and by and large, transdisciplines come into existence to service them, as the utility companies come into existence to service already existing buildings that house people and businesses already dealing with each other, sometimes with their own primitive sources of power (for example). The transdisciplines thus exist to serve—and only then come to exist as disciplines in their own right. Although they deserve to be seen as disciplines, they are tool disciplines—in other terminology, one might say that they are essentially symbiotic in origin, or that they are driven from the bottom up rather than from the top down.

Some of the transdisciplines emerged very early in the history of the disciplines. Some did not: It is obvious that most substantial disciplines developed without statistics, design theory, or computer software, and many preceded formal logic. Informal logic, on the other hand, emerged as early as most philosophy, although perhaps not as early as anything recognizable as a discipline of history or theology or music. Something that at least included a sketch of a discipline of informal logic was in existence by the time of the Sophists, who made a living by teaching a version of it mixed with some rhetoric and philosophy.

Of course, the *practices* of informal logic and evaluation long antedated any of the academic disciplines or *their* precursors in practice. The practice of informal logic, like that of grammar, grew up with the native language that antedated the academic disciplines, because they cannot develop without language. The practice of evaluation may well have predated language, because it was an integral part of the development of the earliest artefacts and the hunter-warrior protodisciplines. One can see its antecedents—perhaps even a limited version of it—in predators considering alternative approaches when stalking prey.

Now, it might appear that without language there are no true disciplines because the metatheory cannot exist, and even the least articulate physical disciplines have their self-concept strongly linked to a metatheory. But a case can be made that a metatheory can be implicit in the practice and teaching-by-example of leading practitioners. It must be capable of providing (implicit) answers to the kind of question listed above, but even that is possible in principle with most of the questions. One must conclude that quite elaborate protodisciplines, even if not fully self-conscious, self-assessing disciplines, are possible in late prelinguistic or largely ritualistic groups.

The practice of the early transdisciplines such as informal logic and evaluation developed into disciplines in their own right as knowledge was increasingly converted from implicit to explicit status and the inevitable questions generated answers[23]. In the Country of the Mind, while facts are the ground itself, the *practice* of logic is the cement and mortar used for all construction and on which all success depends; if it fails us, the roads and buildings will fail. It rarely needs reformulation, having worked well for millenia, except for special uses. The *discipline* of logic is also a building in the Philosophy estate. Like the others, it has its own metatheory—its plans and architecture—but unlike most of them it also serves as a transdiscipline, providing services to all the disciplines[24]. Like evaluation, logic is in use everywhere, but seen as a useful service to research only occasionally, when the most fundamental assumptions about reasoning are questioned—for example, when quantum theorists started looking at the possibility of using multivalued logic to express the properties of particles, or when theologians try one more time to work out a new 'logic of religious discourse'. Nevertheless, it is the logicians who provide us with the basics for *teaching* logic and improving the efficiency of logical analysis, and a palace revolution in the headquarters building has recently produced a massive shift away from the latter-day Latin of formal logic to a new and more useful approach.

Technical advice from the applied evaluation groups, on the other hand, is is called on frequently and increasingly, because it is something we can not pick up in the course of a normal education until the graduate level, and it involves a substantial range of concepts, terminology, and methodology. As with logic, there is a homegrown variety in every discipline, but by contrast with logic, there are serious weaknesses in that homegrown version. In the Country of the Mind, whether the electricity is homegrown or not, it's still electricity—evaluation is ubiquitous. But the homegrown variety is neither the most economical, the most reliable, nor the most powerful supply. Those

---

[23] The antiquity of logic, and of grammar, is reason to forgive them for having taking a wrong turn when they did this; both tried for a more formal status than was appropriate for their subject matter, following the success of early mathematics and physics. The disciplines that emerged—formal logic, and classical grammar—became academic dead ends, of negligible practical or pedagogical value. It took a more sophisticated era, when tolerance of ambiguity (and of fuzziness) became acceptable, for us to move to accepting informal logic and transformational grammar as explicatory devices with sub-deterministic powers.

[24] Ethics is another exception.

18

benefits accrue from connecting to the power grid—that is, to the combination of specialized applications, general logic, methods, and metatheory of evaluation that is to be found at the headquarters estate. Doing so also provides benefits because of the connection to a grid that serves the other estates, which once in a while will be able to help with special problems by kicking in their reserve generators.

By contrast with logic and statistics, however, the headquarters building—the Great House—for evaluation is almost entirely allegorical. There is an Evaluation estate, and it has several buildings on it, inhabited by what should be satellite applications—product evaluation, policy analysis, program evaluation, and so on, each of them complete buildings. But in the real world there is no center around which the satellites should be revolving, a place where work proceeds on the core subject of evaluation, the subject that provides the general logic, the general methodology, and the theory and metatheory of evaluation as a whole. This lack costs the satellite applications heavily in terms of a lack of coordination of their efforts, from the definitional level to the methodological one, and a lack of a general theoretical and metatheoretical corpus from which their problems can be attacked. In turn, it costs those connected to the evaluation 'grid'. Historically, this lack is probably due to the taboo on recognizing evaluation as a legitimate area of study, which meant the applied fields could not spin off from an parent discipline as with logic, ethics, and statistics. The result is that there is as yet no discipline of evaluation; the applications cannot have that status without an overarching theory and metatheory, either alone or in combination. Absent the headquarters for a core discipline, program evaluation is just the latest of the applications to talk as if *it* was 'evaluation'; but the claim is absurd under scrutiny and emerges only because there is a vacuum to fill.

We need to establish a House of Evaluation to provide a base for help to the applications, whether on the estate or on other sites—and to develop its own studies of evaluation. The present work is an attempt to sketch a plan for that structure, and start to build on the ancient foundation stones already on the site; but it has to begin by appealing against the discriminatory zoning laws specifically intended to exclude a Great House of Evaluation. Meanwhile, the allegory can perhaps provide a sense of place, a vision of a homeland, to encourage those workers indentured to other Houses who will have to provide the bulk of the support for developing the core discipline of evaluation[25].

---

[25] In the absence of a headquarters slot in the usual academic scheme of

Finally, two notes about the geography and building industry in the Country of the Mind. First, where are the arts to be found? Craft County is well populated and welcomes those that meet some disciplinary standards, but the 'formless arts' live in caves on the outer borders of the country, unable to construct buildings because they will not accept the construction standards required if buildings are to support their own weight. Although the Great Houses in Craft County have a lower profile because they lack a theory floor, they still have space for methods and metatheory. There may not be a theory *of* jewelry, but there are many theories *about* it to be found in the application floor of other Houses such as the History of Art. The spiritual and physical disciplines occupy neighboring counties, sometimes with—and sometimes earnestly rejecting—a theory floor, but distinguished from mere practices by elaborate metatheory if not theory, and always with extensive methodology floors above the practice halls.

The building trades in the Country of the Mind—an export from the applications offices on the Engineering estate—are kept busy with alterations and with new construction. New houses—sharing the same estate, or new Great Houses built nearby—are constructed when (i) one wing of a Great House needs to expand and can't increase the size of the wing without distorting the whole structure; (ii) small applications, living in a cottage nearby, and originally directly serviced by one or two parent disciplines, become so large as to need their own mansion; or (iii) someone discovers extensive duplication of effort in various houses, and gets the workgroups to merge and set up house together in a new house. New disciplines may be spun off from standard disciplines (as molecular biology emerged from biology, psychology from philosophy) or from transdisciplines (as biostatistics developed from statistics). Quite commonly, their workers will retain part-time jobs in the parent establishment as well as the spin-off, al-

things, the burden of constructing the surrogate core discipline—albeit only for program evaluation—has fallen on workers in the applied fields, especially (i) on research groups at the few universities that ignored the rigidities of the standard plan—notably Stanford and Illinois; (ii) on the contract research shops and institutes, notably Western Michigan, RAND, Boston College, and CIRCE; and to a remarkable extent on (iii) enlightened government agency and foundation staff. As the sense grows that evaluation needs an autonomous core discipline, more of the necessary work will get done in these ways, with or without direct funding. The advantage of this shoestring approach is a relentless pressure to keep any theorizing in touch with the reality of practice, the reason no doubt why a recent book that takes a very serious look at theoretical work on program evaluation has the subtitle "Theories of Practice".

20

though that is often a hazardous arrangement because it raises the question of divided loyalty. The fiefdoms are jealous employers, grudging about the issuance of passports and work permits.

10. More on metatheories: (i) The metatheory is sometimes an explicit theory about the nature of the field, but quite often it is just an assemblage of general claims, rules, and rubrics about the field or research in it. It may be very informal, expressed in passing remarks and after-dinner speeches rather than in treatises. It may be largely implicit in the practice of experts, a driving or orienting conception of the field, learned by role modeling the gurus, but it must be sophisticated enough to include answers to most of the questions about the nature of the discipline that generate a metatheory. Disciplines do not exist without those answers, although they are often practiced unselfconsciously. Individuals have their own metatheories about the disciplines, which are sometimes quite enlightening about the education they received and the *weltanschaung* (a recent example: "But you can't really do *research* in philosophy can you—it's just a matter of writing down what you think, isn't it?") and sometimes quite enlightening about the state of public understanding (e.g., this comment from a professional: "A faculty evaluation questionnaire must be biased if it calls for student responses on 32 possible faults in the instructor, and only provides check boxes for 20 possible virtues.").

(ii) Sometimes the metatheory is dominated by one conspicuous metaphor—usually identified as a 'paradigm'—but sometimes there really is no paradigm, although there is never a shortage of claimants for the title[26]. When there is no paradigm, the metatheory consists of the rest of the cast of characters (including subparadigms, applicable to limited areas) always present but often thrown into shadow by the spotlight on a solo paradigm. Apart from the ones mentioned, these 'shaping elements' may include *a set of* orienting models, analogies, metaphors, highly distinctive methods described in very general terms, ideal types, standards, axiomatic principles, and reasons for thinking all these appropriate in part or all of the field.

(iii) The metatheory, as is now commonly recognized, belies its usual unobtrusiveness by exerting enormous power on the direction and magnitude of a discipline's development. When quantum theory

---

[26] Some details of this position are in "Psychology Without a Paradigm", in *Clinical-Cognitive Psychology: Models and Integrations*, edited by Louis Breger, Prentice-Hall, 1969, pp. 9–24. The term "paradigm" is used here to mean an exemplar or model; in the context of metatheory, the term is particularly used to refer to a dominant model of investigation that is substantially affecting the direction and kind of work done in an area.

emerged, the best theoretical physicists found themselves obliged to spend a great deal of time on metatheoretical matters in order to make or consolidate progress; this theme recurs in other well-known examples such as the development of relativity theory, psychology, sociology, ethnic and women's studies, and computer science. The metatheory is latent in practice, and practitioners often think it's just tea-time talk—until they run into it or fall over it. Much good work is possible without discussing metatheory—lifetimes of it, including Nobel laureates' lifetimes. But those working on the legal and physical *external* frontiers of a subject—the boundaries of an estate in the Country of the Mind—especially the theoreticians, need it often and run into it when they least expect it. The rest are profoundly—even if indirectly—affected by it because it defines the frontier and situates the internal roads and bridges. Their work may only involve exploration of internal frontiers, the lakes and woods yet uncharted and uncatalogued, or it may just involve work on the records of other explorers. Such work will rarely call into question the location of the external frontiers, or of the main roads and bridges across the swamps—but it could not have been done unless those decisions had been made and implemented in some workable way[27].

(iv) The term "applications" is used here as elsewhere ("applied mathematics"), although it has the inappropriate connotation of work done by instantiating general theories. In fact, the direction of development is usually bottom-up in the applied areas. The best justification for using the term is as a concession to attempts to provide a 'logical' structure to the subject matter. The pure side involves the fundamental concepts, which are then, in terms of a logical reconstruction, instantiated in the applications. It is also true that the 'pure' side of the discipline is sometimes useful in helping with the formulations and analyses on the applied side and, sometimes, in providing an overview that drives development and coordination. It is essential to recognize that in practice the actual sequence is usually that a body of work in the applied area is built up and *generates the need for adding to the repertoire of concepts in the pure area.* That body of work could never have been derived directly from the preexisting pure field, in mathematics or evaluation. Program evaluation is not reducible to a substitution instance of general evaluation theory, although it must be consistent with it (a two-way constraint). In the allegory, the House of Program Evaluation (for example), is not owned by the House of

---

[27] The current misconceptions about technology, discussed later in this volume, provide a good example of the cost to a subject—and to a society which depends on it—of poor metatheory.

Evaluation, but by a cooperative in which the shareholders are the houses of the applied and core fields.

(v) The pure/applied or theory/practice distinction in scientific disciplines is thus not the same as the metatheory/applications or metatheory/theory distinction, since each discipline *also* has a metatheoretical level. A discipline consists of all three elements, four if we include methodology. The difference with the transdisciplines is that they contain a general theory and methods that service all their applications areas—*each of which has its own local theory, methods, and metatheory*. What we are calling the 'core' of the discipline includes both the *general* theoretical component (the 'pure' part of the general field, covering everything from the definition and logic of the discipline to social and political studies of evaluation, e.g., studies of when it is and when it should be used), the *general* methodology of the field (which overlaps with the logic, and includes general methods for evaluating metatheories), and the metatheory of the general subject (the discipline)—plus a little assorted application work that hasn't yet found a home in the Great Houses in the County of Evaluation Applications. In evaluation, the 'pure' part of the discipline has not so far been extensively developed, although some efforts have been made in the history of axiology and with multiattribute utility analysis. It's inappropriate to duplicate this in each of the semiautonomous evaluation application fields, as often happens now. And these applications cannot constitute disciplines in their own right, not least simply because they are, logically, 'applications' of a more general study. If their metatheory does not record this fact, and the existence and mutual relevance of the other applications, it is crucially defective.

(vi) Most of the examples mentioned here exhibit a feature of metatheory that is in some contrast—although less than many suppose—with the main body of the discipline: they include *incompatible* accounts, models, or paradigms. It is for this reason that it is more accurate to talk of metatheory as the domain for *discussion* of the nature of the subject (etc.), rather than the domain of a single account. We should try for the single account, but we must often settle for understanding the extent of the truth in a number of perspectives.

(vii) The move to a metatheory of evaluation, to the discussion of the essential nature of evaluation and its methodology, first occurs in the recorded literature in the work of Greek philosophers, notably and at some length in Aristotle. But the discussion in the philosophical literature soon became focused on ethical value systems rather than practical ones, and soon on metaethics alone, with the connection to practice being left to the theologians. The name for what they did with it has become a synonym for the abuse of reason—casuistry. It is only in recent years that the applied fields in ethics have acquired some quality and respect, but that development has not led to any serious move back to developing the general logic of practical evaluation. In the present era, the few small steps in that direction have come from the applied fields. The transdisciplines are as dependent for viability on the applications as on work in the core area.

11. The payoff from creating a discipline: The move to the more general approach is an essential part of the same self-analytic process that led to making a science out of metallurgy after six thousand years of developing smelting, coating, annealing, and forging skills. Finding out how and why a process works is a standard route to improving practice and in many cases it leads to great practical advances almost immediately. In probability theory and game theory the story is well known—a gambler and an economist created the foundations of the new discipline in order to further their practice in another area. Research without critical reflection on the process involved is risky and inefficient, and evaluation, that ancient practice, has at last begun to mature in this respect.

The applied areas in evaluation were severely retarded in developing full disciplinary status by the ban on developing the core discipline due to the influence of other metatheories, notably the value-free doctrine in the social sciences. A modern scholarly literature relating to theories of the applied areas has only begun to emerge in the last third of the twentieth century. This was a handicap for the application areas because the move to a more general theory and paradigm of evaluation was required in order to relate the standalone applications to each other (and to the embedded uses of evaluation in the main disciplines), to push evaluation into new areas, and to legitimate it against attacks on its validity.

How far is evaluation from being a new discipline? If we set out some criteria for a new discipline, and expand them in some detail for the case of evaluation, it will be clear that there is still a considerable distance to go.

12. Criteria for a new discipline: In developing the new field of evaluation (and its younger sibling, policy analysis), much use was made of tools and building blocks from other disciplines—for example, the techniques of survey research from sociology, of test bias and design from educational psychology, and the discussions of types of validity from psychology. However, the origins of tools and building blocks are not the origins of a new discipline any more than the source of the tools and bricks used by Frank Lloyd Wright was the source of his architecture. A discipline is an organized intellectual construct, an element in a complex taxonomy; it's not a bag of tricks and bricks. The

substance of a discipline is its work; the key to the discipline is the overall concept, the metatheory.

Recapitulating and expanding some remarks made in the allegorical exposition, we can distinguish four elements in the emergence and development of a new discipline. They are interdependent, so they are not a sequence of phases in an irreversible maturation process.

• First, there is the emergence of *consciousness*—the explicit recognition that something new is afoot or possible—and the *definition* of what is new (mapping its shape and location). Getting the definition or map right takes several tries—it is partly prescriptive and hence creative—and is crucial because it lays the ground rules for what follows. It is the first step toward liberation from inappropriate models and methods, and the first step toward a metatheory.

• Second, there is the identification and development of an appropriate *methodology*—a set of procedures and tools to generate enlightening or useful results in the new field. These are craft techniques and usually involve some customizing of previously available tools and the selection of materials for the new domain, ranging up to the addition of genuinely new tools and materials. The methodology may be highly specific (scoring keys in marking essays), but it may range up to the level of general methods and models of analysis (a program evaluation checklist), at that point merging into the later elements listed here.

• Third, there is the development of *findings*. These consist of (i) *databases* (of facts, reports, information, illustrations, portrayals) and (ii) *general principles and theories*. The element of generality will be present, explicitly or implicitly, at a minimum in the form of new conceptual schemes and their associated terminology, since these are involved in defining the fields in a database. Usually there are explicit taxonomies, and often also laws, generalizations, and theories[28].

---

[28] The work in a field is often divided into pure and applied work, but both generate findings of fact and of theories and principles. Specifically, a branch of pure mathematics such as number theory uncovers large numbers of facts, and formulates many general principles including taxonomies; a branch of applied chemistry like pharmacology also generates facts, generalizations, and theories to account for them, and its own taxonomies. Theories and generalizations are no more the property of pure science than facts are the property of applied science. Consultants, whether physicians or evaluators, may be thought to be one level further down the hierarchy toward the specific and

• Fourth, there is the *metatheory* of the discipline. It provides a framework—even if a loose and almost invisible framework—for the practice. The metatheory is almost always double-edged, that is, both descriptive and prescriptive, usually deriving the latter from insights based on the former. Without a metatheory, an area of study cannot be identified as a new discipline—it has not identified or defined its territory, it cannot justify its procedures, its ontology, or its boundaries. With a metatheory, disciplinary status depends on the quality of the metatheory.

13. The emerging discipline of evaluation: In the new era of *program* evaluation, early work on the metatheory, consisting mainly of proposed models for the field, came largely from the educational evaluators rather than from those in sociology and psychology. The latter were more inclined to maintain the adequacy of the existing conception of social science, and to see evaluation as just a multidisciplinary application within that family of disciplines. Partial exceptions were the methodological specialists and reformers from those disciplines, notably Campbell, Cook, and Cronbach from psychology, and Suchman and Weiss from the policy sciences[29]. But their contributions were mainly to metamethodology and to the sociology and politics part of theory and metatheory, respectively, rather than to new models and paradigms for evaluation.

The scholars from educational research—and Cronbach could as easily be classified there—had two advantages. First, there was a long history of explicit evaluation in their field—the evaluation of student work, on which much of educational psychology and educational measurement was based, albeit somewhat insecurely[30]. Second, they were more at home with the *radically* multidisciplinary array that makes up their own subject—where the history and philosophy of education, the law of education, comparative education, and quantitative techniques already cohabited—and thus took more easily to the prospect of adopting a new methodology. Tyler in 1942 was the ad-

---

away from the general, but even this does not exclude them from studies of the general success of a treatment in a sample of cases. In any case, investigating individual cases of particular interest is as scientific as writing about generalizations, and there are sciences that spend most of their time doing this.

[29] See the discussions of and by some of these writers in *Foundations of Program Evaluation,* by Shadish, Cook, and Leviton (Sage, 1991).

[30] As we saw when the extent to which norm-referencing methodology had taken over testing became clear. To give one example, we had a thousand standardized tests but none for functional literacy, probably the most needed test of all.

vance guard, suggesting a multipurpose model of educational program evaluation that was related to identified behavioral objectives and not just conventional testing. Stufflebeam and his colleagues came up with a different and more detailed model—the CIPP model—as early as 1970[31]. There followed a dozen other ingenious models or paradigms ranging from the connoisseurship model to the jurisprudential one, and House, a decade later, saw the need for—and began work on constructing—the still more radical but still more important connections to argumentation theory and ethical theory[32]. All of this, although it represented considerable progress, still leaves us far short of anything that deals with evaluation *in general*: a general theory, general logic, general studies of the psychology and utilization of evaluation, and a general metatheory—the tasks of the core discipline.

The distinctions made so far may help in understanding the oversimplification in a widely held view, for example: "...the main intellectual roots of evaluation research are to be found in the social sciences..."[33]. The main *intellectual skills* in evaluation research long antedated the social sciences; the main *logical* roots came from philosophy, beginning (as far as we know) with Aristotle; and the 'intellectual roots' of the essential *metatheory*, albeit only for *program* evaluation—without which it could not become a discipline—came from the educational researchers. What came from the social sciences was simply the main *methodological* roots of the new field, but they were accompanied by implacable resistance to the key features of a general metatheory for evaluation, which did a good deal to cancel out the contribution because it made serious validation of evaluative conclusions illicit.

14. Midcourse review: Thus, a substantial field of theoretical and applied research emerged in the in the 1960s and 1970s, with its own methods and a number of elements of metatheory. But it was not yet a discipline of program evaluation—and much further from being a discipline of evaluation—for at least two reasons. First, it was and is conceived and defined too narrowly by essentially all researchers. There was usually a definitional requirement that evaluation was something done in the service of decisions, or that it was done only of interventions, or that it was done only of programs. None of these restrictions make logical sense, because they exclude the evaluation of past pro-

---

[31] In particular, in *Educational Evaluation and Decision-Making* (Peacock, 1971).

[32] *Evaluating With Validity*, Sage, 1980.

[33] Berk and Rossi, *Thinking About Program Evaluation*, Sage, 1990, p. 12.

grams by historians who have no interest in servicing decision-makers, and studies by researchers mainly interested in getting a true account (and a publication). The logic is identical, so the service of decision-makers is not definitionally relevant[34]. So, even as definitions of program evaluation, these were too narrow.

Moreover, all the definitions used, even if they avoided the previous complaints, were much too narrow to define a discipline of *evaluation*, not just for lexical reasons, but for pragmatic reasons. Implicit or explicit exclusion of the other areas of practical evaluation led to mistakes in the choice of methodology and imposed serious limits on the adequacy of the program evaluations that resulted. To mention two of many possible examples: Product evaluation was not even considered as an appropriate and illuminating exemplar *for* the methodology of program evaluation; and personnel evaluation was not seen as an essential element *in* program evaluation. Excluding evaluation in the primary disciplines is equally costly, for them and for the evaluation applications.

Second, the foundations of the new field were excessively shallow. Two of many examples again: it had no solution for the problem of establishing the validity of any direct evaluative conclusions[35]; and it made no serious attempt to distinguish wants from needs, in order to do needs assessments or to weight the relative importance of evaluative criteria, both key components of program evaluation.

This second kind of shortcoming was due to the previously mentioned conflict between the mission of the new discipline and a key plank in the metatheory of the social sciences—the value-free doctrine. This was the conflict which led to the 'paradoxical status of evaluation'. Its traces could not be washed away merely by avoiding

---

[34] Of course, it is *extremely important* but all it does is to bring home something that applies in all cases: the *definitional* requirement that a point of view and a framework of feasibility be specified before evaluations can be done or appraised. This requirement applies to the evaluative historian and evaluation researcher just as much as to the evaluator servicing a decision maker.

[35] A direct conclusion is one that asserts the merit of something, without relativizing it to some set of values from which the researcher withholds endorsement. It may still be heavily qualified, but it is not qualified by assumptions about which values are correct. For example, "Reading program X is better than reading program Y for population Z in circumstances W" is a direct evaluation; but if you add "on the assumption that values V are correct", you have a much weaker conclusion, here called a relativistic or secondary value claim. It is of limited practical use as a guide to action for public officials unless someone can establish the truth of the assumption of V; basically, it's only halfway to doing the job of the evaluator.

direct evaluations in favor of instrumental or relativistic evaluations—that is, by evaluating things as means to someone else's ends, without taking any stand on the correctness of the ends. No discipline can restrict itself to relativistic claims, and certainly not to relativistic evaluative claims. For, if researchers in a field cannot distinguish what is actually—rather than relativistically—a good theory or interpretation from a bad one, the field would have no way to distinguish between discipline and drivel. It would be a double absurdity to have a discipline of evaluation which could not go beyond relativistic conclusions.

15. The key problem: the validation of evaluations: Social scientists have never had a problem with establishing relativistic value claims, nor have they had great difficulty about ascertaining the ends or values of others—or of a market or culture. The latter conclusions are what one might call secondary value claims. These are by no means the same as mere reports of what a subject says to be their values. Such reports are just part of the raw data for an inference to a secondary value claim. The inference to the actual values of a subject (or group) often integrates longitudinal behavioral observations with knowledge of context and culture, and with the verbal reports, to produce a verifiable claim about X's values, one which X may even deny. Hence there is already a difference between what is said by the subjects about themselves, and what is true about the subjects. In this sense, even personal values, so often said to be merely subjective (i.e., incorrigible first-person reports), are third-party verifiable and part of the domain of objectivity.

But serious evaluation must go beyond these secondary value claims. Evaluation, to match other disciplines, must lead to conclusions about what is *in fact* meritorious, or *really* valuable, or what has *true* merit (either compared to other things or compared to stated and verified standards). Of course, any such claims are subject to the usual background qualifications about the ubiquitous possibility of error, but that is a quite different kind of qualification. These are *primary* value claims; they are not secondary or relativistic claims. These are claims that something *is* the case, not just that it would be the case if something else were the case, or that someone believes it to be the case. This is the type of conclusion that we find in and demand from other disciplines—from scientists and other scholars and craftleaders—and which we must get from at least some evaluations. Sometimes we will be able to make such claims after we have verified the truth of value *premises* that claim to offer standards from which we can draw evaluative conclusions; sometimes we will need to verify the *inferences* by which evaluative conclusions are derived from

29

factual and analytical premises. The key question is: How can this be done, how can evaluative claims be validated?

Because the value-free doctrine in the social sciences was committed to the view that this cannot be done, the social scientists coming to program evaluation—including those in educational research with social science training—had to bypass the key question, or break free of their intellectual heritage. The first option proved more attractive. The best they could do with the problem was to use—but not evaluate— the values of those connected with the program, the planners or the consumers or both. They were thus necessarily restricted to doing secondary or 'second-hand evaluation'—evaluation from the point of view of others. This put them in a position rather like astronomers working for astrologers: "Relative to your beliefs, this would be an auspicious time for an Aries to marry a Leo". All the hazards of the hired gun became pressing. Presumably some code of professional ethics would prevent them from the possibility of giving a favorable evaluation of the effective use of torture by secret police. Can such a code be justified? If you believe it can, you have of course conceded that direct *ethical* evaluation, the hardest type of all to justify, is legitimate. One can hardly then avoid conceding the legitimacy of primary or direct conclusions about practical programs—for example, the conclusion that preschool program X *is* unsafe or that the new drug therapy program Y *is* without merit for AIDS patients[36].

The example of the ethical codes will not impress the committed value-free social scientist, who will argue that the code of ethics cannot *really* be justified, and is adopted only for reasons of expediency; *or* that it can only be justified in terms of one's values as a citizen, not as a scientist; *or* only in terms of one's values as a scientist but not the values of science. If any of these moves were sound, legitimate evaluation would be restricted to relativistic evaluation. To become a respectable discipline, evaluation must find a foundation that is immune to these complaints, or it will be built on sand.

Remember that in all this, the social scientists were operating with double standards because they were, as scientists, continually involved in the creation, criticism, and application of scientific evaluative standards within scientific research and applications, within the

---

[36] Of course, we've never had a problem about coming to such conclusions about drugs, because product evaluation has never had the value-free hangup—but the program evaluators did not consider product evaluation a legitimate paradigm, and there was no credible core discipline to call them to account for this expensive indulgence in second-rate philosophy.

teaching of science, and in talking about the nature of their subjects[37]. As citizens and consumers, too, they were often making rational evaluations, or critically rejecting some of those made by others. So they already had, and had used, paradigms of scientific, pragmatic, and ethical evaluation. On the ethical side, the American Psychological Association (APA)—and other professional societies—produced detailed and laudable standards for the ethical use of psychological tests, made decisions about proper practice in psychotherapy and on the APA's social and ethical responsibilities. But when it came to doing evaluation as part of the job of program evaluation—instead of as part of the job of grading students, reviewing articles, selecting or designing instruments or experiments, or prescribing how to behave as a professional on the job—then their willingness to extend these paradigms failed.

Could this have been due to the feeling that in program evaluation they lacked crucial relevant facts that in the other cases they had in their possession through necessary professional familiarity? This seems unlikely, because any facts they needed for evaluation—even for ethical evaluation—of a program could be made a target for discovery in the course of the program evaluation. Could they perhaps argue that the problem lay in the impossibility of *endorsing* rather than discovering the values they would need in order to judge the program? But there's nothing harder about working out what values to use ("endorse") in evaluating a program than in evaluating scientific work or ethical codes or student talent and they were able to reach categorical conclusions about the latter; you endorse the relevant ethical and practical values, no more and no less. Those are the values one "endorses" in writing an article or a report, or in dealing with a client or student or salesperson.

In sum, they had the tools for determining appropriate values, they had or could get the relevant facts, and they had legitimated the use of the tools 'internally' (dealing with their own professional behavior, with their students, and with research in their field); but they rejected

---

[37] The double standard is often embarassingly visible in discussions of the value-free position itself. To elaborate on an earlier note, those supporting it are essentially arguing for the position that value judgments within science are *improper* or *illegitimate*. Because this formulation is a value claim itself, one that is said to be rationally defensible in terms of the usual scientific standards of evidence and inference, it thereby becomes self-refuting: "Value claims have no legitimate place within science, and I can prove that scientifically." (If no such proof is possible, then this is simply a value claim, not better or worse than its denial, hence not worth mentioning let alone respecting.)

the 'external' legitimacy of the tools—their use in dealing with the performance of a program 'out there', the kind of program they were supposedly evaluating. The *logic* of evaluation can hardly be different for 'objects out there' by contrast with objects in here, and it was the logic they were rejecting.

Usually, they went further, and denied that tools for evaluating were legitimate anywhere, preaching the doctrine of value-free science to their students as if it were not refuted by their own professional activities. For problems of 'external' evaluation, this left them in the position of doing values *description* and values *clarification*—doing second-hand evaluation—but not in the position of *doing evaluation*. Although their approach can certainly be useful for some clients, it is only halfway to a new discipline; and for many clients it is simply not addressing the key question, namely: Which program *is* better—for these patients in this setting?

In terms of the view presented here, this failure to provide an answer to the key question—how to validate evaluative conclusions—and the consequent limitation to, at best, relativistic claims—would of itself exclude the field from the title of an autonomous discipline. What we have instead is a package of tools for clarifying the implications of the value premises held by various audiences and clients, some models of the activity of (conditional) program evaluation, and some general notions, many of them enlightening and useful. There is no doubt that this package establishes the existence of a new service, even a new *field*. It cannot be a new *discipline*, a new knowledge taxon, for this reason in addition to those already listed: it cannot deal with the key question of validating its own conclusions.

Of course, the restriction of evaluation to second-hand claims makes it much more plausible to say that evaluation is a branch of applied social science, because that approach to evaluation is as old as the social sciences themselves. Even in the first two decades of the twentieth century, as the doctrine of value-free social science was being cast into concrete, social scientists were clearly saying that they could tell you what the consequences of alternative value commitments would be, but that speaking as scientists, they could not tell you which value commitments to make and hence which value conclusions you should draw. (This point was often put in terms of the means/end distinction.) If that were the best we could do today, then we would not have a new discipline.

But evaluation *is* a new discipline, if properly conceived, and we need to tie the new models and methods to a better core conception. That conception must not only handle the question of validation, but it must begin with a better idea of the scope of evaluation.

32

16. The scope of evaluation: Why did the educational researchers and the (other) social scientists miss that crucial point on the 'consciousness criterion'—the first of the criteria listed above as markers for a new discipline—a reasonable definition of territory? Although the educational researchers—much more aware that something really new was happening—produced a series of imaginative and enlightening models and metaphors for evaluation, based on processes in other fields such as the law, they were much like the social scientists in that they never saw, or at least never made anything of, *the universal and fundamental nature of evaluation.* They persisted in a 'geocentric' approach: Evaluation is what we do, so that is all evaluation is. The center of the evaluation universe must rather be seen as the sun of the core discipline, not one of the planets, even if all life were on them.

This mistake was perhaps partly due to the fact that both groups lacked analytic experience with—by contrast with use of—the fields of evaluation that long antedated program evaluation, of which the most sophisticated was probably product evaluation (although a case could be made for adding applied ethics). But in part it was the lack of training in logical analysis as a discipline in its own right, for with that orientation one cannot fail to see the transcendent similarities. The whole logic of evaluation, its very vocabulary, carries over from field to field in just the way that the logic of probability does, or the logic of explanation, or the logics of measurement, statistical inference, or decisions. There is no difference in the way that one goes about establishing—or refuting—an evaluative conclusion concerning malfeasance in a law court, inferior design in four-wheel-drive differentials, bad arguments in a student paper, weaknesses in Linnaean taxonomy, or poor performance in a program. The metatheory of many program evaluators contains some hints of reasons for maintaining the distinctions: "People aren't things, so program and personnel evaluation can't be done like product evaluation". But it's equally true that people *are* things, and we weigh them and measure them and run tests on them in clinics, just in order to benefit them. One needs to say *in what respects and why people* are not to be treated as things, in order to avoid error, and the metatheory has no specific suggestions on those points.

If one accepts the view that there is a far-reaching practice of evaluation, highly developed in several of its applications, and that we now have a respectable body of models and theories attached to slices of that practice, with an increasing amount emerging about its common features, then one has accepted the fundamental limitation in the concept of evaluation as part of applied social science. Although that is the home of a few of its applications, it is not the home of the discipline itself, any more than it is the home of statistics.

Evaluation is thus a subject in its own right, not to be buried in subheadings under education, health, law enforcement, or "Social Sciences, Sundry". One might as well argue that there is no subject of statistics, only agricultural statistics, biostatistics, demographics, and so on; no logic, only criticism of propaganda, and so on. The Library of Congress has now recognized evaluation's independence by allocating a special classification for general works in evaluation, paralleling the one for general works on research methodology. The second edition of this book was the straw that broke the back of many years' resistance; it was clearly inappropriate to classify it under any preexisting discipline.

Liberating the discipline from the confines of social science has immediate benefits such as the freedom—and the need—to look at validating the hypothesized values in relativistic claims. Another important expansion of scope comes from swifter recognition of the self-referent nature of evaluation, that is, from seeing that the evaluation of *evaluations* must be part of the discipline. The sociologists came to the analogous conclusion, when they saw that the sociology of sociology must be part of sociology. Evaluation, when treated as part of applied social science, was slow in making this move. One major cost of this tardiness was the breakaway of many federal agencies, who often found the glacial pace of the large social research projects that were being sold to them as evaluations useless for practical purposes and moved to 'inspections'—fast looks at key issues. The grip of the social science research model thus constrained the development of new and more useful models of evaluation. More serious attention to the evaluation of the evaluations that were being done should have come from the evaluators, not from their clients. The problem was not one of how to improve utilization as such but one of how to do useful evaluations.

Although seeing the similarities in evaluation across the realm of systematic thought generates a broader and more defensible concept of evaluation—even of program evaluation—than setting its location in the social sciences, it does not generate a solution to the key question of how to validate evaluations. It only suggests that any answer to the key question should work across every discipline, and hence, because there are answers that work very well—for example, in product evaluation or the evaluation of experimental designs—there should be an answer that will work in program and personnel evaluation.

However, instead of looking for other areas of a broadly conceived

34

discipline of evaluation, where the problem had been solved, the opposite reaction predominated: Those other fields were defined out of the official territory. There were three ways in which this was rationalized in metatheoretical discussions. It was argued that evaluation, unlike 'real' scientific research—(i) is only concerned with supporting decisions, not with generating conclusions (i.e., knowledge, i.e. science); (ii) is only productive of situation-specific results and not of generalizable ones; and (iii) is only a matter of evaluating certain entitities, rather than a toolkit that could be applied to almost anything in the universe. The first two of these moves are discussed in the thesaurus entries, but the third is worth a few sentences here. Granted that one needs to become specific in order to give specific suggestions, what actually happened was much less defensible.

17. Semantic symptoms of scope control: What occurred was an interesting semantic phenomenon, which illustrates the pervasiveness of a generally restrictive attitude to the scope of evaluation. Despite the relatively recent emergence of anything like a discipline of evaluation, the term "evaluation" has been widely used in the titles of texts in psychology and educational psychology from the early decades of the twentieth century until now—for example, in Thorndike and Hagen's classic *Measurement and Evaluation in Psychology and Education,* 4th. edition, (Wiley, 1977; 5th. edition due in 1991). Although the term "evaluation" was used without any qualifications, it only meant "evaluation of student work". The idea that anything else in education and psychology needed evaluation, or could be evaluated—teachers, clinicians, approaches, curricula, policies, schools, and so on—was so unthinkable that no explanation or apology was given for not including any reference or application to these other obvious fields of educational evaluation. The term "evaluation" was simply restricted to evaluation of the powerless[38].

When the New Era in evaluation began and program evaluation became (quasi) legitimate, the same telltale abuse of the term recurred one level up. This time "evaluation" was used to mean "program evaluation". Few books with the unqualified term "evaluation" in the title, published in the last five years, refer to anything but program evaluation—including the leading text, Rossi and Freeman's *Evaluation: A Systematic Approach,* 4th edition, (Sage, 1989). There is no reference to the many fields of evaluation that long predated any

---

[38] In recent years, this situation has changed in education because of the work on many evaluation fronts that has occurred there. Nevertheless, a book called *Evaluation in Education,* by Richard M. Wolf (3rd. edition, 1990, Praeger) is only concerned with program evaluation.

discussions of program evaluation—they are treated as if they never existed. You will not even find a reference to those branches of evaluation which are obviously part of a systematic approach to program evaluation, namely personnel evaluation and product evaluation. Nor will you find any explanation of the failure to discuss them[39].

The failure to include any evaluation of the personnel who make up programs, the equipment they use, or the materials they often produce is remarkable because the first two of these items are obvious topics for evaluation in both formative and summative modes. After all, they are: (i) essential parts of programs, (ii) use up most of the budget, and (iii) are highly improvable. Even more remarkable is the less frequent, but still common, failure to discuss the evaluation *procedures* used for personnel, equipment, and products. The result of these omissions, to put it kindly, is seriously inadequate program evaluation. And the cause is the narrow-mindedness of the specialists, perhaps based on an unconscious recognition that they lack the expertise to handle personnel and product evaluation, but certainly based on acceptance of a narrow conception, not just of evaluation but also of program evaluation. The lack of expertise in many subject matter fields is something that evaluators are used to handling by collaborating with or hiring specialists to strengthen the evaluation team; but where the lack of expertise relates to part of evaluation, it does not occur to them to do it[40].

Thus the name for what was intended to be a new discipline of

---

[39] An analogous disregard is often visible in the early pages of books on evaluation where one finds a *redefinition* of a term like "evaluation" or "evaluation research" to *mean* "the evaluation of social programs". One might as well write a book called *Statistics: A New Approach* where you redefine "statistics" in the early pages to mean descriptive population statistics. In doing this, you have just made the title of your book a lie and many people and libraries will waste money to buy it. Authorship does not legitimate lexical imperialism. You also reveal something significant about your own limited vision.

[40] In a related situation, one finds social scientists complaining that it's inappropriate to include analysis of money management in the program evaluation agenda. But it's simply part of efficient management, and hence accountability requires that it be covered. This is one reason why the Inspectors General always check it, and one reason they broke away from traditional program evaluation designs. If social scientists can't do it, they should get competent help to do it, not redefine the field to exclude it. No one has to cover everything in every program evaluation, but one does have to make sure that one's selection matches the needs of the client, and this is surely a legitimate need.

36

evaluation was used in a way that put a false front on major gaps in the very conception of it. This is reminiscent of the use of the term "man" as in "man's knowledge of the universe", another use of a term that casually preempted what it conspicuously excluded.

18. Final review: The present approach makes two distinctive claims. The first claim is that there is one and only one discipline of evaluation, a 'transdiscipline'. It consists of: (a) a wide range of substantial practical applications of evaluation in various fields, some of them long-established primary disciplines, some of them semiautonomous, with a title that includes the term "evaluation"—each of the latter with its own theory and metatheory about a part of evaluation; (b) a nascent core discipline devoted to developing a distinctive and valid logic, general methods for evaluation, and theories about evaluation, its applications and its methods, from various perspectives including ethical, political, psychological, and sociological perspectives; and (c) a metatheory that includes various still more general and less explicit overviews and models or perceptions of evaluation's nature and presuppositions.

The second claim is that the dozen or so fields of evaluation that have achieved some recognition—program, product, policy, and personnel evaluation, for example—and that have developed a healthy repertoire of their own tools can be massively improved by recognizing their connections to the core discipline, to their sibling applications, and to evaluation practices in the primary disciplines. In this direction, it is suggested, lies part of the future of evaluation, the rest lying in improving the work on the core discipline.

To support the first claim, this work explicates the basic logic of evaluation by exhibiting and explicating paradigms for it and the logical concepts that underpin it, and defending these against common criticisms as well as technical difficulties. It goes on to develop a number of other aspects of the theoretical and metatheoretical areas of the transdiscipline, in order to provide further support for the transdisciplinary view.

To support the second claim, many examples are given of biases, errors, and limitations that can be remedied by appeal to the core discipline or to solutions found in other fields. Two examples were just mentioned: the omission of personnel and product evaluation when evaluating programs that depend heavily on personnel and products for their success. The most serious example, however, is the way in which goal-based approaches to program evaluation—the standard approaches—are not only biased toward management and against consumers, not only involve large unnecessary costs, but are completely inconsistent with good practice in evaluation, as evidenced in product evaluation. Requiring that the general logic of evaluation methodology be consistent across all fields of evaluation uncovers this inconsistency, reveals the underlying bias, and points the way to a solution—and an explanation of why the inconsistency occurred.

Some more recent examples of the benefits a transdisciplinary approach can confer have occurred within personnel evaluation. New standards for personnel evaluation have been developed and published, based on foundational notions in evaluation rather than just statistical and measurement concepts. More recently still, serious flaws in standard personnel evaluation practices have become apparent simply by applying the analogous standards from other fields—in this case, medical diagnosis and legal reasoning. At the metalevel, if we attempt to evaluate research on, for example, teaching, we find a sorry record of irresponsibility. Three volumes of a thousand pages or more have been published under the title *Handbook of Research on Teaching*, by the leading professional educational research association; they span the years from 1963 to 1986, contain hundreds of articles by the leading researchers—and essentially nothing in them is connected to the improvement of teaching. There is nothing at all on the evaluation of school teachers, a couple of pages on the evaluation of college teaching, and not even a definition of good teaching. If one can't define and identify merit in teaching, the connection of one's research with the improvement of teaching will be accidental and unrecognized. Although one might try to justify this orgy of largely useless research as pure research—the editors do not attempt this gambit—education is presumably an applied field, of its very nature, so the idea that *all* 'research on teaching' worthy of inclusion in a handbook should be pure research is at best dubious, at worst ludicrous. Imagine researchers in pharmacology ignoring all research connected to patient health[41].

Evaluation of work in economics and political science leads to even

---

[41] Others in the educational research field finally reacted to this curious omission in research on teaching, and in 1981 and 1990 the association produced the first and second *Handbook of Teacher Evaluation*. But the appearance of the first of these had no effect on the content of the next *Handbook of Research on Teaching*, which appeared five years later. The 'researchers' still did not think that research on or using teacher evaluation—basically, research on or connected to criteria for good teaching—counted as research on teaching. This example is a good indication of the still-sturdy grip of the value-free doctrine on research in education. It would be much more appropriate—and impossibly declassé—for the AERA to organize research around and publish MedaLists every year or two, for the three best reading programs, the three most effective teacher training techniques, and so on.

more serious conclusions. As examples one could point to the slow death of welfare economics and the decades of disinterest in the justification of democracy. In sum, the failure of nerve about evaluation diverted the energies of tens of thousands of researchers into what could at best be called pure research, when applied research—which of course requires evaluative notions like success or merit—was desperately needed.

Even in the well-developed applied field of product evaluation, the transdisciplinary approach has uncovered, and detailed, serious flaws in computer product evaluation and in Consumers Union procedures.

These examples are intended to provide support for the claimed payoff from the comprehensive view of evaluation presented here, a view that is topographically considerably deeper and broader than its predecessors. The view is deeper than prior efforts simply in the sense of extending its foundations further down into the underlying logic, psychology, sociology (and so on) of evaluation. It is broader in three respects—particularly by comparison with the 'applied social science' view—but there is one respect in which it is narrower than some other current views of evaluation.

19. A broader view—in most respects: The transdisciplinary view is broader, first, in that it claims evaluation makes up a crucial part of every discipline—and of many areas of everyday life and craft—and the study and improvement of all these uses of evaluation is said to be part of the proper subject matter of evaluation[42]. Second, sound evaluation in a particular case is said to (often) require that we investigate and weight a broader range of considerations than has usually been the case—although this does not mean that it will lead to lengthier evaluations. For example, it is said that program evaluation should nearly always look at the personnel and products used by the program (at least, at the way they are evaluated), and sometimes look at the program's money management. It should also look more seriously at the needs that clients have for fast evaluation with easily understood reports, as in the 'inspection' model. These considerations take it further away from traditional social science approaches and bring in newer subjects like communications, rhetoric, informal logic, and data visualization, as well as the multidisciplinary repertoire it has long re-

---

[42] In particular, evaluation is not restricted to the policy-support role, the decision-servicing role, or the assessment of potential or actual social interventions. Nor is it limited to the academic disciplines; the crafts and rule-governed physical activities like t'ai chi are often and properly referred to as disciplines, and evaluation is what shapes the novice and identifies the experts there, too.

quired. (This suggestion is essentially an extrapolation of earlier suggestions that are now widely accepted, such as the need to include cost analysis.)

Third, evaluation as a discipline is here taken to include the whole *vertical* range of concerns, from the most abstract matters of evaluative logic to the most mundane aspects of combining cost analysis with decibel measurements in environmental impact studies of computer printers. Everything that concerns evaluation as a process, and evaluations as products, is part of evaluation as a discipline; no theoretical questions are above its head, no practical ones beneath its dignity.

However, in a fourth respect the present view is very narrow compared to some currently popular or emerging ones. It rejects as incidental to the purpose of evaluation (i) nearly all causal microanalysis[43] in summative evaluation, and all of its big brother, descriptive 'program theory', in both formative and summative evaluation; (ii) most 'normative' (prescriptive) theories about the entities being evaluated; (iii) much of the focus on remediation and other recommendations; and (iv) most, though by no means all, of the concern about utilization (apart from research on the subject). In saying that these matters are incidental to the primary purpose of evaluation, it is not being said that evaluation is incidental to *them*. In some cases, studies of these matters cannot even begin without evaluations on which to build (for example, policy studies that aim at recommendations), and in many cases they can scarcely be justified as research efforts unless they are related to an evaluation. It is because they are neither themselves evaluative nor a necessary part of the process of getting evaluations done that they must be segregated—not precisely or rigidly, of course, but generally and firmly. (And regretfully, too; so one should watch for the quite common cases where some useful conclusions of these kinds are windfalls from an evaluation.) It seems likely that a lack of precision about the logic and province of evaluation has combined with the natural attraction of taking on exciting and potentially powerful roles to allow these peripheral matters to move into the limelight.

20. The state of current practice in program evaluation In sociological terms, the profession of evaluation has become a substantial area. There are professional associations in four countries with a total of several thousand members; it now has four of its own encyclopedias[44],

---

[43] The term "causal microanalysis" refers to all causal analysis other than the macro question of identifying the effects of the entity being evaluated.

[44] The most recent and notable of these is *The International Encyclopedia of Educational Evaluation*, edited by Walberg and Haertel (Pergamon, 1990). Its

40

perhaps a dozen of its own periodicals and a dozen more hybrids, and an annual production of a score or more of new anthologies, texts, and monographs. These might be—one must surely consider the possibility—just the trappings of a new discipline, no proof of lasting value. The fashion might surely fade, the journals die. That is a real possibility with some 'new disciplines'; with others, it is essentially absurd. It would be absurd to suggest that a point of view axiomatic to women's studies—the view of women as a long-oppressed class, and of women's achievements as massively undervalued for centuries in texts and references authored by males—might ebb with the tides of intellectual fashion and revert to the establishment view of the first half of this century. It would be no more absurd to suggest that molecular biology might revert to a pre-DNA viewpoint.

Evaluation shares something important with the example of women's studies. It is a discipline that was repressed for centuries—even in the first half of this one, part of its practice was specifically outlawed. In those days, scholarly journals would not consider evaluation reports for publication, *Consumer Reports* was blacklisted by ANPA, and Consumers Union was on the Attorney General's list of subversive organizations. Evaluation was repressed for a reason: It is a dangerous subject. It is the investigative journalism of commerce, social services, and the academy; it is the auditor's voice; it is the threat of judgment bruising to one's self-concept; the threat of an outsider treading one's own turf, a threat of loss of power. Once liberated from the model of merely relativistic, merely fiscal, merely managerial evaluation, this point of view cannot again be confined because it has discovered too much, created too many new ways to see things that repeatedly prove to be valuable. Indeed, it soon moves into niches in the establishment: the Food and Drug Administration adopts excellent product evaluation techniques, the Office of Technology Assessment and the Inspector General positions are created to help Congress make decisions by doing competent nonpartisan evaluations, the General Accounting Office has moved from fiscal auditing to serious program evaluation. Liberation of oppressed classes, suppressed activities, and banned perspectives are not just a matter of fashion, and not reversible this side of total despotism.

Although the state of the art in program evaluation has progressed far beyond the simplistic goal–achievement approach, it is probably true that most current program evaluations still follow that path.

---

150 articles and 800 pages bear on most of the area of human services evaluation, not just education, but they only include four pages on educational personnel evaluation and none on educational product evaluation.

Common practice is often a long way behind best practice in a field where most practitioners had little training in the subject, lack primary professional loyalty to it, and do not keep up with developments in it. Although there are now strong professional associations, many evaluators do not bother to join them and are not evaluated for the currency of their knowledge of it because their supervisors often see the field as something simpler than it is and expect little more than monitoring. A significant part of the profession works in conditions where academic publication is not common or important; acquiring supporters in the agency is the key to success, mainly an exercise in office politics. Moreover, there are relatively few training programs in evaluation—less than in policy studies—from which candidates might be sought, so people with what is little more than peripheral training still move into quite senior positions in the field.

However, the key federal agencies like the OIGs, OTA, and the GAO are now providing a powerful role model of competent broad-spectrum evaluation close to the kind advocated here. Of course, they are not encouraged to second-guess legislative decisions (as the conscientious evaluator must often do), but even in that respect they are remarkably independent.

Even the weight of their influence, however, will not quickly overbalance the powerful prejudice built into the fact that most evaluation studies are still commissioned by managers with some investment in whatever is being evaluated. This usually means the studies are biased in favor of a manager's point of view—that is, toward a conception of evaluation as simply monitoring progress toward the goals of the program—by contrast with the point of view of consumers, who are naturally more interested in whether their needs are met, or taxpayers who are naturally more interested in whether their investment is cost-effective. (There's nothing illicit about monitoring; it just isn't evaluation.) Only a massive movement toward professionalism, together with pressure from consumers and their representatives will change this. Such an effort needs to be able to point to a better conception of evaluation than monitoring or other value-free approaches, and this book is intended to provide one[45].

---

[45] It will not help if it is fundamentally unsound, and in deciding on that the reader may wish to consult a thorough criticism of much of the author's earlier work in *Foundations of Program Evaluation: Theories of Practice* by Shadish, Cook, and Leviton (Sage, 1991), especially pp. 94–118. A hint that something survives the criticisms may be provided by the fact that the authors still found it in their (admittedly kindly) hearts to dedicate the book to Donald Campbell, Carol Weiss, and the present author.

21. Why does all this matter? Doing evaluation and doing it well matters in *pragmatic* terms because bad products and services cost lives and health, destroy the quality of life, and waste the resources of those who cannot afford waste. In *ethical* terms, evaluation is a key tool in the service of justice, in program as well as in personnel evaluation. In *social and business* terms, evaluation directs effort where it is most needed, and endorses the 'new and better way' when it is better than the traditional way—and the traditional way where it's better than the new high-tech way. In *intellectual* terms, it refines the tools of thought and exposes a pervasive and disgraceful prejudice—a further step toward demythologizing the disciplines. In *personal* terms, it provides the only basis for justifiable self-esteem. These considerations are intimately related: the intellectual conception drives practice and is driven by it, the business applications support, direct, and reflect the consumers' concerns, all interact with the ethical dimension, and these in turn with the psychology and politics of evaluation. This interconnection of so many elements is a mark of the importance of the whole, but it makes change very hard—and slow—even when sorely and quickly needed. In the end, the best way to deal with this Gordian knot is to cut it with the knife of a new paradigm. A knife will not do all the work that needs to be done, but it makes a fresh start possible—and it is time for a fresh start in evaluation.

CONVENTIONS

These are reasonably self-evident but are set out here for reference.
- Alphabetization proceeds without regard to hyphens and inter-word spaces, because these are not well standardized with recently emerged terms.
- Single quotes flag a dubious, quizzical, informal, or novel use of a term.
- Double quotes are used only to identify material quoted from other places, a typical but not specific remark, or a term where it is important to make clear that reference is being made to the term itself and not to what it means.
- Cross-references to another entry are in **bold lower case**—but this slightly distracting flag is not waved more than once in any entry, for a particular term. There is sometimes a slightly imperfect match between the emboldened term, if used in a sentence, and the entry, to preserve sense; but never so much as to impede locating it.
- *Italics* are used for emphasis and for foreign phrases that are not yet naturalized.
- ***Bold italics*** are used for the names of books or journals; or for adddding emphasis to words already in italics.
- <u>Underlining</u> is used to highlight terms or distinctions related to the current entry that are being incidentally defined or distinguished—that is, they are not defined elsewhere—particularly when the use of italics might incorrectly suggest emphasis.
- ACRONYMS and other capitalized abbreviations are unpacked in a list at the end; a few of particular importance to evaluation or evaluators are also included in the main alphabetical listing.

A

ABSOLUTE EVALUATION Evaluation that is expressed categorically or unconditionally rather than relative to (conditional on the truth of) a stated set of values. Example: "Robinson's performance on the clinical part of the test was the best in the class" vs. "Robinson's performance was the best, if you use the criteria Accuracy, Completeness, Organization, Expression, weighted equally and with cutoffs." The term "absolute" serves as a red flag for many people, usually because they think it involves accepting some standards which are not open to question, and for this reason is usually referred to here as 'direct evaluation' (by contrast with 'indirect evaluation') or as 'first-hand evaluation' (by contrast with 'second-hand evaluation'). Direct evaluation does involve accepting standards, but they are not arbitrary or divinely ordained; they can be challenged and defended in just the same way as the factual elements in an evaluative claim (in the preceding example, the fact that Robinson's scores were as claimed). A measurement claim also involves a comparison with a standard, but is epistemologically less hazardous than an evaluative claim because the scale involved is defined arbitrarily (originally) and thus involves no claim of validity only a convention. But many of the most important kinds of scientific claim are absolute in the same sense as an unconditional evaluative claim. For example, the claim "About a third of the kudu in the reserve are infected with the K virus", based on autopsies of a carefully selected and appropriately sized sample, is absolute by comparison with "About a third are infected, if our sample is typical". In evaluation, as in science, you have to establish premises and then go forward on the assumption that they are sound. You can't keep listing them as conditions—but they never cease to be challengeable.

ABSOLUTE VALUES Values which transcend a person or situation, sometimes intended to mean values which transcend all people and situations. The first type is common—for example, legal standards—and there is a sense in which ethical standards are of the second kind. But their transcendence is only due to certain very general features of the human condition. (See **Ethics**.) The contrast to an absolute value is a relative value, such as the market value of gold at a particular time or the value of vintage burgundy to different people.

45

ACCOUNTABILITY Responsibility for the justification of expenditures, decisions, or the results of one's own efforts. Program managers and teachers should be, it is often said, accountable for their salaries and expenditures and time, or accountable for pupils' achievement, or both. Accountability thus often requires some kind of cost-effectiveness evaluation where it is taken to imply more than the ability to *explain* how one spent the money ("fiscal accountability"), but it is also expected that one be able to *justify* this in terms of the achieved results. Teachers have sometimes been held wholly accountable for their students' achievement scores (19th-century England), which is of course entirely inappropriate because their contribution to these scores is only one of several factors (the most frequently cited other influences are student ability, support from parents, support from peers, and support from the rest of the school environment outside the classroom). On the other hand, a teacher *can* appropriately be held accountable for the *difference* between the learning gains in his or her pupils and those of other teachers of essentially similar pupils.

A common fallacy associated with accountability is to suppose that justice requires the formulation of precise goals and objectives if there is to be any accountability; but in fact one may be held accountable for what one does, within even the most general conception of professional work, for example, for "teaching social studies in the sixth grade", where one might be picking a fresh (unprescribed) topic every day, or every hour, in the light of one's best judgment as to what contemporary social events and the class capabilities make appropriate. Less specificity makes valid measurement more difficult, but not impossible. Captains of vessels are held accountable for their actions in wholly unforeseen circumstances. It is true, however, that any measurement process has to be very carefully selected and applied if educational accountability is to be enforced in an equitable way. This does not mean that the test must be matched to what is taught (because what is taught may have been wrongly chosen), but it does mean that any tests must be very carefully justified, for example, by reference to reasonable expectations as to what should have been (or could justifiably have been) covered, given the need and ability of the students and the general language of the curriculum. It would often be the case that a range of alternatives would have to be recognized by the testing process or that the process would look only at rather general features of what was done.

ACCREDITATION The award of credentials to programs or institutions, in particular the award of membership in one of the regional associations of educational institutions or in one of the professional organizations that attempt to maintain certain quality standards for membership. The "accreditation process" is the process whereby these organizations determine eligibility for membership and encourage self-improvement toward achieving or maintaining the status. The accreditation process, as commonly practiced, has two phases: In the first, the institution undertakes a self-study and self-evaluation exercise against its own mission statement. In the second phase the (regional) accrediting commission sends in a team of people familiar with similar institutions to examine the self-study and its results and to look at a very large number of particular features of the institution, using data that is supplied by the institution together with a checklist. (*Evaluative Criteria* is the best known of these, published by the National Society for School Evaluation, for use at the high-school level). The results of this process are then pulled together in an informal synthesis process. At the elementary level, schools are typically not visited (although one of the handful of regional accrediting commissions is an exception to this); at the high -chool level a substantial team visit is involved, and the same is true at the college level. Accrediting of professional schools, particularly law schools and medical schools, is also widespread and done by the relevant professional organizations; it operates in a similar way. Accrediting of schools of education that award credentials—for example, for teaching in elementary schools—is done by the state; there is also a private organization (NCATE) that evaluates such schools.

Accreditation is probably the oldest form of institutional evaluation in this country, but there are grave problems with it as currently practiced. These include the use of amateur site-visitors, that is, people unskilled in the now-accepted standards for serious program evaluation—such teams, among other faults, change the interpretation of the standards on an idiosyncratic basis; visits that are too frequent for a settling-down process (less than two years, in some cases); disinterest in looking at learning achievements by contrast to process indicators; the inconsistency between regions (particularly bad news for multistate institutions); inconsistency between its practice and the claim that it accepts the institution's own goals; the **shared-bias** problem; the brevity of the visits; the institutional veto and middle-of-the-road bias in selecting team members; the lack of concern with costs; the failure to compensate for the fact that the costs of accreditation are paid by the in-group and hence create a prima facie bias against admitting competitors; and so on. Overall, there is a strong tendency toward the rejection of innovations simply because they are unfamiliar and a strong tendency to use secondary indicators of unproven validity. Examples include appeal to library size (instead of, for example, electronic database access) although credible figures on library *use* are not available for the institutions whose representatives appeal to this criterion; use of seat hours instead of learning outcomes (even if seat hours are supervised hours, they may not match the hours that a student will put into a work-related project). See **Institutional evaluation, Assessment, Incestuous relations.**

ACHIEVEMENT vs. APTITUDE (THE APTITUDE/-ACHIEVEMENT DISTINCTION) It's obvious enough that there's a difference between the two; Mozart presumably had more early aptitude for the piano than you or I, even if he'd never been shown one. But statistical testing methodology has always had a hard time over the distinction because statistics isn't subtle enough to cope with the point of the distinction, just as it isn't subtle enough to cope with the distinction between correlation and causation. No one has achievement who doesn't have aptitude, by definition, so there's a one-way correlation; and it's very hard to show that someone has an aptitude without giving them a test that actually measures (at least embryonic) achievement. Temerarious testing types have thus sometimes been led to deny that there is any *real* distinction, whereas the fact is only that they lack the tools to detect it. Distinctions only have to be conceptually clear, not statistically simple, and the distinction between a capacity (an aptitude) and a manifested performance (achievement) is conceptually perfectly clear. *Empirically,* we may never find good tests of aptitude that aren't mini-achievement tests. (Ref. *The Aptitude Achievement Distinction*, D. R. Green, ed., [McGraw-Hill, 1974])

ACTION RESEARCH 1. A little-known subfield in the social sciences that can be seen as a precursor of evaluation. 2. More commonly today, the name for research by teachers on classroom or school phenomena. An excellent idea, but one with a very poor track record.

ACTORS Social science (and now evaluation) jargon term for those participating in an evaluation, typically evaluator, client, and evaluee (if a person or his/her program is being evaluated). May also be used to refer to all active stakeholders.

ADMINISTRATOR EVALUATION A species of personnel evaluation that repeats many of the problems of teacher evaluation in that there is a tendency to appeal to style criteria. Because the research evidence appears not to support the existence of a demonstrably superior administrative style (e.g., with respect to democratic versus authoritarian leadership), this is an unpromising start. It is rendered completely useless because style variables cannot be used at all in personnel evaluation, for the reasons outlined under **personnel evaluation.** A better approach is as follows, illustrated for school administrators,

48

but readily translated. Here the assumption is that a principal is being evaluated, and that the evaluation is done by someone at the assistant-superintendent or higher level; again, it is easy to make the adjustments for evaluation of someone at a higher or lower level.

The three main components of administratior evaluation should be:

(I) judgmental ratings of global performance as an administrator, with a request to give an example of: (a) a good performance (if possible), (b) a bad performance (if possible), that have been *directly observed* by the respondent; and (c) a rating of overall performance on an A–F scale (excellent to incompetent) of performance as an administrator, as directly observed. These ratings are provided by a group of ten or twelve "highly interactive others"—people who have seen a great deal of the evaluee. This group is identified by: (a) a preliminary request for a list of about 10–15 from the administrator to be evaluated, to which is attached the comment that the search will also be instigated from the groups at the other end of the interaction; (b) a request for nominations to groups representing subordinates, superordinates, and peers (always including representation of office staff, consumers and/or public, professional staff, student government, same-level administrators, and senior administrators other than the evaluator); and (c) a selection of about 10 individuals from the combined lists by the evaluator, who should be able to select only one of every two nominees and does not release any names at all.

(II) A study of objective measures of effectiveness, such as turnaround time on urgently requested materials, vandalism and truancy rates, comparison of evaluations of staff who have moved on—by looking at their later track record and evaluations by others—with the evaluations of the same staff by this administrator, staff turnover rates, track record data on successful innovations, and so on. Often, it is only changes in these that should be weighted, and even then improvements—for example, on state assessment scores—only yield bonus points rather than part of what is necessary for acceptable performance, because the baseline may already be the maximum feasible. The list of measures is jointly developed by the district principals and district office, from a duties list and from their experience in identifying signs of excellence and difficulty.

(III) Paper-and-pencil or interview and/or simulation tests of relevant knowledge and skills, in particular of (i) knowledge and skills that provide the foundation for operations ("How do you handle a teacher that appears to be an incipient alcoholic?", "How do you reward outstanding teachers?", "Can you ask a paraprofessional to assist with lunch-room supervision?", "What are your plans for next

49

year's priorities, based on what needs-assessment?", etc.); (ii) new knowledge and understanding (e.g., research and legal changes) that have become important since the time of the last review; (iii) knowledge that must be in mind in order to handle emergencies ("Who do you call, in what order, when a fire breaks out in the science lab?", "Who is the school liaison officer at police HQ?", etc.); and (iv) self-evaluation. Increments in knowledge of types (i)–(iii) should be incorporated in a quarterly newsletter from the superintendent's office. This test can be combined with the annual review. Two of the key skills are self-evaluation and remediation/innovation planning, and a short document from the evaluee covering these points, sent in a week ahead, would always be discussed at these sessions, as would any **demurrers** from prima facie implications of the data from the other two sources. The quality of responses to this data would also be rated, and time might be allowed upon request, to produce a more reflective reaction and remediation plan where appropriate. This type of evaluation is thus closely tied to development, so that it should be a productive and supportive experience. In special cases, input from expert others might also be solicited. The use of performance (behavioral) objectives in administrator evaluation is usually rather easy for a skilled con artist to exploit, and hard to defend because of its lack of input from most of the people that have most of the evaluation-relevant knowledge; it also tends to discourage creative management because of the lack of rewards for handling "targets of opportunity"—indeed, there are usually de facto punishments for trying to introduce them as new objectives. It also has the other weaknesses of any **goal-based evaluation**. However, it can be built in as part of the development plan in the third component above, as indicated.

Administrators are often rightly nervous about the kind of approach listed here, because they understand that most of the people with whom they interact have a poor grasp of the administrator's extensive responsibilities and burdens. The questionnaire must therefore carefully delimit the requested response to rating (globally) the *observed* performance; the rest of the objection is taken care of by the comprehensive nature of the group responding (peers, superiors, and subordinates), supplemented by the objective measures. The results from the three components should be combined using cutoffs on each scale and combining performance above the cutoffs for a possible further cutoff on the total score. **Qualitative weigh and sum** provides more details.

ADVOCATE-ADVERSARY EVALUATION (THE ADVERSARY APPROACH) A type of evaluation in which, during the process and/or in the final report, presentations are made by two individuals or teams whose goal is to provide the strongest possible case for (and against) a particular view or evaluation of the program (for example). There may or may not be an attempt at providing a synthesis, perhaps by means of a judge or a jury or both. The techniques were developed very extensively in the early 1970s, from the initial example in which Stake and Denny were the advocate and the adversary (the TCITY evaluation), through Bob Wolf, Murray Levine, Tom Owens, and others. There are still great difficulties in answering the question, "When does this give a better picture and does it tend to falsify the picture of a program?" The search for justice—the home of the adversary approach—is not the same as the search for truth; nevertheless, there are great advantages in stating and attempting to legitimate radically different appraisals, such as the competitive element. One of the most interesting reactive phenomena in the history of evaluation was the effect of the original advocate-adversary evaluation; many members of its audience were extremely upset by the fact that the highly critical adversary report had been printed as part of the evaluation. They were unable to temper this reaction by recognition of the equal legitimacy accorded to the advocate position. The significance of this phenomenon is partly that it reveals the enormous pressures toward bland evaluation, whether they are explicit or below the surface. In 'purely logical' terms, one might think there wasn't much difference between giving two contradictory viewpoints equal status, on the one hand, and giving a merely neutral presentation. But the effect on the audience shows that this is not the case; and indeed, a more practically oriented logic suggests that important information is conveyed by the former method of presentation that is absent from the latter, namely the *range* of (reasonably defensible) interpretations. See also Relativism, Judicial model.

ADVOCATE TEAMS APPROACH (Stufflebeam) Not to be confused with the advocate/adversary approach to evaluation. A procedure for developing in detail the leading options for a decision-maker, as a preliminary to an evaluation of them. Part of the input phase in the CIPP model of evaluation. See also Critical Competitors.

AESTHETIC EVALUATION Often perceived by social scientists as the articulation of prejudice, it can involve a substantial objective component. See Architectural evaluation, Literary criticism.

AESTHETICISM The tendency to overweight characteristics that are essentially aesthetic. It is common in interview-based personnel evaluation and in consumer magazines, notably in road tests. This fault is simply a limiting case of style-based evaluation and hence of the use of irrelevant criteria.

AFFECT, AFFECTIVE (Bloom) Emotion, feeling, and attitude, usually supposed to be noncognitive. However, feelings and attitudes, and most emotions, have considerable cognitive components, so the assumed contrast between the affective and the cognitive domains (and even the psychomotor domain) is not sharp. For example, self-esteem and **locus of control** are often said to be affective variables, but many items or interview questions that are said to measure these actually (and appropriately) call for estimates of self-worth, which are evaluative claims, or judgments of locus of control, which are straight propositional claims about one's power in the world. Both are almost entirely cognitive. Treating the results as simply indicators of affect is part of the often confused thinking about affect, a type of confusion that often springs from the idea that the realm of valuing is not propositional but merely attitudinal, a fallout error from the **value-free** ideology in social science. Claims about one's ability or merit or worth are on a par with claims about one's strength and are verified or falsified by testing or evaluation. Although feelings are tied to some attitudes and may be considered affect, many valuations—whether or not they are associated with attitudes—are simply scientifically testable assertions.

Many so-called 'feelings' are just indicators of degree of belief. For example, "I *feel* perfectly capable of managing my own life, selecting an appropriate career and mate (etc.)" is often intended to be just a milder version of the claim "I *am* perfectly capable of...". The reference to feeling simply internalizes the claim—makes it more of a personal judgment—and thus draws back slightly from the riskier 'external-world' claim. One might think of it as inserting the words "but maybe I'm wrong" after the claim. The claim can still be properly attacked on the grounds that the view expressed (after the words "I feel") is false. But claims about feelings are ambiguous out of context: they may also be intended as entirely autobiographical, in which case the error sources are lying and lack of self-knowledge, but not facts about the external world. One is safer in making the feeling claim, but both are usually cognitive claims. At best, one must recognize that test items including claims like these are cognitive tests of affective variables, something from the realms of high-inference work and not straight measurement.

The use of affective measures—often politically obligatory—beyond the simplest expressions of pleasure, is extremely dubious because of (i) these conceptual confusions between affect and cognition, (ii) deliberate falsification of responses, (iii) unconscious misrepresentation, (iv) dubious assumptions made by the interpreter, for example, that increases in self-esteem are desirable (obviously false beyond a certain usually unknown point), (v) invasion of privacy, (vi) lack of even basic validation, (vii) high lability of much affect, and/or (viii) high stability of other affect. An expert on the measurement of affect once said that the only known-valid measure of affect relates to locus of control and that is fixed by the age of two. He may have been optimistic.

Despite these powerful grounds for scepticism, it is wrong to discard all concern with the affective domain. It is worth distinguishing what might be called "accessible affect" from the rest. For example, it is not only important to teach criticial thinking skills (or inquiry skills or composition skills or groupwork skills) as tricks that students can perform on demand, that is, as items in the cognitive skill repertoire—but also to teach the importance of their use, that is, *personally* valuing them. And one can better measure the extent to which they are valued, not by asking about it (the respondent know the expected reply) but by looking at the amount of effort that is made to use them when use is not obligatory, for example, in the job environment, or in project work where a narrower range of skills is being rewarded, but measures of—for example—library use can be obtained unobtrusively and not for judgmental purposes; attitudes to drug use are similarly reflected—but not simply—in drug arrest figures. Another measurement approach involves looking at the extent of generalization of the basic commitment, using some assumption about the affective commitment revealing itself in this way. For example, one may look at the accuracy of self-evaluations as an indicator of the extent of the affective commitment to the importance of evaluation. Again, one can get good estimates of the perceived value of items of this teachable kind from the respondent in well-designed and administered alumni interviews, without running into problems about privacy and into areas which one does not have a right to try to change.

It can also be argued with some plausibility that attitudes toward drugs, the environment, other races and sexes (for example) are affective variables that we should make some effort to measure in, for example, evaluating citizenship education—perhaps also in personnel evaluation—and that *do* change with experience and media exposure, even if less often with education of the traditional kinds. Still, there is an element of intrusiveness here; the key issue is not whether a teacher, for example, *feels* just the same about girls as about boys, but whether s/he *exhibits* sexist behavior. Thus, ironically, a case can be made for a behaviorist approach on ethical grounds rather than methodological ones. In sum, there is no doubt that the affective dimension is important; what is doubtful is the extent to which we can measure it reliably and the extent to which we should try to affect it

53

directly. The indirect approach to measurement and to modification—the cognitive approach—is often the best approach. See also **Objectives.**

AFFECTED POPULATION (a.k.a. impacted population) A program (or product, etc.) impacts the true **consumers** and its own staff. In program evaluation both effects must be considered though they have quite different ethical standings. At one stage, it looked as if the Headstart program could be justified (only) because of the considerable benefits to those it employed.

AFFIRMATIVE ACTION Often incorrectly seen as an legal imposition upon "proper" or "scientific" evaluation, or as an ethical requirement (and 'hence' separate from the real process of evaluation). This 'add-on' perception is one reason why women/minorities are still in fact discriminated against even by those with the best intentions. The gross excesses of many affirmative-action programs should not be allowed to obscure the underlying *scientific* (as well as ethical) rationale for special procedures that equalize treatment of candidates from groups against which there has been sustained discrimination in the past. Extended antinepotism rules, for example, like excessively strong job requirements, are two examples of about ten that have to be avoided, not just to meet 'intrusive' affirmative action requirements, but *so that the best candidate can be selected.* Opponents of affirmative-action think it necessarily represents a *reduction* of commitment to the principle of selection on merit. See **Personnel evaluation.**

AKA (or a.k.a.) Also known as, a contribution from police procedure (in describing aliases) to the vocabulary of the thesaurus.

ALLOCATION See Apportionment.

ALPHA TEST The first serious test of a new product, done in-house. Cf. **Beta test.**

ALTERNATIVE METHODOLOGIES (in evaluation or other research) The use of this term in the evaluation field has gone through three phases. In the first phase (late 1970s), it meant any approach other than true experiments. In the second, it referred to a specific list of methodological alternatives such as ethnographic, historical, comparative. Currently, there is some support for a shift of the term to the metalevel, so that the alternatives are positivism, postpositivism, constructivism, and critical theory. (Ref: *The Paradigm Dialog*, ed. Egon Guba [Sage, 1990]).

ANALYTIC or ANALYTICAL (grading or evaluation) An approach to the evaluation of something which involves evaluating its parts or aspects, either as a means to an overall evaluation or without the final **synthesis.** (See **fragmentary.**) The contrast is with **global** evaluation. On the basis of the analogy to the two approaches in economics referred to as the macro and micro approaches, analytic evaluation would be called microevaluation; global evaluation would be macroevaluation. In the methodological language of psychology, the terms would be molecular and molar. There are two main varieties of analytic evaluation: **component** evaluation (evaluation of the parts) and **dimensional** evaluation (evaluation of the aspects); combinations are possible, as in program evaluation. It is often thought that causal analysis (**etiology**), **diagnosis**, or **remedial** suggestions are part of analytic (typically **formative**) evaluation, but they are not, strictly speaking, part of evaluation at all. Although analytical evaluation is normally the approach of choice for formative purposes, there are cases where its much higher cost or lower validity may make this a mistake.

ANCHORING (ANCHOR POINTS) Rating scales that use numbers (e.g., 1-6, 1-10) or letters (A-F) should normally provide some translation of the labeled points on the scale, or at least the endpoints and midpoint. It is common, in providing these anchors, to confuse grading language with ranking language, for example by defining A-F as "Excellent... Average... Poor" which has two absolute and one relative descriptors and hence is useless if most of the evaluands are or may be excellent (or poor). Some, probably most, anchors for letter grades create an asymmetrical distribution of merit, for example because the range of performances that D (potentially) describes is narrower than the B range; this invalidates (though *possibly* not seriously) the numerical conversion of letter grades to grade points. It may be a virtue, if conversion is *not* essential. In another but related sense of anchoring, it means crosscalibration of, for example, several reading tests, so as to identify (more or less) equivalent scores.

ANONYMITY The preservation of the anonymity of respondents sometimes requires very great ingenuity. Although even bulletproof systems do not achieve honest responses from everyone in personnel evaluation, because of secret-contract bias, leaky systems get honesty from almost no one because of fear of reprisal. The new legal requirements for open files have further endangered this crucial source of evaluation input; but not without substantial ethical basis. The use of a 'filter' (a person who removes identifying information, usually the person in charge of the evaluation) is usually essential; a suggestion box, a phone with a recorder on it to which respondents can talk (disguising their voice), checklists that avoid the necessity for (recognizable) handwriting, forms that can be photocopied to avoid watermark identifiers, money instead of stamps or reply-paid envelopes (which can be invisibly coded) are all possibilities. Typical further problems: What if you want to provide an *incentive* for responding—how can you tell who to reward? What if, like a vasectomy, you wish to be able to reverse the anonymyzing process (e.g., to get help to a respondent in great distress)? There are complex answers, and the questions illustrate the extent to which this issue in evaluation design takes us beyond standard survey techniques.

APPLES & ORANGES (As in "comparing apples and oranges") Certain evaluation problems evoke the complaint, particularly from individuals trained in the traditional social sciences, that any solution would be "like comparing apples and oranges". Careful study shows that *any* true evaluation problem (as opposed to the unidimensional measurement problem) involves the comparison of unlike quantities, (usually) with the intent of achieving a **synthesis**. It is the nature of the beast. On the other hand, far from being impossible, the simile itself suggests the solution; we do of course compare apples and oranges in the market, selecting the one or the other on the basis of various considerations, such as cost, quality relative to the appropriate standards for each fruit, nutritional value, and the preferences of those for whom we are purchasing. Indeed, we commonly consider two or more of these factors and rationally amalgamate the results into an appropriate purchase. Although there are occasions on which the considerations just mentioned do not point to a single winner, and the choice may be made arbitrarily, this is typically not the case. Complaining about the apples-and-oranges difficulty is a pretty good sign that the complainer has not thought very hard about the nature of evaluation.

APPORTIONMENT (ALLOCATION, DISTRIBUTION) The process or result of dividing a given quantity of resources between a set of competing demands, such as dividing tax revenue or a departmental budget between projects or programs. This is often said to be the defining problem of the science of economics—"the science of the allocation of limited resources among competing demands"— but, extraordinarily, it is a problem that is rarely addressed directly or in practical terms within the economic literature, although the most important basic concept required has a prominent position in economic theory. The reason for this is presumably because almost any solution requires making assumptions about the so-called "interpersonal comparison of utility", that is, about the relative worth of providing goods to different individuals. Thus the **value-free conception** of the social sciences has made it impossible to provide practical solutions to the fundamental problem of economics, the apportionment problem. (An exception is the **zero-based budgeting** approach—one can hardly call it a literature, and it rarely gets referenced in an economics text.)

Apportionment of something valued can be thought of as a separate evaluation process, distinct from grading, ranking, and scoring, although all of those are involved in it. It can also be seen as a decision that has to be based on them as the primitive evaluation predicates, but this turns out to be somewhat convoluted. Of all the evaluation predicates it is probably the closest to the decision-maker's modal evaluation process. Various patently inappropriate solutions are quite frequently used to solve apportionment problems—when, for example, the overall budget is cut. The "across-the-board cut" is often used, although this not only rewards the padding of budgets, and hence automatically leads to increased padding the following year, but it also results in some funding at below the critical-mass level, a complete waste of money. Another inappropriate solution involves asking the program managers to make the cuts; this of course results in the blackmail strategy of setting the critical-mass levels too high, in order to get more than is absolutely necessary.

The only appropriate kind of solution involves some evaluation by a person external to the program, typically in conjunction with each program manager, and the first task of such a review must be to eliminate anything that looks like fat in each budget. Later steps in the process involve segmentation of each program, identification of alternative workable packaging of the segments, grading the cost-effectiveness of the progressively larger systems in each sequence of add-ons, and consideration of interactions between program components that could reduce the cost of each at certain points. Given an estimate of the "return value" of the money (the good it would do if not used for this set of programs), and the ethical (or democratic) commitment to prima facie equality of interpersonal worth, one then has an effective algorithm for spending the available budget in the most effective way. It will typically be the case that some funding of each of the programs will occur (unless the minimum critical mass is too large), because of the declining marginal utility of the services to each of the (semioverlapping) impacted populations, the long-term advisability of retaining capability in each area, and the political considerations involved in reaching larger numbers.

The process just described, although independently developed, is similar to the procedure for zero-based budgeting, an innovation of which the Carter Administration made a good deal in the first years of his presidency; but serious discussion of the methodology for it never seemed to emerge, and the practice was naturally well behind that. (See *Evaluation News*, Dec. 1978). In some conceptual sense, this is a complex application of the simple notion of marginal analysis, combined with the use of interpersonal comparisons of utility. Procedurally, it is an elaborate extension of one of the most brilliant examples of **bias control** methodology in the history of evaluation: the solution to the problem of dividing an irregularly shaped portion of food or land into two fair shares—"You divide, and I'll choose". That, in turn, is a micro version of the "veil of ignorance" or antecedent probability approach to the justification of justice and ethics in Rawls, *A Theory of Justice* (Harvard, 1971), and in Scriven, *Primary Philosophy* (McGraw-Hill, 1966). It is not surprising that ethics and evaluation share a common border here, because justice is often said to be a distributional concept.

Apportionment may be logically reducible to a very complex combination of grading and ranking, on multiple scales; but the reverse is also as likely. In any case, it may be better to use one extra—even though possibly redundant—predicate in setting up the logical foundations of evaluation, in the interest of perpicuity, as we often do in developing the foundations of mathematics or symbolic logic.

APPRAISAL A term for **evaluation**, occasionally used with specific connotations, especially that of establishing a market value for a house or products such as jewelry.

APPROXIMATION One of the ways in which evaluation reports and recommendations should differ from research reports concerns the use of approximation to avoid irrelevant and confusing precision. Careful investigation discloses that the use of approximation in science is more pervasive than appears if one only looks for explicit statements of approximation; for example, the laws of nature, stated categorically though they may be, are in fact almost all just approximations—and not even close approximations. The size of the error in the general gas law, for example, is often several hundred percent. The trade-off is comprehensibility; the escape phrase—in that example, a reference to 'perfect gases'—is often not mentioned. The lesson for the evaluator is a key part of the pragmatics of evaluation reporting—and of data presentation in general. KISS is the acronym—Keep It Simple, Stupid. Use ideal types, key anecdotes, approximations, **summaries** with a compression ratio of 1000:1.

ARBITRATION One of the triumvirate of **mediation**, negotiation, and arbitration, which are regarded as key components of industrial or personnel management. Reflection on these processes reveals a number of important lessons for the evaluator, in dealing with relations between evaluator and evaluee and between evaluator and client. For example, the notions of **credibility, ethics, therapeutic role,** legal role, and limitations are all involved in both tasks, and the way that arbitration—based on its longer track record—handles these aspects of its own process is illuminating.

ARCHITECTURAL EVALUATION Like the evaluation of detective

58

stories and many novels (see **literary criticism**), this field involves a framework of logic and a skin of aesthetics; it is frequently treated as if only one of these components were important. The solution to the problems of traffic flow and energy conservation, the use of durable fixtures that are not overpriced, the provision of adequate floor space and storage, meeting the requirements of expandability, budget, safety, and the law—these are the logical constraints. The aesthetic constraints are no less important and no easier to achieve. Unfortunately, architecture has a poor record of learning by experience, that is, poor commitment to functional evaluation; every new school building incorporates errors of the simplest kind (such as classroom entries at the front of the room), and colleges of architecture when designed by members of their faculty not only make these errors but are often and widely thought to be the ugliest buildings on the campus. (Cf. evaluators who write reports readable only by evaluators.) It is significant that the Ford Foundation's brilliant conception of a center for school architecture, after several years' operation, sank without a trace. It is not much good unless it gets used, after all; the reasons why it wasn't used are right up there with the reasons we do not use the results of serious evaluation of reading programs—see **Power**.

ARCHIVES Repository of records in which, for example, minutes of key meetings, old budgets, prior evaluations, and other **found data** are located.

ARGUMENTATION House has argued that evaluation is a form of argumentation (*Evaluating With Validity*, Sage, 1980) and hence that insights about it may be implicit in studies of reasoning such as the 'New Rhetoric'. It is not easy to pin this idea down to specifics. A more general source would be the literature of the **informal logic** movement, which includes the journal *Argumentation*, hence is consistent in spirit with his suggestion.

ARGUMENT EVALUATION In recent years, the chains of formal logic have been cut away from logic by the development of the informal logic movement. This process has involved, among many other features, a movement away from the all-or-none approach to classifying arguments as valid or invalid, toward a more typically evaluative approach that integrates several dimensions of merit (notably the probability of premises with the strength of the inference) and evaluates arguments as stronger or weaker, better or worse. Argument evaluation is only one part of informal logic, which is also concerned with the evaluation of claims and accounts, presentations and implications; and with the construction of good arguments.

ARTEFACT, ARTIFACT (of an experiment, evaluation, analytical, or

59

statistical procedure) An artificial result, one merely due to (created by) the investigatory or analytic procedures used in an experiment, an evaluation, or a statistical analysis, and not a real property of the phenomenon investigated. (For an example, see **Ceiling effect**.) Typically uncovered—and in good designs guarded against—by using multiple independent methods of investigation/analysis.

ASSESSMENT Often used as a synonym for evaluation, but sometimes the subject of valiant efforts to differentiate it, presumably to avoid some of the opprobrium associated with the term "evaluation" in the minds of people for whom the term is more important than the process. None of these efforts are worth much, either in terms of intrinsic logic or adoption. For one example, the term is sometimes recommended for restriction to processes that are focused on quantitative and/or testing approaches and less on judgment; the quantity may be money (as in assessment of real estate for tax purposes, by the county assessor), or numbers and scores (as in the National Assessment of Educational Progress). However, these appear to be mainly cases of evaluation in which the judgment is built into the context of the numerical results. Raw scores on a test of no known content or construct validity would not be assessment; it is only when the test is—for example—of basic mathematical competence that reporting the results constitutes assessment in the appropriate sense, and of course the judgment of validity is the key evaluative component in this.

Another recent effort has been made to restrict the term entirely to personnel evaluation, a move that would of course exclude the National Assessment of Educational Progress and many other well-established uses and is contrary to other moves mentioned above. See **Clinical performance evaluation.**

In the 1980s, this term became a war cry for a movement to address once more, in a different way, several of the standard problems in the evaluation of students and colleges. An excellent overview of the higher-education side of this is provided by Ewell in the 1991 *Review of Research in Education,* published by AERA. On the program-evaluation side, not much has emerged that isn't already part of the standard program-evaluation repertoire, except that large numbers of colleges are for the first time doing what minimum accountability requires. Another part of the assessment movement, strongly supported in schools as well as colleges, is the move away from paper-and-pencil testing toward something more judgmental and global (hence in the opposite direction from the first sense above). Somewhat independently, moves away from multiple-choice tests are also well supported. So far, these well-intentioned moves away from

60

the rigidities of the multiple choice test show little sign of coming up with something new that will meet reasonable standards of utility and justice; but they might yet, so they should be welcomed—cautiously. A well-balanced view of the new forms of student assessment appears in the volume cited above. Another approach is to develop improved and very different forms of machine-scorable tests (a better name than "objective tests"); see **Multiple rating item** and also **Clinical performance evaluation.**

ASYMMETRY (of evaluation criteria) One often enounters the naive view that evaluative checklists or questionnaires that have more potentially negative points than positive ones are biased. On the contrary, in the context of formative evaluation, a good case can be made for having *only* negative checkpoints (a list of all possible errors is the perfect guide to identifying areas needing improvement). In the summative context, for example in personnel evaluation, one needs to understand that merit isn't a symmetrical notion with respect to duties— regularly missing classes without notification is grounds for dismissal, regularly attending them is no reason for congratulation. Of course, credibility or stress reduction may dictate minor concessions on this point, but basic education in evaluation would be a better solution. The one kind of 'symmetry' that one can demand is that an evaluation approach must be capable of validly supporting both favorable and unfavorable results; something that, for example, **teacher evaluation** based on classroom visits cannot do, but that a personnel or product checklist mentioning all possible errors can do very well.

ATTENUATION (Stat.) In the technical sense this refers to the reduction in correlation due to errors of measurement.

ATTITUDE, EVALUATIVE See **Evaluation skills.**

ATTITUDES The compound of cognitive and affective variables describing a person's mental set toward another person, thing, or state. It may be evaluative or simply preferential; that is, someone may think that running is good for you, or simply enjoy it, or both; enjoying it does not entail thinking it is meritorious, nor vice versa, contrary to many suggested analyses of attitudes. Attitudes are inferred from behavior, including speech behavior, and from inner states. No one, including the person whose attitudes we are trying to determine, is infallible about attitudinal conclusions, even though that person is in a *nearly* infallible position with respect to his or her own *inner states*, which are not the same as attitudes. Notice that there is no sharp line between attitudes and beliefs; many attitudes are evinced through beliefs (which may be true or false), and attitudes can sometimes be evaluated as right or wrong, or good or bad, in an objective way (e.g., attitudes toward "the world owing one a living", work, women (men), and so on). See **Affective.**

ATTRITION The loss of subjects in the experimental or control/-comparison groups during the period of the study. This is often so large as to destroy the experimental design—60% loss within a year is not uncommon in the schools and 98% is not unknown. Hence all choice of numbers in the groups must be based upon a good estimate of attrition plus a substantial margin of error.

AUDIENCE (of or for an evaluation) A special term for the **consumers** of the *evaluation*: those who will or should read or hear of the evaluation, either during or at the end of the evaluation process, including many who are and many who are not being evaluated. The audiences usually go well beyond, but include, the **clients.** To give an example, the audiences for an evaluation of any substantial state-funded educational program include the following: the legislature in general and especially its relevant committees, the office of the legislative analyst (in particular, the principal analyst assigned to the program), the state department of finance (and the relevant principal analyst there), the governor's office, related federal agencies, private foundations with an interest in the area, parents' associations, school administrators' associations, taxpayers' associations, and so on. Audiences of the *program*, where it is the kind of thing that has audiences (such as a television program), are covered as **recipients** (immediate consumers) of it. An evaluation report needs to be carefully planned, perhaps done in several versions, to serve the several audiences that are commonly involved. (The term originates with Robert Stake, but the present definition is something of an extension of his.)

AUDIT, AUDITOR Apart from the original sense of this term, which refers to a check on the books of a company or institution by an independent accountant, the use of the term in evaluation refers to a third-party evaluation or external evaluation, often of an evaluation. Hence—and this is the standard usage in California—an auditor may be a **meta-evaluator,** typically serving in a formative and summative role. In the more general usage, an auditor may be simply an external evaluator working either for the same client as the primary evaluator or for another client. There are other occasions when the auditor is halfway between the original kind of auditor and an evaluation auditor; for example, the Audit Agency of HEW (later HHS/ED) was originally set up to monitor compliance with fiscal guidelines, but its staff is now frequently looking at the methodology and overall utility of evaluations. The same is true of GAO and OMB 'audits'.

On the original front, the fiscal auditor does serve a kind of evaluation function. As Abraham Briloff demonstrated in his 1973 classic,

Unaccountable Accounting, they are not very good at picking up fundamental flaws in accounting, if the flaws involve novel abuses of good practice. It is a lesson with some significance for evaluators in other fields. But then, auditors can teach something very useful to evaluators without accounting backgrounds—how to find out whether a program is rotten at the fiscal core, surely a very relevant consideration for program evaluation.

AUTHENTIC MEASURE Buzzword for a test that is nearer to measuring the real ability or achievement level (or cognitive structure) than traditional tests, especially multiple-choice tests. Authentic measures are often said to involve more complexity, or breadth, or depth, or number of dimensions of the performance, and to provide realistically ill-structured problems to solve rather than artificially structured ones. An example sometimes used is having students think aloud while problem-solving, so that the quality of the process can be evaluated. The approach is certainly worth exploring—testing specialists have been doing so for a century—and may lead to something valuable, but is so far mostly whistling in the dark, because the trade-offs in validity and cost outweigh the gains. Still, the music sounds good. For a slightly different approach to the same problem, see **Multiple-rating item**; see also **Assessment**.

AUTONOMOUS (criteria) In personnel evaluation, especially, it is worth distinguishing these from what are called **compensatory** criteria. An autonomous (or 'standalone') criterion is a requirement that must be met, usually at a certain level, without invoking trade-offs from above-minimum achievements on other criteria. For example, knowledge of subject matter to a level that depends on the grades being taught is an autonomous criterion for a school teacher; that level is sometimes called an 'absolute minimum'. Knowledge far beyond that level is tradeable to make up for deficits in compensatory criteria. See also **Multiple-hurdle**.

AXIOLOGY A relatively archaic term for the field within philosophy that deals with values. Some efforts in that area have been devoted to formalization of evaluative reasoning, without any particular attention to the fundamental problem of validating evaluative conclusions. A term used by axiologists focusing on this aspect of their subject is "deontic logic".

B

BACKGROUND & CONTEXT Evaluations are like some ethnographic research studies in their extreme dependence on contextual factors for determining correct design. For example, if an evaluation is being done in a context of strong opposition to evaluation, or subsequent to an earlier catastrophic attempt at evaluation, the credibility will have to be bolstered by various devices, and data access will have to be thought out very carefully. Again, it may be clear from a study of the ambience that certain aspects of the program's performance are agreed to by all parties; the evaluator needs only to make a quick check on these and can focus on contested matters. Identification of stakeholders is an important part of the B&C effort; more details under **Key evaluation checklist**.

BALANCE OF POWER A desirable feature of evaluation design, summed up in the formula: "The power relation of evaluator, evaluee, and client should be as nearly symmetrical as possible". If the power is out of balance, the search for truth is quickly converted into a search for a politically acceptable solution. For example, evaluees should have the right to have their reactions to the evaluation and the evaluator(s) appended to the report when it goes to the client (see **Demurrer**); that is, they should have the opportunity to evaluate the evaluator. Even the client should undertake to be evaluated in the typical situation where the contract identifies a third party as the evaluee, if this has not already been done. For example, school administrators who are not being properly evaluated have little reason to expect teachers to cooperate fully in being evaluated themselves; school boards who hire superintendents or consultants to evaluate school staff should themselves be evaluated. Nor are these evaluations to be done only by remote others: It is a crucial part of the balance of power approach that each party has effective input to the evaluation of the others, and, in general, they should all have access to at least an anonymized version of the report.

Note that participant involvement does not mean that the evaluation is *completely done* by the evaluees (the 'Toledo' model of teacher evaluation). That process leads to **secret-contract bias** (pulling punches in the hope that the other party will do the same for you). It only means that *input* from the evaluees is sought and incorporated to

64

the satisfaction of the evaluee, up to the point of attachment in uncensored form, *not* up to the point where the evaluation itself must be approved by the evaluee. (Among evaluators, MacDonald advocates the veto power for evaluees—see **Illuminative evaluation**.)

Meta-evaluation and **goal-free evaluation** are both part of the balance of power concept. Panels used in evaluation should exhibit a balance of power, not a lack of **bias** as it is conventionally perceived. There are ethical as well as political and practical reasons for arranging a balance of power; they relate to the concept of fairness.

BANDING A useful technique for avoiding sharp **cutting scores** when defining grade levels, and so on, on very important tests. Consumers often react to sharp distinctions by saying, "You mean that if I (or "my son") had scored one more point, I (he) would have got a different grade/been admitted to Harvard, and so on." Clearly the validation process does not support the implied precision of sharp cutting scores, and yet one does not want to use the term 'arbitrary' about something on which so much depends. Banding indicates the grey area using a fuzzy band instead of a line. For example, current graphing tools make it easy to use so-called 'spray guns' that will paint—for example—two bands of dots, centered on the mean, one of which is two standard deviations wide and one of which is four sigmas wide. One must adjust the decision rule so as to make this meaningful; best done by two-stage or multistage scoring.

BASELINE (data or measures) Facts about the condition or performance of subjects prior to **treatment**. The essential result of the pretest part of the pretest-posttest approach. Gathering baseline data is one of the key reasons for starting an evaluation before a program starts, something that always seems odd to budgetary bureaucrats. See **Preformative**.

BEHAVIORAL OBJECTIVES Specific goals of, for example, a program, stated in terms that will enable their attainment to be checked by observation or test/measurement. An idea that is variously seen as 1984/Skinnerian/dehumanizing, and so on, or as a minimum requirement for the avoidance of empty verbalisms. Some people now use the term "measurable objectives" to avoid the miasma associated with the connotations of behaviorism. In general, people are now more tolerant of objectives that are somewhat more abstractly specified—provided that leading verification/falsification conditions can be spelled out—than they were in the early days of the behavioral objectives movement, in the 1960s. This is because the attempt to spell everything out (and skip the statement of intermediate-level goals) produces 7,633 behavioral objectives for reading, which is an incomprehensible mess. Thus educational research has rediscovered the reason for the failure of the precisely analogous move by positivist philosophers of science to eliminate all theoretical terms in favor of observational terms. The only legitimate scientific requirement here is that terms have a *reliable use* and *agreed-upon empirical content*, not a *short translation into observational language*—the latter is just one way to the former and not always possible. Fortunately, scientific training can lead to the reliable (enough) use of theoretical terms; that is, they can be unpacked into the contextually relevant, measurable indicators upon demand. This avoids the loss of the main cognitive organizers above the taxonomical level, and hence of all understanding, that would result from the total translation project, even if it were possible. The same conclusion applies to the use of somewhat general goal statements.

BENCHMARKS, BENCHMARKING Terms used to refer to the process of running computers through standardized performance tests of the whole system. These used to be designed to diagnose roadblocks in the system, for example, by testing the i/o (input/output) channel speed; more recently there has been an increased focus on consumer-relevant tasks, for example, by defining a standard spreadsheet whose speed of recalculation is measured. The earlier approach led to some specific measures, for example, mips (millions of instructions per second), Whetstones, Dhrystones, and so on, which are still useful for very crude indications of power. See **Technicism**.

BENEFITS Valued outcomes or processes. See **cost analysis** for a matrix that can be used to guide a search for those who benefit, types of benefit, and time of benefit.

BETA TEST The first *external hands-off* evaluation of a new or revised product or service. There are sometimes two phases of this: the first one has support staff standing by (the 'hothouse' phase); the second is hands-off. At least the second must be a part of any serious R&D process. The people using the product in a beta-test should be typical users, leavened with some experts on that type of product. The whole process has been massively corrupted in many U.S. companies, including some who make big claims for their leadership in quality assurance. Typical errors include: using only experts as beta testers (so you miss all the design errors that will trap beginners); using the beta test as a sales effort pitched at buyers for large accounts instead of end-users (buyers often can't even use the programs they order for their organization, but are flattered to be asked to help improve it, and certainly stupid enough to buy bad products as a result); not sampling a wide range of working conditions (one classic example was Apple beta testing hard drives in noisy work places where you can't tell that they will be extremely obtrusive at home); doing shoddy evaluation—

usually by using poor forms or interviewing—so that the results from the test are invalid or incomplete; and running your development timeline off marketing considerations, so there turns out to be no time to make corrections in the light of faults turned up in the beta test. Because it is flattering to be chosen as a beta tester, for most people, there is a conflict of interest in the structuring of this approach to formative evaluation; the best corrective is to reward the identification of faults and identify the best fault-detectors for future use. Cf. **Focus groups.**

BIAS There are two crucially distinct senses of this term, not well distinguished in dictionaries up through the OED: one of them is evaluative, the other is not. In the evaluative sense, "bias" means much the same as "prejudice", and its antonyms are "objectivity", "fairness", "impartiality". In the descriptive sense, "bias" means much the same as "preference" (or—nearly—"commitment"), and its antonym is "disinterest" (or—nearly—"neutrality"). On the whole, the core sense—certainly the sense used in educational and psychological measurement—appears to be the evaluative one, in which it refers to systematic errors or a disposition to errors of a kind that are likely to adversely affect humans. The errors are often due to a tendency to prejudge issues because of beliefs or emotions that are wrong or irrelevant. It seems likely that the nonevaluative usage comes from (i) the desire not to have to make a judgment about who is in error, and/or (ii) the recognition that *for purposes of deciding who is right*—for example, in a court of law or in a scientific forum—one cannot suppose that the issue of truth is predeterminable. One needs *credibility* to both parties in selecting the jurist for such cases, not just *objectivity*, and hence "lack of prior commitment" is just as important as "lack of prejudice"—that is, lack of prior erroneous commitment. Note that there are serious drawbacks about this approach to impartiality, and there are alternatives to it, discussed below.

One reason for thinking that the evaluative use is the fundamental one is that it alone supports the notion of *accusing* someone (or a test) of bias; it would be absurd to accuse people of something that has no negative connotations (holding strong true beliefs). A second reason is that the legal situation, where great matters hinge on the interpretation of the term, clearly favors the disqualification of judges only on the basis of absence of *impartiality*, not on the basis of prior beliefs held; and of jurors only on the basis of the inability to decide without *prejudice* (*Black's Law Dictionary*, 5th edition, West, 1979). A third reason is that there are clearly situations in which one wants to say that being neutral is a sign of bias, for example, being neutral in the debate about the occurrence of the Holocaust or in the dispute between Christian Scientists and others about the truth of the atomic theory; but to say that would be a contradiction according to the nonevaluative use of the term.

Being neutral is often a sign of error in a given dispute and can be a sign of bias; more often it is a sign of ignorance, sometimes of culpable or disabling ignorance. It therefore seems better not to require that evaluation panels include *only* neutral panelists at the (common) cost of including ignoramuses or cowards and getting superficial, easily dismissed reports. Better to allow the selection of trained and knowledgeable people with commitments both for and against whatever approach, program, and so on, is being evaluated (where such factions exist). The neutral faction, if reasonably knowledgeable, should be represented just as any other faction. Selecting a neutral *chair* may be good psychology or politics (and that is part of good evaluation design, too) but not because s/he is any more likely to be a good judge.

If the evaluative use is adopted and the nonevaluative use rejected (as in this volume), one has to make some adjustments in the way that evaluation standards are formulated. For example, the glossary of *Evaluation Standards*, (McGraw-Hill, 1980), defines bias as "a consistent alignment with one point of view", which would of course imply that anyone adopting the *Evaluation Standards* is biased, an undesirable phrasing given that the standards encourage one to avoid bias.

Bias may be a feature of an experimental or evaluation design, as well as of judges and judgments; for instance, a sample of the students enrolled in a school is biased against lower economic groups if it is selected from those present on a particular day, because absenteeism rates are usually higher among lower economic groups. Hence, if we are investigating an effect that may be related to economic class, using such a sample would constitute a design bias. On the other hand, bias is *not* demonstrated by showing, as is common in politically driven bias checks, that minorities or women do less well on a test or in a selection process than others; or that the content of an item is less likely to be familiar to them than to a white male. Bias detection requires deeper analysis of the use to be made of item scores in the interpretation process.

Ralph Tyler, one of the first and sharpest program evaluators of the modern era, has suggested that avoidable bias is the evaluator's white-collar crime. It certainly deserves more attention than it currently gets. At the moment in the U.S., while some types of bias have become severely constrained, the extent of ageism shows how little the moral lesson has been learned. Ask yourself: if a much-published and still-productive scholar and excellent teacher who had taken early retirement were to apply for a junior, assistant-professor opening at a university you know, in competition with the usual group of just-past Ph.D. candidates, would he or she be appointed? Most people respond to the question by trotting out the same kind of generic rationalizations for not doing so that were used to select against women applicants in the bad old days. Study of the data available for several leading universities makes clear they are completely blind to this kind of bias. See also **Shared bias, Selectivity bias, Conflict of interest, Item bias, Research-based personnel evaluation, General positive bias.**

BIAS CONTROL A key part of evaluation design. It should be seen, not as an attempt to exclude the influence of definite views, but to limit the influence of unjustified views, e.g., premature or irrelevant views. For example, the use of (some) external evaluators is a part of good bias control, not because it will eliminate the choice of people with definite views about the type of program being evaluated, but because it tends to eliminate people who are likely to favor it for the irrelevant (and hence error-conducive) reasons of ego involvement or income preservation (cf. also **Halo effect**). Usually, however, program managers avoid the use of an external evaluator with a known negative view of programs such as theirs, even for formative evaluation. That practice confuses bias with preference. Enemies are one of the *best* sources of useful criticism; it's irrelevant to a professional that one doesn't enjoy it. Even if it is politically necessary to take account of a manager's opposition to the use of a negatively disposed summative evaluator, it should be done by adding a second evaluator, also knowledgeable, to whom there is no objection, not by looking for someone neutral as such, because neutrality is just as likely to be biased and more likely to be based on ignorance—a key point. The general principle of bias control illustrated here is the principle of *balancing* (possible) bias in a group of evaluators rather than *eliminating* bias by selecting only 'unbiased' evaluators. "Unbiased" is usually and wrongly interpreted as meaning uncommitted, hence—all-too-often—ignorant or cowardly evaluators. Of course it makes sense to begin by screening out everyone whose views are *plainly* biased, that is, unjustified (e.g., sexists).

Other key aspects of bias control involve further separation of the rewards channel from the evaluation reporting/designing/hiring channel, for example by never allowing the agency monitor for a program to be the monitor for the evaluation contract on that program (violated in the PLATO evaluation), never allowing a program contractor to be responsible for letting the contract to evaluate that program (violated in the Sesame Street evaluation), and so on. The ultimate bias of contracted evaluations resides in the fact that the agencies that fund programs fund most or all of their evaluations and hence want favorable ones, a fact that evaluation contractors are (usually extremely) aware of, and that does a great deal to explain the vast preponderance of favorable evaluations in a world of rather poor programs. Even GAO, although effectively beyond Congressional influence for most purposes, is not immune enough for Congress to regard them as totally credible, hence—in part—the creation of the CBO (Congressional Budget Office) and the Offices of the Inspectors General. Even though they are deliberately given some independence of the agencies, the fact remains that they are instrumentalities of the federal government, which is not always thrilled to have bad news come out about its programs. Unrecorded conversations can make this clear to the IGs. However, OIGs represent a major step toward external evaluation of government operations, including the FBI.

The possible merits of an evaluation 'judiciary', isolated from most pressures by lifetime appointment, deserve consideration. Another principle of bias control reminds us of the instability of independence or externality—today's external evaluator is tomorrow's co-author (or spurned contributor).

For more details, see "Evaluation Bias and Its Control", in *Evaluation Studies Review Annual*, Vol.1, G. Glass, ed., (Sage, 1976). The possibility of neat solutions to bias-control design problems is kept alive in the face of the above adversities by remembering the Pie-Slicing Principle: "You slice and I'll select". See also **Local experts, External, General positive bias, Technicism, Fallacy of irrelevant expertise.**

BIG FOOTPRINT APPROACH This is an outcomes-oriented visual metaphor for project and program evaluation and planning. It is intended to remind the evaluator and planner that the true merit of social intervention programs lies in the extent to which they make a dent in the needs of individual humans. It is intended as a countermeasure to some other approaches, implicit or explicit, which tend to adopt other indicators of merit. These include: (i) being well intentioned; (ii) being successful in their own terms; (iii) being part of a research effort—no matter how prestigious or promising; (iv) cooperating with power groups to do what seems important to them; (v) getting enthusiastic endorsements from a community, and so on.

The Big Footprint approach unpacks into a homely measure of merit by looking at six dimensions of program impact in terms of footprint parameters: depth, length, breadth, number, direction, and location. It is best to begin with the impact of each individual project that is a component of the program. The depth of the project's footprint is the importance of the effect on the average individual affected. It involves two considerations: the size of the impact on the individual and the significance of that impact in terms of the need of the individual. The breadth is the number of individuals affected, including those affected who were not supposed to be affected, and those who are affected through ripple effects from the direct recipients. The length is the duration of the effects, consisting of the heelprint—which refers to the period of direct project support—and the soleprint—which refers to the duration of effects beyond the termination of support. Number of footprints reflects the number of discrete efforts within the project, or projects within the program, or replications inspired by the project; this might sometimes include the number of distinguishable populations affected if they were addressed differently. The crudest aspect of direction—forward or backward—gives us the difference between progress (benefits) and regress (negative impacts such as bad environmental impact). Another aspect of direction concerns the extent to which the program effort moves steadily ahead rather than wandering around aimlessly. A third aspect extends the second, to look at the extent to which this effort builds on prior efforts, so that direction is consistent in the longer temporal framework. The fourth extends the framework into the future, to ensure that considerations of future needs and developments have been incorporated into the program's 'direction', that is, design and implementation. Location involves two considerations. First—and of particular importance to the planner—there is the question of whether the program is being located in territory where, with the resources available, it is feasible to leave a big footprint, perhaps because the ground is relatively untrodden—or, on the other hand, whether the ground is heavily compressed by the footprints of others or is rocky ground, on which footprints are hard to make. Second, there is the question of the relationship between this effort and others; under this subheading we look at issues of symbiosis, synergy, redundancy, resource-sharing, generalizability, and liaison aimed at improving efficiency.

NOTES: (i) Multiproject programs can be evaluated by looking at the number of tracks made by the set of projects they include; the same applies to multicomponent projects and to replications inspired by the original project. The extent to which these tracks cover the target territory is a topic under Location. (ii) In looking at the footprint itself, the metaphor requires that the only measure of size is individual needs met. There's nothing to prevent playing out the metaphor on a different ground (i.e., in terms of a different currency), for example, a shadow ground that represents institutional needs. But footprints on that ground are footprints in the air as far as having a worthwhile effect on individuals is concerned, even if the institutions are intended as vehicles for delivering services to individuals and do their best in that direction. Either the evaluator has to estimate the actual effects on individuals, or one has to do a second evaluation to determine them directly. (iii) Statistical significance leaves no footprint at all in the sands of time. Effect size is everything, in units (JNDs) of needs met, with a multiplier for the importance of the needs met. Statistical significance is just a certification stamp that we put on the footprints—when we can—to show they are real and not illusory. (iv) Good intentions or goals leave no footprints in the ground. The road to hell may be paved with them, but the road to progress doesn't record them at all. Intentions are the maps we make in advance of the journey, sensibly enough, and they may be of interest to the biographer, concerned to estimate our accuracy as planners; they are of no interest to the impactees or the Book of Project Judgments. (v) Cost and ethical issues apply as usual, as the cost (and cost-effectiveness) and the ethics of the process of making the footprints. Similarly, causal issues are unchanged—you have to prove it was your program that made the footprints; similarly, you have to decide how long to wait for a footprint to appear. (Theoretically, there could be soleprints without heelprints.) Long-term studies come back for another look; but remember, the sands blow over footprints and eventually wipe them out. (vi) Synergistic effects are represented by the spontaneous appearance of extra footprints, or of extra breadth/depth/length to the footprints directly caused by the program. (vii) When there are negative and positive effects, if the negatives outweigh the positives, the steps are backward steps; if the positives outweigh the negatives, the effects are netted to give a less deep footprint. (Cases of traumatic negative impact may best be likened to a footprint that involves stepping—forward or backward—on your cat. Mixed effects may involve making—for example—one step forward and two steps back, or a step sideways.) (viii) **Recoil effects** have analogies like jarring your heel, spraining your ankle, strengthening your capabilities, and so on. (ix) A main virtue of the metaphor is its visual power for presentations and midcourse corrections. People find it very easy to see the force of criticisms or suggested improvements in terms of their effect on 'the footprint'. It is a more graphic representation than a checklist.

(The name originated from some experiences doing meta-evaluation of a community development project in the forests of Michigan's Upper Peninsula, home of the fabled creature Bigfoot. It seemed that the program efforts there should have been producing bigger foot-

72

prints than they were, given the local tradition of Big Footprints. Since then, it has been used in very different contexts, for example, urban community development programs, where issues of location become important, such as whether the footprints are to be made/found in the lifespace of city dwellers or the 'shadow' lifespace of community organizations.)

BIG SHOPS The "big shops" in evaluation are the five to ten that carry most of the large evaluation contracts; they have included Abt Associates, AIR, ETS, RAND, RMC, SDC, and SRI (translations in the Acronyms & Abbreviations appendix). The trade-offs between the big shops and the small shops run something like this, assuming for the moment that you can afford either: The big shops have enormous resources of every kind, from personnel to computers; they have an ongoing stability that pretty well ensures the job will be done with at least a minimum of competence; and their reputation is important enough to them that they are likely to meet deadlines and do other good things of a paper-churning kind such as producing a nicely bound report, staying within budget, and so on. In all of these respects they are a better bet, often a much better bet, than the small shops—of course, there are exceptions.

On the other hand, you don't know who you are going to get to work for you in a big shop, beginning with the fact that the proposal writer/evaluation designer may be full-time on proposal writing, hence never executing what s/he designed. In fact, big shops move their project managers around as the press of business ebbs and flows and as their people move on to other positions; they are rather more hidebound by their own bureaucratic procedures than a small shop; and they are likely to be a good deal more expensive for the same amount of work, because they are carrying a large staff through the intervals between jobs that are inevitable, no matter how well they are run. A small shop is often carrying a proportionately smaller overhead during those times because its principals have other jobs and may be working out of a more modest establishment, the staff taking some of their payments in the pleasures of independence.

It's much easier to get a satisfactory estimate of competence about the large shops than it is about the small shops; but of course what you do learn about the personnel of a small shop is more likely to apply to the people that do your work. There's an essential place for both of them; small shops simply can't manage the big projects competently, although they sometimes try, and the big shops simply can't afford to handle the small contracts. If some more serious evaluation of the quality of the work done were involved in government review procedures—and the increasing strength of GAO in meta-evaluation gives some promise of this—then small shops might fit better into the scheme of things, rather as they do in the management consulting field and in the medical specialties. We're buying too much mediocre work for our tax dollar at the moment, because the system of rewards and punishments, while it is (quite rightly) set up to punish people that don't deliver the report on time, is not set up to reward those who produce an outstanding report by comparison with a mediocre one.

BIMODAL (Stat.) See **Mode.**

BLACK BOX EVALUATION A term, usually employed pejoratively, that refers to **global summative evaluation,** in which an overall and frequently brief evaluation is provided, without any suggestions for improvements, causes of troubles, and so on. Although the client (sometimes) and the scientist (nearly always) would prefer more, there is nothing essentially invalid or incomplete about black box evaluation. It is frequently all that is needed and extremely valuable (e.g., most consumer product evaluations) and is frequently far more valid than any analytical evaluation that could be done within the same time line with the same staff, and for the same budget. It is, therefore, frequently the best that can be done, and it has the great advantage of brevity. Although there are many contexts in which it will not provide the needed information—for example, where analytical formative evaluation is required—it is simply fallacious to suppose that such cases are universal or even that they predominate. (Note that black box evaluation may even be extremely useful in the .formative situation.) The attack on the black box approach is currently spearheaded by Huey-Tsyh Chen; see his *Theory-Driven Evaluations* (Sage, 1990). Cf. **Medical model.**

BOILERPLATE Stock paragraphs or sections that are dumped into RFPs or reports (for example, from storage in a word processor) to fill them out or fulfilll legal requirements. RFPs from some agencies are 90 percent boilerplate; one can scarcely find the specific material in them.

BUDGET Regardless of the form that particular agencies prefer, it's desirable to develop a procedure for project budgeting that remains constant across projects so that your own staff can become familiar with the categories and to give you a basis for comparison. It can always be converted into a particular required format if it is thoroughly understood. The main categories might be direct labor costs, other direct costs (materials, supplies, and so on), indirect expenses (space and energy costs), and other indirect costs (administrative expenses or "general and administrative" [G&A] expenses). The difference between ordinary overhead and G&A is not sharp, but the idea is that ordinary overhead should be those costs that are incurred at a ratio proportional to staff salaries on the project, this proportion being the *overhead rate*, for example, retirement, insurance, and so on. G&A will include indirect costs not directly related to project or staff size (for example, license fees and profit). A number of indirect costs such as accounting services, interest charges, and so on could be justifiably put under either category. See **Cost.**

C

CAI Computer-assisted instruction. The computer presents the course material or at least the tests on it. An approach that turns out be less effective but more cost-effective than any other well-documented intervention, but that is still done very poorly compared to what is easily possible. Cf. **CMI**.

CALIBRATION Conventionally refers to the process of ensuring that the readings of an instrument match a prior standard. In evaluation this would include identification of the correct **cutting scores** (which define the grades) on a new version of a test, traditionally done by administering the old and the new test to the same group of students (half getting the old one first, half the new). A less common but equally important use is with respect to the standardization of *judges* who are on, for example, a site-visit or proposal-reviewing panel. They should *always* be run through two or three calibration examples, specially constructed to illustrate: (i) a wide *range* of merit; and (ii) common *difficulties*, for example (in proposal evaluation) the difficulty of comparing low probability of a big payoff with high probability of a modest payoff. Although it is not crucial to get everyone to give the same rating (interjudge reliability)—indeed pushing for it *per se* decreases validity—it is highly desirable to avoid: (i) gross intrajudge inconsistency; (ii) extreme compression of an individual's ratings, for example, at the top, bottom, or middle, unless the implications and alternatives are thoroughly understood and desirable; (iii) drift of each judge's standards as they "learn on the job" (let them sort out their standards on the calibration examples); and (iv) the intrusion of the panel's possibly turbulent group dynamics into the first few ratings (let it stabilize during the calibration period, and possibly rerun early examples later). Although the time-cost of calibration may appear to be serious, in fact it is not, if the development of suitable scales and anchor points is undertaken when doing the calibration examples, because the use of these (plus, for example, **salience scoring**) *greatly* increases speed. And, if anyone really cares about validity, or interpanel reliability (that is, justice), calibration is an essential step. See also **Anchoring**.

CASE-STUDY METHOD The case-study method is at the opposite end of one dimension of the spectrum of methods from the survey method, the micro end rather than the macro end. Both may involve intensive or casual testing or interviewing, but observing, on the other hand, is more characteristic of case-study method than of large-scale surveys. The case-study approach is typical of the clinician, as opposed to the pollster; it is nearer to the historian and anthropologist than it is to the demographer. Causation is usually determined in case studies by the **modus operandi method**, rather than by comparison of an experimental with a control group, although one could in principle do a comparison case-study of a matched case. The case-study approach is frequently used as an excuse for substituting rich detail for evaluative conclusions, a risk inherent in **responsive evaluation, transactional evaluation**, and **illuminative evaluation**. At its best, a case study can uncover causation where no statistical analysis could (but statistical analysis of the results of **true experiments** sometimes trump this trick against the case study); and can block or suggest interpretations that are far deeper than survey data can reveal. On the other hand, the patterns that emerge from properly done large-scale quantitative research cannot be detected in case studies, and the two are thus naturally complementary processes for a complete investigation of, for example, the health or law enforcement services in a city. Note that quantitative methods can often be applied on an intracase basis. One can get an adequate n either from multiple responses (Skinner) or from multiple independently validated measures (Campbell). See also **Naturalistic**.

CAUSATION The relation between mosquitos and mosquito bites. Easily understood by both parties but never satisfactorily defined by philosophers or scientists. Correlation is neither a necessary nor a sufficient condition for causation; not necessary because causation can be established by eliminative induction (ruling out all other possible causes), and not sufficient because the correlated variables may both be effects of a third factor and have no direct influence on each other (e.g., yellowing of eye whites is not a cause of yellowing skin; if they correlate it's because you have jaundice, probably caused by liver disease). The necessary condition analysis (a cause is a factor without which the effect would not have occurred) is vitiated by cases of overdetermination and so is Mackie's analysis, sometimes called the counterfactual analysis (roughly, a cause is a contextually sufficient condition). In the end the element of manipulability is crucial; Don Campbell saw this but thought it was analyzable in terms of the counterfactual definition. He rightly never let go of his conviction that there could be legitimate claims of causal connection in individual cases even if no general laws supported the claim. The historian of course works all the time with such cases.

The other key feature of causal claims is their irreplaceably context-dependent nature. A cause is usually the differentiating factor between the case in point and a contrast case that is obvious from the context of the discussion, but varies completely between contexts. Hence, context-free definitions will always fail. Details in, for example, "Causes, Connections, and Conditions in History", *Philosophical Analysis and History*, edited by William Dray (Harper & Row, 1966).

CEILING EFFECT The result of scoring near the top of a scale—which makes it harder (even impossible) to improve as easily as from a point further down. Sometimes described as "lack of headroom". Scales on which raters score almost everyone near the top will consequently provide little opportunity for anyone to distinguish themselves by outstanding (comparative) performance. This is typical of teacher evaluation forms. Usually they (or the way they are used) should be reconstructed to avoid this; it's not hard to do this by providing deflationary instructions, redefining the anchor points, rephrasing as a ranking questionnaire, or using 'constrained scoring' systems (see **Scoring**). The fourth approach can run into difficulties; the U.S. Air Force once found itself faced with a paper rebellion when it introduced an officer rating procedure with limits on the number of highest ratings you could give, to counteract a problem of getting nothing but A+ ratings.

There are some occasions on which the high scores correctly represent the relevant range of the rated variable, and then creating differences would simply be a measurement artefact. After all, if all students get all the answers right on a difficult test, there *shouldn't* be any headroom above their grades on your scale. (You would want to use a different test, however, if you *had* to get a ranking.) The best control that avoids artefacts is to evaluate the evaluators on their evaluations.

CENTRAL TENDENCY (Measure of) The somewhat misleading technical term for a statistic that describes the middle or average of a distribution, as opposed to the extent to which it is spread thin or lumped, the latter being the dispersion or variability of the distribution.

CERTIFICATION Unfortunately, this term has two substantially different meanings. 1. In one sense, it means roughly the same as "licensure", "credentialing", or "accreditation", and refers to the permission granted by some official body to someone, entitling them to practice a craft or profession. This is the entry-level sense. 2. In the second sense, it refers to the award of some official recognition of advanced status, typically based on a midcareer evaluation process. This often relates to a specialized area of practice, but it may also refer to a higher level of general practice. Certification in this sense may also be an officially required ticket for admission to specialized practice, or a de facto requirement for jobs in the specialty. This is the advanced standing sense. The tests required in either case may be trivial or severe, as with medical boards or certified public accountants. Given the number of synonyms available for the first sense, it makes good sense to reserve 'certification' for midcareer awards; unfortunately, language doesn't always follow common sense.

The certification of evaluators—in one or the other sense—has recently been discussed rather extensively and raises a number of the usual questions: who would be the super evaluators who decide on the rules of the game (and referee it), what would be the enforcement procedures, how would the cost be handled, and so on. Certification is a two-faced process that is sometimes represented as a consumer-protection device, which it can be, and sometimes as a turf-protection device for the guild members, i.e., a restraint of trade process, which it frequently is. Medical certification was responsible for driving out the midwives, probably at a substantial cost to the consumer; on the other hand, it was also responsible for keeping a large number of complete charlatans from exploiting the public. It certainly contributed to the unethical magnitude of physicians' and lawyers' salaries/fees; and in this respect is consumer-exploitative. The abuses of the big-league auditors, to take another example, are well documented in *Unaccountable Accounting* by Abraham Briloff (Knopf, 1973). When the state gets into the act, as it does with the certification of psychologists in many states, and of teachers in almost all, various political abuses are added to the above. In areas such as architecture, where noncertificated and certificated designers of domestic structures compete against each other, one can see tangible evidence for advantages to both approaches; there is very little evidence supporting a single overall conclusion as to the direction that is best for the citizenry, or even for the whole group of practitioners. A well-set-up certification approach would undoubtedly be the best; the catch is always in the political compromises involved in setting it up. In other countries, the process is sometimes handled better and sometimes worse, depending upon variations in the political process.

CERTIFICATION OF EVALUATORS See **Evaluation registry.**

CHANGE AGENT One of the roles of the evaluator that has received little attention as such is the role of constituting an intervention with its own effects. A goal-free approach minimizes this; the **evaluability assessment** approach maximizes it. But it is often much larger than is realized by the evaluator; **meta-evaluators** should always watch for it. Ref: "Evaluators as Change Agents", by Randal Joy Thompson, in *Evaluation and Program Planning*, v. 13, no. 4, Fall, 1990. See also

Proactive.

CHECKLIST APPROACH In many areas of practical evaluation, checklists (of criteria or indicators of merit) are used as the principal instrument. (Note that they are also used in other ways, inside and outside evaluation. For example, within evaluation they are almost essential when investigating the thoroughness of **implementation.** Outside evaluation, checklists are often used in medical diagnosis or engine troubleshooting. See **Etiology.**) An evaluation checklist should identify all significant relevant **dimensions** of value, ideally in measurable terms and preferably without overlap, and may also display their weights by importance. (It may also [or only] refer to **components.**) The checklist provides an extremely versatile instrument for determining the quality of many kinds of work, programs, activities, and products and may be used to guide observation or a series of measurement efforts. Using a checklist reduces the probability of omitting a crucial factor and hence cuts into a common cause of low reliability. It reduces artificial overweighting of certain factors by careful definition of the checklist items, so as to avoid overlap (sometimes one must tolerate overlap, for example in the interest of greatly increased comprehensibility of the dimensions). It reduces possible **halo effect** and **Rorschach effect.** It does not require a theory and should avoid depending on one as much as possible. (Of course, it constitutes an implicit definition of what merit amounts to with respect to the particular evaluand to which it refers, but that's below the level of anything worth calling a theory.) Checkpoints—if there are many—should be grouped under headings that have an obvious meaning, to facilitate interpretation and weighting. A checklist should be tied to an appropriate combinatorial procedure, especially if the dimensions are highly interactive, one of the cases where the linear or weighted sum approach to **synthesis** fails. Checklists may list *desiderata* or *necessitata.* The former accrue points, the latter represent minimum necessary standards; this distinction is related to the **multiple-hurdle** vs. **compensatory.** (A single checkpoint [dimension] may involve both.) It's advisable to asterisk all absolute requirements and check them first, to avoid wasted time. (See **Fire at the horses first.**)

The checklist is of course a mnemonic device, and the design of good checklists should be related to ease of recall and understanding as well as comprehensiveness and ease of implementation. Another payoff from good checklists comes from the way they break down a complex and unreliable global judgment into ones that can be made more reliably—without depending on program theory to do it. Relatively simple though those considerations may be, the approach raises some more complex methodological issues even within evaluation. One might begin a study with a set of well–developed evaluation checklists such as those used by road-testers, skilled senior administrators when evaluating supervisors, biologists doing environmental impact reports, Congress' Office of Technology Assessment, and computer software reviewers. There are strong elements that are field–specific, but there are also many elements and questions common to all of these checklists. Can we specify criteria of adequacy and merit for any such list? More specifically, can we say anything about the relative importance of: (i) omissions of a criterion, (ii) overlap between them, (iii) the limits on the use of indicators to replace variables not directly accessible, (iv) what to use for weights and whether to weight at the most specific level or some higher level, (v) whether to use constrained weightings (fixed number of weighting points), (vi) how best to standardize performance measures, (vii) how to combine weights with performance ratings, and (viii) how to avoid inappropriate assumptions about scaling, and (ix) how to balance other virtues against reliability of application. Examples of general program evaluation checklists are the **Key evaluation checklist** and the **GAO** Checklist; the Duties of the Teacher checklist is a different kind of example.

CIPP An evaluation model expounded in *Educational Evaluation and Decision Making* by Guba, Stufflebeam et al. (Peacock, 1971). The acronym refers to Context, Input, Process, and Product evaluation, the four phases of evaluation they distinguish; it should be noted that these terms are used in a slightly special way. This was probably the first sophisticated model for program evaluation, and possibly still the most elaborate and carefully thought-out model extant. It emphasizes systematic procedures to cover the multifaceted effort of program evaluation. In also emphasizing evaluation for support of decision making, it underemphasizes evaluation for accountability or for scientific interest, where the issue can't be related to decision options in the usual way.

CITATION INDEX The number of times that a publication or person is referenced in other publications. If used for personnel evaluation (a common practice in universities looking for a way to back up judgments of the merit of research), this is an example of a spurious quantitative measure. It invalidly discriminates against those working on the leading edge and/or in areas with few others; against the young; against those working on unfashionable topics; it does not in fact identify a third of the Nobel laureates; it invalidly discriminates in favor of people who invent new terms ("summative evaluation" has an astronomical citation index, but it was just a handy term, not the special theory of relativity), and so on. Citation-index data can be used

81

for awarding a few bonus points, with care, but wider use would require someone to write an expert, rule-based, application handbook. In any case, there have to be other ways to get the same points, for example, indicators of pathbreaking in new fields. The most plausible use is in evaluating the *significance* of a particular journal article *within* a field, that is, in history-of-ideas research; its significance in this sense is very loosely related to merit.

CLASSIFICATION In the evaluation context, this is a personnel decision that may occur at hiring or later (or both) and that determines the salary and duties of the candidate. It may be driven largely by matching qualifications to job descriptions, and to this extent it is descriptive, but it almost always involves at least some judgment about merit and is hence evaluative. Because the classification into which the individual is being fitted is hierarchical, this is understandable; because it is not possible to ensure nonevaluative operation in advance, it is best to treat this as an evaluative procedure.

CLIENT The person, group, or agency, that has commissioned an evaluation and to whom the evaluator has legal responsibility; *not* the employer of whoever hires the evaluator nor, often, the instigator of the evaluation. Clients usually constitute one—often the most important—of the immediate consumers (**recipients**) of the evaluation, hence one of its **audiences**, but are not the only audiences to whom it is delivered. The term "client" is often used for recipients of social services that involve some client-professional relationship. It's somewhat better, when discussing an evaluation, to use the term "**recipients**" for the latter group, remembering that there are other groups of **consumers**.

CLIENTELE The population directly served by the subset of programs which involve supplying professional assistance; usually referred to here as **recipients,** to avoid the confusion with "client" in the sense defined above.

CLINICAL EVALUATION See **Psychological evaluation.**

CLINICAL PERFORMANCE EVALUATION In the health field, and to an increasing extent elsewhere (e.g., in the **evaluation of teaching**), the term "clinical" is being used to stress a hands-on kind of approach that is seen as very different from paper-and-pencil tests. It normally involves carefully done structured observations by trained and **calibrated** observers. The term may be allowed to apply to appropriate **simulations**, of the kind used in some of the medical board exams. However, standard simulations have inherited a great deal of the artificiality of the paper-and-pencil tests. For example, they rarely involve "parallel processing", that is, the necessity of handling two or three tasks simultaneously. A serious clinical simulation would start the candidates on one problem, providing charts and histories, and then—just as, or before, this was beginning to make sense—a new problem with emergency overtones would be thrust at them, and just before they reached the point of making a preliminary emergency decision on that, a third and even more pressing problem would be thrown at them. Given that there is some anxiety associated with test-taking for most people, one could probably come close to simulating clinical settings in this respect. We have long since developed simulations that involve the provision of supplementary information when requested by the testee, part of the scoring being tied to the making of appropriate requests. More advanced simulations presuppose careful **job analysis** *a n d* evaluative analysis of what a practitioner ought to be able to do.

CLUSTER EVALUATION A procedure favored by the Kellogg foundation, where the individual evaluators from a group of projects cooperate with a 'cluster evaluator' to identify special problems that they may be able to solve jointly.

CMI Computer-managed instruction. Records are kept by the computer, usually on every test item and every student's performance to date. Important for large-scale individualized instruction. The computer may do diagnoses of poor performance on the basis of test results and instruct student as to materials that should be used. The extent of the feedback to student varies considerably; the main aim is feedback to course manager(s). Cf. **CAI**.

COGNITIVE The domain of the propositionally knowable or doable; consisting of "knowledge-that" (knowing *that* something is the case) or "knowledge-how" (knowing *how* to perform *intellectual* tasks). The distinction is due to Gilbert Ryle.

COHORT A term used to designate one group among many in a study, for example, "the first cohort" may be the first group to have been through the training program being evaluated. Cf. **Echelon**.

COMPENSATORY criteria are those indicators or dimensions of merit on which performance can be traded off against the performance on others, in order to calculate a total score. The opposite of compensatory criteria are standalone or autonomous criteria—standards that must be met on their own terms. Grade points in the usual college requirements are compensatory (for example, when you calculate a grade point average that must exceed C in order to graduate); in courses required for the major they are often standalone criteria ("you must get a C in *this* course"). It is sometimes difficult with compensatory criteria to explain to testees what the 'passing mark' amounts to in terms of performance, since there is no cutoff on the compensating tests; this also makes it somewhat harder to design a remedial program. See **Multiple-cutoff, Multiple-hurdle,** and **Synthesis.**

COMPETENCY-BASED An approach to teaching or training or evaluating that focuses on identifying the competencies needed by the trainee and on teaching/evaluating to mastery level on these, rather than on teaching allegedly relevant academic subjects to various subjectively determined achievement levels. Nice idea, but most attempts at it either fail to specify the mastery level in clearly identifiable terms or fail to show why that level should be regarded as the mastery level. ("Performance-based" is often used with the same meaning.) Competency-Based Teacher Education (CBTE) was a fashion in the mid-70s but the catch was that no one could validate the competencies. Even where **style research** has found characteristics of successful teachers, that doesn't show they are appropriate requirements for certification, nor that one can use them for evaluation. There is always the subject matter competency requirement, of course, too often ignored in K-12 teacher training while being treated as the only one in the post-secondary domain; but CBTE was talking about *pedagogical* competencies—teaching method skills. See also **Minimum competency testing, Mastery level, Research-based teacher evaluation.**

COMPLIANCE CHECK, COMPLIANCE REVIEW An aspect of **monitoring**: usually means the specific task of checking to see if the legal requirements for a type of program are met.

COMPONENT One listing of the components of a program would include: the delivery system; the support system (or "infrastructure")—for example, administrators, office staff, training staff, maintenance staff, internal evaluation team, consultants; the equipment (vehicles, computers, copiers, etc.); the buildings; and the environment. The components of a product would normally be taken to be the items listed on the parts listing, but there are often more useful groupings of these. Analytic evaluation and often formative evaluation are likely to need identification of components, since components are directly improvable (less true of **dimensions**).

COMPONENT EVALUATION One of the two types of analytic evaluation, the other being **dimensional** evaluation. A component of an **evaluand** is typically a physically or temporally discrete part of it, but more precisely it is any segment that can be said to combine with others to make up the whole evaluand. Typically, we distinguish between the components and their relationships in talking about the evaluand as a system made up of parts or components, and in component evaluation we look at both. The **global** or (w)holistic evaluation of something, by contrast, does not involve any identification, let alone evaluation, of its components; also, an eval-

84

uation of components alone does not automatically imply an evaluation of the whole evaluand, since excellent components for an amplifier (or a school, or a teaching style) will not make a good amplifier (etc.) unless they are correctly integrated by good design and assembly procedures. (The result would be a **fragmentary** or unconsummated evaluation.) However, since components are frequently of variable quality, and since we are frequently looking for diagnoses that will lead to improvement, evaluating the components is sometimes a useful approach to **formative evaluation**. If we can also evaluate their organization, we may have a very helpful kind of (especially) formative evaluation—how helpful will depend upon the extent to which the "fixes" for defective components (and design and assembly) are self-evident or easily determined. Component evaluation is distinguished from dimensional evaluation, the other kind of **analytical** evaluation, by this relatively greater ease of manipulating components in a constructive way, by comparison with dimensions (which may be **statistical artefacts** or **perspectives**).

Note that a mere evaluation of components, without study of the way they are combined (a 'components-only' evaluation) is an incomplete evaluation of the evaluand except where it is provably impossible to do more. Doing components-only evaluations—or, for that matter, dimensions-only evaluations—is one of the approaches that appeals to people who shy at the last fence, the **synthesis** process, sometimes feeling they can stay nearer to the **value-free** approach by so doing. But the evaluation—and even the synthesis—involved in the last step is not the only one involved in component evaluation. It is crucial to remember that the component-only evaluation approach often looks better than it is, because it's sometimes very hard to evaluate the way the components are combined. There is a long record in technology of brilliant designs of artefacts that would all flunk a component-only approach, just because they are designed to work with components of highly variable quality.

COMPUTER PRODUCT EVALUATION See **Product evaluation**.

COMPUTERS AS EVALUATORS The current state of the art in artificial intelligence is that logic-based systems, rule-based systems, and neural networks are all at about the same performance level, albeit on different tasks, and show little sign of making a quantum jump beyond it. That is, they can all form the basis for impressive performances in limited (and different) areas of human intelligence, in many cases outperforming the expert human. But they are still nowhere near matching what we call common sense or the general problem solving ability of a reasonably bright high school student. This means they are a long way from matching the general purpose evaluator.

One should also temper one's admiration for what they can do in the light of the Meehl and Dawes findings on what can be done with an empirically fitted linear regression equation *without* a computer; in general, you can outperform almost any expert on a wide range of tasks including those where observation and interviews are thought to be important and where the experts perform them. If you add 12,000 rules and debug their interactions for a decade or so, you may do better than the linear regression equation, but only on a very restricted problem (in this case, helping a sales rep to fit DEC computer components to the needs of a client). So there's no great difficulty about having a computer select students for the Yale entering class better than the current panel, assuming that the panel is selecting for success at Yale, and the computer can look at the back files. The same will be true for many other evaluation tasks, perhaps up to somewhere in the region of the roadtester and most job selection interviewers. In many other cases—large program evaluations, for example—it will not be true. We should explore the differential validity and costs thoroughly, and respond to the challenge. That prospect will no doubt cause many evaluators to show signs of evaluation anxiety. Ref: Marvin Minsky "Logical vs. Analogical, etc.", *Artificial Intelligence* (Summer, 1991).

COMPUTERS IN EVALUATION The obvious uses include: (i) the usual housekeeping tasks in the process of managing and doing evaluations, which can be assisted to the point where the solo evaluation consultant can get along without secretarial help (by using word processing and electronic communications), or even without bookkeeping and tax consultant help (using accounting and tax software). (ii) Data storing and data analysis using DBMS, spreadsheet software, DSS, and special statistical packages such as SPSS, SAS, and Systat. Most of these basic uses are competently covered in two of the monographs in the Sage series Quantitative Applications in the Social Sciences.

There are also some rapidly developing uses that deserve special mention. (iii) Computers are now used for interactive testing so that the choice of the next item is made on the basis of performance on items so far; hence there can be a focus on items of a relevant level of difficulty or in an appropriate area. This leads to time savings or accuracy gains of up to two thirds. This approach is moving rapidly toward so-called 'intelligent testing' (see "The Four Generations of Computerized Educational Measurement" by Bunderson et al., in *Educational Measurement, 3rd edition,* edited by Robert Linn [Macmillan, 1989]). (iv) **Project management** software provides large gains in management efficiency. (v) **Qualitative evaluation** can be significantly assisted (also see **spreadsheet in evaluation**), as can (vi) **data visualization**. (vii) Special software has been written for data entry work like the coding of elements in interviews, a large part of much qualitative evaluation. There is some discussion in Michael Patton's book *Qualitative Evaluation and Research Methods, 2nd edition* (Sage, 1990), but a great deal (possibly more) can be done using features of current high-end applications such as hideable notes, the zoom and assembly capabilities in some outliners, and the powerful macro resources of many programs. (viii) See **Virtual reality.** Beyond these tool uses there lies the domain of the artificial evaluator, covered in the next entry, **Computers as evaluators.**

A new chapter in field work instrumentation is being written with the help of laptop, notebook, and palm-top computers, and this will be radically extended with the assistance of the new generation of stylus-input machines using new operating systems that recognize gestures as well as hand printing. Most structured field or phone interviews can be managed with one of these, without any need for a keyboard or keyboarding skills.

CONCEPTUAL SCHEME A set of concepts ranging up through refined metaphors to a taxonomy, in terms of which one can organize and often understand the data/results/observations/evaluations in an area of investigation. Unlike theories, conceptual schemes involve no assertions or generalizations (other than the miniscule presuppositions of referential constancy), but they do generate hypotheses and simplify descriptions. The evaluation of conceptual schemes is extremely difficult to codify, although it is one of the most essential processes in any disciplined enterprise, including those used in crafts—for example, the woodworker has complex schemes for describing quality stock in terms of burl and figure (and so on), and even for describing shavings and chips removed in various processes from turning to planing or carving. Some more details in the case of **taxonomies** are mentioned under that heading.

CONCLUSION-ORIENTED RESEARCH (Contrasted with decision-oriented research.) Cronbach and Suppes' distinction between two types of educational research is sometimes thought to illuminate the difference between evaluation research (supposedly decision-oriented) and academic social science research (conclusion-oriented). This view is based on two fallacies: first, the fallacy of supposing that conclusions about merit and value (evaluative conclusions) aren't legitimate conclusions for the social scientist, a relative of the positivistic, **value-free doctrine** that value-judgments are not testable propositions and hence are unscientific; second, the fallacy of supposing that all evaluation is done to inform some decision. (The evaluation of many historical phenomena—for example, of a reign or a leader—is not.) Incidentally, one has to infer far more conclusions to get to the point where one can support a decision, so decision support is the harder task. See **Recommendation**.

CONCURRENT VALIDITY The validity of an instrument that is supposed to inform us about the *simultaneous* state of another system or variable. Cf. predictive validity, content validity, construct validity.

CONDITIONALLY EVALUATIVE (terms) This is a subspecies of **contextually evaluative** terminology, namely cases where 'purely descriptive' accounts of characteristics or performances are given, but in a context where *some* of the audience is known to value that performance. For example, fringe area reception in TV sets is always given by *Consumer Reports*, but only those readers living in fringe areas will value it. Again, many cost analysis details in program evaluation may be irrelevant to the wealthy client; they are only conditionally evaluative.

CONFIDENTIALITY One of the requirements that surfaces under the Process checkpoint in the **Key evaluation checklist**. Confidentiality, as it is presently construed, relates to the protection of data about individuals from casual perusal by other individuals, not to the protection of evaluative judgments on an individual from inspection by that individual. The requirement that individuals be able to inspect an evaluative judgment made about them, or at least summaries of these, with some attempt at preserving anonymity of those who made them, is a relatively recent constraint on personnel evaluation. It is widely thought to have undermined the process quite seriously, since people can no longer say what they think of the candidate if they have any worry about the possibility of the candidate knowing or inferring their authorship and taking reprisals or thinking badly of them (if the evaluation was critical). It should be noted that most large systems of personnel evaluation have failed, because people are unwilling to do this even when complete anonymity was guaranteed. This is generally true of the armed services systems and many state college systems. There is no doubt that even among universities of the first rank there has been a negative effect of the open files requirement. There are usually ways to preserve complete anonymity, under most laws, but it it is generally better to move toward **performance-based evaluation**. See also **Anonymity**.

CONFLICT OF INTEREST (COI) One of many sources of bias, not always fatal to objectivity, but fatal to credibility and hence incompatible with public or other responsible office. The legal definition relates to the clash between private pecuniary interest and the public interest, but in evaluation COI has a much wider scope and its effects on validity and professionalism, not just on credibility, must be examined. While an evaluator evaluating his/her own products is involved in a conflict of interest, the result may still be better than an evaluation done by an external judge, because the latter's lack of intimate knowledge of and experience with the product, and with evaluation methodology, may not compensate for lack of ego-involvement. Since COI *may* affect validity, and almost always reduces credibility, it is normally better to try to minimize the risk of it by using at least a mixture of **internal** and **external** evaluators in the development process. In choosing panels for evaluation, the effort to pick panelists who have no COI is usually misplaced or excessive; it is better to choose a panel with a mix (not even an exact balance) of conflicting interests, since they are likely to know more about the area than those with no interests in it, or against it, and to have more reason to argue seriously. To avoid block voting and the influence of 'heavies', reasons for decisions need to be developed independently and recorded before discussion occurs; those reasons and the final versions should be made public, reviewed for bias, and panelists should be held accountable for error and concealment.

The general level of thought about COI, in the media, in education, among politicians, and in legislation (as opposed to legal thought) is abysmal. Example: the son of the president of the U.S. is given a very highly paid job with essentially no duties by Corporation X, then negotiates a very large loan for Corporation X from the bank on whose board he was already serving, although X would not have received that loan without his intercession. He argues in public that this situation is not improper, but the media do not condemn his view as ludicrous. Is this just because of his father's position? No, because the media treat others in the savings and loan debacle who behaved similarly in the same casual way. A bank president makes large loans at absurdly low rates to the bank's chief auditor and argues that there is nothing improper about that; the media react in the same way. Here we are facing proof of impoverished ethical sensitivity and education.

Preexisting financial, personal, and social ties are not simply better or worse than preexisting intellectual commitments with respect to COI, although none of them guarantee **bias**. In particular cases, all can produce better insights as well as worse judgments. However, these commitments should be disclosed, they do preclude appointment as a sole evaluator, and they do militate against appointment as a member of a small or unbalanced panel. In managing COI, not only commitments but claimed reasons for commitment should be public, and the validity of the arguments should be scrutinized at some point by experts and consumer reps with other or no relevant COI. For example, in this work, there are a good many recommendations for using external evaluators; and the author is partly in the business of being an external evaluator. Hence, conflict of interest—but whether or not it's a bias depends on how well the reasons given support the position.

Considerable confusion about conflict of interest is built into official regulations, which suffer from the usual problem of fail-safe overcontrol, designed to protect the bureaucrat. For example, *past* fiscal involvement with one of the bidders is, but should not be, grounds for excluding a panel member on conflict of interest grounds. Past involvement is the best route to an insider's knowledge of capability without getting into real COI problems.

Most legislatures are clearly in conflict of interest on a number of issues they discuss, for example, 'no-fault' insurance for drivers, or caps on contingency fees, since most legislators are attorneys who can make a good deal of money from this trade and have no tenure as legislators. Dentists, including Consumers Union's dental consultants, are not the people to ask about whether the practice—common in our grandparents' time—of replacing deteriorating teeth with dental plates is sensible, since doing so would eliminate a large slice of all dental practice. Similarly, it is obvious that many people could save a large amount of money by purchasing generic eyeglasses at a drug store; Consumers Union apparently has a problem in getting professional opticians to say that (since they've never mentioned this possibility), presumably because it would take too much money out of their pockets. They can and do get endorsements of generic drugs, on the other hand—although for many years they could not—because the physician doesn't make money from the prescriptions. In program evaluation, the same mistake is involved in the use of psychiatrists as the criterion for identifying patients with institutionalizable mental illness instead of using patients, their families and employers. The **conflict of interest** is obvious, and the results were predictable. Antidote: use at least one 'GP' evaluator on the review team.

In the scholarly world, confusion also reigns. For example, many journal editors will not use as a reviewer of a book or manuscript someone who is known to have strongly opposing views; they often say it's 'unfair' to do otherwise. This is the usual confusion between conviction and bias. The reactions of the established opposition are not only likely to be of considerable interest to readers, but may well uncover flaws that someone less intimately involved with the subject will never see. When such considerations arise, editors should try to commission shorter double reviews of important books, as they always do for manuscripts; one of the reviews being by a supposedly neutral party. It's true that you then run into the fact that many (neutral) reviewers do not like this kind of assignment, since the deficiencies in their own review may then be too apparent. If it's too hot in the professional kitchen, you're not obliged to stay there. See Enemies list, and compare Fallacy of irrelevant expertise.

CONJUNCTIVE MODEL More or less synonymous with the multiple-cutoff model for combining multiple data sources.

CONNOISSEUR Someone with specialized interest in, affection for, and knowledge about (typically) a category of art objects or comestibles. Their tastes are usually quite different from those of the average consumer, and it is widely believed that their taste is superior. That belief has little foundation unless one is thinking of laying down a cellar of fine wines (etc.) as an investment, where the opinion-makers' opinions control market value. If you plan on doing many decades of serious wine drinking, you might bet that your taste will tend to converge toward that of the experts, but the likelihood of that may depend heavily on whether you can convince yourself that it should. In most other cases, connoisseurs are likely to be a bad guide for your purchases—they are simply a group with different tastes from you (tastes that are almost always much more expensive to satisfy), and often with massive conflicts of interest that should render their recommendations suspect as well as irrelevant. From one point of view, much of their judgment involves the fallacy of technicism, of coming to value what has no value other than what is given it. To a limited extent, however, they may be good guides to 'real' quality, for example, in identifying oriental rugs that will in fact wear longer. What happens is that their ability to identify quality is extrapolated into domains of mere taste, and the consumer is often unable to distinguish the two.

People who enjoy what they get at a fast food restaurant, on a particular occasion, are not always poor or insensitive; they are sometimes getting the ideal meal. "Best meal available" doesn't work like "best drug for diabetes", where you know that others have relevant knowledge that will lead to benefits for you. If you don't find that the other available meals, in fancy restaurants, taste substantially better and you do find them to take longer to arrive and cost more than you usually care to spend on eating, the fact that a restaurant connoisseur wouldn't like (or wouldn't be seen dead in) a fast food place is completely irrelevant. It was foolish or self-indulgent of them to let their taste get out of hand so that it cut them off from more readily available and—for those whose taste is not corrupted—equally delightful meals. See next entry and Fallacy of irrelevant expertise.

CONNOISSEURSHIP MODEL Elliott Eisner's nontraditional approach to evaluation is based on the premise that artistic and humanistic considerations are more important in evaluation than scientific ones. No quantitative analysis is used, but instead the connoisseur-evaluator observes firsthand the program or product being evaluated. The final report is a detailed descriptive narrative about the subject of the evaluation. This may generate a valuable perspective, but it abandons much of the requirement of validity. In particular it is vulnerable to the **fallacy of irrelevant expertise**, because connoisseurs are at best a bad guide to merit for the novice—and also affected by the swing of fashion's pendulum. Cf. **Literary criticism, Aesthetic evaluation, Naturalistic, Responsive evaluation, Sensory evaluation, and Models.**

CONSONANCE/DISSONANCE The phenomena of cognitive consonance and dissonance, often associated with the work of the social scientist Leon Festinger, are a major and usually underrated threat to the validity of client satisfaction surveys and follow-up interviews as guides to program or product merit. (The limiting case is the tendency of the U.S. public to accept presidential decisions about wars.) Cognitive consonance, not unrelated to the older notion of rationalization, occurs when the subject's perception of the merit of X is changed by his or her having made a strong commitment to X, for example, by purchasing it or spending a great deal of time and hope on it by taking it as therapy, and so on. Thus a Ford Pinto may be rated as considerably better than a VW Rabbit *after* it has been purchased than before, although no new evidence has emerged that justifies this evaluation shift; more seriously, this applies to revolutions. The self-justificatory aspect of this is the conflict-of-interest side of a coin whose other side is increased knowledge of (for example) the product. Some approaches to controlling this source of bias include very careful separation of needs assessment from performance assessment, the selection of subjects having experience with both (or several) options, serious task analysis by the *same* trained observers, looking at recent purchasers of *both* cars, and so on. The approval of boot camp by Marines and of dehumanizing initiation rites by fraternity brothers is a striking and important case—called "initiation-justification bias" in *The Logic of Evaluation*. (These phenomena also apply to the metalevel, yielding spurious positive metaevaluations by clients.) See **Revolutions, evaluation of,** and **'Boot camp is beautful' bias**

CONSTRUCTIONISM, CONSTRUCTIVISM (Sometimes distinguished, but not with general acceptance.) A radical position in contemporary epistemology and research methodology, with an influential following among evaluation theorists, notably Guba and Lincoln. The position originated with the hermeneutic school, which regarded objectivity as a sensible ideal, but current versions tend to favor epis-

92

temological relativism and hence quickly run into problems about how to justify themselves, because any approach to justification is, in their view, based on unprovable assumptions. The name refers loosely to the idea that reality is not 'out there' but is constructed by each of us. The reasons given by constructivists for adopting epistemological relativism are rather easily handled by those unwilling to abandon the idea of an external reality. See *The Paradigm Dialog*, edited by Guba (Sage, 1990), especially Guba's introduction and Phillips' balanced treatment—the latter being the only contribution from a professional philosopher.

CONSTRUCT VALIDITY The validity of an instrument (e.g., a test or an observer) as an indicator of the presence of (a particular amount of) a theoretical construct. The construct validity of a thermometer as an indicator of temperature is high, if it has been correctly calibrated. The key feature of construct validity is that there can be no simple test of it, because there is no simple test of the presence or absence of a theoretical construct. We can only infer that presence from the interrelationships of a number of indicators and a theory that has been indirectly confirmed in other ways. The main contrast is with **predictive** and **concurrent validity**, which relate the readings on an instrument to another directly observable variable. Thus the predictive validity of a test for successful graduation from a college, administered before admission, is visible on graduation day some years later. But the construct validity of a thermometer to test temperature cannot be established by comparing its readings with the real temperature; in fact, looking at a thermometer is as near as we get to looking at the temperature.

Over the history of thermodynamics, we have had four different theoretical definitions of temperature. Thus, what the thermometer has "read" has referred to four different theoretical constructs and its validity as an indicator of one of these is not at all the same as its validity as an indicator of another. No thermometer reads anything at all in the region immediately above absolute zero, because all gases and liquids have solidified at that point; nevertheless, this is a temperature range, and we infer what the temperature there is, by complicated theoretical calculations from other variables. The validity of almost all tests used for evaluative purposes is *ultimately* construct validity, because the construct toward which they point (e.g., "excellent computational skills") is a complex construct and not observable in itself. This follows from the very nature of evaluation as involving a synthesis of several performance scales. But of course it does not follow that evaluative conclusions are essentially less reliable than those from tests with demonstrated predictive validity, since predictive validities are entirely dependent upon the persistence through time (often long periods of time) of a relationship—a dependency that is often shakier than the inference to an intellectual skill such as computational excellence from a series of observations of a very talented student faced with an array of previously unseen computational tasks. Thermometers are highly accurate though they "only" have construct validity. Construct validity is rather more easily attainable with respect to constructs that figure in a **conceptual scheme** that does *not* involve a theory and hence has only to meet the requirements of taxonomical merit (clarity, comprehensiveness, insight, fertility, and so on), not confirmation of the axioms and laws of the theory. (Such constructs are still called "theoretical constructs", perhaps because conceptual schemes shade and evolve into theories so fluidly.) See also **Content validity.**

CONSULTANT, CONSULTING "A consultant is someone who borrows your watch in order to tell you what time it is." You didn't laugh? Start practising. Consultants aren't despised quite so much as lawyers, but in some circles it's close, and if that bothers you, don't get into the game. You'll have to be able to smile when something not too amusing is said at your expense.

Consultants are not just people hired for advice on a short-term basis, as one might suppose from the term; they include a number of people who are in fact regular (but not tenured) staff members of state agencies, where some budgetary or bureaucratic restriction prevents the addition of permanent staff, but allows a semipermanent status to the consultant. (One significant consequence of this usage is that an evaluation consultant is often inappropriate as an external evaluator.) Such positions may or may not provide offices, secretarial support, fringe benefits, and so on. They are a hybrid between the solo consultant career and the salaried professional appointment and are referred to here as staff (evaluation) consultants (by contrast with staff evaluators, as well as by contrast with other kinds of consultants).

Many people work as consultants in addition to their basic jobs. They may even set up a corporation and hire a substantial support staff; again, this is a hybrid role, and such consultants are referred to here as moonlighters. Here we focus on the limiting case, the solo (or standalone) consultant, because most people who do—or consider doing—some consulting dream a little about that possibility, often not very carefully. The independence of the solo consultant is most attractive—work when you like, on what you like, and live where you like—but largely illusory.

The basic problem about being a solo evaluation consultant is that you're competing with the moonlighters, typically university faculty who have a regular salary, accommodation, and support guaranteed. They often charge very little, sometimes nothing, because: (i) they find the experience useful for keeping in touch with the real world; (ii) they find it interesting for a change; (iii) they are happy to help; (iv) they are flattered by being asked for their opinion; and/or (v) the dean tells them they should do some of this sort of thing. Or, if analytical, they charge at the rate they estimate will repay them for the opportunity cost of lost research and recreation (which they often underestimate considerably). You, on the other hand, have to make enough, on the days you're working at all, to (i) carry you through the days when you're not working and (ii) cover your overhead, for example, office rent, secretarial costs, books, subscriptions, memberships, meeting costs, communications, computers, retirement plan, health and other insurance; quite apart from (iii) your personal housing, grocery and utility bills, commuting costs, furniture, entertainment, vacations, and so on.

In the real world, jobs will not be kind enough to fill your time exactly, even if that were desirable. There are 2,080 working hours in a year of 40-hour weeks, and if you allow yourself 2 weeks vacation a year that conveniently reduces to 2,000. (Of course, there will often be weeks with 60 hours of work in them, but you can average them against some of the 10 hour ones where you spent much of your time at a convention, and so on.) A common rule of thumb in the consultants' world is to figure that you will, or should, only bill 1,000 hours a year; the remaining time can and probably should be filled by attending meetings, writing proposals, talking to prospective clients, reading the announcements of federal RFPs in *Commerce Business Daily* or in newsletters specific to your field, and doing research, travel, and writing that keeps you up to date—*and* you must have a fair amount of slack time in order to be available when a client (new or old) needs you, or you risk losing them.

Suppose you set the very modest goal of netting an average of $45,000 (1991 dollars) before taxes, but after expenses, averaged across ten years. It's unwise to consider this career if you can't think in terms of a ten-year run, because it's a slow start-up business. Even the many contacts you may have made during previous consulting work as a moonlighter can evaporate once you switch to the standalone rates. Given the talents it takes to be a successful solo consultant, you can probably make—very likely, you have in fact been making—at least this much in a salaried position. If you think you wouldn't go solo unless you can make 80K ($80,000), it's simple to adjust the figures in what follows.

First, you must realize that you aren't likely to make your target salary in the first few years, because you have to establish new contacts to support your much larger needs for work, and—with some of the savvy employers—you have to establish a new track record as a solo consultant instead of a moonlighter. So, as start-up capital, you'll need at least half of your annual salary for three years, in addition to the cost of furnishing and computerizing an office if you haven't already done this. Second, you must realize that this amount has to be recovered sometime, and that there will also be lean years after the start-up period (when the economy is down or you have medical or family problems), as well as good ones. So, like a farmer or a shopkeeper, you have to resist the temptation to spend in the good years; you should save anything you make over 45K.

Even with that prudence, you will need to gross at least 66K before taxes to pay the overhead and other costs just mentioned, if you plan on an outside office and any secretarial help. You may just be able to keep this to 55K if you do without the secretary *and* use an office in the home (since that cuts commuting as well as office rental), but don't think you can get below that—the rule of thumb is 25% of base for the fringe benefits, and even if you can trim that a little, you've got a lot more to cover than fringe benefits. Now 66K is only $33/hr, if you were paid on a salary basis, but you're only going to be able to bill half the hours, so you must bill it at $66/hr. Even if you only shoot for 55K, you'll have to charge $55/hr. In either case, we can approximate by saying you're going to be needing around $500/day plus expenses. (To be exact, it's $440–$528, but for our purposes it's near enough to call it 'around $500'.)

One perspective on this amount is that the top management consultants get that much *per hour*, and no self-respecting lawyer from one of the better firms will work for *that little.* However, that perspective won't do you much good. The reality is that many clients, including the federal government, think that $500/day is excessive, because they can get salaried faculty to do the work for half that or less; a common cap (upper limit) is $300/day. And few writers or other homeworkers make that much.

Of course, this is often said, by solo consultants, to be 'unfair' to the solo consultant, but you should bear in mind that the federal government is paying a good deal to support universities and could with some reason regard lower consultant rates as part of the quid pro quo. Industries are paying a large slice of those taxes. (In Australia, industry often feels that it shouldn't have to pay *any* fees for faculty consultants.) These days, university regulations usually and rightly require disclosure of consulting income and sources, and place both qualitative and quantitative limits on it. But the pool is pretty large, so that won't avoid stiff competition for you. Moreover, to a greater extent than before, universities encourage consulting as a way to keep in touch with reality, which tends to increase the pool size.

There is sometimes a way around these caps for the independent, if you can establish—that is, have audited—an overhead rate for yourself, which normally means setting up as a corporation. But that only *legitimizes* higher rates; it doesn't mean that agencies/foundations/organizations will be willing to pay them, since they are on a budget as well as under their own restrictions. Moreover, going corporate substantially increases your own costs and has few of the payoffs of yesteryear, such as company cars. Often the only feasible consultants, as well as the most cost-effective ones, from the client's point of view, are moonlighters. Independent consultants who take umbrage at this, or at complaints about their rates, are in the wrong line of work.

The bottom line from this kind of analysis appears to be that you shouldn't go solo in evaluation unless you are swamped with demand (that is, are turning down half) for your services at the fee level you'll need to survive (*not* at your marginal, i.e., moonlighting fee level). But there are probably more than a thousand independent evaluation consultants in the U.S. who do survive, although few of them are making as much as the base salary of an associate professor. How do they do it? (i) By doing fixed-fee or contract work faster than the contractor projected or the competition can manage, hence getting more per actual hour of work. (ii) By forming a work group that can fill that 1,000-hour 'void' for their employees/associates, via multiple contracts and spreading the load. (iii) By providing the ability to work full-time on a job, an edge on the faculty consultant for jobs with a short timeline. (iv) By developing contacts who come to trust them more than anyone else they know. (v) By making clear that they do not have other primary loyalties such as 'publish or perish'; clients *want* you at their mercy. (vi) By taking on more than just evaluation; for example, by doing training or remediation in some specific areas, or by writing documentation. (vii) By being better than those otherwise available—at least in some narrow specialty. (viii) By taking on contracts that no one else wants to do. (ix) By tough cost-cutting, for example by 'going co-op' with some of the office equipment, using the downtown business branch of the public library for the *Commerce Business Daily,* and so forth. Not near a business library? Go online; CompuServe has a version of *CBD* posted every day, and also a valuable consultant forum (GO CONSULT) that will yield help and, sometimes, leads to work.

Note that some of these options require special skills, for example, management skills or training skills. Don't assume that you have these unless you've run a number of contracts involving them; management skills are nontrivial—*especially the skill of estimating what it will cost you to perform the work required*—and training skills are not the same as college teaching skills. (However, online skills are easy to acquire.) Also note that several of the options involve giving up substantial alleged advantages of going solo. See also **Evaluation skills, Dumping, Quantum of effort, Computers in evaluation, Scaling,** and **Fitting the lock to the key.**

CONSUMER Strictly speaking, anyone affected by a program or product, directly or indirectly, intentionally or unintentionally—the 'impacted group'. May also include *potentially* impacted groups, because programs are often faulted for not reaching people that they could and should have reached (the terms "market" and "potential market" are often used to refer to that group). In common parlance, "consumer" is taken to mean the users or recipients, the *immediately impacted downstream* group. But the impacted group—the "true consumers"—also includes those downstream who are *indirectly* affected by what are sometimes called **ripple effects** (such as effects on the family of users or recipients). These should be distinguished from **side-effects,** which are effects other than intended effects; for example, increased alcohol consumption resulting from a crackdown on marijuana. (There are of course ripples from side-effects.) Anyone to whom any of these effects occur is a consumer in the broad sense. So, too, are those at the providing or payment end (the staff and supporters of the program)—where we call the results **recoil effects.** In the most extended sense, impactees include the taxpayers—when we are dealing with publicly funded programs (even if they opposed the program). Of course, the impact on any one person in these extended groups may be insignificant. Serious evaluation must always check for significant effects on *all* impacted groups, that is, on consumers in the widest sense. (For example, future employers are consumers of the product of an educational institution or a clinic.) Even the recipients' group, let alone the total 'true consumers' group, is usually very different from, although it was meant to be the same as, the *target* population. The differences go both ways: The consumer group usually includes some nontargeted people as well as excluding some of the target group.

The staff of a program are of course affected by the program, but at the upstream or producing or providing end, and the (recoil) effects on them can usually be segregated from downstream effects. While one does not usually want to think of programs as existing *for the purpose of* employing their staff—the WPA (Works Projects Administration) is a counterexample—the issue in evaluation is not intentions but

98

reality.

NOTES: (i) In the evaluation—especially formative evaluation—of service organizations, it is nearly always imperative to identify *internal* consumers, and encourage units to regard them with all the respect that external consumers (for example, counter customers) are expected to receive. (ii) The line between recipients and other consumers is not sharp; the important point is to get all of them identified. For example, it's not clear whether one should say that the recipients of a school band program include the nonband members who hear the music or just the band; but both are certainly consumers. (iii) The immediate consumers of an *evaluation* are its **audiences**, which include the **client**. (iv) How much you need to know about the consumers will vary from case to case; typically, if you're evaluating a training program for neurosurgery, you'll need to know something about the incoming level of skill and knowledge.

CONSUMER-BASED EVALUATION An approach to the evaluation of (typically) a program that *starts with* and *focuses on* the impact on the consumer or clientele or—to be more exact—the whole impacted population. It might or might not be done **goal-free**, though clearly that is the methodology of choice for consumer-based evaluation. It will make a particular effort to include the identification of nontarget populations that are impacted, unintended effects, hidden costs to the consumer and society, and so on. Much of the history of evaluation in the modern era (the last 25 years) is the history of moving away from a management bias (the **goal-achievement model**) to a consumer-based model.

CONSUMMATING (an evaluation) Used here to refer to completing the **synthesis** process, rather than just submitting subevaluations—for example, of the **dimensions** or **components**.

CONTENT ANALYSIS The process of systematically determining the characteristics of a body of material or practices, for example, tests, books, courses, or jobs. A great many techniques have been developed for doing this, running from frequency counts on words of certain kinds (e.g., personal references), to analysis of plot structure in illustrative stories to determine whether the dominant figure is, for example, male or female, white or nonwhite. The use of content analysis is just as important in determining whether the evaluand matches the official description of it as it is in determining what it is and what it does in other dimensions than those involved in the "truth in packaging" issue. Thus, a social studies chart entitled "Great Americans" could be subjected to content analysis in order to determine whether those listed were actually great Americans (truth in labeling); but even if it passed that test, it would be subject to further content

99

analysis for, for example, sexism, because a list that did not contain the names of the great women suffragists would show a deformed sense of values, although it might be too harsh to argue that it was not correctly labeled. Notice that none of this refers to a study of the effects of the product (**payoff** or **outcome evaluation**) but is one of the legitimate types of **process evaluation**. Neither completely preempts the other; for example, teaching literal falsehoods—a process 'error'—may be the best pedagogical device for getting the student to remember truths—a desired outcome. Teaching the correct but much more complicated account may lead to less accurate residual learning than teaching the incorrect account.

It is not an exaggeration to say that most elementary science courses follow the model of teaching untruths in order to get approximate truths instilled in the brains of the students. A more radical view would hold that human brains in general require knowledge to be presented in the form of rather simple untruths rather than true complexities. An excellent brief discussion of content analysis by Sam Ball is found on pp. 82-84 of the *Encyclopedia of Educational Evaluation*, (Jossey-Bass, 1976).

CONTENT VALIDITY The property of tests that, after appropriate content analysis, appear to meet all requirements for congruence between claimed and actual content. Thus a test of netmaking ability should contain an adequate (weighted) sampling of *all* and *only* those skills that the expert netmaker exhibits. Note that this example comes from a (mainly) psychomotor domain of skills; content validity is not restricted to the cognitive or verbal areas. Content validity is one step more sophisticated than **face validity** and one step less sophisticated than **construct validity**. So it can be seen as a more scientific approach to face validity or as a less-than-comprehensive approach to construct validity (which also takes into account all known empirical and theoretical connections). The kind of evaluation that is involved in credentialing someone as a teacher of, for example, upper secondary mathematics (in the U.S.) is content *invalid* because of its absurd failure to require mathematical skills at anything like an appropriate level (e.g., at about the median of college sophomores majoring in mathematics). In general, as with other forms of process evaluation, content validity checks are considerably quicker than construct validity approaches and frequently provide a rather highly reliable *negative* result, while being less decisive on the affirmative side, since content validity is a necessary but not sufficient condition for merit. Content validity is a good example of a concept developed in one evaluation environment (testing, that is, evaluation of students or patients) that transfers well to another, namely, personnel evaluation (candidates and employees),

100

once one starts thinking about evaluation as a single discipline, logically speaking. In the personnel field, predictive and concurrent validity have been overweighted severely; their use in most personnel evaluation is invalid, whereas content-valid tests are acceptable.

CONTEXT (of evaluation or evaluand). The ambient social circumstances that do or may influence the evaluand or evaluation; by contrast with ambient physical circumstances that would normally go under Description. Context includes attitudes and expectations by stakeholders (these factors also apply to Consumers, but are covered under that heading in the KEC), access to documents and sites, community status. Context has a longitudinal (historical, diachronic) and a cross-sectional (concurrent, synchronic) aspect. Here, the term "background" is used to identify the former. Context is often crucial for identifying **causation**, and for identifying **contextually evaluative** terms. Note that a major issue in an applied field is achieving a certain level of credibility as well as certainty with your eventual conclusion, and this is where you discover what those levels have to be; the pure researcher normally skips over this in the search for 'truth in our time'.

CONTEXTUALLY EVALUATIVE (terms; a.k.a. "implicitly evaluative") Terms that are intrinsically descriptive but in a particular context are imbued with evaluative significance and treated exactly as if they were evaluative. Examples include the time a car takes to get from standstill to sixty, having a degree from Harvard, or religious commitment. These are value-imbued by certain contexts and may swing from having positive to negative value depending on the context. The context analysis needed to discover the evaluative loading often includes discussant interrogation. Compare with **Crypto-evaluative** (where a term's intrinsic meaning involves evaluative concepts, although that many not be obvious on the face of it).

CONTRACT See Funding.

CONTRACT TYPES The usual categories of contract types (this particular classification comes from the Eckman Center's *The Project Manager's Workplan (TPMWP)* are (i) fixed price, (ii) time and materials, (iii) cost reimbursement, (iv) cost plus fixed fee, (v) cost plus incentive fee, (vi) cost plus sliding fee, and (vii) joint powers of agreement. Explaining the differences beyond those obvious from the terms would be telling you more than you want to know unless you are about to become a large-project manager, in which case you'll need *TPMWP*, and may be able to afford it (priced upward of $30); it can be ordered from the Eckman Center, P.O. Box 621, Woodland Hills, CA 91365. That's the technical stuff, but at the minimalist level, it's a good idea to have something in writing that covers the basics, for example, when payments are to be made (and under what conditions they will not be made) and who is empowered to release the results (and when). Dan Stufflebeam has the best checklist for this, in his monograph in the monograph series from the Evaluation Center, Western Michigan University, Kalamazoo, Michigan.

CONTROL GROUP A group that does not receive the "treatment" (e.g., a service or product) being evaluated. The group that does receive it is the experimental group, a term that is used even though the study may be **ex post facto** and not experimental. The function of the control group is to determine the extent to which the same effect occurs without the treatment. If the extent is the same, this would *tend* to show that the treatment was not causing whatever changes were observed in the experimental group. To perform this function, the control group must be "matched", that is, so chosen as to be closely similar—not identical to—the experimental group in relevant respects. The more careful the matching is done (e.g., by using so-called "identical twins"), the more sure one can be that differences in outcome are due to the experimental treatment.

A great improvement is achieved if you can *randomly assign* matched subjects to the two groups, and arbitrarily designate one as the experimental and the other as the control group. This is a "true experiment"; other cases are weaker and include *ex post facto* studies. Matching would ideally cover all environmental variables as well as genetic ones—all variables *except* the experimental one(s)—but common sense means that we match only on variables that we think are likely to affect the results significantly, for example, sex, age, or schooling. Matching on each specific characteristic (stratification) is not essential, it is just more efficient. A perfectly good control group can be set up by using a (much larger) random sample of the population as the control group (and, if possible, for the experimental or treatment group). The same degree of confidence in the results can thus be achieved either by comparing small, closely matched groups (experimental and control) or large, entirely randomly selected groups.

Of course, if you're likely to be wrong—or if you're in doubt—about which variables to match on, the large random sample is a better bet even though it is more expensive and slower. It should be noted that it is sometimes important to run several "control groups" and that one can then equally well call them all experimental groups or comparison groups. This is a key point in the design of evaluations. The classical control group is the "no treatment" group, but it's not usually the most relevant to practical decision making. Indeed, it's often not even clear what "no treatment" *means*, for example, if you

102

withhold *your* treatment from a control group in evaluating psychotherapy, they create their own, and may change behavior just *because* you withheld treatment—they may get divorced, get religion, change or lose their job, and so on. So you finish up comparing psychotherapy with *something else*, usually a mixture of things, not with nothing; not even with no psychotherapy, only with no psychotherapy of the particular brand you wish to study. Hence it's better to have control groups that get one or several *standard* alternative treatments than "leave them to their own devices", a condition into which the 'no treatment' groups often degenerate. And in evaluation, that's exactly where you bring in the critical competitors. In medicine, that's why the control group gets a placebo.

It is crucial in understanding the logic of control groups to realize they only provide a one-way test of causation. If there *is* a difference between the dependent variable(s) as between the two groups (and if the matching is not at fault) then the experimental treatment has been (probably) shown to have an effect. But if there is *no* difference, it has not been shown that the treatment has no effect, only no *greater* effect than whatever (mixture of treatments) happened to the control group. A corollary of this is that the differential effect size, when there is one, cannot be identified as the total effect size of the treatment, except in a situation where the control is an *absolute* nontreatment group—more feasible in agriculture than mammalian research.

CONVERGENCE GROUP (Stufflebeam) A team whose task is to develop the best version of a treatment from various **stakeholder** or **advocate** suggestions. A generalization of the term, to convergence *sessions*, covers the process that should follow the use of parallel (teams of) evaluators, namely, the comparison of their *written* reports and an attempt to resolve disagreements. This should be done in the first place by the separate teams, with a referee (group) present to prevent bullying; it may later be best to use a separate convergence (**synthesis**) group.

CORRECTION FOR GUESSING In multiple-choice exams with n alternatives in each question, the average testee would get $1/n$ of the marks by guessing alone. Thus if a student fails to complete such an exam, it has been suggested that one should add $1/n$th of the number of unanswered question to his or her score, to get a fair comparison with the score of testees who answer all the questions, possibly by guessing the ones they do not have time to do seriously. There are difficulties both with this suggestion ("applying the correction for guessing") and with not using it; the correct procedure will depend on a careful analysis of the exact case. Another version of the correction for guessing involves subtracting the number of answers that one would expect to get by guessing from the total score, whether the test is completed or not. These two approaches give essentially the same (grading or ranking but not scoring) results, but their effects may interact differently with different instructions on the test and different degrees of condition in the testees. In general, ethics requires that if such corrections will be used, they be preexplained to testees. It's better to avoid this kind of problem and gain many other benefits by using either differential scoring, which will penalize guessers, or objective tests that are not multiple-choice, such as **multiple-rating items.**

CORRELATION The relationship of concomitant occurrence or covariation. Its relevance to evaluation is (i) as a hint that a casual relation exists (showing an effect to be present), or (ii) to establish the validity of a predictive **indicator.** The validity of evaluative indicators for product but not personnel evaluation can also be established. The range is from -1 to +1, with 0 showing random relationship and 1 showing perfect (100%) correlation (+1) or perfect avoidance (-1).

COST Informally, the cost of something is what it takes to acquire (or make) and keep it; but many evaluations require a considerably more exact analysis. To be more exact, we have to begin with a definition of cost itself as the *negative utility* (a.k.a. disutility) incurred in the making or getting of something. The most fundamental examples of costs are distaste, pain, and dislike; less directly felt examples include the transfer of money, time, or other things one considers valuable. Accountants prefer to treat costs as equivalent to financial outlays, but that excludes opportunity costs and misses nonmoney costs. Economists, whom one might suppose to be the relevant experts in defining cost, go exactly the other way. They incorrectly define cost as opportunity cost, that is, as "the value of the most valued forgone alternative", thereby excluding experiential costs such as pain—a counterintuitive decision—and eliminating the distinction between ordinary costs and opportunity costs.

A major reason for thinking this is an error and not just a sacrifice of intuition for conceptual advantages is the following (more details in "Cost in Evaluation: Concept and Practice", in *The Costs of Evaluation*, edited by Alkin and Solomon [Sage, 1983]). The economists' definition requires that in order to determine the cost of something you must be able to judge or calculate the value of the alternatives, so as to determine which is "the most valued". In doing this, we surely cannot assume that all alternative choices are pure unadulterated pleasure. In the real world, to which this definition is supposed to apply, there are negative elements involved in many alternatives—for example, pain, anxiety, distaste. Pain is not just the absence of pleasure—it's something we actively dislike, disvalue. So, to

104

apply this definition, we already need to understand the concept of disvalue, i.e., cost; but that's the concept this definition is supposed to be replacing, so it's a circular definition. A second reason for avoiding the identification of cost with opportunity cost is that it often requires a great deal of expertise to identify the "most valuable alternative"; it's very often something that nobody had even thought of. In such cases it seems awkward to say that the true cost was deeply buried—better to say that one hadn't realized what opportunities one had missed. See **Critical competitor.**

The notion of opportunity cost is an extremely valuable one, but it can't *replace* the notion of cost—in fact, the relation is the exact opposite: opportunity cost only makes sense in terms of the concept of cost. Opportunity costs are best seen as one perspective on costs, rather than as the true meaning of cost. Opportunity cost analysis will sometimes turn up a perspective we've overlooked and is in that sense 'another' cost; in that respect it is something like maintenance cost. See also **Zero-based budgeting, Budget, Price.** It should also be noted that negatively valued *outcomes* are not normally regarded as costs, but become so from the viewpoint of overall accounting of the evaluand. While this is typically the point of view of social costing, as in **technology assessment,** for example, it is still relevant for the individual: if my expensive pet leopard mauls me, the total cost of *owning it*—by contrast with getting it—goes up.

It's amusing that economics, the only social 'science' that gets Nobel prizes, can't define its key term correctly and hardly scratches the surface of the problem that is said to define the whole subject (see **Apportionment**). The committee that added economics to the Nobel list—rather than, say, psychology—was presumably confused into thinking economics is scientific by the quantitative smokescreen with which it surrounds itself. But few economists can even do serious **cost analysis** on a real example, a situation comparable to physicists not being able to solve the verbal problems on a high school physics test—and the record suggests that none can do reliable economic forecasting. That situation is better thought of as demonstrating a quantitative veneer rather than quantitative sophistication.

COST ANALYSIS The practical process of calculating the costs of something, in particular something that is being evaluated. Economists tend to think it's beneath them—they refer you to the business school. The business school thinks it's done in their accounting courses. However, accounting deals only with a *limited range* of *money* costs. Cost analysis goes further than accountants do, even with money costs: for example, it includes the identification of nontrivial opportunity costs and externalities (unanticipated outcomes) and goes far beyond money costs into that part of the costs in time, space, anxiety, political rights, expertise, and so on that is not translatable into money terms. Moreover, good cost analysis involves, explicitly or implicitly, a three-dimensional matrix not normally seen in accounting texts, a description of which follows.

When people talk about "the cost of X" they often talk in a context that makes clear that they are only referring to one aspect of true total cost, even if they do not realize this; sometimes they may only be referring to price. For serious evaluation, even for personal decisions, one must try to identify the full range of costs. The three key questions that set up the axes of the matrix are: (i) "Cost to whom?", (ii) "Cost of what type?", and (iii) "Cost during what period?" The matrix can usefully show types of cost as row headings, "payers" as column heads (or vice versa), with time phases represented by the slices (the depth dimension). It is increasingly easy to find electronic spreadsheets that will allow this in one set-up, but you can always do it in even the simpler programs by defining a set of spreadsheets, one for each time phase.

This process is much more difficult than most evaluators (and decision-makers) think; on the first point, for example, you have to force yourself to look at your assumptions about who is to count in cost calculations. College administrators will often make changes in various arrangements in order to achieve 'cost savings', *without allocating any figure to the cost of student time*. That approach provides good fuel for resentment and sometimes for revolutions, either of which is very expensive for a college. (See **Perspectival evaluation.**)

The time phases are the easiest to remember: basically, the main heads are preparation, installation, operation, termination. The following breakout of costs under these headings is intended to be rather general, but in some cases is still longer than you will need. In the <u>preparation</u> phase, one must cost out: planning time including research, travel, discussions, consultants and workshops; perhaps trial rentals; getting and paying for clearances, licenses, and approvals; site preparation (may include costs of new construction, wiring, subpanels, infrastructure equipment, and so on); training. <u>Installation</u> covers down payment or total purchase cost, transportation, set-up, and conversion of practices or records. <u>Operation</u> costs involve: payments (if a loan is involved), insurance, taxes, maintenance of equipment, space costs (rent or amortization, janitorial, heating and cooling, building maintenance), supplies and utilities, and upgrades to keep pace (by contrast with improvements to increase capability, which should be treated as separate items); continued training for new staff and new users; revivification counseling/training for continuing staff; money

106

set aside to cover future replacement costs; salaries plus fringes for staff, and cost of external consultants and evaluators; and a slice of remaining overhead (central administration, institutional evaluation, etc.). <u>Termination</u> involves packing, moving, returning, selling, lay-off payments or retraining, rehabilitation of space, possibly penalties for nonstandard wind-up of loans, and rentals or leases, or allowances for vacancy period.

The column headings refer to payers of the costs (impactees), beginning with recipients and those to whom costs are passed on from them (e.g., parents, sibs, peers, friends, teachers/students, counselors, neighbors, other agencies); other **consumers** such as taxpayers, volunteers, communities; program staff; and other consumers and **stakeholders**.

The row headings refer to types of cost. Of course, this starts with money (including price, fees, salaries, travel, and so on—the usual list, well covered in most references), and the other costs are best treated as *net of what money can buy.* So it's incorrect to say that time is a cost if it's simply charged as overtime to people who are glad of the extra income. Time is a cost when it has to be paid for as time taken from or contributed by those who value it to the extent that they do not feel recompensed by payment or cannot be paid. The same applies to other currencies: materials and equipment (the usual list of these); space—both quantity and quality of space (sun, light, shade, view); energy (of all mechanical and human kinds, such as enthusiasm); other environmental impacts (besides energy use); expertise; unskilled labor; transportation; quality of personal life and worklife (noise, heat, humidity, stress, morale, social relations, etc.); societal costs (crime rate, unemployment, discrimination, etc.); and other opportunity costs for all parties (lost learning, achievements, attitude shifts—the loss of innocence etc.). Thus cost analysis always involves looking at opportunity costs, but that's not all it does (whereas, if the economists' definition of cost were correct, that's all it would do). See also **Time costs**.

It also involves looking at all costs incurred, whether intentionally or not, whether directly or not. In particular, it involves the cost of side-effects, including spatially or temporally remote effects (loss of a salmon run from the heat pollution of a power plant, for example). In many cases one has to resort to artifice to get any kind of estimate—'shadow costing' is one such device. The "human capital" or "human resources" approach to cost analysis stresses one nonmonetary component. "Marginal analysis" looks at the relative *add-on* costs, from a given cost-level and is often both more relevant to the decision-maker's choices at that basic cost-level and more easily calculated. Cf.

107

Apportionment, Zero-based budgeting, Budget.

Cost analysis is one of the three fundamental components in the phrase sometimes used to sum up the 'meat and potatoes' part of evaluation—determining *comparative cost-effectiveness* (within the constraints of ethics and the law). Without cost analysis, in fact, one can scarcely determine which elements to compare, so it, like outcomes analysis, is really fundamental. Cost analysis is also the sharp end of economics, without which one can hardly apply the theories, but it is rarely done—let alone done well—by economists, particularly not guru economists (Henry Levin is a major exception) as they join many educational researchers in following the Newtonian dream into lemming oblivion. It is notable that even at Stanford, where Levin teaches, the graduate program in evaluation does not require his course. One might as well not require arithmetic competency in a mathematics major. See **Cost-effectiveness.**

COST AVOIDANCE The first principle of cost management—avoiding costs is better than reducing them. A word processor *avoids* the cost of reproofing unchanged material, but it only *reduces* the (incremental and time) cost of retyping corrected drafts. The distinction is crucial in evaluating new systems (and they include, for example, new technology or managers, since both inevitably lead to new systems). One should look for cost avoidance first and cost savings on carry-over procedures second, though they are all cost savings in a more general sense.

COST-BENEFIT OR BENEFIT-COST ANALYSIS The term is often used loosely to refer to what is in fact correctly called **cost-effectiveness analysis.** Strictly speaking, cost-benefit analysis is both more limited and more powerful than cost-effectiveness analysis in that it estimates the overall cost and benefit of each alternative (product or program) *in terms of a single quantity,* usually money. This analysis will, where feasible, provide an answer to the question: Is this program or product worth its cost? Or: Which of the options has the highest benefit/cost ratio? This is only possible when all values involved can be converted into money terms. This is not normally possible in the case of ethical, intrinsic, temporal, or aesthetic elements. The concept, which is extremely useful in certain cases, originated with the Army Corps of Engineers, who were trying to decide when it was worthwhile to build a dam. They added up the money benefits in terms of increased crop yields, reduced flood damage, and so on, and put them against the dam, and the cost of acreage and housing reimbursement. They did not foresee the costs in terms of spawning runs, kayaking. and other wild river values, which we would today add to the analysis.

COST-EFFECTIVENESS ANALYSIS The purpose of this type of analysis is to go beyond **cost-benefit analysis** in order to determine what a program or procedure costs against what it does (effectiveness) *when these cannot all be reduced to any single dimension of payoff* (usually money). Payoffs and costs might be in terms of a set of valued commodities such as space, time, expertise, gains on standardized tests, increased attendance at a clinic, and so forth. This procedure, while more general, does not provide an automatic answer to the question: Is this program or product worth its cost? The evaluator will have to weight and synthesize the needs and preferences data and combine them with some weighting of any absolute values involved—for example, legal and ethical values—to get an answer, and even that may be equivocal. But cost-effectiveness analysis always clarifies the choices considerably. Ref: Henry Levin, *Cost Effectiveness: A Primer*, Sage, 1983, and his essential essay on the pathetically limited implementation of this approach in *Evaluation and Education at Quarter Century* (NSSE/University of Chicago, 1991).

COST-FEASIBILITY ANALYSIS Determining on a Yes or No basis whether something can be afforded. This means determining whether you can afford the initial *and* the continuing costs.

COST-FREE EVALUATION The doctrine that nonmandated evaluations should, if properly designed and implemented, provide a net positive return, on the average. They may do this either by reducing investment in ineffective programs, procedures, or purchases, or by an increase in productivity or quality from existing resources/levels of effort. The equivalence tables between costs and benefits should be set up to match the client's values and accepted by the client before the evaluation begins, so as to avoid undue pressure to be cost free by cost cutting only, instead of by quality improvement as well as cost cutting—if the latter is requested at all. (Strictly speaking, the doctrine does not eliminate the cost of evaluation, but only the net cost.) Evaluation should be a good investment—and it is often an extremely good investment; but it is usually budgeted without regard to payoff, sometimes so low that the payoff findings are unattainable, sometimes so high that the payoff can't cover it. During an experimental period when a practitioner offered to forego fees until the payoff was established—an approach with which there is a little experience in management consulting—there was a notable increase in client attention to matching the scale of the evaluation to the potential benefits. The key aim of focusing on cost-free or cost-effective evaluation is to eliminate the false dilemma of choosing between spending resources on evaluation and spending them on services; see the NSF anecdote under **Evaluation**. Evaluation may also have to be done for accountability or legal reasons, whether or not it provides returns on investment in the usual currencies; but that is best seen as providing a return in the currency of accountability, in the short run, and cost-reduction (in the long run, because of increased attention to efficiency).

COST PLUS One basis for calculating budgets on contracts is the "cost plus" basis, which allows the contractor to charge for costs plus a margin of profit; depending on how **"profit"** is defined, this may mean the contractor is making less than if the money were in a savings account and s/he was on a salary at some other job, or a good deal more. Cost-plus contracts, since they often lack any real controls to keep costs down, provide an incentive to increase costs, since the "plus" is often a percentage of the basic cost, in which case they are not ideal for the taxpayer either. This has promoted the introduction of the "cost plus fixed fee" contract, where the fee is fixed and not proportional to the size of the contract. That's sometimes better, but sometimes—when the scope of work is enlarged during the project by the discovery of difficulties or (subtly) by the agency—it shrinks the profit below a reasonable level. The profit, after all, has to carry the contractor through periods when contracts do not abut perfectly, pay the interest on the capital investment, and provide some recompense for high risk. The argument for cost-plus contracts is clear in circumstances where it is difficult to foresee what the costs will be and no sane contractor is going to undertake something with an unknown cost. Another advantage is that it allows the agency to retain the option of changing the conditions that are to be met, the hardware that is to be used, and so on, perhaps in the light of obsolescence of the materials available at the beginning. Competitive bidding is still possible, after all.

COST-UTILITY ANALYSIS The more accurate name for what is here called, following common usage, **cost-effectiveness analysis**.

COUNTENANCE MODEL A name given to Bob Stake's first published account of an approach to educational evaluation ("The Countenance of Educational Evaluation", *Teachers College Record*, 1967), which he now finds distressing. See, instead, **Responsive evaluation**.

CREDIBILITY Evaluations often need to be not only valid but such that their audiences will believe that they are valid. (Cf. "It is not enough that justice be done, it must also be seen to be done.") This may require extra care about avoiding (apparent) **conflict of interest,** for example, even if in a particular case the apparent conflict is not in fact going to affect validity. It should not be forgotten that credibility

110

to the *internal* audience (the staff) is often important in a formative evaluation; credibility is not just something for an external audience. Internal credibility is a major reason for using a **local expert**, who knows the jargon, has subject matter area status, understands "the cross we all bear", and so on; but only in conjunction with an evaluator external to the field, or else the usual problems of shared bias become overwhelming, and of course *external credibility* deteriorates. Professions and professional schools, like schools of law and medicine, never think that's a problem because they have such high opinions of themselves (nursing schools, on the other hand, use external evaluators very frequently). But the failure to subject themselves to external scrutiny, along with price-gouging, contributes to the low public opinion poll ratings of the 'senior' professions—and correctly so.

CRITERION, CRITERIA 1. In the language of tests and measurement, a criterion (variable) is whatever is to count as success; the "payoff". For example, graduating from college or the grade point average in college is often the "criterion measure" against which we validate a predictive test such as a college entrance examination. Ability to balance a checkbook might be one "criterion behavior" against which we evaluate a practical math course. Note that it is common for there to be more than one criterion, which raises the question of how they are to be assembled into a variable whose correlation with the indicators under study can be measured. (Cf. **Standard, Indicator, Synthesis, Qualitative weight and sum.**)

2. In the language of evaluation, the term is sometimes used in a looser way, to include *indicators* of success or merit, variables that are not part of success itself (or definitionally connected with it), but rather tied to it by empirical research. Thus in evaluating teachers, one may describe highly organized lesson planning as a criterion of merit. In personnel evaluation (by contrast with product evaluation), this is illicit and leads to unjust and inefficient personnel action; see **Research-based personnel evaluation.** One should distinguish between **compensatory criteria** and **autonomous** or standalone criteria; and between **primary** and **secondary** indicators, only the former being criteria in the essential sense; see **Primary indicator** for examples.

3. In the language of **probative logic**, the relation between concepts and criteria for them replaces the relation in classical logic between concepts and their defining features. A criterion for X is a property from a set x_i with the following properties: (i) some of them (perhaps many, perhaps most of them) must, definitionally, be present when X is present; (ii) the conjunction of all of them form a

111

sufficient condition for X (although that conjunction may never occur or may form a contradiction); (iii) at most some of them are necessary conditions for X. In the real world of learning language, what we see are clusters of criteria—not always the same set, but bearing a family resemblance—and the typical cluster gets the name.

CRITERION-REFERENCED TEST This type of test provides information about an individual's (or a group's) knowledge or performance on a specific, independently defined criterion. The test scores are thus interpreted by comparison with predetermined performance criteria rather than by comparison with the scores of a reference group (see Norm-referenced test). The *value* of such tests (CRTs) depends completely on the (educational or other) significance of the criteria and on the technical soundness of the test. Trivial criterion, trivial test; theory-impregnated criterion, theory-dependent test; survival skill criterion, crucial test; and so on. Some of the commercial test companies cashed in on the swing to CRTs and sold CRTs whose criteria have been developed from some dubious theory, for example, a theory about reading. One has no idea whether it's worth training to those criteria; yet districts bought millions of dollars worth of the tests, because they were 'criterion-referenced'. By contrast, we still lack a good selection of functional literacy tests to choose from, even though that is a case where the criterion is independently known to be valuable. (Cf. Ranking.)

CRITICAL COMPETITORS Viable alternatives to the evaluand that may produce comparably valuable benefits at comparable or lesser cost. They must be considered in almost all evaluations because it is almost always important to find out whether the *best* use of the resources involved is being made, as opposed to the pragmatically less interesting question of whether it's just being thrown away (efficiency rather than effectiveness, in one evaluative parlance). Critical competitors: (i) may not be the same kind of object as the evaluand—critical competitors for a team of trainers include a computer with CBT package, and a text; (ii) may have to be created especially for the exercise; (iii) may cost about the same or substantially more or less (depending on how important money and the prospective benefits are to the needs of the client or consumer); (iv) may not have been thought of before the evaluation began; and (v) rarely include the no-treatment alternative, thus distinguishing the normal approach in evaluation from that in experimental design for research purposes. They are only more or less functionally equivalent to the evaluand; each may offer significant particular advantages in order to be competitive. Look particularly for critical competitors that are only on the horizon now, but are sure to arrive during the time period when the evaluand

112

would be in place. (See ELMR for an example.)

Critical competitors that should figure in the evaluation of a $20 text might therefore include: another at $20 that is reputed to be much better, one that is just as good (or better) for $10 (or $5), or even one that is much better for $25. One should also include a film (if there is one), lectures, TV, a job or internship, and so on, where they or an assemblage of them cover similar learning. The *absence* of a text—the "no treatment" alternative—is rarely a real option. The usual choices are the *old* treatment, *another innovative one, both,* or a *hybrid*—or something no one has so far seen as relevant (or perhaps not even put together). Thinking up or finding these unrecognized or "created" critical competitors is often the most valuable contribution an evaluator makes to an entire evaluation and coming up with them requires creativity, local knowledge, and scepticism combined with realism. In economics, concepts such as **cost** are often defined in terms of (what amounts to being the) critical competitors, but it is often assumed that identifying them is easy. Standard critical competitors in an evaluation of rug shampoos (for example) are easy to identify—everything called rug shampoo—but the nonstandard ones are the most important. In this case *Consumer Reports* included a dilute solution of the leading detergent, which outperformed *and* undercut the cost of all the shampoos by a country mile. It's always worth including an *el cheapo* critical competitor, namely, whatever you can get that's like the evaluand but at no more than half the price. There are some classic cases in education where the *el cheapo* version beat the deluxe original, perhaps because it was less confusing/distracting to the child.

Identifying critical competitors often requires reference to the client and context, but one has to remember to use the term carefully. One might think that the 'critical competitor' in evaluating our local high school basketball team is the perennial league leader from another school, which the locals have never beaten. In formative evaluation, this is likely to be an inappropriate choice if the leader comes from a much larger school with much greater support from wealthier alumni. The coach and principal at our school—for that matter, the community—can't afford that alternative. For this community, one critical competitor is the same team with a different coach; for the present coach, critical competitors include a different style or player selection procedure. Summatively, one must distinguish *actual* competitors or *socially defined* competitors from critical competitors (the appropriate comparisons); and, relatedly, distinguish *ideals* from *appropriate standards*. The other team in this example performs at a higher level, a level that might even qualify as an *ideal* for the local school, but it's just a play on the word "competitor" to identify them as a crit-

113

ical competitor. 'Aiming high' as in this example, is, strictly speaking, inappropriate, and could be discouraging; sometimes, however, it is inspiring.

The converse mistake is setting your sights too low in selecting critical competitors and that has no redeeming features. For example, it's a serious but common error in comparative road tests to run the Lexus 400 series against the BMW 5 series because they're in the same price bracket; the correct comparison is with the far more expensive BMW 7 series, because the overall performance is comparable. Superiority to the 5 series then is generated as a by-product of the evaluation (adding the well-supported premise that the 7s are better than the 5s), and an important extra conclusion is achieved. Another example of context influencing the choice of critical competitors: if you are evaluating something simply because you've got to save money (and this or something else will have to be cut), you might want to focus entirely on a family of radically cheaper critical competitors, all the way down to the zero or no-treatment case (cancel the program entirely).

The crucial role of critical competitors in evaluative thinking and reasoning is now receiving confirmation from studies of general reasoning skills, where it is increasingly being emphasized that the identification of realistic alternatives is a key component in effective reasoning and its teaching. Ref. *Teaching Thinking Skills: Theory and Practice*, edited by Boykoff and Sternberg (Freeman, 1987). See also **Proactive**.

CRITICAL INCIDENT TECHNIQUE (Flanagan) This approach, tied to the analysis of longitudinal records, attempts to identify significant events or times in an individual's life (or an institution's life, etc.) that in some way appear to have altered the whole direction of subsequent events. It offers a way of identifying the effects of, for example, schooling, in circumstances where a full experimental study is impossible. It is, of course, fraught with hazards. (Ref. John Flanagan, *Psychological Bulletin*, 1954, pp. 327-358.)

CRITICAL THEORY The name for a number of schools of modern thought that combine some elements of epistemological relativism with a radical ideology; for example, neo-Marxism, psychoanalytic social research, and some radical feminism. Their self-descriptions focus on the rejection of the value-free doctrine, and it is no accident that all favor strong ideologies. They often 'defend' these on the grounds that the claims of science and logic to have a value-free investigatory paradigm were bogus and hence ideology can only be judged in political terms. Unfortunately, the first part of this position leaves them without the right to appeal to reasons for making any

114

choice between political alternatives; nevertheless, they do so at considerable length. A much more sophisticated treatment of the problem of defining truth for critical theorists exists, and is admirably summarized in Shwandt's paper in *The Paradigm Dialog*, Sage, 1990. **CRITICAL THINKING** The name of an approach to or a subject within the curriculum that might equally well be called 'evaluative thinking', and skill at CT is a key component in evaluation. The term "critical" here is not meant in the sense of being negative but rather in the sense of "thoughtful" or "analytic". The result of critical thinking is in fact often to provide better support for a position under consideration or to create and support a new position. This approach or subject is often taught in the first-year college curriculum, increasingly in earlier years; in some states, such a course is mandated. In recent years, a movement has developed to use CT as a vehicle or framework for teaching mainstream subjects. At the college level, it is increasingly replacing 'baby logic', the introduction to symbolic logic that was traditionally taught by philosophy departments. The analytic skills or logic embedded in a systematic approach to critical thinking are now usually discussed as **informal logic.**

CRITICISM In the humanities, this is the term usually employed to refer to evaluation of creative subject matter, as in "literary criticism".

CROSS-SECTIONAL (study) If you want to get the results that a longitudinal study would give you, but you can't wait around to do one, then you can use a cross-sectional study as a substitute. Its validity will depend upon certain assumptions about the world. In a cross-sectional study, you look at today's first-year students and today's graduating seniors and infer, for example, that the college experience has produced or can be expected to accompany the difference between them; in a longitudinal study you would look at today's first-year students and wait and see how they change by the time they become graduating seniors. The cross-sectional study substitutes today's graduating seniors for a population that you cannot inspect for another four years, namely the seniors that today's first-year students will become. The assumptions involved are that no significant changes in the demographics have occurred since the present seniors formed the entering class and that no significant changes in the college have occurred since that time. (For certain inferences, the assumptions will be in the other direction in time.)

CRYPTO-EVALUATIVE TERM A term that appears to be purely descriptive, and is often used as descriptive, but whose meaning necessarily (definitionally) involves evaluative concepts. Examples include: intelligent, true, deduction, explanation, and scientific. Note that a crypto-evaluative term is not a pseudo-descriptive term, since it is *genuinely* descriptive. It *also* has evaluative properties; one must not think of the two as exclusive. See also **Conditionally evaluative**; compare **Contextually evaluative**.

CULTURE-FAIR/CULTURE-FREE A culture-free test avoids bias for or against certain cultures. Depending upon how generally culture is defined, and on how the test is used, this bias may or may not invalidate the test. Certain types of problem-solving tests—finding food in an artificial desert to avoid starvation, for example—are about as near to culture-free as makes any sense, but they are a little impractical to use. To discover that a test discriminates between, for example, races with respect to the numbers who pass a given standard has absolutely no relevance to the question of whether the test is culture-fair, contrary to the usual political pitch. If a particular race has been oppressed for a sufficiently long time, then its members will not be able to provide adequate support for intellectual development (or athletic development, depending upon the type of oppression) and may not provide the role models that stimulate achievement in certain directions. Hence, *quite apart from any affects on the gene pool*, it is to be expected that that racial group will perform worse on certain types of tests—if it did not, the argument that serious oppression has occurred would be weakened. Systematic procedures are now used to avoid clear cases of cultural bias in test items, but these are poorly understood. Even distinguished educators will sometimes point to the occurrence of a term like "chandelier" in a reading vocabulary test as a sign of cultural bias, on the grounds that oppressed groups are not likely to have chandeliers in their houses. Indeed they are not, but that's irrelevant; the question is whether the term reliably indicates wide reading. Validity studies will show whether members of the oppressor group picked up the term through labeling an object in the environment rather than through wide reading. That's an empirical question, not an a priori one.

A similar point comes up in looking at the use of test scores for admission selection. Validation of a cut-off is properly based on prior experience with the test for this institution and may be based on a mainly white population. In such a case, the use of the same cutting score for minorities does often *favor* them, as the APA's committee discovered. Efforts to develop culture-fair tests, by those objecting to current tests, have led to tests that correlate extremely highly with the present ones. Cultural bias in tests is considerably more subtle than the usual discussion suggests.

CURRICULUM EVALUATION Curriculum evaluation can be treated as a kind of **product evaluation**, with the emphasis on out-

116

come studies of those using the curriculum; or it can be approached in terms of **content validity**—more of a **process evaluation** approach. ("Curriculum" can refer to content only or include the sequencing of lessons and courses.)

Wood and Davis identify the following components in curriculum evaluation: determining the actual nature of the curriculum (and its support system of counselors, other curricula, catalogs, and so on) as compared with the official descriptions (e.g., via transcript analysis, curriculum analysis of class notes); evaluating its academic quality; examining the procedures used for its evaluation and revision; assessing student learning; student surveys including exit and alumni interviews; faculty surveys; surveys of employers and potential employers; reviews by professional curriculum experts; comparison with any standards provided by relevant professional associations; checking with leading schools or colleges to see if they have improvements/-updates that should be considered. (Ref. *Designing and Evaluating Higher Education Curriculum*, Lynn Wood and Barbara Gross Davis, AAHE, 1978). The KEC approach would suggest: adding cost analysis—with particular attention to psychological costs—and generalizability to this very useful list; strengthening the needs assessment in various directions (e.g., to include future-oriented analyses); addressing the **shared bias** problem of experts in the same field by ensuring the use of some radical critics; checking independently for the presence of the usual across-the-curriculum learnings (notably writing skills, critical thinking skills, and computer skills) and for ethical standards (avoidance of unfair tests, sexist language, etc.).

A popular fallacy in the area involves the supposition that good tests used in a curriculum evaluation should match the goals of the curriculum or at least its content; on the contrary, if they are to be tests *of* the curriculum, they must be independently constructed, by reference to the needs of the user population in the general domain of the curriculum, without regard to its specific content, goals, and objectives. (See **Homeopathic fallacy, Testing to the teaching**.) Another issue concerns the extent to which long-term effects should be the decisive ones; since they are usually inaccessible because of time or budget considerations, it is often thought that judgments about curricula cannot be made reliably. But essentially all long-term effects are best predicted by short-term effects, which *can* be measured. Moreover, causal inferences drawn from temporally remote data, even if we could wait to study the long-term situation, are so much less reliable that any gains from the long-term study would likely be illusory.

One of the most serious errors in a great deal of curriculum evaluation involves the assumption that curricula are implemented in

117

much the same way by different teachers or in different schools. Even if a quite thorough checklist is used to ensure implementation, there is still a great deal of slippage in the teaching process. In the more general sense of "curriculum", which refers to the sequence of courses taken by a student, the slippage occurs via the granting of exceptions, the use of less-than-valid challenge exams, the substitution of different instructors for others on leave, and so on. Despite these difficulties, curriculum materials and curriculum sequences should be evaluated for gross differences in their effectiveness and veracity/comprehensiveness/relevance to the needs of the students. The differences between good and bad are so large and so common that, despite all the difficulties, very much improved versions and choices can result from even rough-and-ready evaluation of content and teachability.

CUTOFF A minimum standard or score that must be met in order to pass an evaluand forward for further consideration. What the term adds to "requirement" or "standard" is the quantitative element. Note that this is not the same as the **cutting score** for a passing grade on the dimension, since it involves the further decision that scores below pass level cannot be compensated for by other scores or ratings above that level on other dimensions. The term "hurdle" is also used for the same notion. See **Compensatory, Multiple-cutoff.**

CUTTING SCORE A score that marks the line between grades, between mastery and nonmastery, and so on. Always arbitrary to some degree, it is more easily justified in circumstances where a number of such scores will eventually be synthesized. But in a final report, only cutting *zones* make sense and the grades should indicate this, for example, A, A-, AB, B+, and so on, where the AB indicates a zone or borderline area. Many opponents of minimum competency testing complain about the arbitrariness of any cutoff *point*. The response should be to use a *zone*, that is, three grades instead of two (clearly not competent; uncertain competence; clearly competent); and tie the decisions to these. Although there is still a cutting score between each of these, the action connected to each can be softened appropriately, for example by allowing retakes for the buffer zone. Eventually, of course, the objection reduces to an objection to making any distinctions at all, no matter how large the performance distinction—an absurdity. So one makes concessions in the direction of softening impact, knowing that at some point, the bullet must be bit, but trying to educate the upset evaluees or their representative about the real necessity. See **Banding.**

D

DATA ACCESS Data access in evaluation is often very difficult because of confidentiality controls, because the gatekeepers are afraid that the data may be used against them, because the point of entry is too late, or because appropriate records were never kept. Often a serious effort toward building trust should be part of the early work; normally it will include guarantees that the evaluees will be sent a draft of the report before it is sent to the client, for correction or the attachment of **demurrers**. Sometimes this is impossible; and sometimes a professional evaluation is ruled out simply because data access is too restricted. This is one reason to plan programs for **evaluability** in the first place.

DATA SYNTHESIS The semialgorithmic, semijudgmental process of producing comprehensible facts from raw data via descriptive or inferential statistics, plus interpretation in terms of concepts, hypotheses, or theories.

DATA VISUALIZATION The name for what is now emerging as a new type of computer application software; "data presentation" might be a better term. It began with the use of graphs—now generated automatically by all leading spreadsheet and many database programs, and this led to specialized graphing programs that routinely generate a hundred different types of (customizable) graphs. It branched into the specialized area of 'presentation software', which incorporated outlining and word charts, and sophisticated graphic techniques such as shading of backgrounds. Meanwhile, on the big mainframes and CAT scanners, the use of pseudo-coloring to represent bands of a continuous variable became a standard way to represent results, notably in medicine (tomography scans), astrophysics (the comet probe photos), satellite survey work, and shock wave research, the latter especially from the Livermore Labs. Parallel work developed improved ways to display statistical data sets, including coloring to indicate, for example, recency of data or sex of subject, and the use of rotation and real time to convey a four-dimensional picture of the data. The value of these approaches has made **exploratory data analysis** much more powerful and successful—and it has deskilled it substantially. In the 1990s, much of this power has been made available on microcomputers and it transforms the empirical side of research (including evaluation) as well as the presentation of results. For future possibilities, see **Virtual reality.**

DECILE (Stat.) See **Percentile.**

DECISION-MAKER It is sometimes important to distinguish between making decisions about the truth of various propositions about X and making decisions about the disposition of (or appropriate action about) X. Although the scholar automatically falls into the first category, s/he typically only serves as a consultant to a decision-maker of the second type—in the program evaluation context. But much of the use of evaluation today occurs in product evaluation, and in much of that the evaluator is one of the decision-makers (a.k.a. **consumer**), so one has to be careful not to make too much of the distinction.

DECISION-ORIENTED RESEARCH See **Conclusion-oriented research.**

DECISION RULE A link between an evaluation and action, for example "Those with a grade below C must repeat the course"; "Hypotheses that are not significant at the .01 level should be abandoned." (The latter example is a common decision rule but logically improper; see **Null hypothesis.**) It is widely supposed that evaluations imply **recommendations** by their very nature, but in fact they rarely do so, and even more rarely are such recommendations ordered for priority, exhaustive, and well-based on the necessary local expertise.

DELIVERY SYSTEM The link between a product or service and the immediate consumer (the recipient population)—which may or may not consist of those that need or want it. It is important to identify this in evaluation, because it helps avoid the fallacy of supposing that the existence of the need justifies the development of something to meet the need. It does so *only if* one can find and use an existing delivery system—or develop a new one—that reaches the needy. (A **marketing** system is normally aimed at those with wants, which may or may not happen to be needs.)

DELPHI TECHNIQUE A procedure used in group problem solving or evaluating, involving—for instance—circulating a preliminary version of the problem or a questionnaire to all participants, calling for suggested rephrasings (or, less ideally, preliminary solutions). The rephrasings or preliminary solutions are then circulated for a vote on the version that seems most fruitful (and/or the preliminary solutions are circulated for rank ordering). When the rank orderings have been synthesized, *these* are circulated for another vote. Innumerable variations on this procedure are practiced under the title "Delphi Technique", and there is a considerable literature on it. It is often done in a way that overconstricts the input, for example, with a badly designed first questionnaire, which ruins it before it begins. In any case, the intellect of the organizer must be the equal of the participants or the best suggestions won't be recognized as such. A phone conference call may be more effective, faster, and cheaper, perhaps with a second session after some written afterthoughts. But phone and face-to-face are subject to excessive influence by forceful participants. A *good* Delphi, using mail or fax, is worthwhile; they are rare. Originally used for forecasting, there are many possible uses in evaluation, with possible reductions in travel costs, etc. However, the choice of manager is crucial, and checks on censorship and the validity of synopses usually need to be arranged. Serious research on evaluation applications of this potentially useful methodology is badly needed.

DEMOGRAPHICS The characteristics of a population other than those under investigation. Often defined in terms of age, sex, level of education, occupation, place of birth, residence, IQ, and/or attitude.

DEMURRER The rejoinder to an evaluation, which the evaluee(s) should have the opportunity to make prior to the submission of the evaluation report to the client. This should either result in changes to the evaluation, which in the opinion of the evaluee make a demurrer to the second edition unnecessary; or the demurrer should be forwarded to the client along with the evaluation report—and the evaluator's response to the demurrer. This response should, where possible, be shown to the evaluee at the same time that proposed changes to the evaluation, if any, made in response to the demurrer, are conveyed. These arrangements have a simple justification in terms of improving validity; but they also have a psychological and ethical basis. See **Balance of power, Meta-evaluation.**

DEONTIC LOGIC See **Axiology.**

DEPENDENT VARIABLE One that represents the outcome—the contrast is with the independent variables that are the ones we (or nature) can manipulate directly. This definition is at least semicircular because the notion of 'outcome' is no easier to explain than 'dependent variable'. So are all other attempted definitions of the concept. The distinction between dependent and independent variables is an ultimate notion in science, definable only in terms of other such notions, for example, **randomness** or **causation.**

DESCRIPTION One of the hardest parts of an evaluation for beginners, partly because they think it's the easiest part. They confuse labels, which (like names) are easily attached to things, with descriptions, which have to be constructed from the common language so that their meaning identifies the thing. The first task is to determine the task the description is to serve. Making the description complete enough for checking implementation of the treatment at another site is hard enough, but making it good enough to enable replication of the treatment being evaluated is sometimes much harder and should rarely be required of an evaluator. Description may also include describing the true function of something, which—in program evaluation particularly—often requires deep analysis. (Describing DNA would normally refer to its function; description is rarely restricted to what can be directly observed.) Keeping the description concise—often important—by restricting it to salient features requires a needs assessment done on the audiences for the evaluation, as does the choice of language level. Descriptions provided by the client should be treated as claims for verification, not premises. **Stakeholders** normally provide multiple inconsistent descriptions, all of which are usually wrong (or too vague to be acceptable.) The delivery system and support system should usually be included in the total description.

There is no sharp line between the Description and Process checkpoints in the KEC, but the intent is to use the latter for evaluative conclusions and keep the former relatively descriptive. Sometimes, too, as in product evaluation, the former is clearly the description of an object, and the latter refers only to its use and has a relatively small role to play.

Describing often includes low-level evaluative language ("You can't miss it; it's the near-perfect 1976 Porsche 911S near the end of the row."). In evaluation, however, it's usually desirable to separate the description from any *controversial* evaluative account; as with screening out theory-impregnated language in describing a physics experiment, this turns out to be hard. Again, the distinction between description and evaluation is strongly context-dependent, so what counts as description in one context will, under the microscope of another context (where microscopes are relevant) show up as evaluative.

The description sometimes turns out to be all that matters about the evaluation, since the context of the evaluation may clearly establish all the relevant values, and there only remains the task of describing/measuring to 'settle' the evaluation (e.g., a court case or a challenge race). See **Contextually evaluative.**

DESCRIPTIVE (account or language) The usual contrast is with normative, but we reject that here because normative means "referred to norms", and many norms are descriptive. The two contrasts that need to be preserved are descriptive/prescriptive and descriptive/-evaluative. "Prescriptive" is usually taken to cover "evaluative", but in fact it has its own meaning, which refers to *laying down* how things are to be, as in stating the rules of a game or office procedures, by contrast with describing how things are. The language is often predictive language ("Senior managers will always wear suits") or uses terms like "should/ought" or "must". Evaluative language, on the other hand, is principally concerned with the language of merit— "good", "better", and so on. Similarly, "descriptive" is usually taken to cover "predictive", although these are not the same at all—what scientists describe is almost always the present, not the future. (Science fiction novelists describe the future.) In this work, the idea is to develop a useful working language rather than to get all the details right, so we accept the looser use of "prescriptive" and "descriptive". Three cautions. (i) These distinctions are highly context-dependent, and it is often misleading to talk of terms out of context as being descriptive or evaluative (see **crypto-evaluative**); (ii) in a functional sense, evaluative language *is* descriptive language. One of its values is its function as extremely compressed description ("She's a straight-A student.") and (iii) many accounts including theories in the physical sciences are double-edged, that is, they are both descriptive and prescriptive and the more useful for that. (There are also cases where scientists are seriously confused about whether they are providing descriptive or prescriptive analyses; decision theory abounds with such examples, and so does work on mathematical problem-solving.) So, the contrasts referred to here are useful, but there are two reasons for thinking they are not absolute.

DESCRIPTIVE STATISTICS The part of statistics concerned with providing illuminating perspectives on or reductions of a mass of data (cf. inferential statistics); typically this can be done as a translation, involving no risk. For example, calculating the mean score of a class from its individual scores is straight deduction and no probability is involved. But *estimating* the mean score of the class from the actual mean of a random sample of the class is of course inferential statistics.

DESIGN (of an evaluation) The process of stipulating the investigatory procedures to be followed in doing a certain evaluation—and the product of that process. See **Key evaluation checklist, Product evaluation**.

DIAGNOSIS The process of determining the nature of an affliction, of a putative symptom of disorder, or of poor performance, and/or the report resulting from that process. This may or may not happen to involve identification of the cause of the condition (see **Etiology**), but it always involves classifying the condition in terms of an accepted typology of afflictions or malfunctions, hence the terms it uses are evaluative (typically, names for *diseases*). Diagnosis is not a primary type of evaluation; it presupposes that a true evaluation—such as the annual check-up—has already occurred, and has led to the conclusion that something is wrong. The task of diagnosis is classificatory. **Analytical evaluation** sometimes but not always spins off a diagnosis: for example, if it becomes clear that something is wrong with a program (the primary evaluation) and we can discern what it is, we may say "The trouble with this program is bad management (not underfunding or the absence of need)". In general, the task of evaluation is to determine the merit, worth, or value of something, as a whole or by parts, and that often does not lead to the identification of a standard disorder, most obviously when the performance is outstanding but also when the trouble is idiosyncratic. In particular, medical diagnosis does not require a theory of the well organism, and program diagnosis does not require a theory of the well-functioning program. See **Program theory**.

DIFFUSION The process of spreading information about a product or program. Diffusion is deliberately and somewhat artificially contrasted with **dissemination**. Note that both apply to evaluation findings and suffer from the usual asymmetry of newsworthiness; the favorable results of the Sesame Street evaluation are known to millions, the fact that they're not justified, as shown in the published re-evaluations, is known to few.

DIMENSIONAL EVALUATION A species of **analytical evaluation** (by contrast with **global** evaluation) in which the performance of the entity to be evaluated is analyzed into a set of dimensions that are independent and exhaustive and, preferably, familiar from other contexts or easily grasped. (Hence factors from factor analysis are only rarely valuable for this purpose.) For example, the performance of a TV set can be broken out into: color purity, resolution, convergence, picture stability, fringe area reception, audio quality, and so on; and programs may be analyzed into the KEC dimensions. The dimensions may include some that are descriptive (as in KEC), others that are evaluative, and many that are implicitly or conditionally evaluative as in the TV example. It may be used **prescriptively** as well as analytically; for example, the scoring system used in judging Olympic diving has the two dimensions of degree of difficulty (descriptive) and skill in execution (evaluative). It is useful when explaining the meaning of an overall evaluation (e.g., in teacher evaluation, where one can refer to, say, nine intelligible dimensions of job performance that cover more than a hundred indicators). **Component evaluation** is more useful for explaining the **cause** of an evaluated performance and sometimes more useful for providing **remedial** suggestions. Dimensions are sometimes like perspectives, but the exhaustiveness requirement does not apply to **perspectival evaluation**.

DIRECT EVALUATION An evaluative claim not relativized to a set of unendorsed values, as is a **relativistic evaluation**. Example: "Randomized patrol patterns are better police procedure" vs. "On the criteria provided by (assumptions made by, values endorsed by) the San Rafael police department, randomized patrol patterns are better". Direct evaluation is sometimes also called 'unconditional', 'absolute', or 'first-hand' evaluation.

DISCREPANCY EVALUATION (Provus) Evaluation conceived of as identifying the gaps between time-tied objectives ("milestones" in the language of project management) and actual performance on the dimensions of the objectives. A slight elaboration of the over-simplified **goal-achievement** model of evaluation; a good basis for **monitoring**.

DISJUNCTIVE MODEL A way of combining the results from several data sources into an overall evaluation (that is, a **synthesis** procedure) which allows the best of several tests (interviews, etc.) to count. Since errors of measurement will get many candidates through a disjunctive approach, although they lack the minimum competence, this is a poor way to select personnel unless the passing mark is set high to compensate for the retake process. (Teacher re-certification usually uses a disjunctive process without compensation of the passing score, and a limited item pool to compound the felony.)

DISPERSION (Stat.) The extent to which distribution is "spread" across the range of its variables, as opposed to where it is "centered"—the latter being described by measures of "central tendency", such as **mean, median,** and **mode.** Dispersion is measured in terms of, for example, **standard deviation** or **semi-interquartile range.**

DISSEMINATION The process of distributing (typically) a product itself, rather than information about it (cf. diffusion). Also used as jargon synonym for distribution.

DISSONANCE See **Consonance.**

DOMAIN-REFERENCED TESTING (DRT) The purpose of testing is not usually to determine the testee's ability to answer the questions on the test, but to provide a basis for conclusions about the testee's ability with regard to a much wider *domain*. Criterion-referenced tests identify ability to perform at a certain (criterion) level on—typically—a particular *dimension*, for example, two-digit multiplication. DRT is a slight generalization of that to cover cases such as social studies education where it seems misleading to suggest that there is *a* criterion. One can think of a domain as defined by a large *set* of criteria, from which we sample, just as—at the other end—the test samples from the testee's abilities. The major problem with DRT is defining domains in a useful way. J. R. Popham has a usefully specific discussion in his

Educational Evaluation (Prentice-Hall, 1975).

DOUBLE-EDGED Having both a descriptive and an evaluative (or prescriptive) meaning. It is a common misconception that these notions are mutually exclusive; in many circumstances they are complementary. The physical sciences, seen as the models of descriptive accounts, in fact have always used ideal types to formulate their laws—for example, ideal gases, perfectly elastic solids and particles, point-masses. The laws *prescribe* what the ideal types do, as an indirect way to *describe* what real things do. This process is complex but not confused, in fact it is optimal in dealing with some kinds of loose data patterns. Ideal types are also common in the social sciences and so are theories that are both descriptive and evaluative or prescriptive, such as organizational and decision theories. (Sometimes the two *are* confused, but sometimes they are said to be confused on the basis of the false a priori assumption that they cannot cohabit.)

DREYFUS CASE The limiting but not atypical case of refusal to acknowledge the results of evaluation. It involved the French Army's recommendation that an innocent man should end his days on Devil's Island rather than that the Army should confess error in sending him there, the Army's grounds being that the loss of credibility of the Army would be worse for France than the ruin of an innocent man's life. It is a common argument when police forces reject civilian review boards. *Consumer Reports* presumably argues in a similar way when it refuses to publish clear examples of errors in its evaluations. Commitment to evaluation begins at home—which means where the evaluator lives—and there's no surer way to show you lack that commitment than to arrange that some other group (for example, teachers or students) be evaluated whereas your group, which does the evaluation (school administrators or teachers, respectively) is not evaluated. In the Dreyfus case, and in cases of police or judicial or political corruption, the analogous argument is simply that justice has to be most sternly respected and rigidly enforced when it bears on the instruments of justice itself, if they are to make clear that they are committed to justice and not merely to self-interest. See **Self-reference**.

DUMPING The practice of unloading funds rapidly near the end of the fiscal year so that they will not be returned to the central bureaucracy, which would be taken as a sign that next year's budget could be reduced by that amount since it wasn't needed this year. Dumping may be done with all the trappings of an **RFP**, that is, via a contract, but it's a situation where the difference between a **contract** and a **grant** tends to evaporate because the contract is so unspecific (because of lack of time for writing the RFP carefully) that it has essentially the status of a grant. From the agency's point of view, dumping is a sign of inadequate staff size, not a lack of need for the work that is RFP'd (as Congress often infers).

DUTIES-BASED TEACHER (OR PERSONNEL) EVALUATION (DBTE) An approach to evaluation that begins by asking what one can legally and morally require, instead of beginning with a vague idea of good teaching (for example) as it might appear to an observer. Our capacity to define or identify the latter in objective terms has been notoriously unsuccessful and even then is of dubious validity for evaluation. The DBTE approach is not as closely connected with improvement of teaching as the traditional or **RBTE** approaches; but then, medical diagnosis is a completely separate art from therapy—much of diagnosis would be discarded if it were restricted to cases where therapy is possible. Far from being a flaw, this separation is one reason DBTE is superior, since in the real world tightening the connection reduces validity. DBTE rests on a clear conception of the difference between teacher evaluation and teacher improvement, and a clear sense that accountability and serving the cause of students *requires* the first and only *hopes* to be able to provide the second. The duties of a teacher are the rest of the iceberg under a job description as it appears in an advertisement for the job; the latter only shows the duties that are different from those of other teachers. In one version (details obtainable from the author), the main headings or dimensions of the duties are:

1. Knowledge of subject matter (A. In the fields of special competence, B. In across-the-curriculum subjects); 2. Instructional ability (A. Communication skills, B. Management skills, C. Instructional design); 3. Evaluating student performance (A. Observation and classification of students, B. Test construction and administration, C. Grading/-ranking/scoring, D. Reporting student achievement); 4. Professionalism (A. Professional ethics, B. Professional attitude, C. Professional development, D. Service to the profession); 5. Other services to the school. (A fuller but earlier version of this checklist is in "Evaluating Teachers as Professionals", in *Teacher Evaluation: six prescriptions for success*, ed. J. and S. Popham [ASCD, 1988]; the most recent one is available from the author.)

E

ECHELON A term like "cohort", sometimes used interchangeably with the latter, but better restricted to a group (or group of groups) that is time-staggered with regard to its entry. If a new group of trainees, for example, comes on board every four weeks for five months, followed by a three-month gap in the entry flow (while they are being trained), and then the whole process begins again, the first three groups are called the first echelon; each of them is a cohort.

ECONOMIES OF SCALE They do exist, but are offset by the problems of scaling—the inefficiencies of size. Evaluators need to be careful, when making recommendations, not to assume that replications lead to economies of scale. They may—or they may not, or the economies may be offset by loss of effect from scaling problems.

EDUCATIONAL ROLE (of the evaluator) Evaluators often report with some surprise that they find half their time on-site is spent in educating program staff and managers about the nature of evaluation and the potential benefits from the current evaluation. It is both empirically and desirably the case that this educational role is of the greatest importance, at worst second only to the truthfinding role. This is partly because few people have been properly educated as to either the importance or the techniques of evaluation and such education can massively improve their effectiveness. It is also because the discipline will probably always seem unimportant until it (or its neglect) bites you, and quick education about *that particular* branch or application of evaluation will then become very important. No professional who is unsophisticated about personnel, product, proposal, and program evaluation in his or her field *is* a professional; but even when this sophistication is widespread, application of it to oneself and to one's own programs will not be easy, and the evaluator can help to teach professionals how to handle the process and its results. When Socrates said, "The unexamined life is not worth living", he was identifying himself as an an evaluator, but it is not *accidental* that he is best-known as a teacher. Nor is it accidental that he was killed for combining the two roles. Robert Wise argues that one way the evaluator is in a good position to be an educator is that few people have as good an overview of a project or program. See also **Valuephobia, Therapeutic role, Professional imperative.**

128

EDUCATIONAL SIGNIFICANCE See **Significance.**

EFFECT An **outcome** or *type* of outcome. The following effects in the sense of outcome types have their own entries here: **Ceiling, Enthusiasm, Halo, Hawthorne, John Henry, Longterm, Placebo, Practice, Pseudo-negative, Pseudo-positive, Pygmalion, Reactive, Recoil, Ripple, Rorschach, Sequencing, Side, Trickle.**

EFFECTIVENESS Often but not necessarily used to refer to the conclusion of a **goal-achievement** evaluation, with all its limitations. Various indexes of effectiveness were developed around mid-century, when evaluation was widely thought of as simply goal-achievement measurement for social action programs. "**Success**" is roughly equivalent to this sense. Although effectiveness can be construed more generally as referring to achieving an outcome that may not have been part of the aims of a program, it always refers to some goal, even if not the original one; it is a means-end notion. **Merit** and **worth** are the more important evaluation predicates, and include **efficiency,** often contrasted with **effectiveness.**

EFFICIENCY Efficiency goes beyond **effectiveness** by bringing in a reference to the amount of resources involved. It implies the absence of wastage for a given output; it can be increased by increasing the output for a given input. It does not guarantee that the results are of any useful size. For this reason, in many contexts, planners conventionally require that a social intervention must be both effective and efficient.

EFFORT, LEVEL OF A measure used in RFPs and in evaluation as an index of resource input—hence important in evaluation of, for example, efficiency. Often measured in terms of person-years or person-months of work. However, such measures, although virtually essential, have to be treated with a great deal of care (i.e., not too seriously). For example, one of the rules about level of effort in writing computer programs is that if a program takes a good programmer one month to write, it will take ten good programmers ten months to write—and won't be as good.

EIR See **Environmental impact report.**

ELMR (Evaluation of Learning Materials Resource) ELMR (Elmer) was invented to provide a critical competitor to ERIC, the computerized federal educational research information database. ERIC (Eric) is enormous and never purged, since dropping records reduces the size of the database and doing that reduces the size of someone's turf. Consequently, it contains masses of contradictory and outdated records, and a vast amount of material that reports on badly designed studies that someone let into the zoo. ELMR, by contrast, is a four-drawer file cabinet that contains a folder for each major practical issue

129

about which educators request (or need) advice. The drawers refer to curriculum, management, teaching, and facilities/equipment. A typical folder might be called Reading Programs, and it would contain a few sheets *summarizing* the results of the best and latest studies on the efficacy, cost, support requirements, training time, and so on, for various grade levels and types of students. A group of experts would be responsible for each folder, and would update it quarterly. Dissident opinions would be included to supplement the group's opinion. The permanent support staff would be one receptionist to take calls, and one secretary to service them by photocopying the contents of a folder—plus recording the inquiry and jogging the resource folk for updates. This would cost less than 1% of the current ERIC budget, and deal with most of the high-need inquiries—plus a great many that aren't made because people do not have the time to sort through the usual vast pile of vaguely relevant and mixed quality material. A small subsidy—say, 5% of the present budget—to the educational research organizations would support them for setting up a *research* database. ELMR's impact should be considerably more beneficial than ERIC's in the first year and improve thereafter. If it works well, it could all be put onto a micro with mirrored back-up, and released in ASCII on a diskette for those who want to search the whole package, with semiannual updates. (Its size would always be restricted to what fits on one diskette.) Not surprisingly, the ELMR proposal never received much support from the ERIC staff, and the 'consumer groups' such as ASCD or the national PTA association tend to get lost in their own affairs and process theories rather than going for the heart of their information needs.

EMPIRICISM The everyday use of the term "empiricist" refers to someone who is essentially practical in her or his orientation. The more technical use refers to an epistemological doctrine that stresses the primacy of sensory knowledge. In the philosophy of science, the (logical) positivists were among the most prominent and extreme empiricists. (Russell described himself as a "logical empiricist", that is, as being at one important remove.) The contrast is with the (allegedly) evil tribe of metaphysicians who tend to be "idealists" (in the *technical* sense of believing that the mind, not the senses, is the primary source of knowledge) or "rationalists" (again in a technical sense, ascribing the source of knowledge to reason rather than the senses). The diluted version of empiricism that became the dominant ideology of the social sciences stressed the superiority of experiments and (public) observations over a priori reasoning and introspection. But it also involved a key holdover prejudice of the positivists, namely the rejection of all evaluative terms. Although it is plausible to say that such terms do not refer to observable properties, it was wrong to conclude that they lacked objective reference since there is another legitimate category of terms, namely those referring to so-called theoretical terms, that is, terms referring to unobservable entities/processes/states whose existence can be inferred from (i.e., explains) the observable phenomena.

The logical positivists were originally keen to eliminate most unobservables as metaphysical entities, value terms along with them, but this unfortunately leaves one without either extrapolable taxonomies, adequate explanations, or guides for future microexplorations. The empiricist social scientists quickly drifted into acceptance of at least middle-level theories and their concepts, but failed to check whether the taboo terms of the evaluative vocabulary were thereby legitimated. (Of course, they were using these terms all the time, in distinguishing good experimental designs from bad ones, good instruments from bad, and so on.) The best excuse is perhaps that evaluative language consists of "theoretical terms" that relate to functions, not observations—but then so does much of the language of mathematics and linguistics. The inexcusable behavior was the failure to reconcile the obviously legitimate use of methodical evaluation and consumer product evaluation with the continued support for the doctrine of value-free social science. See **Valuephobia**.

ENEMIES LIST Worst enemies make best critics. They have three advantages over friends, in that they are more motivated to prove you wrong, are less concerned about the effect on you, and are more experienced with a radically different viewpoint. Hence they will often probe deep enough to uncover assumptions you have not noticed and destroy complacency about the impregnability of your inferences. Obviously we should use them for meta-evaluation and pay them well. But who enjoys working with, thanking, and paying an enemy? The answer is: a good evaluator. This is a key test of the "evaluation attitude" that makes up an important part of **professionalism** (see also **Evaluation skills**). The fact that many of us care little about improvement and too much about making life easy for ourselves shows up nowhere more clearly than on this issue.

A good example is the distribution of teaching-evaluation forms to students in a college class, normally done near the end of the semester. But where are your enemies then? Long gone; only the self-selected remain. Even for summative purposes, you should distribute the forms to every warm body that crosses the threshold on the first day and any later date; to be turned in to their seat-neighbor or via campus mail when they decide not to come back. The ones who leave can often tell you the most—by now you will know most of what the stalwarts will say. If you value quality, reach out for suggestions to

131

those who think *you* lack it. Much is written in methodology texts about the need to search for rival explanations and negative cases, but no one seems to mention the obvious source for them or even the role-conflict that you are in while searching for them. Use the enemies list; of course you have to find those who will cooperate, perhaps on a barter basis. The hardened evaluator may reflect: With enemies like these, who needs friends?

ENGINEERING MODEL See Medical model.

ENJOYMENT In the general context of evaluation, enjoyment is the value one measures through market surveys and is a lower priority than need, which one gets from needs assessments. Nevertheless, enjoyment will drive evaluation in the absence of overriding needs and societal standards. There's nothing flawed about inferences to evaluative conclusions concerning cruise liners' itineraries and operation, even if the value premises are hedonic. Similarly, in mixed environments, one can't discount the enjoyment to zero. Thus, for example, although it is an error in educational evaluation to treat enjoyment as primary and learning as not worth direct inspection, there's no justification for not counting enjoyment at all. Kohlberg once commented on the evaluations of the big early childhood programs that it was too bad no one bothered to check whether at least the kids *cried less* in Headstart centers than at home. The situation in certain special cases, for example in aesthetic education, is much nearer to one where enjoyment is a primary goal. A common fallacy is to argue that since it would be a serious mistake to teach K-3 children some cognitive skills at the expense of making them hate school, we should therefore make *sure* they *enjoy* school and *try* to teach them skills. That prioritization of effort reduces the already meager interest in teaching something valuable and has never been validated for its gains in positive attitude toward school. The teacher is in conflict of interest here, since finger-painting takes less preparation than spatial skill-building.

ENTHUSIASM EFFECT The **Hawthorne effect**, the **John Henry effect**, and the **placebo effect** are important effects to bear in mind when designing and interpreting evaluations since they—rather than the evaluand—may be causative of the observed outcomes. There is another psychological effect which is often subsumed under them but should be distinguished. All of those effects can occur without any special effort or manifest belief by the service provider, and indeed in the absence of any such person. They operate, as far as we know, because of the perception of the 'treatment' by the recipient. But there is a powerful effect that is due to the manifest beliefs of the *providers*, sometimes beliefs in the potency of the specific treatment or the potency of those supposedly originating or associated with it. The most

132

familiar examples of this effect are faith-healing (but 'bedside manner' sometimes relies entirely on placebo effect), charismatic leadership (e.g., in battle), and super-salesmanship. As with the other effects, the principal reason for the concern of evaluators is that programs and products are often exported without the original delivery staff and the evaluation is often supposed to report on the effects that *will* carry over to new sites. See **Generalizability**.

ENVIRONMENTAL IMPACT REPORT (EIR) Often required by law prior to granting building or business permits or variance. A form of evaluation focusing on ecosystem effects. Currently based mainly on bioscience and/or traffic analysis, these tend to be thin on the evaluation of opportunity costs, indirect costs, ethics contingency trees, and so on. See also **Technology assessment**.

EPISTEMOLOGY Theory of knowledge. The subject concerned with what kinds of knowledge we have or can get by the various investigatory means at our disposal. A key area in the foundations of a new discipline, as the history of quantum mechanics, relativity, the social sciences, and evaluation make clear. Metatheories always contain epistemological commitments. The best discussion of the evaluation implications is in *Foundations of Program Evaluation: Theories of Practice* by Shadish, Cook, and Leviton (Sage, 1990).

ERRORS OF MEASUREMENT It is a truism that all measurement involves some error; it is more interesting to notice exactly how these errors can get one into trouble in evaluation studies. For example, it is obvious that if we select the students with the lowest scores on a test for remedial work, then some of these will be in the group because of errors of measurement. That is, their performance on the particular test items that were used does not give an accurate picture of their ability; that is, they were unlucky—or distracted. It follows that an immediate remeasurement, using a test of matched difficulty, would place them somewhat higher. Hence on a posttest, which is essentially a delayed version of such a retesting, they will come out looking better, even if the intervening treatment lacked all merit. This result—their improvement—is simply a statistical artefact due to errors of measurement (specifically, a regression effect). It also follows that matching two groups on their entry level skills, where we plan to use one of them as the control in a *quasi*-experimental study (that is, a study where the two groups are not created by random assignment) will get us into trouble because the errors of measurement on the two groups cannot be assumed to be the same, and hence the regression effect will be different in size. Another nasty effect of errors of measurement is to reduce correlation coefficients; one may intuitively feel that if the errors of measurement are relatively random, they

133

should "average out" when one comes to look at the correlations, but the fact is that the larger the errors of measurement, the smaller the correlations will appear. There are design controls for these problems. See **Regression to the mean.**

ESCROW A neutral individual or secure place where identifying data can be deposited until completion of an evaluation and/or destruction of the data. (The term originated in the commercial sector and law.)

ETHICS Ethics is the emperor of the social sciences, imperial because it refers to considerations that supervene above all others, such as obligations to science, prudence, culture, and nation. It is, from one perspective, an application of evaluation (to social systems and actions within them), from another a key support discipline that, like history or testing, contributes an element to many evaluations and to much other research. That it is (logically) a social science is of course denied by virtually all social scientists, who have been brought up on the doctrine of **value-free** science, and for this or other reasons tend to get agitated about the suggestion that even *nonethical* value-judgments have a place in science. But that's just prejudice now that policy studies are well established: What is ethics but the principles of the most general kind of social policy, and what is policy analysis supposed to do with general questions—look the other way? Lexical analysis of the term "ethics" suggests that it refers to a particular policy—the policy of treating adult humans as having prima facie equal rights—and its costs and benefits can be analyzed as with any other policy.

In fact, developments in many areas of the social sciences have made it increasingly embarrassing to avoid this one great topic in policy analysis. These include work in game-theory (especially the treatment of the **prisoner's dilemma**), decision theory, latent function analysis, democratic theory in political science, moral stage theory, welfare economics, analytical and social jurisprudence, behavioral genetics, the codification and refinement of professional ethics, and many aspects of policy analysis. Some help, which should not have been necessary, is provided by three key developments outside the normal turf of social science—the emergence of the 'good reasons' approach to ethics within philosophy, the emergence of informal logic, and the re-emergence of studies of the general logic of evaluation. Thus, all the bricks have been baked for the building, and it's mere superstition to argue that some mysterious force prohibits putting one on top of another.

The Constitution and the Bill of Rights are sets of ethical propositions with two properties: first, there are, as most citizens believe, good reasons for adopting them; second, they are treated as legal ax-
134

ioms that generate sound laws. The arguments for them (e.g., Mill's essay "On Liberty", or the discussions of the French constitution that had so much influence on the founding fathers) are as good social science as you'll find in a long day's walk through the professional journals, and the inferences to specific laws about freedom of speech and so on, are well tested. It follows that all the well-known arguments for 'law and order' are arguments for the (secular) ethics of the Constitution and thus for the principle of equal rights from which *it* flows, just as the arguments for the existence of atoms are the first stage of the arguments for the existence of electrons. Ethics is simply a general social strategy and no more immune to evaluation and improvement by social science than the death penalty or excise taxes or behavior therapy or police strikes. To believe otherwise is to cut the social sciences off from the most important area to which they can make a contribution. And it leads to ragged edges on and inconsistencies within the sciences themselves. For an example, see the excellent discussion of the "ethics-or-else" dilemma for allocation theory, in "The Social Rationale of Welfare Economics", Chapter 58 of *Cost-Benefit Analysis*, by E. J. Mishan (Praeger, 1976). Significantly enough, although a large part of that book is about evaluation (e.g., Chapter 5 is called "Consistency in Project Evaluation"), neither that term nor the author's frequently-used variation "valuation" gets into the index. Valuephobia runs deep.

Ethics is thus, lexically and optimally, the set of rules governing behavior and attitudes based on the doctrine of prima facie equal rights (a.k.a. the Golden Rule, the categorical imperative, etc.). The paradox of justifying ethics is like that of justifying the best strategy in the Prisoner's Dilemma. Relatively simple analysis suggests that ethics is an overwhelmingly superior policy when founded on the ethical attitude (that is, *believing* that all humans have prima facie equal rights), but at best a locally optimal policy if founded on rational self-interest. The two remaining policy issues are therefore (i) whether it is sensible for an individual to *adopt* the moral attitude in a society in which that is uncommon; and (ii) whether it is sensible for individuals and a society to *teach* the ethical attitude to children (rather than enlightened self-interest). Note that if one adopts the ethical attitude, one no longer calculates payoffs in terms of just one's own benefits. Affirmative answers to these questions can also be demonstrated, and it seems clear that moral training of the young is an ancient, largely intuitive, theologically rationalized, imperfect effort at a solution. (Most of the detailed argument is in *Primary Philosophy* (McGraw-Hill, 1966).

Ethics has traditionally been allocated to the department of phi-

135

losophy in the academic scheme of things, which for many years was a highly effective way of dismissing it. But in recent years *applied* ethics, like *practical* logic, has stepped out of the ivory tower and become one of the most active and socially—and educationally—valuable research and practice areas in the academy. The often-derided demand for relevance contributed much of the fuel for this, and medical ethics was the first subspecialty to become highly independent. For some years to come, more joint appointments between the philosophy department and one or more social science departments would seem to be the best solution to the jurisdictional problem, since the skills at ethical theory that philosophy developed are very important for providing depth support—and avoiding fallacies—in applied ethics. See also **Ethics in evaluation, Prisoner's dilemma, Valuephobia, Responsibility evaluation, Logic of evaluation.**

NOTE: Essentially none of the views in this work about various fields and methods of evaluation depend on accepting the view of ethics in this entry. The point of view that generated them leads one on to the conclusion here, but it is not presupposed elsewhere.

ETHICS IN EVALUATION Ethics appears to come into evaluation in two ways; either as professional ethics governing practice—here as in any other science or profession—or as part of the subject matter. Social scientists have never had trouble with the former sense, but they have never been willing to face up to the latter, although they ran a ringer instead. The ringer was the 'external' or nonparticipant study of codes of conduct; but the other half of treating ethics as subject matter is *doing* ethics. (Psychotherapists not only *study* psychotherapy, they also *do* it.) Although it is not inconsistent for physicians or lawyers to separate these two roles of ethics and treat only the formulation of a code of professional ethics as part of their duty, it was bizarre for the social scientists to do likewise, once they had developed one of these codes to govern their own behavior, a code for which they believed there were good arguments. From this achievement it followed that they believed good reasons could be given for some codes of conduct and not for some of the alternatives to them. Hence it followed that what they would call normative ethics is a legitimate subject. Now, since it concerns, governs, and depends on human behavior, it can hardly be located somewhere other than in the purview of the social sciences. (This doesn't mean that it should be part of one of the existing social sciences, just one of the set.)

This turns out not to be just an issue of turf. When it came to the emergence of evaluation as a discipline, the evaluators who came from social science were in a serious dilemma. They either had to ignore ethical aspect of programs—with or without saying that it was

136

improper to draw ethical conclusions—or they had to actually draw ethical conclusions about practices they observed, and include these in their evaluations. The former was unethical, the latter unscientific (according to the current doctrine). Most of them took the first option; the leading text, Rossi and Freeman's *Evaluation: A Systematic Approach*, 4th edition (Sage, 1989), doesn't bother to put the word in the index.

Examples of great importance abound. In evaluating drug and personal relations rehab programs, for instance, major ethical issues surround the theistic foundations of the 12-step approaches (such as Alcoholics Anonymous). Is it ethically appropriate to tie a theistic commitment to admission or continuance with one of these services: (i) with, and (ii) absent, government funding for them? Does the 'disease theory' to which they are committed involve reduction of responsibility in a way that is ethically undesirable? One can hardly be said to have evaluated them without some answer to such questions. See **Ethics** and **Evaluation ethics**.

ETIOLOGY The causation of a condition. Evaluation will sometimes uncover the cause of success or of failure, of merit or of incompetence—but not always, nor is that its duty, nor should that be its aim. Even if it does, it will not always point the way to remediation. It is often assumed by clients—and, all too often, by evaluators—that they are capable of, and appropriate choices for, the task of identifying causes and providing recommendations for remediation. That may or may not be true in a particular case, but it certainly isn't part of the requirements for being a good or outstanding evaluator—the television evaluators at Consumers Union are not revealed to be incompetent because they are not electronics engineers or for that matter repair technicians. Although these extra abilities are sometimes helpful, they are also sometimes distracting, diverting analytic efforts into consideration of 'how it works' (and why it doesn't work well) and away from 'how well it works'. The key task for the evaluator is to evaluate; if trouble emerges, the limit of the evaluator's task is to determine the general area of trouble, but no more than that and sometimes less. In particular, it is not the evaluator's task to determine the etiology of the trouble. As in the case of the general practitioner, the matter is turned over to specialists in the focus area, for detailed diagnosis and treatment. No one can be a specialist in all areas, and acting as if program evaluators or personnel evaluators are exceptions to this is naive, and part of the reason for evaluators getting a bad name with some clients. Many professionals have to learn some skills in addition to evaluation, including causal analysis—a teacher is a good example—but it is not the case that teachers who are good at the

137

evaluation of students (for example, by constructing valid tests) are thereby rendered good at working out why a pupil continues to make a particular error (let alone how to fix it).

EVALUABILITY 1. The natural sense of the term. Projects and programs—and the plans for them—are often, but not often enough, scrutinized for evaluability, that is, for the extent to which they can be evaluated. In the planning stage, concern for evaluability must not be allowed to become a case of the evaluation driving the project but it cannot be ignored and often leads to major program improvements through sharpening focus and improving the early warning system. It should be thought of as the first commandment of **accountability** or as the last refinement of Popper's requirement of **falsifiability**. The underlying principle can be expressed in several ways, for example as "It is not enough that good works be done, it must be possible to *show that*—and also, *when*—good works have been done", or as "You can't learn by trial and error if there's no way to identify the errors." The bare requirement of an evaluation component in a proposal has been around for a while; what's new recently is a more serious effort to make it feasible and appropriate by keeping it in mind during program design. That presupposes more expertise in evaluation than most program designers, review panels, and project monitors have, but that may come. Evaluability should be checked and improved at the planning and **preformative** stages. Requiring evaluability of new programs is analogous to requiring serviceability in a new car; obvious enough, but who besides fleet owners (and GSA) knew that there was for many years a 2:1 difference in standard service costs between Ford and GM? Congress may some day learn that low evaluability has a high price.

2. The technical sense of the term. Beginning with Wholey and others at the Urban Institute in the early 1970s, Evaluability Assessment (EA) was introduced as a response to the excessive delay and lack of value of summative evaluations of the period. It involves an inexpensive early peek at the program, to determine whether the program is in shape for an evaluation (i.e., for Wholey, is being managed for results) and to assist the program to define its goals and outcomes; it also focusses on whether an evaluation would contribute to performance (be cost-effective). It is followed by other steps aimed at the same kind of constructive results. It is part of what might be called helpful management assistance and is only intended as a lead-in to a bulletproof summative evaluation, if the program 'deserves' one. There is a danger of substituting it and what follows it in Wholey's multistep approach for a serious summative evaluation; other dangers include excessive co-authoring, and the usual problems of **goal-based**

138

evaluation models. Ref: *Evaluability Assessment*, M. F. Smith, (Kluwer, 1989).

EVALUAND A generic term for whatever is being evaluated—person, performance, program, proposal, product, possibility, and so on—by analogy with "multiplicand", "analysand", and so on. If it is a person, the term "evaluee" is used here; although "evaluatee" parallels "evaluator", the analogy with "examinee" and "testee" and the greater brevity seemed more appealing. (Precedent exists for contracting the predicate term, for example, in "progenitor/progeny".) It is often possible and always desirable to avoid using this neologism, for example, by using 'candidate' or 'entry' or 'option'; but there are some cases in discussing the logic of evaluation where existing terms have inappropriate connotations, sometimes because the former suggests that people are involved, and the latter that some kind of competition is involved.

EVALUATE, EVALUATION Four possibly different senses of the term are distinguished here.

1. The key sense of the term "evaluation" refers to the process of determining the **merit, worth,** or **value** of something, or the product of that process. Terms used to refer to this process or part of it include: appraise, analyze, assess, critique, examine, grade, inspect, judge, rate, rank, review, study, test. A longer list, involving nouns as well as verbs, and including a number of terms that are only used evaluatively in special contexts, would also include: accredit(ate), adjudicate, allocate, apportion, appraise, appreciation, audit, benchmark, beta-test, check, check-up, classify, comment, criticism, determination, distribution, estimate, finding, field test, follow-up, gauge, interpretation, investigation, judge, mark, measure, monitor, overview, quality control, perspective, rank, referee, report, 'road test' or 'test drive' (now used metaphorically), scale, score, scrutiny, sea trial, survey, synthesis, tryout, weigh, verdict. The evaluation process normally involves some identification of relevant standards of merit, worth, or value; some investigation of the performance of evaluands on these standards; and some integration or synthesis of the results to achieve an overall evaluation or a set of associated evaluations. It contrasts with the measurement process, which also involves the comparison of observations against standards, in that (i) measurement is characteristically not concerned with merit, only with 'purely descriptive' properties, and (ii) those properties are characteristically unidimensional, which avoids the need for the integrating step. The integration process is sometimes judgmental, sometimes the result of complex calculation, very commonly a hybrid of the two.

In this sense evaluation is what distinguishes food from garbage, lies from truth, and science from superstition. In short, it is the sine qua non of intelligent thought and action and in particular of professional practice. But it has also been an intellectual outcast for most of the history of intellectual investigations: the only one of the cognitive processes not to be covered in the science curriculum, the only one that so tainted articles submitted to professional journals that until the late 1960s they were automatically rejected.

Now, evaluation is not so difficult that one can explain its neglect as simply due to being 'put in the Too Hard basket', as the Australians say; it was in fact extensively practiced by those who denied its legitimacy. The explanation appears to be in part that for many people and organizations, evaluation is one of the most threatening phenomena in their experience. Some of them—the **valuephobes**—will lie, cheat, steal, and plot to avoid its occurrence or its impact, a phenomenon that often takes novice evaluators by surprise when they become the victim of character assassination. The *conscientious* practice of evaluation is thus more hazardous as well as more far-reaching than most applied social science research. People are often surprised to learn that Consumers Union, the bastion of product evaluation, was put on the Attorney General's list of subversive organizations in the war against Japan and Germany, and that a the current Director of the National Bureau of Standards was dismissed for providing, at Congressional request, an unfavorable although valid evaluation of a battery additive. They should remember that a large number of conscientious professionals in medicine as in journalism have lost their jobs for doing nothing more than what ethics requires with the results of good evaluations. Moreover, they should understand that the practice of evaluation is hard on evaluators for its own reasons, independently of the machinations of hostile evaluees. It is hard to maintain objectivity in the face of caused pain or joy and to decline bribe and threat combinations of various degrees of severity. The avoidance of evaluation thus achieves considerable support from many of those who would be obliged to do it, as well as those who would be subject to it.

If evaluation causes anxiety and the erection of defenses in many people, it is a source of power—over those who have not come to terms with it. As usual, this leads to efforts to reserve the power for a priesthood. This perspective on evaluation has an ancient history. In the Garden of Eden it is significantly the fruit of the tree of knowledge of good and evil that is taboo, indeed seriously taboo: God says, "in the day that thou eatest thereof, thou shalt surely die". The serpent inaugurates independent evaluation with this comment: "Ye shall not surely die: for God doth know that in the day that ye eat thereof, your

140

eyes shall be opened, and ye shall be as gods, knowing good and evil". The serpent is right on both counts. Nobody dies for the crime (an early counterexample to claims that God is omniscient and trustworthy), and God confirms: "Behold, the man is become as one of us, to know good and evil" (no mention of Eve, of course). The serpent turns out to be the only one of the four actors without moral flaw in the scenario—God lies, breaches contract, and acts unjustly, the other two try to blame someone else for their disobedience—and for this God curses the serpent "above every beast of the field". The parable thus tells us something about the risks of evaluation as well as about the connection of power to evaluative knowledge.

Myths apart, evaluation often acquires power because of its ties to possible action by decision-makers but more generally because of its potential threat to self-esteem. See **Balance of power, Whistle-blowers, Going native, Phenomenology of evaluation.**

2. The name of an autonomous discipline (now with its own Library of Congress classification); it refers to the study and application of procedures for doing objective and systematic evaluation (in the first sense). Semiautonomous applied areas include program, product, personnel, performance, proposal, and policy evaluation ('the Big Six'); other autonomous applied fields include **technology assessment,** medical or psychological evaluation, and **quality control;** other applications that reside within disciplines include **curriculum, sensory, aesthetic,** and **proposal** evaluation, and **literary criticism.**

Evaluation as a particular kind of investigative discipline is distinguished from, for example, traditional empirical research in the social sciences or from literary criticism, criminalistics, or investigative reporting, partly by its extraordinary multidisciplinarity. It typically requires consideration of costs, comparisons, needs, and ethics; political, psychological, legal, and presentational dimensions; the design of outcome studies; sources of bias; reactive effects; and a focus on the techniques for supporting and integrating value judgments—rather than on purely aesthetic matters, or on hypothesis-testing, theory-building, and taxonomy. Although aspects of the relevant part of these concerns—often quite primitive—are to be found in the social sciences, evaluation is not, contrary to the authors of most leading texts and references, a branch of applied social science, nor a study of human interventions, nor a subject whose intellectual origins are in the social sciences. It is a much older and more general discipline. Not only do systematic approaches to product and personnel evaluation predate the whole of social science by millenia, but so do the intellectual roots of the core discipline, the study of its methodology and models. Even if thought of in the limited sense in which it covers

141

some of the territory that social science should have been covering since it began, it still antedates social science, and has frequently used quite distinctive methods, not just existing social science tools. Examples include the key elements of functional analysis and its crucial connection to evaluation which came from Aristotle, the repertoire of logical assessment which goes to the preSocratics or earlier. Other elements like ethics, the study of self-referent evaluation, the relation of evaluation to political power, statistics, large-scale testing, cost analysis, models of legal reasoning, experimental design, and the logic of evaluative inference, all came from outside social science and often go back millenia instead of a century. Evaluation is properly conceived of as a discipline in its own right, an analytical discipline like mathematics (on the one hand, less precise, but on the other, much more general, useful, and fundamental to the human condition), covering a range of activities from quality control in manufacturing to the marking of student papers. Its occurrences in the social sciences should be seen as applications of the general discipline, not as applications of social science methods. It is one of the transdisciplines, although more multidisciplinary than any of them.

Evaluation—properly done—can be said to be 'a science' in a loose sense, as can, for example, teaching; but it can with equal justice to be said to be an art, an interpersonal skill like arbitration, and the logic implicit in the reasoning of judges and juries and literary critics and real estate assessors and jewelry appraisers—and thus not "one of the sciences". (See **Meta-evaluation**.)

Evaluation is normally contrasted with description, but this is only true in a particular context or from a certain point of view. "How would *you* describe the candidate, since you've known him for a long time?" is often followed by an account that is partly evaluative, and the questioner will not feel this is inappropriate. The function and hence the logic of evaluation is often to provide an extremely concise description of one aspect of something—its merit or worth. The letter grade that sums up a semester's work by a student describes the quality of that work. Indicator research is aimed at concise description of the state of the economy or of national health, and the indicators to be useful have to be evaluative, albeit sometimes **contextually evaluative**. A recent article on school process indicators makes clear that these would mainly be evaluative indicators (Andrew Porter, "Creating a System of School Process Indicators" in *Educational Evaluation and Policy Analysis*, Spring 1991).

Many attempts have been made to distinguish (program) evaluation from research—typically, other social science research—for example, in terms of generality or generalizability, replicability, and

142

data types. It is true that the typical efforts of a contract evaluator or of someone whose job title defines them as an evaluator are more likely to be particularistic rather than general, by comparison with the typical efforts of a researcher. But this only corresponds to the difference between research chemists and those with the same qualifications who spend most of their time analyzing water samples for the water company. The latter are employed as practical or applied chemists rather than researchers, but both are chemists. Similarly, the applied evaluator does not own the domain of evaluation; the evaluation researcher, like the research chemist, is just as much a professional in the discipline. The slight difference in the way the term "evaluation" works, by contrast with the names of traditional disciplines, only means that one is a little less likely to say that the evaluation researcher is 'an evaluator' (whereas an inhabitant of either role is said to be 'a chemist')—but this kind of distinction is not unknown in the transdisciplines: the ethicist is someone working at the applied end, while the researcher working on metaethics, is called a philosopher. The distinction appears more attractive in the case of evaluation because there is no clearly identified location or name for—or tradition of—evaluation research in the academy. But eventually, "evaluation researcher" should be as recognizable a label as "cryogenics researcher".

In any applied field, meaning one that services clients with real-world problems, there is always one criterion for good work that is absent from the research field, namely the immediate utility of the conclusions. This will include their timeliness and cost-effectiveness, and bringing in these considerations means that the mission of getting the right answer will sometimes have to be compromised by conversion into 'getting the best answer possible under certain time/budget constraints'. In the end, this is not an alien approach, because most of what we refer to as 'laws of nature' are simply convenient approximations, but it does have to be clearly understood.

Stressing the difference between research and evaluation by using that phrasing is unfortunate, because it tends to support the same kind of mistake teachers make when they distinguish teaching from testing. The fact is that testing is an essential part of teaching; similarly, practical evaluation is an essential part of evaluation research, and research is an essential part of practical evaluation. Stressing this, for example by stressing that an estimate of generalizability (external validity) should be part of every program evaluation, is more constructive and productive than stressing the difference.

What distinguishes evaluation from other applied research is at

143

most that it leads to evaluative conclusions, and to get to them requires identifying standards and performance data, and the integration of the two. See **Formative** and **Summative evaluation**.

3. The term "evaluation" is sometimes, and unfortunately, used more narrowly to mean only the work done by professional evaluators. For example, a scientist on the National Science Board, when asked why NSF didn't evaluate its own evaluation procedures (e.g., by looking at such matters as interjudge agreement) said, "I don't think we can afford to do an evaluation of our procedures; it would simply divert sorely needed funding away from worthwhile proposals." Of course, she was really saying that she had informally evaluated the procedures and judged them sound enough. She was also recording some scepticism that the cost of a professional evaluation would pay off. But the question to which she responded was raised because of the disquieting evidence that the NSF proposal evaluation process is seriously flawed. (This evidence came from intelligent program administrators within NSF who have had some proposal evaluations done by two independent panels who were not informed that their work was being replicated.) The general idea in science, we are often told, is not to rely on assumptions and informal judgments but to do systematic study. However, she wasn't willing to apply this to her own foundation's procedures. Evaluation begins at home, and if you are evaluating proposals for the use of hundreds of millions of tax dollars, you should look carefully at how you do it, that is, evaluate the process, or get someone less ego-involved to evaluate it, because even a small improvement will pay off handsomely. Of course, the prospect of having these flaws documented involves the risk of loss of credibility and hence funding, so it lacks intrinsic charm.

In this criticism of her remarks no assumption is made that a single professional evaluator would in fact have done something useful. Although evaluation in the broad sense is a necessity for rational behavior or thought, and is indeed the only intellectual process common to all types of science, 'professional'—i.e., paid—evaluation is sometimes worthless, a sham, and/or excessively expensive (as is much other management consulting). Only a team of the best evaluators, working closely with program officers, experienced panelists, and NSF board members, could produce worthwhile results. But, given the facts mentioned here and similar findings elsewhere, those results would cover their costs many times as well as improving the justice of the procedures. Panel rating, as normally done, is a primitive procedure. See **Self-reference, Two-tier, Wild card, General positive bias, Cost-free evaluation**.

4. In what is normally thought to be a completely different sense, the term "evaluate" is also used in mathematics to mean "calculate the value of an expression"—for example, of a polynomial. The gap between these uses is not unbridgeable, however, as one notices when examining the term "evaluation function" in expert system work or "evaluative metering" in camera design. Each of these refers to the process of calculating the sum of several weighted values, just as in evaluating a polynomial. This is the key logical process which distinguishes evaluation from measurement—for example in cost-benefit analysis, or in giving a term grade to a student based on lab work, field work, attendance, and so forth.

EVALUATION ANXIETY Anxiety provoked by the prospect, imagined possibility, or occurrence of an evaluation. In the clinical context, this includes much social anxiety, test anxiety, pregame anxiety, and so on, and is a cause for concern only when it produces incapacitating affect or dysfunction. In the evaluation context, it is often something that deserves serious and direct attention, and dealing with it—especially the phobic version, **valuephobia**—calls for special skills and knowledge. Ref: *Handbook of Social and Evaluation Anxiety*, edited by Harold Leitenberg (Plenum, 1990). See also **Reactive evaluation**.

EVALUATION CONSULTANT See **Consultant**.

EVALUATION EDUCATION Consumer education (e.g., in home economics courses in the schools, or in the usual media presentations) is still very weak on training in evaluation, which should be its most important component. More commonly it simply involves doing evaluation on some limited topic with limited generalizability beyond the sources used. There are many other contexts besides those in which one's role is that of the consumer where evaluation education would be most valuable, notably in the manager role, parenting role, or the service-provider/professional role. Few teachers (or, for that matter, other professionals) have any idea how they or others can or should evaluate their own work or that of others, although this is surely a minimum requirement of **professionalism**. The last decades have seen considerable federal and state effort to provide reasonable standards of quality that will protect the consumer in a number of areas, but these agencies have not yet really understood that the superimposition of standards is a poor substitute for understanding the justification for them and having the skills to generalize them to new areas. **Evaluation training** is the training of (mainly professional) evaluators; evaluation education is the training of the citizenry in evaluation techniques, traps, and resource finding and is the only satisfactory long-run approach to improving the quality of our lives without extraordinary wastage of resources. It should begin with **critical think-**

ing instruction. See also **Evaluator as teacher.**

EVALUATION ETHICS AND ETIQUETTE Because evaluation in practice so often involves tricky interpersonal relations, it has much to learn from the ethics and etiquette developed in areas like diplomacy, arbitration, **mediation**, negotiation, and management (especially personnel management). Unfortunately, the wisdom of these areas is poorly encapsulated into learning and training materials, which are mainly truistic or anecdotal. The correct approach would appear to be via the refinement of guiding principles and the collateral development of extensive calibration examples, rather as in developing skill in applied ethical analysis (casuistry.) An example: You are the only first-timer on a site-visit team to a prestigious institution, and you gradually realize, as the time slips away in socializing and reading or listening to reports from administrators and administration-selected faculty, that no serious evaluation is going to occur unless *you* do something about it. What should you do? There is a precise (flow-chartable) solution that specifies a sequence of actions and utterances, each contingent upon the particular outcome of the previous act, and that avoids unethical behavior while minimizing distress. Mature professionals without evaluation experience never get it right; some very experienced and thoughtful evaluators come very close; a group containing both reaches complete consensus on it after a twenty-minute discussion. Like so much in evaluation, this shows that the right procedure can be extracted from the standards of common sense, although it is not in our normal repertoires: it surely should be. Another example: A write-in response on an anonymous personnel evaluation form accuses the evaluee of sexual harassment. As the person in charge of the evaluation, what *exactly* should you do? In program evaluation there are also some special issues centering around the "judge not that ye be not judged" theme. See **Balance of power;** and **Ethics in evaluation.**

In addition, there are the usual kinds of 'professional ethics' issues about the practice of evaluation, for example, issues about confidentiality, fairness, harassment, misrepresentation, and misuse. Most of these seem to involve issues common to other social sciences, and to be quite well covered in the professional guidelines of, for example, the American Psychological Association. A more discursive account is in *Ethics and Values in Applied Social Research* by Allan Kimmel (Sage, 1988).

EVALUATION FUNCTION A formula used in expert systems to determine whether a possible solution or move is better or worse than others or than some standard. A chess-playing program like Deep Thought, for example, can look ahead at several sequences of possible moves and countermoves (the number of steps in these is called the number of 'plies') but cannot, usually, come anywhere near to looking ahead to the end of the game. So it must have some means of deciding which of the alternative move sequences to initiate, that is, which of them avoids the worst outcomes and—among those—leads to the best ones. The terminal board position in each sequence is computed by the evaluation function.

EVALUATION IMPERATIVE, THE The obligation to evaluate what one does is part of accountability, notably where one is using funds from others or putting others at risk. It is part of and perhaps the key element in **professionalism**; professionals work without immediate supervision, and do things with potentially serious impact on others; their part of the social contract has to be the taking of reasonable precautions to ensure that what they do when not under scrutiny is at least competent. What does "reasonable precautions" mean? Because we all age, forget, and err; and because what counts as good practice changes as knowledge and practice improve; and because we all know of many examples of professionals who insisted they were competent when it was clear and proven that they were not, usually after they had done a great deal of damage to others; and because for this and other reasons we know we are not good judges of our own merit, "reasonable precautions" must include evaluation by qualified others. Thus evaluation is not something imposed from outside and to be resisted; it is at worst something to be improved. It cannot be eschewed.

Above all, the evaluation imperative applies to evaluators. Evaluators who believe in the discipline must believe that there are benefits from evaluating most deliberate and difficult enterprises and they, better than anyone, must know that the obligations of accountability and professionalism, and of fairness, require them to encourage and facilitate external evaluation of their own work. See **General positive bias**.

EVALUATION MANAGEMENT What to know: everything in this book (including the references), the content of a good graduate program in statistics with an alternative methodologies course on the side, and preferably a law degree. What to believe: don't believe *any* promises. What to expect: promises. How to learn: talk to experienced managers *at great length* (and pay for the lunch). Why it's hard: because you're dealing with a mix of prima donnas and entrepreneurs— as what executives aren't, but that doesn't make it any easier—and your superiors know nothing about evaluation. Useful tricks: get a second opionion on most serious points, without allowing consultation between the two experts; then get them to resolve differences in

147

your presence. The results will pay for themselves many times over. (This should sometimes extend to running duplicate evaluations—of course, you'll need a whole lot of luck to get that budgeted.) The right stuff: an indomitable sense of humor and a firm grasp on the fact that if it wasn't for you, the product would be half as good.

EVALUATION OF EVALUATIONS See **Meta-evaluation**.

EVALUATION OF EVALUATORS Track record, not publications, is the key, but how do you get it? See **Evaluation registry, Big shops, Meta-evaluation, Fitting the lock to the key.**

EVALUATION OF RESEARCH Evaluating the quality and/or worth and/or amount of research (proposed or performed) is crucial for funding decisions and university personnel evaluation, to take two examples. It involves the **worth/merit** distinction—"worth" here refers to the social, institutional, or intellectual payoffs from the research, "merit" to its intrinsic (professional) quality. While some judgment is always involved, that is no excuse for allowing the usual *wholly* judgmental process; one can quantify and in other ways objectify the merit and worth of almost all research performances *to the degree requisite* for personnel evaluation. The solution does not lie in the use of a citation index, but in evaluating research on the basis of its social value *and*, separately, its intellectual value and its value to the campus (not if it represents a net cost); in identifying journals at several levels of quality with different weights; in allowing nonstandard publication under strict controls over independent reviewing of the publication; in determining relative weights for books, texts, articles, and so on.; in arranging for external review when someone claims discrimination, with safeguards against external clique control; in avoiding the usual claims that it's harder to publish in math than in philosophy, since the evidence is against them; and so forth.

EVALUATION OF SERVICE The ugly duckling of the three dimensions on which faculty and staff in colleges and some other institutions are normally evaluated. Usually best divided into service to profession, service to campus, and service to community, each with appropriate and public weights—and cutoffs (required minima), if any—attached by the college. Some points to keep in mind: the overall weight for service should not be so low as to make it impossible to retain people who are now serving as essentially full-time heads of large departments (it's better to rewrite their contracts); while there should be a minimum on campus service, since the campus has to be run and counseling done, it is hard to justify a minimum for professional service; authoring a text can be at least partly entered here as service to the profession or public, rather than under teaching; although a small

148

credit goes there if the book is well reviewed (simply the equivalent of good course notes)—the system should prevent double-weighting; substantial standard-rate paid consulting entered as service to the community should not be penalized because it is paid, but it's a good test of the criteria being used for service to the community whether mere moonlighting counts; mere membership of editorial boards or association committees should get low weight, more being possible on evidence of heavy reviewing or committee load; all of this should be set out in a short handbook; and so on.

EVALUATION PARAMETERS An evaluation can be 'internally' specified by reference to ten parameters or characteristics. Some of these parameters are headings—that is, they unpack into several sub-specifications. They are: field, functions, generality (of conclusions required), analytic level (**global** vs. **component** vs. **dimensional**), logical type (grading, ranking, scoring, apportioning), criteria used, weights for criteria, standards used, synthesis procedure, and metric. Given the values of these for a particular evaluation, one can construct an 'evaluation profile' and this should point to an appropriate design or small group of possible designs. Appeal to six 'external parameters', which give us a profile of the environment for the evaluation, should limit the options still further. Some of these involve brief narrative descriptions, others require only descriptors. They comprise: **client** characteristics (needs, preferences, etc.); **background** (did someone else evaluate the same program [etc.] previously, and what happened then?); **stakeholders** (those who have some investment, ego or other, in the results of the evaluation); **audience**; constraints (ethical, legal, institutional, or ecological—e.g., on data access and news releases); **resources** (including expertise, workspace, finances), and so on. (It is likely that neither list is complete, although much revised.) Major intervening variables that we determine on the way to a design include evaluator credibility and evaluation credibility, both of which give us hints about required evaluator locus and credentials.

From this we develop a specification which might begin: "A rating (not just a ranking) of two alternative programs for training police sergeants in dealing with offers of bribes, neither having been previously evaluated, the client aiming to commit to one of them for three years...".

EVALUATION PREDICATES The distinctively evaluative relations or ascriptions involved in **grading, ranking, scoring,** and **apportioning,** as ways to determine **worth, merit,** or other **value.** A huge list of other evaluative terms are appropriate in particular contexts: for example, **validity** (of tests or news stories), integrity (of security systems or personnel), adequacy, appropriateness, effectiveness, plausibility.

These predicates can be construed as serving an information-compression function in language, combining performance data and needs assessment or standards data into a concise package, of which the letter grade for coursework is the paradigmatic example.

EVALUATION, REASONS FOR See **Reasons for evaluation**.

EVALUATION REGISTRY A concept halfway from complete laissez-faire to the certification or licensing of evaluators. This would operate by encouraging evaluators and their clients to file a copy of their joint contract or letter of agreement with the evaluation registry at the beginning of an evaluation; to this would be appended any modifications made along the way and finally a brief standard report by each party, made independently, assessing the quality and utility of the evaluation and the performance of the client. Each would have a chance to add a brief reaction to the other's evaluation, and the net end result (two pages) would then be available for inspection, for a minimal fee, by potential clients. This arrangement, it is argued, would be of more use to the client than asking an evaluator to suggest former clients as references or simply looking at a list of publications or reports, but would avoid the key problems with licensing—enforcement standards and funding. See the introduction to the *Directory of Evaluation Consultants* (The Foundation Center, 1981).

EVALUATION RESEARCH The original use of this term simply referred to evaluation done in a serious scientific way; the term was popular among supporters of the **social science model** of evaluation. That only made sense as long as there was no clearly mapped area for research *on* evaluation. It now seems preferable to use it exactly as we use terms like 'physics research'—to identify work that goes beyond routine application of long validated principles or techniques. In this sense, evaluation research has subareas corresponding to (i) the various fields of applied evaluation, where both theoretical and applied research can be done, as well as the relatively routine applied work we normally think of as 'evaluation'; (ii) the core subject of evaluation, with its own subdivisions (the logic, history, sociology, etc., of evaluation in general), (iii) certain types of research in other fields where evaluation is of the essence, for example in pharmacology. It is not sharply distinguishable from other research, although it usually has explicitly evaluative conclusions (some work on the history of the subject does not). Other attempts to distinguish research from evaluation—some identify six or eight dimensions—distort or stereotype one or the other. For example, it is often said that evaluations are aimed at conclusions that are 'particularistic' or idiographic rather than general or nomothetic, the latter supposedly being the goal of the scientific researcher. This is wrong in both directions: evaluators are often set or

150

undertake the task of evaluating the success of a newly discovered treatment (e.g., lithium for psychotics, or contract teaching), which of course requires a general conclusion, sampling, etc.; and scientists frequently spend their lives on the study of individual cases (e.g., the geology of the Darling Scarp, the evolution of the universe). Of course, many studies in history or philosophy are essentially evaluative research, and may be studies of individuals or of generalizations or theories.

"Doing evaluations" or "being an evaluator" in the consultant or contract context *may* not involve anything that justifies the use of the term "research", but some applied personnel or program evaluation projects and contracts require a great deal of research and most require more than is usually done. In particular, every serious program evaluation, however constrained by time and budget, should consider the **generalizability** of the findings, since that bears on the value of the program. Publishable research will continue to come from evaluation practitioners as well as academics, as they do from clinical psychologists as well as experimental ones, and practitioners should be strongly encouraged to look for and develop the research issues in their work. The idea that evaluation practice, short of the big federal contracts, is something we can leave to "graduate students and graduates of masters level programs" as a recent article in *Evaluation and Program Planning* put it, seems comparable to the idea that local medical practice should be left to RNs.

"Research *on* evaluation" always refers to work on evaluation methodology, theory, or metatheory. See also **Exploratory research**, and **Reinventing the wheel.**

EVALUATION SKILLS There are long lists of desirable skills for evaluators (Dan Stufflebeam developed one with 234 competencies); as for philosophers, almost any kind of specialized knowledge is advantageous—since it covers the necessary expertise in some area—and the list of the more obvious tool skills (see **Key Evaluation Checklist**) is more demanding than in most other disciplines—it obviously includes statistics, cost analysis, ethical analysis, management theory and practice, pedagogy, social psychology, contract law, interviewing skills, professional politics, presentation graphics, dissemination (for the report); and of course there are some **evaluation-specific** techniques such as **synthesis.** Here we mention five desiderata that are less obvious. First, the evaluative attitude (or temperament). Unless you are committed to the search for quality, in the way that the best of those in the legal or scientific professions are committed to the search for justice or the search for truth, you are in the wrong profession. You will be too easily tempted by the charms of "joining" (e.g., joining the program staff—see **Going native**), too unhappy with the outsider's role, too unwilling to search out and listen to your critics (see **Enemies list**). The virtues of evaluation *must be* their own reward, for the slings and arrows are very painful. Valuing the search for value appears to be a learnable and probably even a teachable characteristic for many people; but some people come by it naturally and others will never acquire it. In particular, self-evaluation has to be regarded as a peculiarly important task for the evaluator, since practicing what you preach is a reasonable test of competence and honesty.

The second package of relatively unproclaimed skills are part of "practical logical analysis" and include skills such as: (i) identifying hidden agendas or unnoticed assumptions about a program's practice or rationale; (ii) identifying mismatches between a goal statement and a needs statement or between a definition of a term and its use; (iii) identifying loopholes in an evaluation design; (iv) the ability to provide accurate summaries one fiftieth the length of the original; (v) the ability to give a nonevaluative, noninterpretive description of a program or treatment; and (vi) the ability to see weaknesses in suggested definitions, for example, of 'need' or 'audience' or 'resource'. See **Critical thinking.**

The third ability is empathy or role-playing ability. Seeing what one is doing as others see it is important for five reasons; (i) to ensure you do not cause unnecessary anxiety or distress; (ii) to generate insights that will, if used thoughtfully, increase your chances of cooperation in order to get better access to data; (iii) to increase the relevance of the evaluation's focus; (iv) to generate better explanations; and (v) to increase chances of implementation if you come up with recommendations. An extension of this skill is part of **Perspectival evaluation.** (See also **Therapeutic model.**)

The fourth ability is teaching—if you are not already a teacher—and, in particular, adult education. If you can't teach the staff of programs you are evaluating—and staff that you are evaluating—what evaluation involves and why and how evaluation it is valuable, even if it is sometimes a cause of extra work and some ego pain, you'll have difficulty getting the cooperation you need and the impact your conclusions should have. But you should also be thinking about teaching because the long-term benefits to programs and personnel from evaluation, if they use it, are much more important than the payoff from your visit and your recommendations on this occasion. To the extent it isn't cutting into your primary duties, you should try to pass that insight and some skills along.

The fifth ability bears on being a **general purpose evaluator** rather than being a local evaluator. It is the skill of being a 'quick study', that is, of being able to catch on very quickly to points of view, terminology, and the state of the art in a field. The reason for this is partly that in many cases you will not have the luxury of teaming with a local expert and the 'window of tolerance' for the outsider is narrower than clients realize, so you need to be talking their lingo and understanding their situation faster than they expect from any new graduate student in their field. In the end, they are not willing to accept advise from someone who is not on top of the situation with all its ramifications (although not all its subject matter expertise), nor are they usually willing to allow a reasonable time for this. A good rule of thumb is that you ought to be making useful contributions to program improvement and no gross errors within half a day, no matter what the subject. Of course, the larger your basic repertoire, the more often you can do this.

The good news is that no one is good at all the relevant skills, and hence that there is room for specialists, and for team members. Partly because of the formidable nature of the relevant skills list, evaluation—unlike computer programming—is a field where teams *if properly employed* are immensely better than soloists. Not only are two heads better than one, six heads—if carefully chosen and appropriately instructed—are almost always better than five. See also **Fitting the lock to the key.**

Do you have what it takes? Here's a one-item aptitude test. Which is the correct way to insert a roll of toilet paper into the holder; with the loose end coming out on top, or underneath? There is only one right answer; the test may seem culturally biased and a well-argued proof that it is or is not constitutes an alternative proof of evaluation competence.

EVALUATION-SPECIFIC METHODOLOGY Much of the methodology used in evaluation studies is derived from other disciplines; the special nature of evaluation lies mainly in the way in which it selects and synthesizes these contributions into an appropriate overall perspective and brings them to bear on the various kinds of evaluation tasks. However, as in any service field, a key issue for the consultant evaluator is deciding on—and designing for—certain levels of credibility and certainty for your eventual conclusion; yours is not the task of determining truth for the ages, but the best possible advice at the time it is needed. You discover what these levels have to be from intelligent inquiry into the **context** of the evaluation, including the needs of the client and other audiences or stakeholders. This is a key distinction from the typical academic research task; but it only applies to some client-centered evaluation, and certainly not to all contract work.

There are also some situations where substantial variations on the usual procedures in scientific research become appropriate. Two examples follow. In survey research, sample size is normally predetermined in the light of statistical considerations and prior evidence about population parameters. In evaluation, although there are occasions when a survey of the classical kind is appropriate, surveys are frequently *investigatory* rather than *formal*, which changes the situation considerably. Suppose that a respondent, in a phone interview evaluation survey of users of a particular service, comes up with a wholly unexpected comment on the service that suggests—let us say—improper behavior by the service-providers. (It might equally well suggest an unexpected and highly beneficial side-effect.) This respondent is the thirtieth interviewee from a planned sample of a hundred. On the standard survey pattern, one would continue, using the same interview form, through the rest of the sample. In evaluations, one will quite often want to alter the form so as to include an explicit question on this point. Of course, one can no longer report the results of the survey as entirely based on a sample of a hundred, with respect to this questions (and any others with which its presence might interact). But one may very well be able to turn up another twenty people that respond under cuing, who would not have produced this as a free response. That result is much more important than salvaging the survey—in most cases. It also points to another feature of the evaluation situation, namely the desirability of time-sequencing the interview or questionnaire responses. Hence one should try to avoid using a single mass mailing, a common practice in survey research; by using sequential mailings one can examine the responses for possible modifications of the instrument.

The second taboo that we may have good reason to break concerns sample size. If we find ourselves getting a highly standard pattern of response to a fairly elaborate questionnaire, we are discovering that the population has less variability than we had expected, and we should alter our estimate of an appropriate sample size in midstream. No point in continuing to fish in the same waters if you don't get a bite after an hour. The generalization of this point is to the use of "emergent", "cascading", or "rolling" designs, where the whole design is varied en route as appropriate. (These terms come from the glossary in the Joint Committee's *Evaluation Standards*.) Open-minded researchers in fields other than evaluation obviously could and should sometimes use these approaches. Note that the traditional response to what are here called 'investigatory' designs is to call them 'exploratory' with the implication that they will eventually lead to serious formulation and testing of a hypothesis—the 'real' research. They *are* real research.

At a more general level, evaluation-specific methodology requires designs that combine the investigation of costs, comparisons, needs, and ethics with political, psychological, and presentational dimensions and use the techniques for supporting and integrating value-judgments—rather than with hypothesis-testing, survey research or taxonomy. This process more than any other might be called evaluation-specific. Other more limited techniques include the use of **parallel teams, calibration of judges, convergence groups, "blind" judges, synthesis, goal-free evaluation, bias balancing**, and so on. See also **Anonymity, Questionnaires, Exploratory research**.

EVALUATION STANDARDS A set of principles for the guidance of (particularly) program evaluators and their clients. The first major effort was aimed at program evaluation, and was led by the joint efforts of representatives of many professional associations, headed by D. Stufflebeam and resulting in the *Evaluation Standards* (McGraw-Hill, 1980); the Evaluation Research Society also produced a set. There are some shared weaknesses—for example, neither includes **needs assessment** in any explicit way—but the former is much more explicit about interpretation, giving specific examples of applications and possible misinterpretations. In general, these are likely to do good by raising clients' consciousness and general performance, and have already had this effect. Fears have been expressed by first-rank evaluators that they may rigidify approaches, stifle research, increase costs (cf. "defensive lab tests" in medical practice today), and give a false impression of sophistication. It's useful to have this list of possible problems in hand, but once warned of them, it seems unlikely that they will constitute a major threat to the utility and validity of the Standards. (See also **Bias**.) The program standards were followed by a set for **personnel evaluation**, referenced under that heading.

EVALUATION SYMBOLS See **Symbols**

EVALUATION THEORY Some evaluation theories are theories about evaluation in a particular field (e.g., theories of program evaluation such as the **discrepancy** model ['local theories']). Some are about evaluation in general (e.g., theories about its political role or logical nature ['general theories']). Partly because of the tendency to call the first field 'evaluation' without qualification, there is some overlap of intent and of relevance. General theories include a wide range of efforts from the logic of evaluative discourse—general accounts of the nature of evaluation and how evaluations can be justified (axiology)— through metamethodology to sociopolitical theories of its role in particular types of environment, to 'models' that are often simply

155

metaphors for, conceptualizations of, or procedural paradigms for evaluation. The latter come closest to being theories in the usual sense; the others are nearer to metatheories. (See *Evaluation Models*, Kluwer, 1983.)

Little work has been funded on this topic, less has borne fruit; a notable exception was NIE's Research on Evaluation project at NWL, a series of studies on radically different metaphors for evaluation edited by Nick Smith. The field was unlucky in that most of the federal funding that could have gone for theoretical work has been allocated (across 20 years) to the Center for the Study of Evaluation at UCLA, which has used most of its support to *do* evaluations, with a little attention to measurement, management, and methodology but almost none to evaluation theory. It has put out a few small items on the theory side, mainly guided and authored by Alkin, who recently reviewed his original definition of evaluation after 21 years, and still could not bring himself to include any reference to merit, worth, or value in it. (He defines it as the collection and presentation of data-summaries for decision-makers, which is of course the definition of MIS—see pp. 93–96, in *Evaluation and Education at Quarter Century* [NSSE/University of Chicago, 1991]). NWL, CIRCE, and the Evaluation Center at Ohio State (now at Western Michigan) probably produced twenty times as much evaluation theory per dollar of support.

Criticism of evaluation theories is often based on a confusion between prescriptive and descriptive theories. For example, theories about how evaluation should be done in order to be valid cannot be criticized on the grounds that these practices are rarely followed or hard to implement. The only issue is whether there are some better alternatives. Otherwise, the original comment stands as correct, and the criticism is irrelevant—it is simply a way of saying that real-world evaluations will be invalid. Although they frequently make this mistake—by criticizing evaluation theories for not describing what evaluators do, even when the theory is intended to describe what they should do—the most detailed and acute analysis of evaluation theories is in *Foundations of Program Evaluation: Theories of Practice* by Shadish, Cook, and Leviton (Sage, 1991).

EVALUATION TRAINING PROGRAMS There is little serious support for these at the moment, despite the large demand (and larger need) for trained evaluators, perhaps a sign of evaluation backlash or of the widely-supported view that any social science training is an adequate background for evaluators. The best places are probably the Evaluation Center at Western Michigan, Boston University, Stanford University Graduate School of Education, and CIRCE at the Uni-

156

versity of Illinois, but some of the **policy studies** graduate programs
are also good. Short courses are more widely available and are advertised in *Evaluation Practice*. See also **Training of evaluators.**

EVALUATIVE (language) Language using the basic vocabulary
"good/bad/right/wrong/valuable/worthless" (etc.) and terms that
cannot be translated without using the basic evaluative vocabulary.
See also **Descriptive, Prescriptive.**

EVALUATIVE ATTITUDE Defined by contrasting example, this is
what is missing from the profession of educational administration
when one discovers that its publications make no effort to communi-
cate news of programs proved successful by comparative field test
(for example, reading programs) that some of their members have
gone to great lengths to obtain by running direct comparative
evaluations. Defined in a wider context, see **Evaluation skills.**

EVALUATOR AS TEACHER Evaluators often report with mild as-
tonishment that they find themselves spending a great deal of time on
site as instructors about evaluation. Additionally, they do a good deal
of teaching without conscious intent. This function is a kind of inservice professional or consumer training and its results may, in the long
run, outweigh anything specific to the evaluation task that brings the
evaluator to the site. This function is not just a bonus, nor is it just
stealing time from the primary obligation: it may be crucial for obtaining cooperation and in particular, mildly skilled cooperation—and
implementation.

EVALUATOR AS THERAPIST See **Therapeutic role of evaluator.**

EVALUEE, EVALUATEE A person being evaluated; the more general term, which covers products and programs, and so on, is
"evaluand".

EXECUTIVE SUMMARY Abstract of results from an evaluation,
usually in (at least relatively) nontechnical language. (The term is revealing; as in other phrases, such as "executive word processor", the
executive is presumed to be technically incompetent in the field s/he
is administering and with the tools that facilitate efficient management. Since both are fairly easy to grasp—*vide* Sculley after switching
from Pepsi to Apple—the stereotype, well based as it is, suggests a serious weakness in executive performance.)

EXIT INTERVIEWS Interviews with subjects as they leave, for example, a training program or clinic, to obtain factual and judgmental
data. A very good time for these, with respect to the evaluation of
courses or teaching in the school or college setting, is at the time of
graduation, when: (i) the student will have some perspective on most
of the educational experience; (ii) fear of retribution is low; (iii) response rate can be nearly 100% with careful planning; (iv) judgments

of effects are relatively uncomplicated, for example, by work-experi-ence as an extra causal factor; and (v) memory is still fresh. Later than this—alumni surveys—conditions can and do deteriorate, notably the reduction of return rate to the 10% to 20% level, although there is a partial offset because job relevance can be judged more accurately.

EXPECTANCY A term from decision theory. The product of the probability of an outcome by its utility. See **Risk assessment.**

EXPERIMENT See **True experiment.**

EXPERIMENTAL GROUP The group (or single person, etc.) that is receiving the treatment being studied. Cf. **Control group.**

EXPERTISE The legitimate use of experts is a well-known practice in evaluation, especially the use of 'local' (usually subject matter) experts in educational program evaluation. There is, however, a tendency to overrate experts, not only in the commonly discussed cases of mili-tary, psychological, and environmental issues but also in fields where their expertise is more properly described as connoisseurship. See **Connoisseur, Fallacy of irrelevant expertise.**

EXPLANATION 1. By contrast with evaluation, which identifies the value of something, explanation involves answering a Why or How question about it or a call for some other type of understanding. Often, explanation involves identifying the *cause* of a phenomenon, rather than its *effects* (which is a major part of evaluation). When it is possible, without jeopardizing the main goals of an evaluation, a good evaluation design tries to uncover microexplanations (e.g., by identi-fying those components of the curriculum package that are producing the major part of the good or bad effects, and/or those that are having little effect). The first priority, however, is to resolve the evaluation is-sues (is the package any good at all, the best available? etc.). Too often the research orientation and training of evaluators leads them to do a poor job on evaluation because they became interested in explanation. Even then, an explanation in terms of a **conceptual scheme** may not involve much of a diversion, whereas we can ill afford a search for a **theory.** The realization that the logical nature and investigatory de-mands of evaluation are quite different from those of explanation is as important as the corresponding realization with respect to prediction and explanation, which neopositivist philosophers of science still think are logically the same under the (temporal) skin. Recent work on "program theory" advocates much more effort to use evaluations as a basis for improving or implementing theories about how in-terventions operate (e.g., *Advances in Program Theory*, Leonard Bickman, ed., Jossey-Bass, 1990). That's icing on the cake, good if you can get it without paying too large a bill. See also **Prescriptive.**

2. Explanation *of an evaluation* is something else. It may involve:

158

(i) translating technicalities; (ii) unpacking the quality indicators in the data, that is, justifying the evaluation; (iii) exhibiting the microevaluations on separate dimensions that added up to the global rating; and (iv) giving component evaluations.

EXPLORATORY RESEARCH In conventional social science research, often institutionalized into a requirement on every thesis proposal in a Ph.D. program, only hypothesis-testing counts as true science. Other studies, even ethnographic ones, are classified as exploratory research, from which one will eventually derive an interesting hypothesis to test; doing that will be the 'real science'. This stereotyping of science has crippled it seriously and is now beginning to evaporate. Good evaluations are often essentially protracted exploratory research, as the responsive evaluation enthusiast would be keen to stress. They do not involve an overall hypothesis-testing design, although they do involve constant formulation and checking of hypotheses. That's what the discovery of side-effects involves, and side-effects, being unanticipated, can hardly have been part of a prior design.

EX POST FACTO DESIGN One where we identify a control group "after the fact", that is, after the treatment has occurred. A very much weaker design than the true experiment since there must have been *something* different about the subjects that got the treatment without being assigned to it, in order to explain why they got it, and that something means they're not the same as the control group, in some unknown respect that may be related to the treatment. Support for this approach is sometimes possible if the conditions for one of the quasi-experimental designs can be met.

EXTERNAL (evaluator or evaluation) An external evaluator is someone who is *at least* not on the project or program's regular staff, or someone—in the case of personnel evaluation—other than the individual being evaluated, or their family or staff. It is better if they are not previously known to or paid by the project or by any entity with a commitment to the success or failure of the project. That arrangement is rare outside product evaluation, and even there, many of the 'external' evaluations are done by magazines dependent on advertising by manufacturers and vendors. It is best to regard externality as a continuum along which one tries to score as high as possible, rather than a yes/no attribute of an evaluator or evaluation.

Where or to whom the external evaluator reports is what determines whether the evaluation is formative or summative, *either* of which may be done by external or by internal evaluators (contrary to the common view that external is for summative, internal for formative), and both of which should be done by both. Although each possibility occurs, and has specific value, the most common arrangement is that formative is internal and summative external, for reasons of credibility as well as practicality.

The trade-offs between external and internal are roughly as follows. The internal evaluator knows the program better and so avoids mistakes due to ignorance, knows the people better and hence can talk to them more easily, will be there after the evaluation is finished and hence can facilitate implementation, probably knows the subject matter better, costs less, and is sure to *know of* some other comparable projects for comparison. The external evaluator is less likely to be affected by personal or job-benefit considerations, is often better at evaluation; has often *looked closely at* comparable programs, can speak more frankly because there is less risk of job loss or personal retribution/dislike, and carries some cachet from externality and, as Freud observed, cost.

EXTERNAL VALIDITY By contrast with internal validity, this refers to (some aspects of) the generalizability of the experimental/evaluation findings. Here the traps to avoid include failure to identify key environmental variables that happen to be constant throughout the experiment (but won't be constant on other sites), decreased sensitivity of participants to treatment at posttest due to pretest, reactive effects of the experimental arrangement, or biased selection of participants that might affect the generalizability of the treatment's effect to nonparticipants—thus jeopardizing the external validity. (Ref. *Experimental and Quasi-Experimental Designs for Research*, Campbell and Stanley, Rand McNally & Co., 1972; and *Validity Issues in Evaluative Research*, Bernstein, ed., [Sage, 1976]). The references discuss the classical conception of validity in evaluation, but this is only part of the problem. Content validity is extremely important in evaluation and essentially not discussed in these (typical) references. See Generalizability.

EXTRAPOLATE Infer conclusions about ranges of the variables beyond those measured. Cf. Interpolate.

F

FACE VALIDITY Apparent validity, typically of test items or of tests; there can be skilled and unskilled judgments of face validity. Highly skilled judgments come pretty close to **content validity**, which does require systematic substantiation.

FACT/VALUE DISTINCTION The logical distinction that was put forward as supporting the **value-free** conception of science. It *is* a logically sound distinction, but—like the distinction between observational and theoretical—it is neither a sharp distinction nor independent of context. (The idea that logically sound distinctions must be context-independent is a relic of the days when logic was identified with formal logic.) The distinction does not provide grounds for the value-free doctrine, since one can infer from facts to values—not deductively, but then almost no scientific inference is deductive—as one can see in every issue of *Consumer Reports* or a scientific journal (e.g., in the review of literature or of alternative interpretations of the data). The distinction between facts and values is the distinction between the vocabulary of description and that of evaluation, and in many contexts it's easy to make (e.g., the difference between descriptions of a program and conclusions about its merit). Moreover, in many situations it's crucial that a competent evaluator make this distinction rather carefully, or s/he injects value premises without evidence. But there are plenty of borderline cases—are the terms "intelligent", "tidy", or "visually handicapped" descriptive or evaluative?—and contexts where terms that would be evaluative in other contexts are properly treated as descriptive because they are not the focus of the evaluation task and would not be disputed by anyone—"this candidate had a good degree from a good college" becomes part of the background description when it's not the issue in an evaluation; when we are evaluating 386 DX computers, the best reviewers will often say that a particular brand "uses good components" as part of the description (the evaluation focuses on how well the *package* performs). See also **Logic of evaluation**.

FACULTY EVALUATION The evaluation of college faculty is one of the weakest areas in personnel evaluation. Even in what are thought of as the best universities there are wholly incompetent faculty members, who impose a huge cost on students and/or taxpayers, col-

161

leagues, and on those who need their jobs and could do it much better. It involves three main dimensions, weighted differently for different colleges: teaching, research, and service, the latter being divided into (i) service to the profession, (ii) service to the campus, and (iii) service to the community. The types of service are also weighted very differently—including a zero weight for some—at different colleges. Normally a research university will espouse equal weights for research and service, although the de facto weighting may be six to one—and very different between departments. There is usually no serious control of deviations. A junior college may still give zero weight to research, but the practice may also be different. There is no good reason to avoid individual contracts with specified variant weighting—the University of Georgia was a leader in that approach—with certain global limitations. Common errors include: (i) the failure to recognize the difference between minima (**cutoffs**) and weights; no weighting can accommodate the need for minima on, for example, service to the campus via committee work. (ii) The failure to handle the difference between quantity and quality of research output and teaching load; usually there's a weak sense that you can trade these off. (iii) The failure to define "research" in a way that deals with poetry, consulting, philosophy, and physics in a reasonable way, for example, without allowing promotion for physics professors on the basis of their poetry, or for authors of elementary school texts on the basis that it is applied research using a theory of cognitive development. (iv) The failure to use student ratings, or, more commonly, the use of invalid forms to gather them. Students are expert witnesses on fifty items, and merely prejudiced on another fifty that turn up in widely used forms. See **Style research.**

FADING Technique used in programmed texts, where a first answer (or set of a few answers) is given completely, the next one (or set) is given in part with gaps, then an answer with just a single cue, until finally answers are called for without help. A key technique in training and **calibrating** evaluators.

FAIRNESS A major reason for (valid) evaluation. Distributional justice requires that the distribution of goods or taxes—or praise or blame—be done according to merit on the relevant dimensions. When students' academic work is graded on the basis of effort alone, rather than quality, or on the basis of gender or favoritism, they are treated unjustly and a better system of evaluation is needed. When teachers are graded on the basis of tiny samples of staged classroom behavior, they are being treated unjustly, since the job involves so much more and less than that. Fairness requires a better system of teacher evaluation. For an example where product evaluation violates principles of

162

fairness, see **Pseudo-evaluation.**

FALLACY OF IRRELEVANT EXPERTISE A group of errors in evaluation that arise because expertise often isn't. More precisely, they arise because an administrator or evaluator (often including an expert evaluator) incorrectly defines expertise—for example, by accepting *related* expertise as *relevant* expertise. Some examples: (i) Expert tasters of wine or tea may simply have developed different tastes from people who drink the product with the usual moderate frequency and may be inappropriate judges to use in evaluation of products for use by normal consumers. One example is the preference among many layout designers for ragged right line endings; the alleged research to support this is invalid or irrelevant, a mere rationalization for a taste. For other examples, see **Connoisseur** and **Sensory evaluation.** (ii) Expert testers of consumer products may come to value performance on measurement standards originally introduced to improve objectivity, even in regions where the performance has no perceptible or pragmatic significance. (See **Technicism**). (iii) Evaluators of teaching are often affected by theories or research about teaching which suggests certain styles are more successful than others, and may downgrade those using the opposite style, although it is working very well for this teacher and this class. See **Teacher evaluation.** (iv) Movie critics often detect aesthetic or other 'flaws' that will be invisible to most viewers; it's generally better to use the Consumers Union poll of nonexpert viewers. (v) Turning the tables on CU, to avoid being misled by *their* auto experts' tastes, one should supplement the CU car evaluations with the J. D. Power surveys of owner satisfaction. (vi) It is common to suppose that experts *in* a field are qualified to be expert *evaluators* in that field, for example, of research, faculty, students, programs, or proposals. In reality, there are half a dozen clear categories of cases where they are very bad at it. For example, experts are sometimes psychologically incapable of appreciating approaches that implicitly reject their own; indeed, this attitude is part of one success syndrome for preeminence. Some evaluation skills are necessarily involved in being an expert, but these do not include all of the evaluation skills relevant to the teaching and practice of the discipline. (The mistake is essentially the same as supposing that physics Ph.D.s would make good high school science teachers.) Another example: those who grew up with and mastered IBM microcomputers often advise beginners to get one, although learning its esoteric operating system is beyond many first-time users and a complete waste of time for any others since one can match the performance with less effort on a Macintosh (as shown by the evidence of time required to train to mastery). Compare **Conflict of interest,** a different case.

163

FALSE POSITIVE/NEGATIVE It is important in experimental design, evaluation, policy research, and decision theory to distinguish two different kinds of error. One type refers to the case when an event is predicted (for example) and does not occur; the other refers to the case where the event is not predicted and does occur. These are related to a classification of errors in statistics that are unhelpfully known as Type I and Type II errors. These refer only to errors about the null hypothesis and also leave you having to remember which is which (see Hypothesis testing). Here we use the much more general terms 'false positive' and 'false negative', and it's relatively easy to remember that a 'positive' statement—in this case a prediction—is a claim that something will happen, a 'negative' is a claim that it won't. Hence a false positive is a case where it is said that something will happen, although in fact it doesn't; and a false negative is a case where it is said that something won't happen, although it does. (The terms "incorrect acceptance" and "incorrect rejection" are even more understandable, but are less commonly used.)

In personnel evaluation a false positive in the process of picking a short list of promising candidates only costs you a little extra work interviewing one extra candidate; a false negative may lose you the best of all the candidates. So you 'fail-safe' by setting the cutting scores on the low side. When it comes to the actual picking of a candidate from a pool containing both poor and excellent candidates, in a situation where they will get de facto or real tenure, the situation changes radically. Either choice will cost the same in money terms, and that cost may easily be a million dollars. The false positive guarantees you, say, 30 years of poor work, the false negative will only lose you 30 years of excellent work if combined with a false positive. Either outcome is extremely expensive to you, but the first is the worst in most cases and the moral is that one should be prepared to spend a great deal more on teacher selection than is common today, in order to bring down the number of false positives. See Teacher evaluation.

FALSIFIABILITY A famous criterion or principle used in the evaluation of scientific theories. It was generally taken to be obvious that scientific theories or hypotheses had to be true, but Karl Popper proposed an additional requirement—that they had to be *falsifiable in principle*. That is, he said, it must be possible to *describe* what evidence would refute them. If that cannot be done, then the theory, he said, can be telling us nothing informative about the world, since whatever happened would be consistent with it. It would not even be a truism, just a vacuous assertion—or, more likely, a very complex set of assertions with no *net* content. The information content of a scientific law or theory, said Popper, is its claim that the cases that would falsify it do not and will not *in fact* occur. If no such cases are even conceivable, then the theory is not ruling out any possibilities at all, so there is no information content to the theory, hence it has no claim to being a contribution to scientific knowledge. Popper's favorite example of an unfalsifiable and hence unscientific theory was psychoanalysis. G. G. Simpson's favorite example to show that the theory of evolution met the falsifiability criterion was that the theory would collapse instantly if we ever uncovered a fossilized human skeleton in a coal seam. Falsifiability is related to testability, which is in some ways the equivalent, in the scientific domain, of evaluability in the domain of policy and program planning.

Now, Popper was completely wrong in placing this (evaluative) requirement on scientific theories. There are many scientific laws and theories that, in at least one common version, are true by virtue of the definitions of the terms in them (e.g., either one or two of Newton's Laws of Motion, the Ideal Gas Law, Hooke's Law, the Fundamental Law of Economics). In fact, even the presupposition that Popper shared with his predecessors but took too literally is wrong; the laws of physics are not literally true—most of them are only approximations to the truth, and not very good ones for much of their range. Hence they would be falsified by almost all known data, and so the criterion is clearly unacceptable for a second reason. Still, it is of considerable value as a dialectical device to clarify the meaning and content of a theory. The status of mathematics is also somewhat unclear on the falsifiability criterion, since it is widely believed to be tautological and hence not falsifiable, but it can hardly be said to have no information content in any useful sense. In fact, it is informative in much the way that tautological scientific laws are informative.

FAULT TREE ANALYSIS (CAUSE TREE ANALYSIS) These terms emerged about 1965, originally in the literature of management science and sociology. They are sometimes used in a highly technical sense, but are useful in a straightforward sense in which they refer to the kind of troubleshooting chart often found in the pages of, for example, a Volkswagen manual. The branches in the tree identify possible causes of the fault (hence the terms "cause" and "fault" in the phrase), and this method of representation—with various refinements—is used as a device for management consultants, for management training, and so on. Its main use in evaluation is as a basis for needs assessment or when moving from analytic evaluation to remediation.

FIELDS (of evaluation) The Big Six fields are product, personnel, performance, proposal (bid), program, and policy evaluation. Each has its own long history of practice and shorter history of methodological discussion. In the case of program evaluation much of the apparatus of a discipline has been developed, although not the key foundational and relational elements discussed in the introduction to this volume. There are dozens of other fields and subfields of evaluation, many of them quite well-developed as practices, ranging from diamond grading and road testing (subfields of product evaluation) to medical, psychological, and technology assessment, argument evaluation, quality control, the evaluation of preliminary architectural sketches or ideas for a new television series, curriculum evaluation, and literary criticism.

FIELD INITIATED This refers to proposals or projects for the funding of grants or contracts that originate from workers in the field of study rather than from a program announcement of the availability of funds by an agency for work in a certain area (which is known as solicited research or development.)

FIELD TRIAL (FIELD TEST) A dry run, a true test of a product or program (etc.). Absolutely mandatory in any serious evaluation or development activity. It is essential that at least one true field trial should be run in circumstances and with a population that matches the targeted situation and population. Earlier trials ("hothouse trials" or alpha tests) may not meet this standard, for convenience reasons, but the last one must. Unless run by external evaluators (very rare), there is a major risk of bias in the sample, conditions, content, or interpretations used by the developer in the final field trials. In the computer field, alpha tests can be hothouse, but there should also be **beta** tests. Few of the ones run today are true field trials, being notably different with respect to personnel involved and support available.

FILTER Someone who—or a computer that—removes identifying information from evaluative input, to preserve the **anonymity** of the respondent. Also used to refer to one or a series of tests in personnel selection or product evaluation.

FIRE AT THE HORSES FIRST (FATHF) A procedural maxim designed to reduce wasted effort in doing evaluations involving multiple evaluands *or* multiple tests. These evaluations usually involve filling in cells in a matrix with dimensions of merit as row headings and evaluand names as column headings. The FATHF principle recommends that one should never work through an alphabetical listing beginning at the top left cell, or begin with the antecedent favorite, but always proceed by first identifying any nonnegotiable standards, for example, cutoffs on price, speed, or ethicality, and then checking performance on these. One culls the candidates that do not pass any of these, since that often avoids all further work on several candidates. When dealing with a series of tests to be

166

administered to candidates, and you have some experience with the battery of tests, cost considerations become more complex if you have the option not to run everyone through all tests and can score one before you decide who takes the next. A useful procedure is to begin with absolute requirements that are trivial to check (for example, has a high school diploma, writes legibly on the application form), then use cost to select between the ones that candidates most frequently fail and the remaining absolute requirements. Remember that you need to be quite sure of your performance data and the justification for the exclusionary cutoff point, since you can't reconsider incomplete records. Thus validity, and the cost of the test itself, also need to be considered if large-scale testing is to be done.

The name comes from apocryphal advice to riflemen in a circled wagon train when mounted hostiles start an attack, meant to improve on the advice given infantry in earlier battles: "Don't wait till you can see the whites of their eyes, fire at the horses first!". Reasons, for the record (not for the animal liberation advocate): you can hit horses at a much greater distance; one horse down may bring down others; even if you miss the horses you may get lucky and hit a warrior; even hitting horses time-spreads the arrival of the hostiles, making the rate at which they attack more manageable; and so on. In short, do the most damage you can as soon as you can. See **Multiple-hurdle.**

FISCAL EVALUATION The highly developed subfield that involves looking at the worth or probable worth of, for example, investments, programs, companies. See **Return on investment, Payback, Time discounting, Profit.**

FISHING Colloquialism for exploratory (phase of) research; *or* for true nature of large slices of serious—for example—program evaluation; *or* for visits to Washington (or your local center of power) in search of funding support.

FITTING THE LOCK TO THE KEY An expression from the field of personnel evaluation, referring to the possibility of modifying a job to fit an applicant—particularly a talented one. Rendered harder but not impossible by affirmative action legislation (it may require readvertising with a rewritten job description); in a large organization it is often easier because there are other openings available or about to become available. Applies also to midcareer evaluations; it is a mark of a good manager to be flexible in this respect; in the college situation, one should be able to move burnt-out researchers into introductory teaching or administrative areas. Applies also to the use of **consultants;** if you find someone who's exceptionally good at analysis but very poor about submitting timely reports, use them for visits at which you record their remarks (or schedule a short report writing

167

period for an hour before departure) rather than striking them off the list because they don't fit the ideal model of an evaluation consultant. The issue is not your convenience but getting the best advice in a feasible way. Conversely, consultants should be very aware of their limitations and submit bids or select colleagues that work around those limitations.

FLOW CHART A graphic representation of the sequence of decisions, including contingent decisions, that is set up to guide the management of projects (originally, the design of computer programs), including evaluation projects. Usually looks like a sideways organization diagram, being a series of boxes and triangles ("activity blocks", and so on) connected by lines and symbols that indicate simultaneous or sequential activities/decision points, and so on. A **PERT** chart is a special case.

FOCUS (of a program) A more appropriate concept for most evaluations than "goal"; both are theoretical concepts and both serve to limit complaints about things not done to the general area where resources are available and legitimately usable. The focus of a program is often improved by good evaluation. For a different sense, see **Refocusing**.

FOCUS GROUPS A term imported into the evaluation vocabulary from market research, especially in the automobile industry. It originally referred to groups of prospective purchasers brought in to use a new product not yet in final form, essentially a supervised beta test. However, the practice has been corrupted in many organizations to the point where it has been taken away from the engineering division and given to marketing, who uses it as a device for (i) creating an advertising campaign, by discovering what features of the product appeal—and do not appeal—to typical customers; or (ii) soliciting advance orders for a product not yet officially on the market. In this role, the invitees are no longer a sample of typical end-users but purchasers for large accounts, many of whom are simply incompetent evaluators (read their comments in the press releases). Nothing wrong with all this, except (i) invitees are often told that this is a chance to improve the product, though it's long past the last-revision point; and (ii) it substitutes for the beta testing, whose absence is obvious from the many gross flaws in the released products; *Consumer Reports*, buying new cars anonymously, finds an average of about 8–12 faults per car, often serious ones. See **Pseudo-evaluation**.

FOOTPRINT See **Big footprint approach**.

FORMATIVE EVALUATION Formative evaluation is contrasted with **summative** evaluation. It is typically conducted *during* the development or improvement of a program or product (or person, and so on) and it is conducted, often more than once, *for* the in-house staff

168

of the program *with the intent to improve*. The reports normally remain in-house; but serious formative evaluation may be done by an **internal** *or* an **external** evaluator or (preferably) a combination; of course, many program staff are, in an *informal* sense, constantly doing formative evaluation. The distinction between formative and summative evaluation has been well summed up by Bob Stake: "When the cook tastes the soup, that's formative; when the guests taste the soup, that's summative."

In an extended sense, formative evaluation should begin with evaluation of the proposal or concept underlying the proposal—this is sometimes called preformative evaluation. Very often, the difficulties that will later plague the evaluation can be located in poor preformative evaluation; but RFPs are often treated as if they do not need or it is somehow impertinent to suggest that they need evaluation.

Typically, formative evaluation benefits from being designed as an **analytic evaluation**, but **global evaluation** will also work, may sometimes be all that is possible, and is often important as a check on the validity of the analytic approach. Analytic evaluation, in turn, may or may not involve/require/produce causal analysis, so the connection between evaluation and causation is remote, contrary to W. Edwards Deming's oft-quoted remark, "Evaluation is a study of causes". (Troubleshooting requires a knowledge of causes, but it *presupposes* evaluation.) To avoid loading formative evaluation with obligations that will bog it down, or expectations that will be disappointed, it is helpful to keep in mind that one of the most useful kinds of formative evaluation is 'early-warning summative', that is, an evaluation which is essentially a summative evaluation of an early version of the evaluand under development. The trial final examination, scored and returned but not recorded, is a useful device even if it only generates an overall score—a case of formative global evaluation. It's more useful if it locates where your weaknesses are (analytic formative).

Evaluation of the *plans* for a project (housing development or research proposal) can be treated as part of the formative evaluation of the project, or as formative or summative evaluation of the plans. Note that in formative evaluation where it is done at several points in the project's development life, success (in one sense) is inversely proportional to the length of the final report; if all the evaluator's suggestions are adopted after being made, there won't be any left over at the end. Successful formative evaluation is thus like the state in ideal communism—its content should wither away. (The final report should, however, list the suggestions made and their effects, not just the residual ones.) See **Critical competitor**.

169

FOUND DATA Data that exists prior to the evaluation, usually in institutional records—the contrast is with experimental data or test and measurement data. "Archival data" is sometimes used to mean much the same.

FRAGMENTARY EVALUATION A species of incomplete evaluation in which the evaluator stops short of drawing an overall conclusion, although doing so was feasible and would have served the client better (a better term is 'unconsummated evaluation'). The stopping point may be after the performance listings on dimensions or components ("just give them the facts"), or as late as the last step before integrating a set of subevaluations. There are many situations where an overall synthesis is not justified, and there's no special term for them. Sometimes it's better in formative evaluation to list the various items that need improvement without drawing any overall conclusion, but this often has the unfortunate effect of an evaluee not realizing how bad the situation is, and it is often mainly done to avoid the possibility of confrontational stress if the synthesis is made. Evaluations usually stop prematurely because the evaluator holds mistaken beliefs or metatheoretical principles, or lacks nerve. A common mistaken belief underlying the metatheoretical principle that 'you should just give the client the facts' (or subevaluations) is that the integrative step can be made by the client as well or better than by a trained evaluator. If that's true in any complex evaluation, it's true only because the evaluator is incompetent. In most cases, the integration step is one of the hardest, often the one where the most help is needed. On ways to do it, see **Weight and sum**. On the fragmentary fallacy, see "Beyond Formative and Summative" in *Evaluation & Education: At Quarter Century*, edited by McLaughlin and Phillips, NSSE/University of Chicago Press, 1991.

FRONT END EVALUATION A term used by Hood and Hemphill in the Far West Laboratory for evaluating the concept or model, perhaps also the assumptions about need and available methodology, underlying a proposal, program, or RFP. See also **Preformative**.

FUGITIVE DOCUMENT One that is not published through the public channels as a book or journal article. Evaluation reports have often been of this kind. ERIC (Educational Resources Information Center) has picked up some of these, but since its standards for selection are so variable, its selection so limited, and its cleanup nonexistent, time spent in searching it is all too often not cost-effective.

FUNCTIONAL ANALYSIS Anthropologists and sociologists have long been familiar with the distinction between the latent and manifest functions of, for example, religious ceremonies. (One manifest function is to worship or solicit the assistance of deities; one latent

170

function is to strengthen the social fabric of the group, another [claimed] one is to serve as "the opiate of the masses".) There is often some tension between the two, since those believing the former are unwilling to accept what appears to be dismissive reduction to the latter. Functional analysis in biology often describes the functions of organs or coloring in language that sounds like manifest teleology, although the real truth lies in the latent explanation in terms of natural selection. In evaluation, functional analysis is a common basis for the values used to reach an evaluative conclusion. See **Logic of evaluation.**

FUNDING (of evaluations) Done in many ways, but the most common patterns are described here. The evaluation proposal may be "field-initiated", that is unsolicited, or sent in response to (i) a program announcement, (ii) an RFP (Request for Proposal), or (iii) a direct request. Typically the unsolicited request, if successful, results in a grant, the others in a contract. The former identifies a general charge or mission (for example, "to develop improved tests for early childhood affective dimensions") and the latter specifies more or less exactly what is to be done, for example, how many cycles of field tests (and who is to be sampled, how large a sample is to be used, and so on), in a "Scope of Work". The legal difference is that the latter is enforceable for lack of performance, the former is (practically) not. But it scarcely makes sense to use contracts for research (since you usually can't foresee which way it will go), and it is rarely justifiable to use them for the very specific program evaluations required by law. Approach iii, "**sole sourcing**", eliminates competitive bidding and can usually only be justified when only one contractor has much the best combination of relevant expertise or equipment or staff resources; it is much faster and does avoid the common absurdity of 40 bidders, each spending 12K ($12,000) to write a proposal worth 300K to the winner. The wastage there (180K) comes out of overhead costs that are eventually paid by the taxpayer or by bidders going broke because of foolish requirements. A good compromise is the **two-tier system**, all bidders submitting a two- (or five- or ten-) page preliminary proposal, the best few then getting a small grant to develop a full proposal.

Contracts may or may not have to be awarded to the lowest "qualified" bidder; qualification may involve financial resources, stability, prior performance, and so on, as well as technical and management expertise. On big contracts there is usually a "bidders' conference" shortly after publication of the RFP (it's often required that federal agencies publish the RFP in the *Commerce Business Daily* and/or the *Federal Register*). Such a conference officially serves to clarify the RFP; it may in fact be a cross between a con job and a poker game.

171

Examples of traps for young players: if you ask clever questions, others may (i) be scared off or (ii) steal your approach, or (iii) the agency may be sniffing around for a "friendly" evaluator and the evaluators may be trying to look friendly but not so friendly as to eliminate credibility, and so on. Eventually, perhaps after a second bidders' conference, the most promising bidders will be asked for their "best and final" bid and on this basis the agency selects one, often using a sometimes anonymous external review panel to lend credibility to the selection. After the first conference between the winner and the project officer (the agency's representative used to be called the monitor) it often turns out that the agency wants or can be persuaded to want something done that isn't clearly in the contract; the price will then be renegotiated. Or if the price was too low (the RFP will often specify it in terms of "Level of Effort" as N "person-years" of work; this may mean N x 30K or N x 50K in dollar terms, depending on whether overhead is an add-on) to get the job done, the contractor may just go ahead till they run out of money and than ask for more, on the grounds the agency will have sunk so much in and be so irreversibly committed (time-wise) that they have to come through to "save their investment". The contractor of course loses credibility on later bids but that's better than bankruptcy; and the track records are so badly kept that no one may hold it against them (if indeed they should).

In the bad old days, low bids were a facade and renegotiation on trumped-up grounds would often lead to a cost well above that of another and better bidder. Since evaluations are tricky to do in many ways, bidders have to allow a pad in their budget for contingencies— or just cross their fingers, which quickly leads to bankruptcy. Hence another option is to RFP for the best design and per diem and then let the contract for as long as it takes to do it. The form of abuse associated with this **cost-plus** approach is that the contractor is motivated to string it out. So no overall clear saving is attached to either approach; but the latter is still used where the agency wants to be able to change targets as preliminary results come in (a sensible point) and where it has good monitoring staff to prevent excessive overruns (from *estimates* that of course are not binding).

A major weakness in all of these approaches is that innovative proposals will often fail because the agency has appointed a review panel of people committed to the traditional approaches who naturally tend to fund "one of their own". Another major weakness is the complexity of all this, which means that big organizations who can afford to open branches in Washington D.C., pay professional proposal writers and "liaison staff" (that is, lobbyists), have a tremendous edge (but often do poor work, since most of the best people do not work for

172

them). A third key weakness is that the system described favors the production of timely paper rather than the solution of problems, since that's all the monitoring and managing process can identify. Billions of dollars, millions of jobs, thousands of lives are wasted because we have no reward system for really good work, work that produces really important solutions. The reward is for the *proposal*, not the product, and the reward is the contract. Once obtained, only unreliability in delivery or gross negligence jeopardizes future awards. You can see the value system this arrangement produces from the way the vice presidents all move on to work on the next "presentation" as soon as negotiation is complete. It would cost little to change this procedure via (partial) contingency awards and expert panels to review work done instead of proposals.

FUTURISM Since many evaluands are designed to serve future populations and not (just) present ones, much evaluation requires estimating future needs and performance. The simpler aspect of this task involves extrapolation of demographic data; even this is poorly done; for example, the crunch on higher education enrollments was foreseen by only one analyst (Cartter) although the inference was simple enough. The harder task is predicting, for example, vocational patterns twenty years ahead. Here one must fall back on possibility-covering techniques, rather than selection of the most probable outcome, for example by teaching flexibility of attitude or generalizable skills.

G

GAO (Checklist) The General Accounting Office, which is a highly competent evaluation agency, has developed a checklist for program evaluation which is useful in itself, and makes for an interesting comparison with the KEC. It involves ten criteria which fall into three groups: Need for the program, Implementation of the program, and Effects of the program. Need includes Problem magnitude, Problem seriousness, and Duplication. Implementation includes Interrelationships, Fidelity (see **implementation** of treatment), and Administrative efficiency. Effects includes Targeting success, Goal Achievement, Cost-effectiveness, and Other effects. Comments: (i) There is unnecessary Duplication between Duplication and Interrelationships; (ii) ethics and legality gets no mention, the latter omission providing one of the reasons why the Offices of the Inspectors General were created; (iii) comparisons, resources, and generalizability are also slighted; however, they may be buried in the fine print somewhere. Although the KEC had some influence on the earliest version of the GAO's list, GAO's vast experience since then makes the continuing similarity amount to mild mutual confirmation.

GENERALIZABILTY 1. As a feature of evaluations: In the days before the New Era in evaluation, editors gave two reasons for rejecting evaluation reports. The first was that they were essentially subjective, and hence not scientific—since all evaluation was held to be essentially subjective. The second was that evaluation reports had no generalizable content, and hence were not scientific. The second view persists today, even in the evaluation community: R. M. Wolf, for example, in *The Nature of Educational Evaluation*, argues that: "Research is concerned with the production of knowledge that is as generalizable as possible... Evaluation, in contrast, seeks to produce knowledge specific to a particular setting." (Praeger, 1990, p. 8). (i) While it is true that many program evaluations do, in fact, only concern themselves with the immediate issue of evaluating a particular implementation, this is to some degree a fault—at least a limitation—of the evaluation. The Key evaluation checklist recommends that *all* evaluations consider the generalizability of the evaluand as part of evaluating it, although financial constraints may put *extensive* investigation of this checkpoint beyond reach. (ii) Situation-specific evaluations are certainly not the only kind of evaluation—or even the only kind of *program* evaluation—that is or can be done. Comparative evaluations of the leading available hospice programs, done to assist local agencies determine which one to implement, can hardly be said not to be evaluations because they have general significance.

2. As a concept related to external validity: Although external validity (Campbell's term, which he later unsuccessfully tried to rename 'proximal validity') is commonly equated with generalizability, it refers to only part of the latter concept (which includes 'distal validity'). Typically one wants to generalize to populations (and so on) essentially other than the one tested, not just extrapolably other; and it's not just population differences but treatment differences and effect differences that are of interest. (See the Generalizability checkpoint in the KEC.) In short, while the generalizability of external validity is akin to that of **inferential statistics**—we might call it short-distance generalization (so 'proximal' makes sense)—much more than that must be considered by the evaluator or the scientist, who are constantly pushing for long-distance generalization, involving tenuous inductive or imaginative leaps. Generalization is thus often nearer to speculation than to extrapolation and a good evaluation needs to check these possibilities. The value of things or personnel is often crucially affected by their versatility, that is, their utility after transportation. Because the term means much more than the traditional scientific approach takes into account, it is common to suppose that evaluation practitioners are not concerned with it—only researchers. On the contrary, evaluation practitioners often are more concerned with it than researchers (in order to justify the cost of the evaluation and evaluand, and for humanitarian reasons), and should be encouraged to be concerned with it more often than they are; moreover, they are in a much better position to estimate it than the researcher.

NOTES: (i) In formative evaluation, considerations of generalizability can often lead to much improved market size and viability. (ii) With very large multisite projects, interpolation is often as critical as extrapolation. (iii) See also **External validity.**

GENERAL POSITIVE BIAS (GPB) (in evaluation) There is a strong GPB across all evaluation fields—a tendency to turn in more favorable results than are justified. (In exceptional circumstances one finds something like a general negative bias, for example in the U.S. Marine Corps boot camp.) The extent of GPB becomes obvious when one does systematic metaevaluation, and its pervasiveness looks like a case of the '80/20 Rule' that would here be "80% of programs (personnel, products, and so on) get favorably evaluated, whereas only 20% de-

175

serve it". It has some common causes and some specific ones. GPB turns up in the grade inflation that is almost universal in colleges and schools today (C used to be close to the average grade in undergraduate classes, but B is probably the current average, and in some colleges, B+ or A– is the median grade). A common reason for this in colleges is that the administration uses enrollment to determine the survival of courses and hence of instructors, so only As and Bs are given (since the classroom is otherwise empty after the first quiz is returned); or that the instructors' commitment to honesty and professional training is less strong than their dislike for causing pain or fear of retaliation.

GPB is pervasive in program evaluation mainly because of role-conflict. The evaluator is either a staff member, a contractor, or a consultant, and in that role knows that his or her own chance of future employment or contracts usually depends on or is enhanced by giving a favorable report on the program. Sometimes this is because the program manager's career depends on favorable outcomes and the manager has foolishly been give the responsibility of hiring the evaluator; more subtly and commonly these days it is because the program manager's superior—who is letting the evaluation contract—approved the program or its manager in the first place and hence has a stake in it.

One sees GPB in the peer input to personnel evaluations, due to the fear of reprisals if an unfavorable report is seen by the evaluee, or to **secret-contract bias**. In evaluation by supervisors it is often used to create or keep servitors or to avoid hassles. In all evaluation, GPB is generated by those whose dislike of causing distress or disappointment outweighs their commitment to honesty or to the payoffs from evaluation. And those without much faith in their own ability as evaluators are unwilling to take the risk of loss on appeal.

GPB can only be controlled by methods explicitly aimed at it; for example, by developing and enforcing strict standards for evaluation, by regular use of metaevaluation, by explicitly rewarding justified criticism, by taking action against supervisors that exhibit or tolerate GPB, by improving professional training and raising the consciousness of professionals in other ways, and by setting up increasingly independent evaluation units like GAO and the Offices of the Inspectors General (*Consumer Reports* rarely exhibits GPB).

GENERAL PURPOSE EVALUATOR The GP evaluator has a wide range of evaluation expertise, and is not identified with a particular field/area/discipline. (The contrast is with a **local expert**.) In the strong sense, the term also indicates experience outside a *type* of evaluation, for example, outside program evaluation, perhaps in policy/-product/personnel evaluation, or outside the **accreditation** type of

176

evaluation. The GP's weakness is a lack of depth in local knowledge—but this trades off against a lack of the **shared bias** of the disciplinary in-group. The best arrangement is the use of two (or more) evaluators, including at least one local evaluator and one general purpose evaluator. A strong-sense GP evaluator will often see enough in the outer office of a client to ensure that s/he can cover the whole of a program evaluation fee with demonstrable savings in office equipment, the poor choice of which is one of the real holes in the bucket of organization resources. It used to be said that no one was ever fired for buying IBM; today, one can say that if that's true, it's time they were. For what it takes to be a GP evaluator, see **Evaluation skills.**

GLOBAL (scoring/grading/evaluating) The allocation of a single score/grade/evaluation to the overall character or performance of an evaluand; by contrast with **analytical** scoring/grading/evaluating. The global/analytical distinction is related to the macro/micro distinction in economics and to the molar/molecular or gestalt/atomistic distinction in psychology. "Holistic" (or "wholistic") is a sometime synonym, but in the health field "holistic" has another, somewhat confusing, meaning. Jargon can be minimized by using the term "global" rather than "holistic" (or even the alternative spelling "wholistic").

In practical terms, global evaluations are often much faster than analytical ones, so the key question is how their validity compares. The answer is that in some cases, global ratings are more accurate. In the case of mass marking of English compositions in state or national testing, for example, the cost ratio is five to one in favor of the global approach, and the accuracy gain is significant (after suitable training of the graders). This is presumably because of unreliability in the synthesis step, when the analytical ratings (on the subdimensions of spelling, punctuation, grammar, organization, originality, etc.) are pulled together. One should be alerted by this, and by some evidence about the perceptual abilities of great clinicians, and never jump to the usual conclusion that the analytical approach is 'more scientific' and hence better. It nevertheless seems obvious that the analytical approach is more useful for formative purposes; but if the loss of validity is large, especially if it derives from invalidity on the subscale ratings and not just from synthesis invalidity, this may not be true. Global ratings can work very well in the formative role, as in learning to shoot on a pistol or rifle range, where mere scores (without reference to where the bullet went on the 'clock' of the target) provide enough feedback to generate steady improvement.

GOAL The technical sense of this term restricts its use to a rather general description of an intended outcome; more specific descriptions are referred to as **objectives**. It is important to realize that goals cannot be regarded as observable features of programs (or products, services, or systems). There is often an announced, official, or original goal—usually several, in which case the problem of how to weight their relative importance comes up and is rarely answered with enough precision to pin down the correct evaluative conclusion. Usually, too, different stakeholders have different goals—conscious and unconscious—for a program, and most of these change with time. The best one can hope for is to get a general sense of a program's goals as theoretical constructs from the paper trail, interviews, and actions. Beginners often think the goals are the instigator's official original goals, for example, those in the original legislation, just as they think the program's correct description comes from the same source. But the GAO long since learned you have to go back to the prelegislative hearings to get more information, and then onward to the budget negotiations, and then of course there's the problem that the field workers probably haven't read any of that stuff and have their own version of the goals of the program. Great material for a thesis, but quicksand as a basis for a serious evaluation. Since the goal-hunt is not only difficult and expensive but unnecessary and often biasing, one should be very careful to avoid it whenever possible. See **Goal-free evaluation.**

GOAL-ACHIEVEMENT MODEL (of evaluation) The identification of program evaluation with determining whether a program has met its goal or set of goals. This is the minimal version of **goal-based evaluation**, and is nothing more than **monitoring**, not program evaluation in any serious sense. It does not continually question the relevance of the goals to the impacted population, it does not involve any search for side-effects, it does not look at cost (unless cost happens to be one of the goals), it does not find and explore relevant comparisons with other ways to achieve the same goals, it does not include checking on the ethics of process, and so on; it *does* require the sometimes very difficult identification of the goals of a program. Goal-achievement evaluation (GAE) is sometimes legitimate for a special purpose within personnel evaluation, namely evaluation of the program progenitor for the realism of his or her projections. Normally, it should be replaced by **goal-based** or **goal-free evaluation.**

GOAL-BASED EVALUATION Any type of evaluation based on and knowledge of—and referenced to—the goals and objectives of the program, person, or product. While the simplest form of this is **goal-achievement** evaluation, a goal-based evaluation (GBE) can be much more sophisticated and fill many of the gaps in that approach. It may

178

add a needs assessment so that the goals can be looked at critically; it may do some cost analysis or comparisons; perhaps it looks for side-effects and checks on the ethics of the program's process. To the extent it does include these components, they are often *referenced to* the program's (or the person's) goals, and hence the approach is likely to be involved in serious problems such as identifying these goals, handling inconsistencies in them or false assumptions underlying them and changes in them over time, dealing with outcomes that represent shortfall and overrun on the goals, and avoiding the perceptual bias of knowing about them.

GBE is thus flawed, although a thorough approach of this type, done by experienced external evaluators, can cover much of what is needed in program evaluation. The strength of the approach is inversely related to the extent to which the goals are used as standards of merit. Goals have nothing to do with merit, only with management monitoring. Serious program evaluation must dig for the fundamental facts that determine merit—the facts of needs and performance and process—and bypass the bog containing the rhetoric of goals and objectives. (In fact, the digging is better done by people who are unaware of the program's goals; people who know them do not search with quite the same enthusiasm for what are seen as mere side-effects.) The irony is that we do this all the time when we put on our consumer hats; no one evaluates cars in terms of the goals of the design team. Why the difference? The problem is that program evaluation was—and to a large extent still is—instigated by or controlled by managers, not consumers. Managers think in terms of the success of their plans and GBE thus tends to be manager-oriented evaluation, too close to **monitoring** and too far from consumer-oriented evaluation (**goal-free evaluation**).

Four notes: (i) Defining evaluation as the study of the **effectiveness** or **success** of programs is often a sign of (often unconscious) acceptance of GBE, because these are goal-dependent notions. (ii) The problems with goal-based evaluation do not in any way count against *funding constraints*, for example, limitations on the type of grant or residence of grantee that are imposed on a foundation by its deed of gift. Insofar as 'success' is thought of as success within that area, it is a harmless and useful notion; it is only when it is referenced to the *specific* goals of a program or project that it becomes too narrow an approach. (One must move toward determining *comparative cost-effectiveness in meeting ranked true needs, including side-effects, generalizability, and ethical/legal considerations*—to give an oversimplified summary of the KEC.) (iii) The cost of finding, translating, and reconciling goals for major programs is enormous; the fact that it is unnecessary might

179

be a good enough reason to switch to goal-free evaluation, all by it-self. (iv) The best possible GBE approach goes a long way toward a goal-free front-end evaluation, with comments on goal-achievement only coming in at the end. Outstandingly good evaluations can be done using this 'goal-incidental' approach; the GAO approach does this, as does the OIG approach to some extent, and the KEC approach allows it.

GOAL-FREE EVALUATION (GFE) In the pure form of this type of evaluation, the evaluator is not told the purpose of the program but does the evaluation with the purpose of finding out what the program is actually *doing* without being cued as to what it is *trying* to do. If the program *is* achieving its stated goals and objectives, then these achievements should show up (in observation of process and inter-views with consumers not staff); if not, it is argued, they are irrelevant. Merit is determined by relating program effects to the relevant *needs* of the *impacted* population, rather than to the *goals* of the program (whether the goals of the agency, the citizenry, the legislature, or the manager) for the *target* (intended) population. It could equally well be called "needs-based evaluation" or "consumer-oriented evaluation" by contrast with goal-based (or "manager-oriented") evaluation. It does *not* substitute the evaluator's goals nor the goals of the consumer for the program's goals, contrary to a common criticism; the evaluation must justify (via the needs assessment) all assignments of merit. The report should be completely transparent with respect to the evaluator's goals.

One of the major arguments for the pure form is that it is the only systematic or design procedure for improving the detection of side-effects. Evaluators who do not know what the program is *supposed* to be doing look more thoroughly for what it *is* doing. Does this really produce much of an improvement over the sophisticated goal-based evaluator making a serious effort to find side-effects? To date, the au-thor knows of no pure GFE that has failed to uncover new and sub-stantial side-effects after a program has already been evaluated in a goal-based mode. Other arguments for it include: (i) it avoids the often expensive, always speculative, and time-consuming problems involved in determining true current goals and true original goals, reconciling, and weighting them; (ii) it is less intrusive into program activities than GBE; (iii) it is fully adaptable to midstream goal or need shifts; (iv) it is less prone to social, perceptual, and cognitive bias be-cause of reduced interaction with program staff; and (v) it is 'reversible', that is, one can begin an evaluation goal-free and switch to goal-based after a preliminary investigation thereby garnering the preceding benefits (whereas if you begin goal-based, you can't re-

180

verse); (vi) it is less subject to bias arising from the desire to please the client because it's less clear what the client was trying to do.

Of course, in many cases an evaluator can hardly fail to form some idea of what the *general* goals of the program are from observing it—for example, teaching math to ninth-grade students. But there are dozens of programs doing that; this one will have been funded because of some more specific goals, and it is those which are disregarded and not speculated about, let alone made into the basic measuring rod for merit.

Even if one does not adopt the pure form of GFE, one can adopt an *approximation* to it, which means at least that one: makes no effort to pin down details of 'real' goals; keeps knowledge of the alleged goals to as few investigators as possible, and 'segregates' them; uses only very brief and vague descriptions of the goals even to them; and in general tries to make the field people work hard at the process of outcome-hunting across the full range of possibilities, and to make the interpretation staff work hard at tying effects to needs rather than to goals.

A somewhat better compromise is to use a hybrid form: for example, a design with a goal-free 'front end'. This means that one runs goal-free up to the point of a preliminary summary and then reverses. Or one may use a goal-free *strand* in an evaluation, with one or two socially isolated evaluators working on it. These hybrids are arguably superior to pure GFE, especially if the GF mid-stream report is submitted when completed. This ensures that the evaluators work under the pressure of GFE, and also that the manager gets feedback on how what may be a 'grand vision' is succeeding in its own terms.

GFE is generally disliked by both managers/administrators and evaluators, for fairly obvious reasons. For the evaluator, it raises anxiety by its lack of predeterminate structure and greatly increased risk of being shown up as incompetent because one did not discover already-identified effects; for the manager, it raises anxiety by abandoning the standards of success that were built into the contract for the program.

It is also risky for the evaluator because the client may get a nasty shock when the report comes in (no prior hand-holding and early warning) and in the extreme case—euphemistically referred to as 'a learning experience'—the client may refuse to pay because of embarrassment at the prospect of having to pass the evaluation along to their funding agency, even though they requested GFE. (Of course, if the findings are invalid, the client should simply document this and ask for modifications.)

The shock reaction when GFE was introduced in the area of program evaluation—it is of course the standard procedure used by all consumers, including evaluators, when evaluating products—suggests that the grip of management bias on program evaluation was very strong, and it may indicate that managers felt they had achieved considerable control over the outcomes of GBEs. See **General positive bias.**

GFE is somewhat analogous to double-blind design in medical research; even if the evaluator would like to give a favorable report (e.g., because of being paid by the program, or because hoping for future work from them) it is not (generally) easy to tell *how* to 'cheat' under GFE conditions. The fact that the risk of failure by the evaluator is greater in GFE is desirable since it increases effort, identifies incompetence, and improves the **balance of power.**

Doing GFE is a notably different and enlightening experience from doing the usual kind of evaluation. There is a very strong sense of social isolation, and one comes to be extremely conscious of the extent to which GBE evaluations are not really 'independent evaluations' even when they are called that; they are cooperative efforts, and hence easily co-opted efforts. One is also very conscious of the possibility of enormous blunders. It is good practice to use a metaevaluator and very desirable to use a team.

Although GFE is a method, the choice of it does not come from the same box as the choice of what is usually thought of as methods (quantitative vs. qualitative, survey vs. experiment, multiple perspectives vs. one right answer, etc.) It can be combined with any of them, only excluding GBE, and that only for a part of the investigation.

GOING NATIVE The fate of evaluators that get co-opted by the programs they are evaluating. (The term originated with the Experimental Schools Program evaluation in the mid-1960s.) The co-option was often entirely by choice and well illustrates the pressures on, temptations for, and hence the temperamental requirements for being a good evaluator. It can be a very lonely role, and if you start thinking about it in the wrong way you start seeing yourself as a negative force—and who wouldn't rather be a co-author than a (mere) critic? One answer: someone who cares more about quality than kudos. See **Evaluation skills.** In anthropological field research, a closely related phenomenon is known as the "my tribe" syndrome, characterized by proprietary attitudes toward the subjects of one's field work and defensive attitudes toward one's conclusions about them. See **Independence.**

GRADE-EQUIVALENT SCORE A well-meant attempt to generate a meaningful index from the results of standardized testing. If a child has a 7.4 grade-equivalent score, that means s/he is scoring at the average level (estimated to be) achieved by students four months into the seventh grade. Use of the concept has often led to an unjustified worship of average scores as a reasonable standard for individuals and to overlooking the **raw scores** that may tell a very different story. Supposing a beginning eighth grader is scoring at the 7.4 level; parents may be quite upset unless someone points out that on this particular test the 8.0 level is the same as the 7.4 level (because of summer backsliding). In reading, a deficit of two whole grade equivalents is quite often made up in a few months in junior high school if a teacher succeeds in motivating the student for the first time. Again, a student may be a whole grade-equivalent down and be ahead of most of the class—if the average score is calculated as the *mean* not the median. Again, a student in the *fifth* grade scoring 7.2 might flunk the seventh grade reading test completely; 7.2 just means that s/he scores where a seventh grader would score on the *fifth* grade test. A year's deficit from the fifth grade norm isn't comparable to a year's deficit from the fourth grade norm. And so on—that is, use with caution. But don't throw it out unless you have something better for audiences not made up of statisticians.

GRADING ("Rating" is sometimes used as a synonym.) Allocating individuals to an ordered (usually small) set of named categories, the order corresponding to merit—for example, A-F for "letter grading". Those within a category are regarded as tied if the letter grade only is used; but if a numerical grade is also used (**scoring**), they may be ranked within grades. The use of plus and minus grades simply amounts to using more categories. Grading provides a *partial* ranking, but a **ranking** cannot provide a grading without further assumptions about the merit metric, for example, that the best student is good enough for an A, or that "grading on the curve" is justified (essentially never). That is, the grade labels normally are taken to have or are given some independent meaning from the vocabulary of merit (for example, "excellent", "good", "satisfactory", "poor" or "marginally acceptable", "bad" or "unacceptable"). Hence they cannot be treated as simply a sequenced set of categories separated by making arbitrary or predetermined cuts in a ranked sequence of individuals. In short, grades are normally **criterion-referenced**. It is **ranking**, not grading, that is facilitated by **norm-referenced testing**.

The difference between ranking and grading frequently results in confusion. For example, grading of students does not imply the necessity for "beating" other students and does not need to engender "distractive competitiveness" as is often thought. Only *publicized grading on a curve* does that. Pass/Not Pass is a simple form of grading, not a no-grading system. Grades should be treated as quality estimates by an expert and thus constitute essential feedback to the learner or consumer and their advisers, as well as crucial feedback to the teacher. Corrupting that feedback because the external society misuses the grades is abrogation of duty to the learner or consumer, a confusion of **validity** with **utilization**.

Other corruptions are the "A for effort" or the "A for improvement" approach. These have a role in formative evaluation, but only if not used as a substitute currency; that is, either grades should be given for merit as well as effort or improvement, or the context should make clear that the grades are, for the moment, only for effort (or for improvement). Research suggests that grades for effort are pedagogically ineffective, but that grades for improvement are often effective. One of the major drawbacks of mainstreamed classrooms is the difficulty of avoiding the discouraging effect of a steady stream of low grades for handicapped students without using a double standard—which involves lying to them—or abandoning grading for merit for the whole class—which involves abrogation of duty. See the next entry and **Responsibility evaluation**.

GRADING ON THE CURVE The process of allocating grades to a class on the basis of their *relative* performance, usually in terms of a predetermined pattern. For example, the top and bottom 10% may get As and Fs respectively, the adjacent 20% get Bs and Ds, and the middle 40% get Cs. This was one of the sorrier crimes committed in the name of keeping science—in particular, psychology—free from the contamination of value-judgments. (Of course, the same people doing this to their first-year class were happily giving real grades to their graduate students.) The flaws are obvious, for example, the arbitrary choice of percentages, the absence of any adjustment for the difficulty of a particular test, no examination of the F papers to see whether they did in fact deserve to be failed, or of the As to see if they showed real excellence. The defence was that this approach removes the 'subjectivity' from grading. And so it does, as any simple-minded rule for allocating grades will do. It does so because it bypasses the key questions that grading addresses, to which students as well as lecturers need answers—questions such as: Am I really failing to understand this material or just doing less well than others in the class; Am I near to getting everything right, or just nearer than anyone else but still a mile from mastery; Is the teaching conveying erroneous impressions, and so on. The task for psychology was to improve the accuracy with which such questions could be answered, not treat them as improper.

GRANT See **Funding**.

H

HALO EFFECT The tendency of someone's reaction to part or all of a stimulus (e.g., a test, a student's answers to a test, or someone's personality) to spill over into their reaction to other, especially adjacent, parts of the same stimulus. For example, judges of exams involving several essay answers will tend to grade the second answer by a particular student higher if they graded the first one high than they would if this had been the first answer they had read by this student. The error is often as much as a full grade. Halo effect is avoided by having judges assess all the first components before they look at any of the second components, and by concealing from them their grade on the first component when they come to evaluate the second one. The halo effect gets its name from the tendency to suppose that someone who is saintly in one kind of situation must be saintly (and perhaps also clever) in all kinds of situations. But the halo effect also refers to the illicit transfer of a *negative* assessment. The Hartshorne and May work *Studies in Deceit* (Columbia, 1928) suggests there is no good basis for this transfer even across categories of immorality.

HARD (vs. soft; approaches to evaluation) Colloquial way to refer to the differences between the quantitative/testing/measurement/survey/experimental-design approach to evaluation vs. the descriptive/-observational/narrative/interview/ethnographic/participant-observer kind of approach. At a slightly deeper level, hard approaches stress hands-off and summative (plus simulated summative in the formative role) against hand-holding and low-threat designs. Each approach has its uses. See **Soft.**

HARVARD FALLACY The inference that Harvard must be a good university from the outstanding quality of its graduates. This is an example of the flaws in simple outcomes-based evaluation. All you can infer from the performance of graduates is that Harvard didn't seriously damage their brains. As far as you know, the whole of Harvard's contribution comes from one little office, the admissions office, which isn't even on the campus. It's likely that the contribution from Widener, the great Harvard library, is also significant. It's still more likely that peer-group interaction makes a significant contribution. How about the faculty? The curriculum? The texts? (That is, the stuff that is normally thought of as making up a university and on which Harvard spends most of its income.) Who knows? How about the contribution of 'being at Harvard'—what one might call the placebo effect of Harvard? Who knows? It does seem clear that the institutional complacency induced by having successful graduates and a great reputation (and no training in evaluation) undermines serious efforts to improve the more deplorable teaching practices at Harvard, which are more rarely found at universities of lesser reputation since they are more vulnerable. Can you imagine the regional accreditation organization flunking Harvard? Hardly, since its own credibility would not survive the decision. Then you will not be surprised to learn that the modest beneficial effects of the accreditation process, namely the self-study and self-evaluation, have often not filtered down to the faculty level at Harvard. One more reason to worry about the adverse effects of pseudo-evaluation. (To avoid the appearance of discrimination, it should be stressed that Yale, Princeton, Oxford, the Sorbonne, or Berkeley, could also have been chosen for the honor of increased name-recognition by immortalizing them in this fallacy. Well, perhaps not *quite* so appropriately.)

HAWTHORNE EFFECT The tendency of a person or group being investigated, or experimented on, or evaluated, to react positively or negatively to the fact that they are being investigated/evaluated, and hence to perform better (or worse) than they would in the absence of the investigation, thereby making it difficult to identify any effects due to the treatment itself. Not the same as the **placebo effect**, that is, the effect on the consumer of belief by the consumer in the treatment power of provider or recipient, though the term is often used to cover both: the Hawthorne effect can occur without any belief in the **merit** of the treatment. (Recent research suggests that the historical basis for claiming that the effect occurred during experiments at General Electric's Hawthorne plant is unsound.) See **John Henry effect**.

HEADROOM See **Ceiling effect**.

HERMENEUTICS Originally, the term referred to the 'science' of exegesis, explanation, and interpretation or to the study of this process, particularly in textual analysis—for some time this meant mainly in Biblical scholarship. It was extended to a position in the philosophy of science which stressed interpretation and understanding, often of individual experiences, by contrast with the experimental, behaviorist emphasis of the social science of the time. Dilthey was the intellectual leader of this movement. More recently, it refers to an antipositivist and strongly relativist methodology in European philosophy (especially Habermas) that has been appealed to by supporters of qualitative methods or models in evaluation. It represents an empha-

186

sis on 'seeing events from the inside', on empathic understanding, on meaning and significance, by contrast with the subsumption of actions and events under laws of human behavior. Its most serious competition is the more tangible alternative of postpositivist explanation theory, especially the accounts that originated in the analytical philosophy of history—William Dray is one of the most impressive contributors. This is much closer to Dilthey than the Habermas group, and clearly much better argued.

HIERARCHICAL SYSTEM See Two-tier.

HOLISTIC (scoring/grading/evaluating) See Global.

HOMEOPATHIC FALLACY (in evaluation) Refers to various misapplications of the intuitively attractive appeal to similarity. Two examples are of particular importance. (i) The belief that "it takes one to evaluate one", for example, the belief that it takes an experienced teacher to evaluate teachers. This view is almost completely wrong; it obviously does not take a programmer to evaluate a word processing program. The basis for the belief is the fact that knowing how to do something is *sometimes* useful in converting *formative* evaluation into *suggestions for improvement*. However, in summative evaluation such expertise is not only completely unnecessary but often biasing. Common biases are the tendency to give As for effort instead of achievement, the tendency to assume too much knowledge on the part of the consumer, and the tendency to rate those exhibiting one's own style higher than others, even if it is just one of many equally good ones. Even the weaker generalization—that it takes an expert in X to produce useful advice to other people doing X—is unsound; one of the best swimming coaches in the history of the sport, Frank Kiphuth of Yale, could not swim at all, let alone swim well. (Some elaboration of this is in "Beyond Formative and Summative", in *Evaluation & Education: At Quarter Century*, eds. M. McLaughlin and D. Phillips [University of Chicago/National Society for the Study of Education, 1990].)

(ii) The second example of interest is the belief that tests should match the content of the course for which they are testing achievement. It is the basis of the single greatest source of invalidity in teacher-made tests—the usual type at the college level and the modal approach in K–12. Whereas there *should* be a close match between tests for personnel selection and the work on the job, the match in the case of course testing should (mainly) be with the curriculum, not with what was actually covered. Otherwise the students (and the administrators, parents, and teachers) are given a misleading impression of the competence of the student on subject matter. Of course, this will result in an 'unfair' grade for the student but it is the

187

correct grade on the subject matter as defined (and often as required in the following year); and the fault for the unfairness (and the lack of proper preparation) is the teacher's. External examiners, setting and marking exams which test the knowledge required are essential at some points in any serious educational system. See **Testing to the teaching.**

HURDLE A test with a cutoff, as in personnel selection or in the evaluation of investments where, for example, a certain risk level may be one hurdle, and a certain projected rate of return may be another.

HYPERCOGNITIVE The domain beyond the supercognitive, which is the stratosphere of the cognitive. Only occasional individuals demonstrate skills at this level. It includes eidetic imaging; perfect pitch; mathematic calculating at the prodigy level; ESP skills (if they exist). The term "transcognitive" refers to the joint domain of the para-, super- and hyper-cognitive.

HYPOTHESIS TESTING The standard model of scientific research in the classical approach to the social sciences, in which a hypothesis is formulated prior to the design of the experiment, the design is composed so as to test its truth, and the results come out in terms of a probability estimate that the results were solely due to chance ("the null hypothesis"). If the probability is extremely low that only chance was at work, a good design makes it inductively highly likely that the hypothesis being tested was correct by eliminating alternative explanations. What is to count as a high degree of improbability that only chance was at work is usually taken to be either the .05 (one chance in 20) or the .01 (one chance in 100) "level of significance". When dealing with phenomena whose existence is in doubt, a more appropriate level is .0001; where the occurrence of the phenomenon *in this particular situation* is all that is at stake, the higher conventional level is more appropriate. The significance level is thus used as a crude index of the merit of a hypothesis, but it is legitimate as such only to the extent that the design is bulletproof. Since evaluation is not hypothesis testing, little of this is of concern in evaluation, except in checking subsidiary hypotheses, for example, that a treatment caused certain outcomes.

An important distinction in hypothesis testing that carries over to the evaluation context in a useful way is the distinction between Type I and Type II errors. A Type I error is involved when we conclude that the null hypothesis is false although it isn't; a Type II error is involved when we conclude that the null hypothesis is true when in fact it's false. Using a .05 significance level means that in about 5 percent of the cases studied, we will make a Type I error. As we tighten up on our level of significance, we reduce the chance of Type I error, but cor-

188

respondingly increase the chance of a Type II error (and vice versa). It is a key part of evaluation to look carefully at the relative costs of Type I and Type II errors. (In evaluation, of course, the conclusion is about merit rather than truth; or about the truth of merit statements.) A meta-evaluation should carefully spell out the costs of the two kinds of error and scrutinize the evaluation for its failure or success in taking account of these in the analysis, synthesis, and recording phases. For comprehensibility reasons, the Type I/Type II jargon is best replaced by the 'false positive/false negative' dichotomy, which refers to the evaluand directly not the null hypothesis. For example, in quality control procedures in drug manufacture (a type of evaluation), it may be fatal to a prospective user to identify a drug sample as satisfactory when in fact it is not; on the other hand, identifying it as unsatisfactory when it is really satisfactory will only cost the manufacturer whatever that sample costs to make. Hence it is obviously in the interest of the public—and the manufacturer, given the possibility of damage suits—to set up a system that minimizes the chance of false acceptances, even at the expense of a rather high level of false rejections.

I

ILLICIT VALUES The existence of illicit or inappropriate values, something that we all recognize in practice, constitutes one of the most obvious flaws in the usual social science effort to avoid making real value-judgments in evaluation, and to end run the problem by accepting the values of others. (A good example of this attempt is *Multiattribute Evaluation* by Ward Edwards and J. Robert Newman [Sage, 1982].) Values may be illicit in one or another context of evaluation, but not in all, since (for one reason) none of them impact on all evaluations. Illicit values include those that violate moral constraints (e.g., enjoying violent rape), legal constraints (racist police), or logical consistency (some cases of valuing incompatible ends); those that rest on false factual assumptions (e.g., assumptions about what the individual with the values would enjoy in the long run); those that rest on mistakenly displaced value for example, **technicism**; and those which lack appropriate support, for example, those based on a no longer relevant assessment of **need**. See **Values**.

ILLUMINATIVE EVALUATION (Parlett and Hamilton) A type of pure process naturalistic evaluation, very heavy on multiperspective description and interpersonal relations, very light on tough standards, very easy on **valuephobes** and very well defended in *Beyond the Numbers Game* (Macmillan, 1977). Congenial to r esponsive evaluation supporters; not unlike **perspectival evaluation** except more relativistic. Considerable emphasis is placed on 'progressive focusing', related to but not the same as **refocusing**.

IMPACTED POPULATION The population that is crucial in evaluation, by contrast with the **target** population and even the **recipients**. Sometimes called the 'true consumers' or even, in the KEC, the **consumers**. See **Recoil effects**.

IMPACT EVALUATION An evaluation focused on outcomes or payoff rather than **process**, delivery, or **implementation evaluation**.

IMPLEMENTATION (of program or treatment) The degree to which a program or treatment has been instantiated in a particular situation, typically in a field trial of the treatment or an evaluation of it (the GAO calls it "fidelity of implementation"). Ralph Tyler was probably the first person to see the central importance of this in program evaluation—in 1934. The notion of an "index of implementation", from
190

Lou Smith, consisting of a set of scales describing the key features of the treatment, allowing one to measure the extent to which it is implemented along each dimension, is a useful one for checking on implementation. Doing so is fundamental if we are to find out whether the *treatment*, as opposed to this version of it, has merit, but it is surprisingly rare. This is part of the "purely descriptive" effort in evaluation and is handled under the Description, the Background & Context, and the Process checkpoints of the KEC. The Description checkpoint should tell us what actually happens, Background tells us what was supposed to be implemented, and Process pins down the mismatch, if any, and puts a value on the mismatch from the Values checkpoint, which will then affect the overall conclusion. The result of this comparison also bears on the extent to which we can Generalize from the evaluation's outcomes.

IMPLEMENTATION EVALUATION Recent reactions to the often unexciting results of impact evaluations on social action programs have included a shift back to mere monitoring of program delivery a.k.a. 'implementation evaluation'. It's easier to implement; it's harder to improve. (But it's still hard; see **Implementation of program**)

IMPLEMENTATION OF EVALUATIONS Program evaluators frequently complain that evaluations have little effect, a fact which they often describe in terms of lack of implementation. But one can only implement **recommendations**, not evaluations, and many evaluations can only—or should only—come to evaluative conclusions, from which recommendations do not automatically follow. The correct formulation of the problem has to be in terms of **utilization**. So the first problem is that evaluators are not even clear about the difference between evaluation and recommendation. Suppose that an evaluation or policy study does in fact come up with recommendations. There are at least five quite different situations about implementing them, and the total picture is not one that should make evaluators feel their work is often wrongly ignored by incompetent bureaucrats: (i) Many evaluations are invalidly reasoned or based on inadequate data, are recognized as such by the client, and it is highly desirable that recommendations based on them *not* be implemented. (ii) Many evaluations are commissioned or interpreted in such a way that even when done as well as possible they will not be of any use, because they were set up in a way that was irrelevant to the real issues that affect the decision-maker or the consumer; or (iii) they are so underfunded that no sound answer can be obtained. (iv) Some otherwise excellent evaluations are ignored because they are presented badly, written obscurely, not **layered**, or not supplemented with explanations for those with a different background. (v) Some excellent

191

evaluations are ignored because the decision-maker doesn't like (e.g., is threatened by) the results or won't take on the risks or trouble of implementation.

The "lack of implementation" phenomenon thus has little or large implications for the field of evaluation, depending entirely on the distribution of its causes across these five categories. Organized medicine shouldn't worry that patients ignore their doctor's advice, if a great deal of it is bad advice or presented in a way that makes acceptance unlikely or difficult. Nevertheless, as a *citizen* one can scarcely avoid concern about the colossal wastage resulting from the fifth situation. Here is a fairly typical quote from a GAO annual report on their (usually good) evaluations: "The Congress has an excellent opportunity to save billions of dollars by limiting the number of non-combat aircraft to those that can be adequately justified... Dept. of Defense justifications [were]..based on unrealistic data and without adequate consideration of more economical alternatives." GAO has been issuing reports on this topic and in this spirit since 1976 without any effect so far, and the Gulf War did nothing to invalidate these recommendations.

In short, the absence of implementation is no better an indicator of evaluator failure than the death of patients is of a doctor's incompetence; it all depends on the reason for the failure. See **General positive bias, Psychology of evaluation, Phenomenology of evaluation, Risk evaluation, Report.**

IMPLICITLY EVALUATIVE (terms) See **Contextually evaluative.**

IMPROVEMENT, EVALUATION FOR See **Formative evaluation.**

INAPPROPRIATE PRECISION See **Approximation.**

INAPPROPRIATE VALUES One of the most common examples is the use of values that are based on a misconception (usually an out-of-date conception) of **needs**, or of the remedial power of some nostrum. Others are covered under **illicit values**, which deals for the most part with more serious errors.

INCESTUOUS RELATIONS (in evaluation) Refers to extreme **conflict of interest** where the evaluator is "in bed with" the program being evaluated. This is typical of much program monitoring by agencies and foundations where the monitor is usually the godfather of the program, sometimes its inventor, and nearly always its advocate at the agency, hence a co-author of its modifications, as well as—supposedly—its evaluator (or at least the monitor for the evaluation contract as well). **Going native** is one of the consequences of incestuous arrangements, as is outright fraud, but the usual consequence is a contribution to **General positive bias.** One of the less attractive examples is the exclusive use of field-specific evaluators in the process of ac-

192

crediting professional training programs. This practice is a hothouse for **shared bias** and **secret-contract bias.**

INCESTUOUS VALIDATION The practice, common in test construction circles, of dropping items from a test when scores on them do not correlate well with total score. The argument is that this absence of correlation shows that the aberrant items are not measuring the same thing as the rest of the test. The reality is that they may be measuring another aspect of whatever the test is supposed to be measuring. Given that most educationally interesting concepts are multidimensional, often with dimensions that do not correlate highly with each other, this practice frequently reduces the validity of the test. Before dropping an item, therefore, it is crucial to explore its claims to inclusion on the basis of **content and construct validity.** In particular, one should   check for other errors (e.g., irrelevance, ambiguity) perhaps by external judge review, or by rewriting the item(s), hoping the new correlation *won't* be high—because then you have tapped into an independent dimension of criterion performance. An example in personnel evaluation is the common claim that the **compensatory** approach to amalgamating results from several tests or criteria or interviews will be equivalent to the **multiple-cutoff** (or 'conjunctive') approach if the criterion variables are highly correlated. Correlation isn't the issue; the issue is whether they refer to *conceptually* different skills (etc.).

INCREMENTAL NEED An unmet or add-on **need.** Cf. **maintenance** need or met need.

INDEPENDENCE Independence is only a relative notion, but by increasing it, we can decrease certain types of bias. Thus the external evaluator is somewhat more independent than the internal, the consulting medical specialist can provide a more "independent opinion" than the family physician, and so on. But of course both may share certain biases, and there is always the particular bias that the external or "second opinion" is typically hired by the internal one and thus is dependent upon the latter for this or later fees, a not inconsiderable source of **bias.** The more subtle social connections between members of the same profession, for example, evaluators, are an ample basis for suspicion about the true independence of the second or **meta-evaluator's** opinion. The best approach is typically to use more than one 'second opinion' and to sample as widely as possible in selecting these other evaluators, hoping that an inspection of their (independently written) reports will provide a sense of the variation within the field from which one can extrapolate to an estimate of probable errors.

INDEPENDENT VARIABLE See **Dependent variable.**

INDICATOR 1. A factor, variable, or observation that is *empirically*

193

connected with the criterion variable; a correlate. For example, the judgment by students that a course has been valuable to them for pre-professional training is an indicator of that value. **Criteria**, by contrast, *are*—or are *definitionally* connected with—the criterion variables (the real payoff); the truth of the content of a course is a criterion of merit. 2. The term is sometimes used to cover *both* empirically connected factors and definitionally connected factors. In that sense, the distinction between the two is sometimes indicated by referring to primary and secondary indicators, the former being criteria. *Constructed* indicators (or "indexes") are variables *designed* to reflect, for example, the health of the economy (a social indicator) or the effectiveness of a program; they are secondary indicators. Like course grades, they are examples of the frequent need for concise evaluations even at the cost of some accuracy and reliability. (Primary) indicators, unlike criteria, often have a rather fragile validity and can be easily manipulated; furthermore, for other reasons, their use in personnel decision making is almost always illicit (see **Research-based personnel evaluation**).

INFERENTIAL STATISTICS That part of statistics concerned with making inferences from characteristics of samples to characteristics of the population from which the sample comes (cf. **descriptive statistics**). This can of course only be done with a certain degree of probability. Significance tests and confidence intervals are devices for indicating the degree of risk involved in the inference (or "estimate")—but they only cover some dimensions of the risk. For example, they cannot measure the risk due to the presence of unusual and possibly relevant circumstances such as freakish weather, an incipient gas shortage, ESP, and so on. Judgment thus enters into the final determination of the probability of the inferred condition. See **External validity** for the distinction between the inferences in inferential statistics and in **generalization**, or other plausible inferences.

INFORMAL LOGIC Several evaluation theorists consider evaluation to be in some respects or ways a kind of persuasion or argumentation, notably Ernest House, in *Evaluating with Validity* (Sage, 1980). In terms of this view, it is relevant that there are new movements in logic, law, and science that give more play to what have previously been dismissed as "merely psychological" factors, for example, feelings, understanding, plausibility, credibility. The "informal logic movement" parallels that of the **New Rhetoric** movement in law, and some aspects of what is often called **naturalistic** methodology in the social sciences. The title is intended to stress the contrast with formal logic (a.k.a. symbolic logic or mathematical logic). The forte of IL is the analysis of everyday arguments and presentations without appeal to a sophisticated formal apparatus (see **argument evaluation**).

History has shown that the formal approach yields few if any benefits in terms of improved practical skills. Recent efforts to develop a logic of evaluative reasoning come from within the informal logic camp— see **probative logic**. Ref. *Informal Logic*, Johnson and Blair, eds. (Edgepress, 1980).

INFORMED CONSENT The state that one tries to achieve in conscious, rational adults as a good start toward discharging one's ethical obligations toward human subjects. The tough cases involve semirational semiconscious semiadults, and semicomprehension.

INITIATION-JUSTIFICATION BIAS (a.k.a. "Boot camp is beautiful") The tendency to argue that unpleasant experiences one went through oneself are good for others (and oneself), presumably as a way to justify having put up with them. A key source of bias in the use of alumni interviews for program evaluation. See **Consonance/-dissonance**.

INPUT EVALUATION Usually refers to the undesirable practice of using quality of ingredients as an index of quality of output (or of the evaluand), for example, the SAT scores of those being admitted to a college as an index of merit for the college. It has a different and legitimate use in the **CIPP model**, where it is just one part of a whole approach. The **Harvard fallacy** is the converse error: naive evaluation based on looking at output as an index of merit, that is, as if it was not affected by input.

INSIDER TRADING In the financial world, the sin of using information obtained as or from an officer of a company for personal pecuniary gain. In evaluation, any exploitation of a special role, such as serving on an evaluation committee for an appointment or grant, to obtain personal benefit in the present or future. The classic example is the practice of Air Force officers on weapons system review panels who shortly thereafter jumped into early retirement and a lucrative position with the vendor of the winning system. This practice became so scandalous that some official restrictions have now been placed on it.

INSPECTIONS The term used for one type of evaluation done by an evaluator from one of the Offices of the Inspectors General. Typically, they are much shorter (60–180 days), less costly, involve less imposition of data-gathering load on states and agencies, and are more directly aimed at policy issues than the traditional social science, research-like investigations. Technically speaking, separate activities of the OIG cover two other dimensions of evaluation of special governmental concern that were not being covered in traditional program evaluation approaches—fraud and other illegal activities, and money management—but it is common to speak loosely of the 'inspection' as

195

covering all three. This is an impressive list of virtues; of course, it raises the question whether one can get adequately valid answers to most of the relevant questions in the short time-frame. It is clear that experience shows this to be the case. Of course, inspections do not preclude and indeed should occasionally be run in parallel with longer-term, more detailed studies, which have better validity and turn up more effects. See next entry.

INSPECTOR GENERAL One of the earliest examples of an official external evaluator in Euro-Russian history. The office has flourished (and sometimes decayed) in Russian, British, Continental, Australian, and most recently U.S. governments. There is typically an obligation to report to some senior federal officer outside the agency or site being inspected, as well as an obligation to report to the manager or supervisor of the organization or program being inspected, so the function is often both formative and summative, both internal and external. In early 1991, 67 federal agencies had such offices, from a cold start in 1976. There is a definitive reference: *Inspectors General: A New Force in Evaluation* by Hendricks and others (Jossey-Bass, 1990). It would have benefitted from a historical review of IGs in other cultures; cross-cultural perspective is an essential element in self-evaluation, and self-evaluation is a major aim of the book. See **Inspections, Bias control.**

INSTITUTIONAL EVALUATION A complex evaluation, typically involving the evaluation of a set of programs provided by an institution plus an evaluation of the overall management, publicity, personnel policies, and so on of the institution. The **accreditation** of schools and colleges is essentially institutional evaluation, though a very poor example of it. One of the key problems with institutional evaluation is whether to evaluate in terms of the mission of the institution or on some absolute basis. It seems obviously unfair to evaluate an institution against goals that it isn't trying to achieve; on the other hand, the mission statements are usually mostly rhetoric and virtually unusable for generating criteria of merit, and they are at least potentially subject to criticism, for example, because of inappropriateness to need of clientele, internal inconsistencies, impracticality with respect to the available resources, ethical impropriety, and so on. So one must in fact evaluate the goals *and* the performance relative to these goals or do **goal-free evaluation.** Institutional evaluation always involves more than the sum of the component evaluations; for example, one major defect in most universities is departmental dominance, with the attendant costs in rigidifying career tracks, virtually eliminating the role model of the generalist, blocking new disciplines or programs—and preserving outdated ones, since in steady-state new ones have come out of the old departments' budgets, and so on. Most evaluations of schools and colleges fail to consider these system features, which may be more important than any components.

INSTRUMENT Covers not only calipers and so on, but also (especially standardized) paper-and-pencil tests, and a person used as a judge, for example to estimate quality of handwriting. See **Calibration, Measurement.**

INTEGRATION The term is used in evaluation methodology to refer to the process of combining scores on multiple indicators or dimensions, or combining multiple research studies. See **Synthesis.**

INTERACTION Two factors or variables interact if the effect of one, on the phenomenon being studied, depends on the magnitude of the other. For example, math education interacts with age, being more or less effective on children depending on their age, and it interacts with math achievement. There are plenty of interactions between variables governing human feelings, thought, and behavior, but they are extremely difficult to pin down with any precision. The classic example is the search for aptitude-treatment or trait-treatment interactions in education. Everyone knows from their own experience that they learn more from certain teaching styles than from others and that other people do respond favorably to the same styles. Hence there's an interaction between the teaching style (treatment) and the learning style (aptitude) with regard to learning. But despite all our technical armamentarium of tests and measuring instruments, we have virtually no solid results as to the size or even the circumstances under which these ATIs occur. Ref. *The Aptitude-Achievement Distinction*, D.R. Green, ed. (McGraw-Hill, 1974).

INTERACTIVE EVALUATION One in which the evaluees have, for example, the opportunity to react to the content of a first draft of an evaluative report, which is reworked in the light of any valid criticisms or additions. A desirable approach whenever feasible, as long as the evaluator has the courage to make the appropriate criticisms and stick to them despite hostile and defensive responses—unless they are disproved. Very few evaluators have this strength, as one can see by looking at site-visit or personnel reports that are not confidential, by comparison with those that are, for example, verbal supplements by the site visitors. See **Balance of power.**

INTERDISCIPLINE A term whose usage is very close to that of multidiscipline, and somewhat different from that of transdiscipline.

INTERNAL EVALUATOR Internal evaluators (or evaluations) are those done by project staff, even if they are special evaluation staff—that is, even if they are external to the production/writing/teaching/-service part of the project. Usually internal evaluation is part of the formative evaluation effort, but long-term projects have often had special summative evaluators on their staff, despite the low credibility (and probably low validity) that results. As we look at cases where the internal evaluators are separately housed and/or supervised, it becomes clear that the internal/external distinction can be seen as a difference of degree rather than kind; see **Independence**. If the evaluator comes from the same institution but not from the same program we might call the evaluation partially external. Careful management, and high quality evaluation can offset the validity handicape, but not the credibility one. On the relative advantages/disadvantages of internal vs. external, see **External evaluator**. Ref: a special section on internal evaluation, edited by Sandra Mathison, in the Fall, 1991, issue of *Evaluation and Program Planning*.

INTERNAL VALIDITY The kind of validity of an evaluation or experimental design that answers the question: "Does the design prove what it's supposed to prove about the treatment *on the subjects actually studied?*" (cf. **External validity**). In particular, does it prove that the treatment produced the claimed effect in the experimental subjects? (Relates to the Outcomes checkpoint in the **Key Evaluation Checklist**.) Common threats to internal validity include poor instruments, participant maturation, spontaneous change, or assignment bias. Ref. *Experimental and Quasi-Experimental Designs for Research*, Campbell and Stanley (Rand McNally, 1972).

INTEROCULAR DIFFERENCES Fred Mosteller, the great practical statistician, is fond of saying that he's not interested in statistically significant differences, but only in interocular ones—those that hit you between the eyes. (At least, that's what people are fond of saying he's fond of saying.)

INTERPERSONAL COMPARISONS O F UTILITY Does a dollar count as having the same value, no matter to whom it is allocated—the starving person or the rich person? If you can't justify a particular answer to this scientifically, then economics can't make any policy recommendations that involve distributional matters, and that's most of the important ones. This is the stumbling block that has prevented welfare economics from fruition, and hence prevented economics from making the giant social contribution in the 20th century that its subject matter demands. The answer to the question is not very hard, but there's a catch; you have to understand the logic and justification of **ethics**.

INTERPOLATE Infer to conclusions about values of the variables within the range sampled. Cf. **Extrapolate**.

INTERRUPTED TIME SERIES A type of **quasi-experimental design** in which the treatment is applied and then withheld in a certain temporal pattern *with the same subjects*. The somewhat ambiguous term "self-controlled" used to be the name for such designs, since the control group is the same as the experimental group. The simplest version is of course the "aspirin for a headache" design; if the headache goes away, we credit the aspirin. On the other hand, "psychotherapy for a neurosis" provides a weak inference because the length of the treatment is so great and spontaneous recovery rates are so high that the chance of the neurosis ending during that interval for other reasons than the psychotherapy is very significant. (Hence short-term psychotherapy is a better bet, *ceteris paribus*.) The next fancier self-controlled design is the so-called "ABBA" design, where A is the treatment, B the absence of it—or another treatment. Measurements are made at the beginning of each labeled period and at the end. Here we may be able to control for the spontaneous remission possibility and sundry interaction effects. This is quite a good design for experiments on supportive or incremental treatments, for example, we teach 50 words of vocabulary by method A then 50 more by method B—and to eliminate the possibility that B only works when it follows A, we now reverse the order, and apply B first, and then A. Obviously more sophisticated approaches are possible by using curve-fitting to extrapolate (or interpolate) to an expectable future (or past) level and compare that with the actual level.

The classic fallacy in this area is probably that of the governor of Connecticut, who introduced automatic license suspension for the first speeding violation and got a very large reduction in the highway fatality rate immediately, on the basis of which he crowed a good deal and ran for U.S. Senator. But a look at the variability of the fatality rate in previous years would have made a statistician nervous, and sure enough, it soon swung up again in its fairly random way. (Ref. *Interrupted Time Series Designs*, Glass et al. (University of Colorado, 1976.)

INTERVENTIONIST (evaluation) One which, intentionally or inadvertently, produces substantial changes in the evaluand. While this is commonly expected from formative evaluation, it is supposed to occur through a direction change decided on by program management; sometimes it occurs through direct action by the program staff. Summative evaluation of stable ongoing programs often becomes de facto formative, that is, interventionist, when published. But there are also cases where the evaluator meddles, sometimes improperly, sometimes driven by a sense of moral outrage (and still perhaps improperly); these can raise difficult questions of professional ethics. Historical evaluations are immune to this, and of the concurrent approaches, **goal-free** comes closest. See **Proactive.**

INTERVIEWING One of the most common procedures in **personnel evaluation**, particularly though not only used for selection. Much in-

199

terviewing is done at about the level of inkblotreading, as the validity research makes clear. Although sophisticated approaches are possible, it never seems to be a requirement on the usual interviewer (solo or panel member) to know anything about such approaches—and, even more to the point, about the serious errors and illegalities that commonly occur (e.g., questions about arrest record, history of mental illness, or parental status are illicit, as are very short interviews or those for which adequate notes are not taken; and unstructured interviews are legally risky). Extremely important information can be obtained from interviews, if they are reasonably well structured in advance, and well run. (For example, one can agree on potential weaknesses suggested by the dossier and how to follow them up; on descriptions of critical incidents that relate to some or all major job responsibilities, and on a scoring form for assessing the interviewee's responses.) Nevertheless, some experts recommend that interviews not be used for selection at all because they are so rarely used well—instead recommending that one use them to inform, recruit, and display. Frequent errors include asking too few questions; focusing on what applicants are, or are like, rather than whether they can and will do the job (likings have a place, but need to be separately rated); failing to get *independent ratings* from interviewers (on Can Do and Will Do for each responsibility) prior to discussion; going for an overall impression instead of deciding on how the judgments from different interviewers are to be combined; not deciding how the performance on different criteria are to be combined (the separate scores could be compensatory, multiple-hurdle, or multiple-cutoff); not using the same critical incidents for each candidate; overstructuring so that the candidates have no chance to present themselves; not doing interviewer-specific evaluations via follow-up. The key work is *The Employment Interview: Theory, Research, and Practice*, Eder and Ferris, eds. (Sage, 1989) and it should be required reading for anyone who will take part in any interview.

IRRELEVANT EXPERTISE See Fallacy of irrelevant expertise.

IS/OUGHT DISTINCTION Often believed to be the same as the fact/value distinction, and used to support the value-free conception of science. The argument was that one can never derive an 'ought claim'—an assertion about what ought to be the case—from premises that only contain statements of (descriptive) fact—assertions about what is the case. Coupled with the (false) premise that science only contains such statements of fact, this would mean it excludes ought statements. Now, claims about what ought to be done are only a small subset of value claims, so the supposed equivalence between the fact/value distinction and the is/ought distinction is unsound. Even

200

so, ought claims are just as common and legitimate in science as outside it. They are to be found everywhere in science, from the content of lab manuals (which say how equipment ought to be set up, and [often] what the results ought to be), to discussing research and funding priorities (what ought to be done/funded in what order). Such claims are supported, when challenged, by appeal to evidence and definitions, like other scientific claims.

A small subset of all ought claims is found in the moral domain. (Talking to scientists, one often finds that they supposed the value-free doctrine was a way of excluding ethics, not all of evaluation, from science.) Moral ought claims may or may not be part of science, but their *logic* is no different from that of ought claims anywhere else, including the logic of deriving ought claims from 'is claims'. That logic cannot be attacked unless most of science is to be attacked. It's another question whether moral ought claims can always or ever be *substantiated* (this is the question of providing foundations for ethics) in the way that scientific ought claims can be substantiated. Of course, many ought claims in the domain of science are made that cannot be substantiated, so the issue is not whether all ought claims in every system of ethics ever or currently proposed are substantiable. See also **Logic of evaluation**.

ITEM BIAS It is relatively easy to identify *relative* item bias, that is (greater) bias in an item by comparison with a test as a whole. One simply looks for significant *differential* performance on that item by minorities, compared to their performance on the test as a whole (or on a subset of the items in the test that measure the same construct). Of course, this leaves open the question whether the test as a whole is biased, and that's not so easily determined. However, there are several indicators, ranging from content validity, determined by judges, to correlations with other tests or indicators. Excellent summaries of the issues are in the two articles, "Test Bias" and "Item Bias" in the *International Encyclopedia of Educational Evaluation*, Walberg and Haertel, eds. (Pergamon, 1990).

J

JND Just Noticeable Difference. A unit for psychological or phenomenological effects, including utility. In the **qualitative weight and sum** approach, for example, we use a plus as a weight for criteria that have JND status, then a pound sign for 'important' considerations, and a star for 'very important'.

JOB ANALYSIS A description of the work involved in a job by functional components, often necessary to provide remedial recommendations and a framework for **analytical evaluation or needs assessment**. Job analysis is a highly skilled task, which, like computer programming, is frequently done badly by those hired to do it because of the failure of the pay scale to reflect the payoffs from doing it well. But there are also limitations in its conceptualization. For example, it is often misused as the principal basis for job descriptions for hiring purposes. It can only be used in that role if it is supplemented with evaluative analysis that identifies duties and not just current practice. Job analyses of the secondary school math teacher may show that the modal job holder only knows a certain amount of mathematics, but one can't conclude that that amount of mathematics is adequate for the job or that it should be perpetuated by being treated as an ideal in future advertisements of job openings.

JOHN HENRY EFFECT (Gary Saretsky's term) The correlative effect to, or in an extended sense a special case of, the Hawthorne effect. It refers to the tendency of the *control* group to behave differently just because of the realization that they *are* the control group. For example, a control group of teachers using the traditional math program that is being run against an experimental program may—upon realizing that the honor of defending tradition lies upon them—perform much better during the period of the investigation than they would have otherwise, thus yielding an artificial result. The evaluations of performance contracting were remarkable, as Saretsky observed, in that the control groups performed much higher than usual. One cannot of course assume that the Hawthorne effect (on the experimental group) cancels out the John Henry effect. The effect suggests that one should do interrupted time series studies as well as simple comparisons with a control group. Named for a black folk hero in the U.S. who was told that the steam hammer was about to replace track layers and who

202

then performed at an extraordinary level to beat the machine—although the effort killed him.

JUDGMENT It is not accidental that the term "value-judgment" erroneously came to be thought of as the paradigm of evaluative claims; judgment is a very common part of evaluation, as it is of all serious scientific inference. (The absurdity of supposing that "value-judgments" could have no validity, unlike all other judgments, was an additional and gratuitous error.) The function of the discipline of evaluation can be seen as largely a matter of reducing the element of judgment in evaluation, *or* reducing the element of arbitrariness in the necessary judgments, for example, by reducing the sources of bias in the judges by using double-blind design, teams, **parallel panels, convergence groups, calibration** training, and so on. The most important fact about judgment is not that it isn't as objective as measurement (true) but that one can distinguish good judgment from bad judgment (and train good judges).

JUDICIAL or **JURISPRUDENTIAL MODEL** (of evaluation) Bob Wolf's preferred term and a term sometimes used for his version—or, rather, extension—of **advocate-adversary evaluation**. He emphasizes that the law as a metaphor for evaluation involves much more than an adversarial debate—it also includes the fact-finding phase, cross-examination, evidentiary and procedural rules, and so on. It involves a kind of inquiry process that is markedly different from the social scientific one, one that in several ways is tailored to needs more like those of evaluation (the action-related decision, the obligatory simplifications because of time, budget, and audience limitations, the dependence on a particular judge and jury, the fate of individuals at stake, and so forth). Wolf sees the **educational role** of the judicial process (teaching the jury the rules of just inquiry) as a key feature of the judicial model and it is certainly a strong analogy with a common process in evaluation. He provides an excellent brief account of the model in *The International Encyclopedia of Educational Evaluation*, Wahlberg and Haertel, eds. (Pergamon, 1990).

JURY TRIAL A simulation of the legal procedure; used in TA, advocate-adversary evaluation, and see preceding entry.

K

KEY EVALUATION CHECKLIST (KEC) This is a general checklist for many kinds of evaluation, but especially for program evaluation. On a specific evaluation job, it often needs to be supplemented by a well-developed field-specific checklist, but there are four cases where it is valuable by itself: (i) generating or checking field-specific checklists; (ii) working in areas where those are not available; (iii) doing multiprogram evaluation when the range of programs is extremely diverse; and (iv) for meta-evaluation, where again a checklist has to apply to a vast range of fields. On many other occasions, it is a useful supplement to local checklists since the latter are often not founded on a comprehensive approach to evaluation. See also Checklist.

What follows is not intended to be a full explanation of the KEC and its application, something that is more appropriate in a conventional text, where worked examples can be appended. It simply serves to identify the many dimensions that must be explored prior to the final synthesis in an evaluation. It is nearly always essential to check every one: this is not a list of *desiderata*—items that it is desirable to check—but of *'necessitata'*—items that *must* be checked in order to avoid invalidity in the evaluation. A few words are given to indicate the sense in which each of the checkpoint labels is intended, the labels themselves being kept very short to make them mnemonically and referentially useful; all labels are expanded as entries elsewhere in the Thesaurus. (They are not in bold print here, to avoid giving the reader the impression that what follows them is a full thesaurus entry.)

Many iterations of the KEC are involved in a typical evaluation, generating a process of successive approximation. (If the evaluation is to be 'pure' goal-free, the field personnel, at least, will modify the given sequence in the way indicated.)

The KEC underlines the point that evaluation is multidisciplinary in method as well as a discipline in its own right. It cannot be seen as a straightforward application of standard methods in the traditional social science repertoire. In the traditional social sciences, very few of the checkpoints are addressed in anything like the way required in evaluation. Moreover, the use of the KEC is not completed before the evaluation begins; it can serve to generate a proposal, but will also serve to force changes of procedure on the evaluator as new facts and

204

background emerge.

1. DESCRIPTION What is to be evaluated? (Called the 'evaluand'.) A *correct* description/measurement, probably not the official one and possibly not a good match to the vendor's label or descriptive phrases (many of which beg key evaluative questions). The description should provide an overview and a method of identification of the same or similar programs at other sites, not an installation recipe; it is normally couched in nonevaluative language but may use language that involves low-level, here-undisputed, evaluative language ("good parking space"). It should identify **components**, if any, their actual functions, and their relationships (as well as the actual functions of the whole evaluand). It should translate any key terms into operational language and check the translation with the client and perhaps with others (examples: literacy, poverty, bias, ethnicity). It's often useful to divide Description into four parts, corresponding to description of: (1.1) overall nature, function, and operation; (1.2) the components, their functions and relationships (e.g., organization charts, production flow diagrams, staff qualifications); (1.3) the delivery system (interface to **recipients**); and (1.4) the support system or infrastructure, which includes the physical environment, maintenance/service/update system, the instruction/training system for users/providers, the management's monitoring system (if any) for checking on proper use/maintenance/quality.

When the evaluation process begins, the evaluator usually has only the client's descriptions of the evaluand and its functions and so on. As the evaluation proceeds, descriptions from staff, users, monitors, and others will be gathered, and direct observation/tests/measurements will be made. Eventually only the most accurate description will survive under this checkpoint, but the others are important and should be retained—and used as notes for Checkpoint 2 (Background and Context)—because they provide important cues as to what problems (for example, misperceptions or inconsistent perceptions) should be addressed in the evaluation and in the final report.

2. BACKGROUND & CONTEXT The basis for perspective and design. Includes identification of **client** and **stakeholders**, their information needs, and decision options; *intended* function and *supposed* nature of the evaluand; *believed* performance now and in the future; expectations for the evaluation; desired type of evaluation (**formative vs. summative**, serious vs. **ritualistic, global** vs. **analytical, goal-based** vs. **goal-free**, and so on); resources available for the evaluation; history of the program, its relation to other programs; precedents, errors, enemies, allies, connections, perceived options, political constraints, prior evaluation efforts, and so on. Who gave you descrip-

tions or evaluations that were wrong/insightful? Who would or wouldn't cooperate? Why? In **goal-free** mode, much of this will be screened off from the field staff until their preliminary report. But in many cases, this is the checkpoint that guides you toward a feasible and sometimes easily manageable design instead of one that covers everything in the universe of program-related phenomena. Check the **evaluation parameters** list as you zero in on a design.

3. CONSUMER Who is impacted by the direct or indirect effects of the evaluand—or units within the evaluand, when analytic evaluation is being done—the 'downstream impacted group'? Who needs the evaluand and isn't getting it but *could* get it (potential consumers, here called the **market**; reaching them will also depend on Resources, see below). Distinguish recipients from indirectly impacted consumers. Note that the instigator and service providers are impacted, for example by having a job, but this does not make them consumers in the usual sense, because they do not receive the services that the program is set up to deliver. We should, however, consider them when looking at total effects (Outcomes) and can describe them as part of the *total* affected, impacted, or involved group—the impacted population. Taxpayers are usually part of this population. There are no consumers unless there is a delivery system that works, so looking at the delivery system (covered under Description) is one way to discover the true consumers. You don't just want a label for the consumers, you need some information about them; their background, their attitudes, and so on, depending on the case.

The *intended* consumers are identified as part of Background & Context. The difference between intended and actual with respect to the consumer population parallels the difference between intended and actual effects, in the sense of types of effect. Often, unintended consumers are subsumed, generally unconsciously, under 'side-effects'.

4. RESOURCES (Sometimes called the "strengths assessment" by contrast with the needs assessment of the next checkpoint). What is available for use by or for the evaluand? These are not what *is* used up, in, for example, purchase or maintenance, but what *could* be used, because the evaluation should ask whether the program (etc.) reached its potential (did all that was feasible). They include money, expertise, past experience, technology, quality of intake, and flexibility considerations. (Identifying Market, for Checkpoint 2, depends on potential and not just actual resources.) All of this has to take into account the political and legal constraints uncovered in the Context investigation. See **Harvard fallacy.**

5. VALUES The source of standards for converting facts into

evaluative conclusions. Often requires a **needs assessment** of the impacted and potentially impacted populations. But it must look at wants as well as needs; and also at values such as *judged* or believed standards of merit and ideals as well as at those that are relevant (even if their relevance [or existence] was not realized). Standards that must be considered include legal/ethical-moral/political/managerial/aesthetic/hedonic/logical/scientific (or other disciplinary)/-quality of life (and environment) standards; at any other validated or widely accepted standards that apply in the field, especially professional standards; at the defined goals of the program where a goal-based evaluation is undertaken; and at the needs (and so on) of the instigator, staff, inventor, and so on, since they are indirectly impacted. The legitimacy and relative importance of these often conflicting considerations will depend upon ethical, contextual, and functional considerations *and must be considered*; it is unprofessional to do relativistic evaluations in which you accept values from some other source without validation (direct or indirect). For example, you may have to decide whether the political value of a program offsets the substantial inequity that it involves.

It is from this checkpoint alone that one gets the value component in an evaluation—the element that makes it more than an assemblage of data. The values may apply to either process or outcome, and hence will turn up in the synthesis (Significance). NOTE: the very process of doing the needs assessment involves not only generating values, but, along the way, using other values (which you should of course identify and justify) to decide that the status quo needs improvement, or that deprivation of something currently provided would lead to an 'unsatisfactory' state of affairs. Thus, of the three points to which Values are applied—the status quo, the process of change (Process), and the results of change (Outcomes)—the first is already evaluated in this checkpoint.

6. PROCESS At this point, we apply the Values identfied in the last checkpoint to the process that we began to identify under Description. (Next we will apply them to the Outcomes; so this is the second of the three checkpoints that generate evaluative conclusions to go into the synthesis.) Process is here considered to cover everything associated with but not caused by the evaluand, plus (many) things caused by it that are still internal to it (e.g., staff enthusiasm). Thus, under Process we evaluate all aspects of the evaluand's nature, not just its operation. We ask ourselves: what values apply to, and what conclusions can we draw about, the *nature* and normal *operation* of the evaluand? For example, an evaluation done by the Office of the Inspector General in an agency may focus especially on efficient in-

vestment of floating funds and avoidance of fraud. An accreditation visit may focus on the academic qualifications of the teaching staff in a program. (We get the facts about nature and operation from Description and file them under that heading; the Values of course come from Checkpoint 5.)

The Process checkpoint applies equally to product evaluation—for example, we would look at the support and repair system for software, or the scientific accuracy of the contents and the typographical quality of a textbook under this heading. A typical immediate evaluative conclusion might be something like: "Violates safety standard X" or "Meets personnel standard Y". Often we have to do some further investigation of the process to see if the relevant standards are upheld; the results of the investigation will partly improve our Description but will also lead to direct evaluations. From Background and Context (Checkpoint 2), we will have an idea of what the Process is *supposed* to be, and that provides us with another kind of process evaluation, relating to misleading description and misconceptions; here we are likely to use an 'index of **implementation**'.

We can also look for indicators that are known to be correlated with certain long-term outcomes (whose emergence we may not have time to await). This is a common procedure in product evaluation, where we buy using the name and model number of a product tested in a consumer magazine. The brand name, for example, is an indicator of quality, not always reliable, but certainly a 'process' indicator. In personnel evaluation, style indicators (descriptors) are process variables, and usually illicit. We may also spot immediate or very fast Outcomes, whose occurrence overlaps Process; these are different from phenomena that are *part* of the Process.

7. OUTCOMES What effects are produced by the evaluand, whether intended or unintended? Setting up a matrix of possible effects is useful to get one started on the search; population affected x type of effect (cognitive/affective/psychomotor/health/social/environmental) x size of each x time of onset (during program/end of program/later) x duration (e.g., long-term reliability) x each component or dimension (if analytical evaluation is required). NOTES: (i) For some purposes, the intended effects should be separated from the unintended (e.g., program monitoring, legal accountability); for others, the distinction should not be made (consumer-oriented summative evaluation). (ii) Often the emphasis should be on 'value-added' rather than bare causal functioning (see **Harvard fallacy**). (iii) What to count as an outcome is a key design issue: for example, a choice must be made as to whether to count well-trained graduates of a secretarial school as the outcome, or well-employed graduates. (iv) Always dis-
208

tinguish immediate effects from Process—the effects are different from the program itself; the process is not. (v) One 'effect' of running a program is that you spend money; but that's not an outcome, it's simply a cost. (vi) Another 'effect' is that you employ people. This could be treated under Process, but it can best be treated separately as a **recoil effect**. (vii) Do not rely heavily on summary statistics unless the impacted population is homogeneous on the main dimensions of interest. Success with slow learners, minorities, or gifted, may be extremely important even if overall success is negligible. (viii) There are a number of effects that have been identified by name, for which the evaluator needs to watch out. These are not all the equivalent of fallacies in logic, but, along with statistical artefacts, many of them can lead to misleading results. Nearly twenty of them have their own entry here and they are listed under **Effects**.

The key methodology for this checkpoint focuses on the determination of causation. Mainstream social science methodology is often helpful, but often inadequate, and we must turn to models used by jurists, detectives, investigative journalist, clinicians, or historians. (For one approach, see **Modus operandi method**.)

8. COSTS Money vs. psychological vs. personnel vs. time vs. space; initial vs. recurrent; direct vs. indirect; nominal vs. discounted; actual vs. opportunity; by components if appropriate.

9. COMPARISONS with alternative options—include options recognized *and* unrecognized, those now available and those constructable. The leading contenders in this field are the **'critical competitors'** and are identified on cost-effectiveness grounds. They normally include ones that produce similar or better effects for less cost and better effects for a manageable extra cost (check Resources). Often, there is a major choice between governmental and private sector alternatives.

10. GENERALIZABILITY (or 'potential' or 'versatility' [cf. **'external validity'**]). Utility if used by or for other people/places/-times/versions. ("People" refers to staff as well as recipients.) This overlaps with Market considerations (under the Consumer checkpoint), and should be constrained by considerations of deliverability/-saleability/exportability/durability/modifiability.

11. SIGNIFICANCE A rating of overall importance, applied to a **synthesis** of all the above, that is (approximately) a rating on *comparative cost-effectiveness in meeting ranked true needs, including side-effects, generalizability, and ethical/legal considerations*. The process of synthesis cannot normally be left to the client, who is usually ill-equipped by training or objectivity to do it; and the formula approaches of, for example, cost-benefit calculations are only rarely adequate. The **qualita-**

tive **weight and sum** approach is often useful. Judges are sometimes the most feasible and sometimes the best approach to determining overall significance, but their validity is dubious without **calibration**. The validation of the synthesizing procedure is often one of the most difficult tasks in evaluation. Commentary on the extent to which goals have been achieved may or may not be incorporated; other things being equal, it is a service to do so, but this issue is best investigated after a **goal-free approach** has led to its own conclusions.

12. RECOMMENDATIONS These may or may not be requested, and may or may not follow from the evaluation; even if requested it may not be feasible to provide any without a major secondary project, because it is often the case that the only type that would be appropriate is such as to require massive and independent expense for local experts. (Here you need to look carefully at the Resources available for the evaluation.)

13. REPORT Vocabulary, length, format, medium, time, location, and personnel for the presentation(s) need careful scrutiny, as do protection/privacy/publicity and prior screening or circulation of preliminary and/or final drafts. In a formative evaluation, the reporting process extends into an educational process (about what counts as merit, and how it can be improved), which may take as much as half the time. The report has to carry a scientific and commonsensical message, but it is also a case where data visualization and its aesthetic dimension is deeply involved. As the software develops further, we may expect to see more of multimedia and eventually virtual reality techniques used for reporting.

14. META-EVALUATION This checkpoint is the link to a second level of evaluation—the evaluation of the first-level evaluation. Professionalism requires treating one's own product in the same critical way that one does the evaluand. See **Meta-evaluation**. Also see **GAO** for another checklist.

KILL THE MESSENGER (phenomenon) The tendency to punish the bearer of bad tidings, who is often the evaluator. A phenomenon related to **valuephobia**—mindless striking back at the proximate cause of pain, even when it's clear this is neither just punishment nor likely to be curative of the problem. Much of the current attack on testing—for example, minimum competence testing for graduation or teaching licensure—is pure KTM, like many of the elaborately rationalized earlier attacks on course grades. The presence of the rationalizations identify these as specimens of the subspecies AFTOC: Kill The Messenger—After a Fair Trial, Of Course.

KISS Acronym for the advice most often needed by the academic doing evaluation consulting: Keep It Simple, Stupid. Academics aren't

210

used to being called stupid, so they think this is meant metaphorically, to which one should say, "TISS, TISS": Take It Seriously, Stupid. To someone in the field, giving overlong presentations full of inappropriate precision is paradigm stupidity, and that was much of the early history of program evaluation. Evaluation is a pragmatic discipline, and if one can't grasp that and implement the consequences, one isn't very bright. (The bowdlerized version of KISS is Keep it Simple, Sweetheart.)

L

LAISSEZ-FAIRE (evaluation) "Let the facts speak for themselves". But do they? What do they say? Do they say the same thing to different listeners? This is a more extreme version of the refusal to con-summate an evaluation; here, even the subevaluations are balked at. Once in a while this approach is justified, but usually it's simply a cop-out, a refusal to do the hard professional task of synthesis and its justification. The laissez-faire approach is attractive to valuephobes—and to anyone else when the results are going to be controversial. The major risk in the responsive/naturalistic/illuminative approach is sliding into laissez-faire evaluation, that is—to put it *slightly* tendentiously—no evaluation at all.

LAYERING, LAYERED (reports, texts, or designs) Layering is a pro-cedure used in the construction of reports or designs. By contrast with layering, footnotes and appendixes unpack reports by attaching ex-planations of—or more details about—*parts* of the report to the main stem of the report, a *branching* approach. Layers represent a *stacking* approach in which different layers provide different views of the *whole* report. The simplest form of layered report is one that begins with an abstract or an executive summary. Here, the top layer can serve three groups of readers: (i) those who can't tell from the title alone (plus other contextual data such as the organizational source, authors, or journal title) whether they are interested in the details or not, and hence need more information; (ii) those who are definitely interested, but who will not have time to read the whole report; and (iii) those who are going to read it anyway, but like to have—or will read it with more understanding if they get—an advance organizer. Call these diggers, racers, and readers. There are two kinds of abstract: synopses and metadescriptions. Synopses provide summaries of *actual* content; metadescriptions outline the *type* of discussion in the content without summarizing it ("We begin with a review of the literature... identify the dominant view... discuss some of the main objections to the dominant view"). Racers will definitely not benefit from a metadescription, and diggers will probably not benefit from one. Hence, this very common type of abstract is a very poor approach, and editors should normally require synopses. Authors sometimes favor metadescriptions in order to convert racers to readers, but in many cases the strategy loses far more readers than it gains.

In the case of a book, the table of contents often functions as a layer; it can be written so as to fit anywhere on an even longer spectrum that runs from mere numbering, through cryptic labeling metadescription, all the way to summary. Abstracts of long articles sometimes consist in a list of subheads, which is one of the dictionary definitions of "synopsis"; if these are well-phrased they can come close to providing a useful summary; if cryptic, only a metadescription. The layers instanced so far are common practices in the disciplines, but reflection on their logic leads to some more unusual suggestions for use—particularly, but not only—in evaluation.

Layers can, for example, run down other dimensions than level of detail; they can, for example, be useful in dealing with a variety of audience backgrounds. CIRCE has produced outstanding examples of this approach, in which the top layer of a multipage pamphlet provides a nontechnical summary—perhaps only one page in length—and succeeding layers provide reports with increasing amounts of technical analysis. Note how the top layer is different from an abstract (does not use technical language), and how the addition of the other layers differs from branching. (Of course, lower layers might also use branching.) The layering approach might also be used as a vehicle for advocate-adversary reports or other multiperspectival reports. Layers may also interpolate the usual dichotomy of table of contents and text; using a good outliner in a word processor, one can often usefully print a short table of contents, a list of all first-level subheads, and a longer list of all second-level subs, perhaps even with the first lines of the text. While this might not seem useful until you've seen it, it turns out to be rather helpful and to have reactive effects that are sometimes desirable—that is, the author tends to put the point into the first sentence, so that it will show up in that layer. The extra pages for these layered tables of contents will sometimes eliminate half of all labor with the index. It certainly assists diggers and racers and should be considered by the online services as a more-expensive supplement to the abstract they usually provide.

LEARNER VERIFICATION A phrase of Ken Komoski's, then president of EPIE, that refers to the process of (i) establishing that educational products actually work with the intended audience, and (ii) systematically improving them in the light of the results of field tests. At one stage required by law in Florida and being considered for that status elsewhere. The first response of publishers was to submit letters from teachers testifying that the materials worked, something that can usually be done with the worst programs. This is not the

213

R&D process to which the term refers. Some of the early programmed texts were good examples of learner verification. Of course, it's costly, but so are four-color plates and glossy paper. It simply represents the application to educational products of the procedures of quality control and development without which other consumer goods are illegal or dysfunctional or suboptimal.

LEVEL OF EFFORT Level of effort is normally specified in terms of person-years of work (or work-years [originally man-years]), but on a small project it might be specified in terms of person-months. It refers to the amount of direct labor that will be required, and it is presumed that the labor will be of the appropriate professional level; subsidiary help such as clerical and janitorial is either budgeted independently or regarded as part of the support cost, that is, included in a professional person-year of work. RFPs will often not describe the maximum sum in dollars that is countenanced for the proposal, but may instead specify it in terms of person-years. Various translations of a person-year unit into dollars are used; this will depend on the agency, the level of professionalism required, whether or not overhead and clerical support is separately specified, and so on. Figures from $30,000 to over $50,000 per person-year are used at times. More thoughts under **Effort, level of**; see also **Quantum of effort**.

LICENSING (of evaluators) See **Evaluation registry**.

LIMITS OF EVALUATION Most evaluations are, quite properly, addressed to a small subset of the issues about the evaluand that have some possible evaluation relevance. Some are improperly restricted by error or deliberate censorship. Creating a finite task out of the near-infinite possibilities depends heavily on a thorough and accurate reading of the context and background of the evaluation situation; see the Background and Context checkpoint in the **KEC**.

LINEAR COMBINATION APPROACH The commonsense way of combining the performance of evaluands on various dimensions, by weighting each of them and then adding them up. Called "**numerical weight and sum**" here, and contrasted with **qualitative weight and sum**. When used in personnel evaluation—where the 'various dimensions' may also be the ratings of various evaluators—the approach is now usually described as '**compensatory**' (because deficiencies on one scale—or in the view of one evaluator—can be made up on the others). The usual contrast is with **multiple-cutoff** approaches, here usually referred to as ones where there are 'required minima' on some dimensions. Of course, the restriction to *linear* combinations is not essential, although it's well proven that linear combinations do extremely well or better than most supposedly higher-order combinatorial functions; in some cases, however, one would want to use ratios

214

(The bank loan decision is improved by using one ratio [of the six that loan officers believe important], namely debts to assets.)

LITERARY CRITICISM The evaluation of works of literature. In some ways an illuminating model for evaluation—a good corrective for some emphases of the social science model. In other ways, a sorry tale of soft-headed thinking. Various attempts have been made to "tighten up" literary criticism in the last half century, of which the New Criticism movement is perhaps the best known, but they all display rather obvious and unjustified preferences of their own (that is, biases)—exactly what they are created to avoid. Current post-modernism and deconstructionism have even less claim to respect. The time may be right to try again, using what we now know about **sensory evaluation**—and perhaps **responsive** and **illuminative evaluation**—to remind us of how to objectify the objectifiable while illuminating the essentially subjective. Conversely, a good deal can be learned from a study of the efforts of F. R. Leavis (the doyen of the New Critics) and T. S. Eliot in his critical essays to precisify and objectify criticism. Eliot's view that "comparison and analysis are the chief tools of the critic" (Eliot, 1932) and, even more, his practice of displaying very specific and carefully chosen passages to make points would find favor with the responsive evaluators (and others) today. Ezra Pound and Leavis went even further toward exhibiting the concrete instance (rather than the general principle) to make a point. This idiographic, antinomothetic approach is not, contrary to some popular philosophy of science, an alternative to scientific method, but in practice it failed to avoid various style or process biases, and too often (e.g., with Empson) became precious at the expense of logic. One can no more forget the logic of plot, the constraints of philosophical analysis, or the limits of psychological possibility in fiction than the logic of responsibility and evaluation, and the limits of logistical possibility in program evaluation. Ref: "The Objectivity of Aesthetic Evaluation", *The Monist*, Vol. 50, No. 2, April, 1966.

LOCAL EXPERT A local expert (used and, rarely, trained as an evaluator) is someone from the same field as the program or person being evaluated. There's a long spectrum of specialization, from a "health area evaluator", to a nursing program evaluator, to—even more commonly—"someone else from Texas in nursing education" (but without evaluation expertise). The gains are in relatively specific expertise; the losses are **shared bias** and (usually) lack of knowledge of or experience with the more serious aspects of, for instance, program evaluation as a discipline. If you're looking for a friendly evaluator, it's understood that you use a local one—you get a prima facie ally against everyone else, who will nearly always recommend increased resources, and can hardly be separated from hopes of jobs with you in the future, and perhaps also the hope that you will return the favor one day (**Secret-contract bias**). If you want objectivity/validity *always* go for the mix—one local, one **general-purpose**—and ask for separate reports; after you get them, you can always try a convergence session. If your budget is too small for the travel costs or fees of a national-level evaluator, just find a *geographically local* general-purpose program evaluator or at the worst just a local evaluator from another discipline—there are plenty around—to form a team with the one from your locality.

LOCUS OF CONTROL Popular 'affective' variable, referring roughly to the location someone feels is appropriate for the center of power in the universe on a scale from "inside me" to "far, far away". A typical item might ask about the extent to which the subjects feel they control their own destiny. In fact, this is often a simple test of knowledge about reality and not affective (depending on how much stress is put on the feeling part of the item), and where it *is* affective, the affect may be judged as appropriate or inappropriate. These items are often misinterpreted, for example, by taking any movement toward internalization of locus of control as a gain, whereas it may be a sign of loss of contact with reality. See **Affective**.

LOGIC The study of sound reasoning, and the systems of rules resulting from that study. Logic is a **transdiscipline**, and nearly as general as evaluation, but it is junior to evaluation since it is itself prescriptive, that is, evaluative. Of course, the **logic of evaluation**—a reconstructive effort—is a branch of logic; but evaluation began long before language crystallized, let alone logic, as artisans learnt to improve and reject artefacts.

LOGIC OF EVALUATION The key function of evaluative inference is moving validly to evaluative conclusions from factual (and of course definitional) premises; so the key task of the logic of evaluation is to show how this can be justified. Doing this is a task that was and still is thought to be impossible by most logicians and scientists—social scientists in particular. The first part of this entry addresses the problem from a practical point of view, by exhibiting two widely used and respectable paradigms. The second part looks at some semitechnical problems with extending the paradigms to other fields of evaluation, and the third part addresses the problem in the technical language of the logician and philosopher of science. Finally a reference is made to one or two other topics in the logic of evaluation.

1. Whatever the merits of the discussion among logicians, everyday product evaluations demonstrate the feasibility of facts-to-values inference. They begin with facts about the performance of various

216

products, and draw conclusions about their relative or absolute merit. One can hardly argue that every issue of *Consumer Reports* is full of fallacies. For practical purposes, the product evaluation paradigm is sound and generalizable. If one doubts this, one can turn instead to the working scientist's equivalent of product evaluation: the evaluation of data, designs, hypotheses, papers for publication or in publications, instruments, and so on. In each case, the scientist works from factual evidence about performance and gets to an evaluative conclusion; if challenged s/he has no problems with defending the conclusion by appealing to evidence, definitions, and valid inference.

2. The usual attack on the product evaluation paradigm as an example of how to infer evaluative conclusions from factual premises suggests that it relies on shared values among its readers, and this won't transfer to, say, program evaluation. People don't disagree radically about what they value in a dishwashing detergent; but they do disagree about what they want from a drug clinic, or police patrols, or a school curriculum. This criticism involves two mistakes. In the first place, it is not shared values that support the validity of product evaluations. You will have noticed that Consumers Union rarely if ever does a survey to check what people value in appliances and products. Nor do scientists do surveys about what makes a good theory. This is not because they believe they have infallible intuitions about preferences. It is because they share an understanding of the meaning of the terms describing the evaluand. If you know what a watch is, you know that time-keeping accuracy, legibility, and durability are merits in a watch; and if you know that, you know how to establish some (prima facie) evaluative conclusions from factual premises about the comparative merit of watches. (Similarly in the case of scientific theories.) The names of most products and methodological entities have a logic somewhat like that of ideal types—entities long familiar from the scientific field where 'ideal gas', 'perfectly elastic spring', 'blue-collar worker', 'perfect competition', and so on, serve a useful purpose. So, conclusions about watches, dishwashers, theories, and so on, follow directly from understanding the meaning of the terms (their implicit definition, the ideals built into understanding the concept) and the facts about their performance.

These conclusions are not shown to be wrong by the existence of 'aberrant' taste profiles among consumers—people who buy Rolex DayDate watches at $20,000, despite the fact they are much less accurate, harder to read, require more frequent and more expensive maintenance, and are more likely to incite bodily assault on the wearer than the Swiss Microtec at $80 (the current accuracy and luminosity champion). The existence of status buyers does not show that it's

217

wrong to call the Microtec a Best Buy, nor even that it's wrong to list it top for merit *as a watch*. Legitimating that kind of inference is part of the logic of descriptors for products, which are abstractions from a complex of indicators that includes functions. Another part of the same logic is grouping by price: we will often protect a product evaluation against attack by introducing price categories. Then we can recognize superiority at a higher price, as when we say that the Lexus 400 is a better car than the Nissan Maxima, but reserve the right to say that the Maxima is the best car in its price class. The Rolex, on the other hand, isn't a better watch than the Microtec. It's only a better status symbol—and that only among people with limited appreciation of technology—which has almost nothing to do with its merit as a watch.

Real life performance studies, chief source of the facts in product evaluation, involve slightly more than checking performance on the criteria built into the common meaning. The simulated or actual field tests (i) uncover further criteria that are obviously relevant (usually confirmed by unanimous consent of the lab staff, but a focus group might be used), and (ii) lead to connecting the original and new criteria to empirical measures. For example, although (perhaps) not a part of the specific meaning of "electric light bulb", electrical safety is certainly a criterion of merit for them, and measures of this have to be devised. (iii) Testing also assists with the procedure of 'price-slicing', that is, with identifying good cutting points for cost categories (e.g., economy cars, luxury cars) and with function-slicing into function-defined subcategories such as 'family sedan', 'van', 'sports car', and so on. The introduction of subcategories preserves the evaluative conclusions from the charge of invalidity by substituting limited validity. However, these are just refinements; the bottom line is that the product evaluation paradigm survives the attack on fact-value inferences by using functional analysis, rather than the variable and elusive facts of value surveys, to establish its evaluative conclusions from factual premises. Our language implicitly defines ideal types in the product field, as it often does in the psychological and sociological field, and we use them, with the kind of refinements indicated, as the norms against which we rate actual products. The ideal types themselves are based on functional and definitional analysis, not on popularity polls. The same model we use in product evaluation applies—with minor modifications—to candidates via job descriptions, to building plans via specs, and to social programs in a similar way (see below).

So, evaluation does not sneak in dubious hidden premises or arbitrary assumptions about what is good and bad, let alone what is believed to be good and bad. It only needs to use the usual 'definitions',

218

that is, conceptions of functional entities, part of whose conception is that they are better examples of their kind if they perform their defining functions better, itself a definitional truth.

But what about ethical considerations? Should we fault products whose containers do not use recycled material? Those that might hurt inquisitive children, although there are none in our family? The soft answer is to say that the role of ethics here is no different from its role in all professional activities; it has a role, and professional codes exist—or should be created—to spell it out. The hard answer is to say that ethical considerations are simply general considerations of social strategy (analogous to legal considerations), and social strategies are subject to evaluation just as any policies. (See **Ethics**.) So, to the extent that ethics comes in, the ethical issues have to be sorted out before the task is complete; and sorting them out is an evaluative issue, too. This is no different from the fact that personnel issues or fiscal or legal issues may have to be sorted out before we can draw final evaluative conclusions about a program or an institution—or a war.

Another problem that has to be thought out concerns the relative vagueness of the concept of 'proper function of a drug clinic' by contrast with 'proper function of a ball-point pen'. A good analogy here is with 'the proper function of the MMPI (or any standardized test)'. It's not the same as the originally intended or modified function (the fallacy of **goal-achievement evaluation**), but it is a function of the interaction of the needs environment and the resources available. Basically, when we do program evaluation, we have to hammer out the best function and the merit of the program concurrently. It's not a trivial process, but it's no more problematic than doing the same thing with a psychological test or a scientific instrument.

But suppose we were to fall back on surveys. Even there, more objectivity is possible than is commonly supposed. Suppose, for example, that one does a survey of preferences as part of a needs assessment, or in a case where wants are the driving parameters (i.e., where ethics does not supervene). Suppose it turns out that the respondents have a wide range of different views about what is desirable. Suppose, furthermore, that the performance of the candidates on different criteria is not at all the same. This is a fairly common kind of situation and it is one that is often pointed to as a reason for thinking that there cannot be said to be any objectivity about evaluations: "The best X will be quite different for different peoples." In fact, even without using any of the usual segregating, screening, and idealizing procedures, the results are often exceedingly robust and generalizable. That is, the best X will be best for all the players. This obviously occurs when one candidate outscores the others on all criteria, since this makes the differences in the weighting of the criteria irrelevant. But it also occurs in a very wide range of cases where several candidates win on one or another criterion, *but the amount they win by, when multiplied by the (various) weightings of the criterion, is not enough to offset the size and number of wins by the leading candidate.* Hence no relativistic conclusion about evaluation follows from the fact of large differences in the values of consumers, whether or not combined with large differences in the performance of the candidates on the valued dimensions. There still can be, and often are, outright winners, which can be said to be the best for everyone. These are cases where the winners simply overwhelm the opposition.

3. Technical issues. (i) It's clear that a central role is played here by the notion of cluster concepts or 'criterial definitions', by contrast with classical definitions which were substitution rules or sets of logically necessary and sufficient conditions. For example, the meaning of "watch" is said to have definitional criteria like time-keeping ability, which automatically generate criteria of merit. Most terms in the common language and in the technical languages of the disciplines are cluster concepts. This fact destroys the so-called 'open question argument' of G. E. Moore, which was supposed to show that the meaning of evaluative terms could not be 'reduced' to nonevaluative concepts. Suggested reductions were said to commit 'the naturalistic fallacy', but only do so if so simplistic as not to be worth considering. The way in which criteria of merit are built into the concept of "watch" can hardly be said to be fallacious. (Ref. "The Logic of Criteria", *Journal of Philosophy*, October, 1959, reprinted in *Criteria*, ed. John V. Canfield [Garland, 1986]). (ii) Recognizing the nature and ubiquity of cluster concepts also leads to the notion of **probative inference**, the more general concept of inference that subsumes inductive and evaluative inference. (ii) Probative inference generates prima facie conclusions instead of categorical, conditional, or (quantitative) probabilistic ones. Probative inference can be used to generate conclusions using the fundamental *qualitative* meaning of probability ("it's an apple, so the inside is probably a very different color from the skin"), from which the more mathematical versions derive in special cases, and thus it is linked to one type of inductive inference. Inference to the best explanation is also probative inference, as are most inferences to legal or evaluative conclusions. (iv) One aspect of probative inference is its iterative or potentially iterative nature. That is, a first round of probative inference generates prima facie conclusions, which are tested by further investigation and modified in the light of new data, reaching gradually higher levels of justified confidence, but never transcending the possibility of
220

empirical errors. This feature, so characteristic of the process of legal reasoning, is equally characteristic of evaluative inference with its long and multidimensional checklists. It is also characteristic of much scientific reasoning, although scientists appear to forget this when they raise the prima facie nature of evaluative conclusions as a sign that the inference to them is not really scientific. One often hears the question, "But how do you know there aren't some other considerations that will override these ones?" Answer: for the same reason you sometimes know the explanation of a physical phenomenon. You look hard for alternatives; even then, you can never be absolutely sure, but you can become increasingly sure by careful iterative investigation, just as with the process of confirming a tentative hypothesis in a scientific (or criminal) investigation.

Given all that, what can we say in the technical framework about inference from factual premises to evaluative conclusions? It seems obvious that it can't be done by strict deduction, but then almost no scientific and commonsensical inferences are deductive. If one accepts the idea that the only other choice is induction, and one is impressed by Popper's claim that there is no logic of induction—only guessing and confirming—that about closes the door. There appear to be only three possible options. (A) One can find a way around Popper's arguments and establish evaluative inference as inductive; (B) one can invent a new type of logic, which runs the risk of begging the question (why should one assume that giving a fallacy a new name makes it legitimate?); or (C) one can try to pull off a deductive trick that has appeared to be logically impossible to the best logicians of the last couple of centuries. In fact, one can do all three legitimately.

(A) Popper is certainly wrong about the logic of induction—ironically, he was still under the spell of the deductive paradigm. There is a logic of induction, albeit one whose principles cannot be formulated in the way that those of deductive logic are formulated. It is trainable, teachable, evaluable, and performed competently by every scientist all the time, brilliantly by a few (in this respect, it is no different from deduction). Its standards are the standards of scientific argument; its basic concepts are headed by the concept of explanation—the converse of inductive support—and its chief assistant, the concept of criterial definition, the converse of prima facie inference. It is for the most part an implicit logic—just as the grammar of a language is for the most part implicit, but quite precise enough for us to be able to create and distinguish grammatical sentences from ungrammatical ones in almost all cases. The tools of inductive argument and critique are analogies, examples, counterexamples, counterexplanations, and contrasts, more often than they are exact rules, and the statements it does use—

221

such as the 'rules of grammar'—are only rough guides to the truth, that is, hints and heuristics rather than exact laws. We use certain modifiers, like "prima facie", "balance of proof" and "ceteris paribus"—sometimes "probably"—to flag the qualifications involved. One of the paradigm examples of inductive reasoning is evaluative reasoning, and one need go no further than *Consumer Reports* to see how it works.

(B) It may be healthier to start further back, nearer to fundamentals, and couch all this in terms of a new logic that covers much of our everyday reasoning along with scientific and legal reasoning. On one such account—probative logic—logic is treated as necessarily and essentially like grammar, with occasional simple limit cases emerging— the occasional 'grammatical rules', on the one hand, and the rules of deductive logic on the other. (Mathematics is, on this view, a step beyond deductive logic in the direction of science, though not as far as Mill supposed.) In probative logic, context is as important as content; in traditional logic, the nature of logic is to be independent of context. In probative logic, definitions are never substitution rules, only explanations of meaning, capable of indefinite reformulation and refinement by those who understand the terms being defined, whenever they unsuccessful in conveying meaning. In terms of this account, evaluative reasoning is typical probative reasoning, as is most legal, commonsense, and scientific inference. (An extended though still programmatic account of this is to be found in "Probative Logic", in *Argumentation: Across the Lines of Discipline*, edited by van Eemeren, Grootendorst, Blair, and Willard [Foris, 1987]).

(C) Finally, one can (as does John Searle) make a good case that there are cases, albeit rare ones, where straight deduction can be used to break the taboo. (i) Murder is defined as unjustified killing (probably closer to correct usage than the usual dictionary definition of it as unlawful killing). "Unjustified" here means roughly "Not in self-defense, war, execution, or to save another's life". (ii) We can sometimes establish as a matter of fact, perhaps with the assistance of confession, that a murder for selfish reasons, by someone not in dire straits, has occurred. (iii) We can therefore conclude, from definitions and facts, that the responsible agent is a murderer, an evaluative conclusion. There are last-ditch ways to contest this example, notably by attacking the notion of definitions in context (as with the definition of "unjustified"), but they are indeed last ditch since they mean abandoning much of the dictionary's practice in order to save a logician's dogma. This case is closely analogous to the standard inference in product evaluation.

From this it should be clear that the logic of serious practical evaluation is not the invalid deductive inference from "I like X" to "I should have X" (or "I should get X" or "I deserve X"). True, in an appropriate context, that simple case provides the *limiting* case of *one type* of prima facie inference, common enough in product evaluation, the inference from what attributes one wants in a product to the conclusion that one should buy a particular one. It's just that there are many possible traps in the path from that premise to that conclusion, and the logic of evaluation is devoted to dealing with those traps.

There are several other issues that fall under the heading of the logic of evaluation, such as the nature of **needs assessments**—they often appear to be value premises, but seem also to be factual matters—and the problem of specifying the sometimes very complex logical object that is described as an evaluation—the matter of **evaluation parameters**. (Some of these issues were discussed at greater length in *The Logic of Evaluation*, Edgepress, 1981.) The practical logic of evaluation is discussed here in several entries, such as **Qualitative weight and sum, Refocusing, Functional analysis, Is/ought distinction**. See also **Symbols** (for evaluation).

LONGITUDINAL STUDY An investigation in which a particular individual or group of individuals is followed over a substantial period of time, to discover changes due to the influence of an evaluand, or maturation, or environment. The contrast is with a cross-sectional study. Theoretically, a longitudinal study could also be an experimental study, but none of those done on the effect of smoking on lung cancer are of this kind, although the results are almost as solid. In the human services area, it is very likely that longitudinal studies will be uncontrolled, certainly not experimentally controlled.

LONG-TERM EFFECTS In many cases, it is important to examine the effects of the program or product after an extended period of time; often this is the best possible criterion. Unfortunately, it's also the hardest one to pin down—in most fields. Bureaucratic arrangements, such as the difficulty of carrying funds over from one fiscal year to the next, often make investigation of these effects virtually impossible; they are compounded by the short attention span of political bodies. Longitudinal studies where one group is followed up over a long period are commonly recognized as standard procedure in the medical and drug areas, however, and there is an important example in education—the Project Talent study, now in its third decade. See **Overlearning**.

M

MACROEVALUATION See Global evaluation.

MAINTENANCE NEED A need that is currently met but will continue to be a need—for example, the need for a constant supply of oxygen. See Needs assessment.

MANAGEMENT INFORMATION SYSTEMS (MIS) Organized process for presenting management with data that is supposed to facilitate decision making. In many organizations, this is mainly an exercise in computer database design, but in fact, should include the results of many evaluations, only some of them specific to the particular organization.

MANAGEMENT (USE) OF EVALUATION While it would be tedious to elaborate on the theme that evaluation provides management's quality control system, from where the external evaluator sits one can't help noticing a few traps for managers that catch them too frequently. (The language of product evaluation is used here, but the comments apply across the board; and apply more strongly still to internal evaluators.) (i) It is tempting for managers to blame the evaluator or the evaluation for distasteful decisions that s/he later makes in accordance with the evaluation's recommendations. The cost of doing this is to 'poison the wells' for data-gathering on later occasions, and to induce a negative attitude toward evaluation. That's a high price to pay, especially if you're trying to develop a team that's working for better quality; you've set them against their source of feedback on quality. (ii) It is tempting to let Sales (or PR) get hold of the field trial process, as they have done with focus groups and beta testing in many organizations, especially in Detroit and Silicon Valley. The results are disastrous; lies about the process to the test consumers, and loss of vital feedback. Field trials have to fit into the project management plan *before* the design is set in concrete, not after; and the feedback has to go to the R&D team, not sales. (iii) It is tempting to think that your *products* are what need to be evaluated; but your *purchases* (and hires) should be evaluated in a way that sets an example for the evaluation of your products. (iv) It is tempting to let evaluators see that you'd prefer a favorable report to an accurate report. Since they want your business in the future, you're biasing them. *You have to prove to them* that you want a valid evaluation more than a friendly

224

one. They learnt long ago that managers who just *say* they want 'real evaluation' rarely mean it. One way is to spell out to them the costs of a poor product, and that they can save you from those costs; at least that shows you've thought the point through. See also **Personnel evaluation, Fitting the lock to the key, Evaluation management, Utilization.**

MAN-YEARS (properly, person-years or worker-years) See **Level of effort.**

MARKET Potential users, or accessible potential users. The Consumer and Generalizability checkpoints in the KEC both refer to the market for the product or program, because this is one consideration in assessing its importance. But markets do not often seek out what would in fact benefit them, so one must look at marketing mechanisms and experience. Many needed products, especially educational ones, are unsaleable by available means (e.g., good CAI programs). It is only possible to argue for developing such products if there is a special, preferably tested, plan for getting them used. No delivery system, no market penetration. No market penetration, no needs met. (It does not follow that the existence of a market implies needs met, or any other basis for worth.)

MARKING The process of grading or ranking student test or exam papers. More widely used in English-speaking nations outside North America. See **Scoring, Point constancy requirement, Rubric.**

MASSAGING (the data) Irreverent term for (mostly) legitimate synthesis of the raw results into the kind of conclusions that statistics can generate.

MASTERY LEVEL The level of performance actually *needed* on a criterion—sometimes, the level thought to be optimal and feasible. Focus on mastery level training does not accept anything less, and does not care about anything more. In fact, the 'mastery level' is often arbitrary. Closely tied to competency-based approaches. Represents one application of criterion-referenced testing.

MATCHING See **Control group.**

MATERIALS (evaluation) See **Product evaluation.**

MATRIX SAMPLING If you want to evaluate a new approach to preventive health care (or science education), you do not have to give a complete spectrum of tests (perhaps a total of ten) to all those impacted or even to a sample of them. You can perfectly well give one or two tests to each (or each in the sample), taking care that each test is given to a random subsample, and preferably that it is randomly associated with each of the others, if they are administered pairwise (in order to reduce any bias due to interactions between tests). This can yield (i) much less cost to you than full testing of the whole sample,

(ii) less strain on each subject, (iii) some contact with a much larger sample or even with each subject in the population, by contrast with giving all tests to a smaller sample, (iv) ensuring that all of a larger pool of items are used on some students. But—the trade-off—you will not be able to say much about each individual. You are only evaluating the treatment's *overall* value. This is a good example of the importance of getting the evaluation question clear before doing a design. Matrix sampling is exceptionally valuable for pretests aimed at getting a general sense of class preparedness and at gain score determination, since it avoids: (i) long tests; (ii) possible discouragement since students may do badly on a pretest; (iii) the problem of matching pre and post tests for difficulty, since you can draw items from the same pool; and (iv) it gives you better coverage of the domain.

MBO Management By Objectives, that is, state what you're trying to do in language that will make it possible to tell whether you succeeded. Not bad as a guide to planning (though it tends to overrigidify the institution), but disastrous as a model for personnel and program evaluation (though acceptable as *one* element in an evaluation design). See **Goal-achievement model, Administrator evaluation.**

MEAN (Stat.) (Cf. **Median, Mode**) The mean score on a test is that obtained by adding all the scores and dividing by the number of people taking it; one of several exact senses of "average". The mean is, however, heavily affected by the scores of the top and bottom scores in the class, and can thus be very unrepresentative of the majority.

MEASUREMENT Determination of the magnitude of a quantity, not necessarily, though typically, on a criterion-referenced test scale (e.g., by using feeler gauges) or on a continuous numerical scale. There are various types of measurement scale, in the loose sense, ranging from nominal (labeling) through ordinal (grading or ranking) to varieties of cardinal scales (numerical scoring). The standard scientific use refers to the latter only. Whatever is used to do the measurement, usually but not always distinguished from the experimenter, is called the measurement instrument. It may be a questionnaire or a test or an eye or a piece of apparatus. In certain contexts, we treat the observer as the instrument needing **calibration** or validation. Measurement is a common and sometimes large component of *standardized* evaluations; but a very small part of its logic, that is, of the justification for the evaluative conclusions.

MEDIAN (Stat.) The median performance on a test is that score or scores that divide(s) the group into two, as nearly as possible; the 'middle' performance. It provides one (fairly) exact sense for the ambiguous term "average". The median is not affected at all by the performance of the few students at the top and bottom of a class (cf. **mean**). On the other hand, as with the mean, it may be the case that no one scores at or near the median, so that it doesn't identify a "most representative individual" in the way that the **mode** does; and the median is more sensitive to a range of changes than the mode. Scoring at the 50th **percentile** is (usually) the same as having the median score, since about 50% are below you and about 50% above.

MEDIATED EVALUATION A more precise term for what is called (in a loose sense) **process evaluation**, meaning evaluation of something by looking at secondary indicators of merit, for example, name of manufacturer, proportion of Ph.D.s on faculty, or where someone went to college. The term "process evaluation" *also* refers to the *direct* check on valid process indicators, for example, on the ethicality of the process. See **Key evaluation checklist.**

MEDIATION (or ARBITRATION) MODEL (of evaluation). Little attention has been paid to the interesting social role and skills of the mediator or arbitrator—two different roles—that in several ways provide models for the evaluator, such as the combination of distancing with considerable dependence upon reaching agreement, the role of logic *and* persuasion, of ingenuity and empathy. It is a model that is particularly attractive to those who wish to avoid making value-judgments; that, of course, is its Achilles heel.

MEDICAL MODEL (of evaluation) In Sam Messick's version—in the *Encyclopedia of Educational Evaluation* (Jossey-Bass, 1976)—a contrast is drawn between the engineering model and the medical model. The engineering model "focuses upon input-output differences, frequently in relation to cost". The medical model, on the other hand—the one Messick favors—provides a considerably more complex analysis, enough to justify the treatment's generalization into other field settings, remediation suggestions, and side-effect predictions. The problem here is that this model takes us across the boundaries between evaluation and general causal investigations, thereby diluting the distinctive features of evaluation and so expanding its scope as to make results extremely difficult to obtain. It seems more sensible to appreciate *Consumer Reports* for what it gives us, rather than complain that it fails to give us explanations of the underlying mechanisms in the products and services that it rates. Cf. **Global** and **Analytical evaluation, Diagnosis, Etiology.**

MERIT The "intrinsic" value of evaluands, as opposed to extrinsic or system-related value/worth. For example, the merit of researchers lies in their skill and originality, whereas their worth (to the institution that employs them) might include the income they generate through grants, fame, or bequests, attracting other good faculty and students.

227

(Cf. Worth, Success.)

META-ANALYSIS (Gene Glass) The name for a *particular approach* to synthesizing quantitative studies on a common topic, involving the calculation of a special parameter for each ("effect size"). Its promise is to pick up something of value even from studies that do not, alone, meet the usual minimum standards of significance. Its danger is the one referred to in the computer programming field as the GIGO Principle—Garbage In, Garbage Out. While it is clear that a number of studies, none of which is statistically significant, can be integrated by a meta-analyst into a statistically significant result (because the combined N is larger), it is not clear how *invalid* designs can be integrated. Meta-analysis is a special approach to what is called the general problem of research (studies) integration or research synthesis; this array of terms for it reflects the fact that it is an intellectual activity that lies between data synthesis on the one hand and the evaluation of research on the other. As Light points out (in the first reference below) there is a residual element of judgment involved in several places in meta-analysis as in any research synthesis process; clarifying the basis for these judgments is a task for the evaluation methodologist, and Glass' efforts to do so have led to the burgeoning of a very fruitful area of (meta-) research. In the first instance, meta-evaluation is an approach to evaluating a body of knowledge; it's also an example of self-referent research analogous to meta-evaluation.

Note that with qualitative studies, there is no special methodology of meta-analysis; but it is often possible to quantify certain features of the studies such as the occurrence of a certain pattern, and treat this quantitatively, even meta-analytically.

An excellent early review of results and methods is in *Evaluation in Education* (Volume 4, No. 1, 1980), a special issue entitled "Research Integration: The State of the Art"; also excellent and more current is *Meta-Analysis* by Fredric Wolf (Sage, 1986). Levin raises some deeper problems in his essay in *Evaluation and Education at Quarter Century* (NSSE/University of Chicago, 1991).

META-EVALUATION Meta-evaluation is the evaluation of evaluations—indirectly, the evaluation of evaluators—and represents an ethical as well as a scientific obligation when the welfare of others is involved. It can and should be done in the first place by an evaluator on his or her own work; although the credibility of this is poor, the results are considerable gains in validity. Meta-evaluation can be done by applying an evaluation-specific checklist (see below), or a general checklist like the **Key Evaluation Checklist** (KEC) to the evaluation itself; this approach is spelled out in some detail below. (One could also use the **GAO** checklist.)

228

General comments: This practice is not different in principle from any scientific researcher looking over a design checklist before wrapping up a piece of research, or Deep Thought (the leading chess-playing program) reassessing the weights used in its evaluation function when planning strategy, against empirically validated standards. However, the multidimensionality of evaluation designs makes it unusually important. The results of self-evaluation are notoriously unreliable, however (for noncomputers, at least), so it is also desirable, wherever cost-justifiable, to use an independent evaluator for the meta-evaluation. This practice also assists the **balance of power** approach to fairness and validity in that it puts the primary evaluator in a similar position to the evaluee—both are evaluated on their performance. This arrangement can also have the same proactive (reactive) effect in increasing validity and reducing costs (of the evaluation) that the primary evaluation often has in increasing performance (of the primary evaluees). It also gives the evaluator and the evaluees some common ground that can increase their rapport, and it avoids the 'class-distinction' atmosphere stemming from the analogy with the supervisor/supervisee relationship.

Meta-evaluation is the professional imperative of evaluation: it represents the recognition that 'evaluation begins at home', that evaluation is self-referent and not just something one does to others. While it is an obligation of all professionals to ensure their own evaluation—and in some cases, notably psychoanalysis, this is seriously enforced (at least in the preservice phase)—it is especially deplorable if an *evaluator* does not have an immediate answer to the question, Who evaluates the evaluators? (After all, it's twenty centuries since the question achieved the status of an epigram: *Quis custodiet ipsos custodes?*) One answer should be that the evaluees do so, by having the chance to respond and to have that response (a demurrer) incorporated in the evaluation to their satisfaction, or passed on to the client intact. But that is not enough in this now-technical field; it must also be the case, in any serious context, that some professional evaluator is also involved in the meta-evaluation. (Consumers Union, like the French Army in the Dreyfus case, persists in regarding itself as above this obligation, and consequently persists in methodological errors of some importance to their ten million clients. See **Self-reference.**)

Meta-evaluation can be done formatively or summatively or both: Draft summative reports of a meta-evaluation, as in most evaluation, should (where possible) go to the evaluee—in this case, that happens to be the primary evaluator—for the correction of errors or the addition of **demurrers**, or endorsements, and when agreement is not

229

reached, both the report and the demurrers should go to the client. Summative meta-evaluation gives the client independent evidence about the technical competence of the primary evaluator and, where not commissioned by the client, should be considered by the primary evaluator as an evaluation service to the client and a way to improve the primary evaluation.

Who evaluates the meta-evaluator? No infinite regress is generated because investigation shows it usually doesn't pay after the first metalevel on most projects and after the second on any.

Specific checklists developed for evaluating evaluations include the following three; the twenty items in the first one have been gathered from many sources. (i) The Meta-Evaluation Checklist (MEC). An evaluation should be conceptually clear, comprehensible in all details, comprehensive, cost-effective, credible, ethical, explicit about the standards of merit or worth used and about the justification for them, feasible (in terms of the resources available), appropriately but not excessively precise and robust, politically and psychologically sensitive, reported to appropriate audiences in an appropriate way (which often means multiple reports, not necessarily all written), relevant to the client's and audiences' needs, secure, timely, and valid. Validity should be taken to include technical soundness, but may require care with construct validity that goes beyond current technical resources. Note the absence of **implemented** as a criterion; for legitimate indicators from this quarter, see **Utilization**. (ii) Bob Gowin's **QUEMAC** approach provides another checklist addressed specifically at meta-evaluations. So do (iii) the **Evaluation Standards**.

Self-referent use of the KEC: The KEC can be used in two ways for meta-evaluation. It can be used to generate a new evaluation (or design), which can then be compared to the actual one (the **repeated design** approach), or by applying the checklist *to* the original evaluation *as a product* (true meta-evaluation). The latter process might be taken to include the former as an appropriate scientific process consideration, but it *also* requires us to look at, for example, the cost-effectiveness of the evaluation itself, and at the differential costs of false positive and false negative errors in the evaluation. Evaluations should not, however, be evaluated in terms of their actual consequences (except by a historian), but only in terms of their *foreseeable consequences if used appropriately*.

Here's how the KEC looks when translated into an instrument for meta-evaluation.

1. DESCRIPTION The design, staffing, timelines, and so on, of the *evaluation*; the sources of data used for checkpoints and to fix all specifications and parameters; the choice of metaevaluator if there is
230

one.

2. BACKGROUND & CONTEXT Who demanded/requested/opposed this evaluation; were there prior evaluations; why another? Determine antecedent credibility of proposed evaluation approaches.

3. CONSUMER Identify clients and audiences for the evaluation; prior evaluators, other potential audiences that should have been audiences?

4. RESOURCES Resources for the evaluation; the source of constraints on design and hence on evaluation of the design or execution.

5. VALUES Criteria of merit for the evaluation, given the client's needs and relevant professional standards: timeliness, relevance, cost-effectiveness, justice, validity, meeting appropriate and relevant needs of client, and so on. Must be validated and not just quoted. Are any evaluative assumptions of the evaluator evident in the evaluation, or is it appropriately transparent in this respect?

6. PROCESS Was the evaluation designed and executed well; for example, was it set up to facilitate its own evaluation? To best report and disseminate the findings? Did the evaluator respect confidentiality? Enhance credibility? Assess results of false positive vs. false negative errors? Show consideration toward those impacted by the evaluation? Arrange for a balance of power?

7. OUTCOMES Includes reports and their good or bad effects, but only to the extent foreseeable by the evaluator. Also includes effects of the *process* of evaluation; did it increase productivity, weaken morale, use of information in decisions?

8. COSTS What did the evaluation cost? (Especially nondollar costs.) What would the alternatives to it cost (including not doing one at all)?

9. COMPARISONS Critical competitors for the evaluation include not bothering at all, using informed judgment, tossing a coin, and using other evaluation models.

10. GENERALIZABILITY Other uses for the design, for later times, different programs , other sites, and so on.

11. SIGNIFICANCE The synthesis of all the above, to achieve a reading on the value and merit of the evaluation.

12. RECOMMENDATIONS May or may not follow, but might include: reject, repeat (for confirmation), accept, implement.

13. REPORT Of the metaevaluator.

Ref: Daniel Stufflebeam, "Meta-Evaluation: Concepts, Standards and Uses" in *Educational Evaluation Methodology: The State of the Art*, Ronald Berk, ed. (Johns Hopkins, 1981). See also **Consonance.**
METAMETHODOLOGY The theoretical side of the study of

methodology; it forms part of **metatheory**.

METATHEORY A 'theory' about the nature of a field of inquiry, engineering, or craft. It deals with matters such as the definition of the field's boundaries, its differences from neighboring fields or disciplines, the reason why certain methods work well for it and others are inappropriate (the last topic is sometimes called metamethodology). It is often very informal, sometimes entirely implicit, but its existence is a prerequisite for the existence of a discipline, since it is the self-concept of the discipline, and a discipline without a self-concept is just practice in one place rather than another, or on one kind of raw material rather than another. The view of evaluation as applied social science and the view that it is a transdiscipline are planks in metatheories of evaluation; the **value-free doctrine** about the social sciences is a plank in a common metatheory of the social sciences .

METHODOLOGICAL INDIVIDUALISM A doctrine in the philosophy of the social sciences that holds that all claims about social entities (markets, nations, and so on) must be decomposable into claims about individuals. A kind of social atomism. There are significant consequences for evaluation; see, for example, **Big footprint approach**.

MICROANALYSIS This can either refer to (i) an evaluation that includes and may have been constructed from evaluations of the **components** of the evaluand; or (ii) an evaluation broken out by **dimensions** (see **Analytical evaluation**); or (iii) a causal **explanation** of the (valued or disvalued) performance of the evaluand, which is *not* (usually) a concern of the evaluator.

MICROEVALUATION See **Analytical Evaluation**.

MINIMAX A decision strategy that involves acting so as to *mini*mize the *maxi*mum possible loss. The paradigm example is buying fire insurance because it eliminates the worst case of a total uninsured loss. One alternative strategy is maximax (maximizing maximum gain)—for example, entering the lottery with the largest prize, regardless of ticket price or number of tickets sold. These are said to be significant alternatives to optimization, which maximizes expectancy (the product of the utility of an outcome by the probability that it will occur). In fact, insofar as they can be justified at all, they are simply limit cases, only applicable to limited special cases. *Empirically*, they are alternative strategies, and people use them in all sorts of cases; but *evaluatively* that is mainly a sign of irrationality or ignorance or lack of training. See also **Risk assessment**.

MINIMUM COMPETENCY TESTING A basic level of (usually) basic skills is a minimum competency. Success in such tests has been tied to graduation, grade promotion, remedial education, teacher retention; failure has been tied to teacher dismissal, program nonfunding, and so on. With all this at stake, MCT has been a very hot political issue—as well as an ethical one and a measurement one. Introduced with due warning and support it can represent a step toward honest schooling; done carelessly, it is a disaster. See **Cutting score**.

MISSION BUDGETING A generalization of the notion of program budgeting (see PPBS); the idea is to develop a system of budgeting that will answer questions of the type, "How much are we spending on such and such a *mission?*" (by contrast with *program, agency,* and *personnel*—the previous kinds of categories to which budget amounts were tied). One limitation of PPBS has been that a good many programs overlap in the clientele they serve and the services they deliver, so that we may have a very poor idea of how much we're putting into, for example, welfare or bilingual education, by merely looking at agency budgets or even PPBS figures, *unless* we have an extremely clear picture—which decision-makers rarely can have, especially a new Executive Cabinet—of the actual impacted populations and the level of service delivery from each of the programs. The mission budgeting concept, along with **zero-based budgeting**, was popular with the early Carter administration but we heard little about it later in that regime, just as MacNamara's introduction of PPBS (into DOD, from Ford Motor Company) under an earlier administration has faded considerably.

MODE (Stat.) (Cf. **Mean, Median**) The mode is the "most popular" (most frequent) score or score interval. It's more likely that a student about whom you know nothing except their membership in this group scored the modal score of the group than any other score. But it may not be *very* likely; for example, if every student gets a different score, except two who get 100 out of 100, then the mode is 100, but it's not very typical. If the data follows a "normal" curve, on the other hand, as—supposedly—does the distribution of IQ scores in the U.S. population, then the mean, the median, and the mode are all the same value, corresponding to the highest point of the curve. Some distributions, or curves representing them, are described as bimodal, and so on, which means that there are *two* (or more) peaks or modes; this is a looser sense of the term mode, but useful. Conventionally, a flat distribution is said to have no mode.

MODELS (of evaluation) A term loosely used to refer to a conception or approach or sometimes even a method (naturalistic, goal-free) of doing evaluation (or evaluation within a certain area such as program evaluation). Models are to paradigms as hypotheses are to theories, which means less general but with some overlaps. Entries here include the following, frequently referred to as models: **advocate-**

233

adversary, big footprint, black box, checklist, connoisseurship, CIPP, discrepancy, engineering, goal-free, judicial, medical, naturalistic, illuminative, perspectival, responsive, social science, therapeutic, transactional, and transdisciplinary. Possibly the best classification of models is in Stufflebeam and Webster's article in *Evaluation Models*, Madaus et al., eds. (Kluwer, 1983); another very interesting effort by Alkin and Ellett is in *The International Encyclopedia of Educational Evaluation*, ed. Walberg and Haertel (Pergamon, 1990). Apart from taxonomies, a very detailed analysis of the models (and other work) of seven contributors to the field is provided in *Foundations of Program Evaluation: Theories of Practice* by Shadish, Cook, and Leviton (Sage, 1991). The multitude of models illuminatingly reflect the many facets of program evaluation. On the transdisciplinary view, each of these is underpinned by the same logic. See also **Evaluation theories.**

MODUS OPERANDI METHOD (MOM) A procedure for identifying the cause of a certain effect by detailed analysis of the configuration of the chain of events preceding it and of the ambient conditions. MOM is sometimes feasible when a control group is impossible, and it is useful as a check or strengthening of the design even when a control group is possible. The term refers to the characteristic pattern of links in the casual chain, which the detective refers to as the *modus operandi* of a criminal. These can be quantified and often configurally scored; the problem of identifying the cause can thus be converted into a pattern-recognition task for a computer. One strength of the approach is that it can be applied in individual cases, informally, semiformally (as in criminalistics), and formally (full computerization). It also leads to MOM-oriented *designs* that deliberately employ "tracers", that is, idiosyncratic features of a treatment that will show up in the effects. An example would be the use of a particular sequence of items in a student questionnaire disseminated to faculty for instructional development use. Details in a section by this title in *Evaluation in Education*, J.R. Popham, ed. (McCutcheon, 1976.) The MOM approach is in the spirit of Campbell's pattern-matching approach, dating back to 1966; see Cook's essay in *Evaluation and Education: At Quarter Century*, McLaughlin and Phillips, eds. (NSSE/University of Chicago, 1991).

MOLAR See **Global.**

MOLECULAR See **Analytic.**

MONITOR The term "monitor" was the original term for what is now often called by an agency "the project officer", namely the person from the agency staff who is responsible for supervising progress and compliance on a particular contract or grant. "Monitor" was a much clearer term, since "project officer" could equally well refer to some-

234

body whose responsibilities were to the project manager, or to somebody who merely handled the contract paper work (the "contract officer", as the fiscal agent at the agency is sometimes called). But it was apparently thought to have "Big Brother" connotations, or not to reflect adequately the full range of responsibilities, and so on. See **Monitoring.**

MONITORING A monitor (of a project) is usually a representative of the funding agency who watches for proper use of funds, observes progress, provides information to the agency about the project, and vice versa. Monitors badly need and rarely have evaluation skills; if they were all even semicompetent formative evaluators, their (at least quasi-) externality could make them extremely valuable since many projects either lack evaluation staff, or have none worth having, or never supplement them with external evaluation. Monitors have a schizophrenic role that few learn to handle; they have to represent and defend the agency to the project and represent and defend the project to the agency. Can these roles be further complicated by an attempt at evaluation? The roles already include it and the only question is whether it should be done reasonably well.

MOTIVATION The disposition of an organism or institution to expend effort in a particular way or direction. It is best measured by a study of behavior, since self-reports are intrinsically and contextually likely to be unreliable. Cf. **Affect.**

MOTIVATIONAL EVALUATION The deliberate use of evaluation as a management tool to alter motivation. It can be content-dependent or content-independent. If the content of the evaluation is a recommendation that there be a tie between raises and work output, and if this proposal is adopted, it may affect motivation and hence the evaluation will have affected motivation. But the mere announcement of an evaluation even without its occurrence, and certainly the presence of an evaluator, can have very large (good or bad) effects on motivation, as experienced managers well know. Evaluators, on the other hand, are prone to suppose that the contents of their reports are what counts and tend to forget the reactive effects, while they would be the first to suspect the Hawthorne effect in a study done by someone else.

Establishing a sustained level of self-critical awareness—the **evaluative attitude**—requires a sustained effort by a manager or team leader. That effort might comprise arrangements for regular external evaluation, or quality circles, or simply the role modeling of self-evaluation by senior managers. When people say that "in Japan projects are not evaluated for the first ten years" they show a complete misunderstanding of evaluation, treating it as restricted to major-event external summative review, but Japan is just the place where con

235

tinual internal evaluation (for example, by quality circles) has become so well accepted that one can make sense of a long trial period before a stop-or-go review. It would be absurd to do that in the absence of a strong evaluative commitment *and evaluative competence* in the work group. There is no worthwhile commitment to quality without competent and frequent self-evaluation.

MULTIATTRIBUTE UTILITY ANALYSIS The name for one version of the commonsense evaluation procedure that consists in weighting attributes for importance, scoring candidates for performance on each attribute, multiplying the score by the weight, and adding up the results for each candidate, the one with the highest score being the best. The usual versions of this model, including the mathematical versions developed since 1976, involve inappropriate assumptions about the measurement scales involved, a willingness to accept illicit values, and a naive view about the ability of decision-makers to identify relevant criteria and determine appropriate weights. A recent review of the literature is in *Decision Research* by Carroll and Johnson, Sage, 1990. See also **Synthesis, Weight and sum.**

MULTIDISCIPLINE (MULTIDISCIPLINARY) A subject that requires the methods of several disciplines. Cf. **Interdisciplinary, Transdiscipline.**

MULTIPLE-CHOICE TEST (OR ITEM) A test—or question in a test—in which each question (the 'stem') is followed by several alternative answers, one and only one of which is to be selected as the correct or nearest to correct answer. Normally, each right answer gets one point. The advantage is ease and speed of correcting (e.g., machine-scoring is possible), and the reduction of the judgmental error involved in correcting essay answers (but see Objective tests). Multiple-choice items (MCIs) have weaknesses in practice as well as concept. The usual weaknesses in practice are: (i) several of the options are equally good; (ii) only one or two of the options make grammatical sense with the stem, so one has a 50% or 100% chance of being right without any subject matter knowledge; (iii) none of the options is near enough to being correct to deserve approval; and (iv) the minimum pass mark is set close to the guessing level, hence one can pass on the basis of 5%–10% actual knowledge of the right answers. Weaknesses in concept include: (i) without knowing anything, one has a 25% chance of being right (with the usual four options), unlike a short-answer question; (ii) the question-type is unreal, since one almost never encounters a situation in the real world in which one is offered four options, one of them being guaranteed correct or nearly correct; (iii) with very limited subject matter knowledge, one can often narrow down the feasible options and get

236

the answer right without having the slightest reason to think it is right, any understanding of why it's right, or any chance of remembering that it is right; (iv) there is no testing of composing or writing skills, and so on, some of which are nearly always a matter of importance, even to science majors (who may go through four years of college on pure multiple-choice); (v) it's too easy to cheat by quick looks at a neighbor's paper; (vi) constructing the 'distractors' (false options) is extremely time-intensive; and (vii) the tests have to be very long in order to cover a domain at all well. A better approach is the plain or modified **multiple-rating item.**

MULTIPLE-CUTOFF A procedure in personnel evaluation for combining the ratings of a candidate by different evaluators, *or* for combining the scores of a candidate on several different tests (or tasks or requirements). It is sometimes referred to as the conjunctive approach. It requires that a specified minimum score—the cutoff—be achieved on certain (possibly all) ratings or scales, not just on the total score, as with **compensatory** criteria. This approach is also contrasted with the **multiple-hurdle** approach, which is, technically speaking, only different in that the tests or interviews are administered seriatim instead of simultaneously. In practice, however, the cutoffs tend to be lower in the case of concurrent administration of multiple tests, for reasons that are not clear and not obviously valid. Among acceptable candidates, the winner is the one with the largest total score. A possible additional requirement, apparently rarely discussed, is the imposition of a cutoff on the total score as well as on the subscores (or ratings). See **Qualitative weight and sum** and also the next entry.

MULTIPLE-HURDLE Sequentially-administered set of tests with cutoffs on at least the first subset. (See the previous entry and **Compensatory** for alternatives.) This approach is far more efficient than multiple-cutoff when the cost of testing/interviewing is substantial, since it eliminates the cost of many tests for those candidates who fail an early one. Its efficiency is maximized by weighting the probability of failure and the cost of each test, so that harder and more expensive tests are given first. (See **Fire at the horses first.**) It is not efficient if your test data is unreliable or if your reasons for imposing cutoff scores may be second-guessed. Legally speaking, it is of some importance that each test in a battery that is being run in multiple-hurdle mode be checked for adverse impact on minorities or women, not just the overall score (the 'bottom line'). This term has also acquired some currency in the field of rating investments, where a set of standards or requirements, say on rate of return and risk, are all to be met.

MULTIPLE-RATING ITEM (MRI) A type of test item that requires that each of a number of options be rated (perhaps graded, or perhaps

237

evaluated in some other way), instead of one being selected as best, as in a multiple-choice item. Each option may receive any grade; for example, they all might correctly receive the same grade. (The 'modified MRI' option [MMRI] requires two-line explanations of the main reason for the selected grade, on a marked subset or on all responses; these comments are used to confirm authorship, interpret ambiguous performances, and check other skills.) Claimed advantages of MRIs over MCIs or short-answer items include: they call immediately on higher-level cognitive skills (these are verified with the MMRI version), they save item-writer's time (no need to invent three distractors for every correct answer); they retain machine- or template-scorability (plus subsidiary inspection for MMRI); they are more realistic-they match some professional tasks perfectly (e.g., teachers marking student assignments); they provide for algorithmic 'soft' scoring (grades that are adjacent to correct grade get some marks); they invalidate the test strategy of picking the least unlikely without having any idea why it's true; they save paper; and they reduce the payoff from guessing to the point of eliminating any need to apply a correction for guessing (MMRI version only, with random sampling to minimize time costs in marking). An option is 'hard scoring' with a penalty for a very bad answer.

Just as the MRI looks at first sight like a multiple-choice item, although it's radically different, so a variation on it looks like a 'matching' type of test item. In this variation, a set of statements (A, B,... N) is listed in one column and a set of evaluative comments (1, 2,... M) in the adjacent column. M and N are numbers above ten and may be very different. The task is to find the correct evaluative comment for each statement and place its number in the left margin next to the letter identifying the statement. As with the basic MRI—and unlike the standard matching test—no elimination algorithm works; one of the comments may be appropriate for several statements. Soft or hard scoring rubrics may be used, and write-in of a better comment may be allowed—with attendant risks—when none provided seem appropriate.

While many of the options here can be incorporated in MCIs and in a limiting sense MRIs can be regarded as MCIs, they are very different from MCIs as currently used. The rigidity with which MCIs have been retained may be the dislike of the 'tests and measurement' people for treating grades or ratings as objective (of course, they treat them that way when giving them to their own students), a hangover from the value-free doctrine.

MULTIPLISM (sometimes, "critical multiplism") The use of multiple methods in evaluation. The term comes from Shadish and

238

Cook, and an excellent exposition of its application to evaluation will be found in *Foundations of Program Evaluation: Theories of Practice* by Shadish, Cook, and Leviton (Sage, 1991).

MULTI-TIER or MULTIPLE TIER See **Two-tier system.**

"MY TRIBE" SYNDROME See **Going native.**

N

NATURALISTIC (evaluation or methodology). An approach that minimizes much of the paraphernalia of science, for example, technical jargon, prior technical knowledge, statistical inference, the effort to formulate general laws, the separation of the observer from the subject, the commitment to a single correct perspective, theoretical structures, experimental design, predictions and propositional knowledge—sometimes causes. Instead there is a focus on the use of metaphor, analogy, informal (but valid) inference, vividness of description, reasons-explanations, interactiveness, meanings, multiple (legitimate) perspectives, tacit knowledge. For an excellent discussion, see "Appendix B: Naturalistic Evaluation" in *Evaluating with Validity*, E. House (Sage, 1980). Egon Guba and Yvonna Lincoln, Bob Stake, and Bob Wolf have paid particular attention to the naturalistic model, and their definition (Wolf, personal communication) stresses that it: (i) has more orientation toward "current and spontaneous activities, behaviors and expressions rather than to some statement of prestated formal objectives; (ii) responds to educators, administrators, learners, and the public's interest in different kinds of information; and (iii) accounts for the different values and perspectives that exist." It also stresses contextual factors, unstructured interviewing, observation rather than testing, meanings rather than mere behaviors.

Much of the debate about the legitimacy/utility of the naturalistic approach recapitulates the idiographic/nomothetic debate in the methodology of psychology and the debates in the analytical philosophy of history over the role of laws. At this stage of the debate, while the principal exponents of the naturalistic approach may have gone too far in the **laissez-faire** direction (any interpretation the audience makes is allowable), and in caricaturing what they think of as the empiricist approach, their work has shown up the impropriety of many of the formalists' assumptions about the applicability of the **social science model**. Ref: Guba and Lincoln's *Effective Evaluation* (Sage, 1981). See **Illuminative evaluation**.

NEEDS ASSESSMENT (NEEDS ANALYSIS and NEEDS SENSING are other variants) This term has drifted from its literal meaning into jargon status in which it refers to any study of the needs, wants, market preferences, values, or ideals that might be relevant to, for example, a program. This enlarged sense might be called the "values assessment" sense (or process), and it is in fact a perfectly legitimate activity when one is looking for all possible guidance in planning—or justification for continuance (or modification or termination—of a program. Needs assessment in the literal sense is just part of this; but, short of moral imperatives, it is the most important part. Hence, even if the general or values assessment interpretation of needs assessment is taken, one must then sort out the true needs from the rest. Needs provide the first priority for response—with ethics as a framework constraint—just because they are in some sense *necessary*, whereas wants are (merely) *desired* and ideals are *"idealistic"*, that is, often impractical. It is therefore very misleading to produce something as an NA (needs assessment) when in fact it is just a market survey, because it suggests that there is a level of urgency or importance about its findings that simply isn't there. True needs are considerably harder to establish than felt wants (or even than unconscious wants), because true needs are often unknown to those who have them, and may even be contrary to what they want, as in the case of a boy who needs a certain diet and wants an entirely different one.

The most widely used definition of need—the discrepancy definition (Kaufman, *Educational System Planning* [Prentice-Hall, 1972])—does not confuse needs with wants (although some users of this model make that mistake) but does confuse them with ideals. It defines need as the gap between the actual and the ideal (or whatever it takes to bridge that gap). This definition has even been written into law in some states. But the gap between your actual income and your ideal income is quite different (and much larger) than the gap between your actual income and what you really need. We have to drop the use of the ideal level as the key reference level in the definition of need—which is just as well, because it is very difficult to get much agreement on what the ideal curriculum (for example) is like, and if we had to do that before we can argue for any curriculum needs, it would be hard to get started.

A second fatal flaw in the discrepancy definition is its fallacious identification of needs with one particular subset of needs, namely *unmet* needs. But there are many things we absolutely need—like oxygen in the air, or vitamins in our diet—that are already there. To say we need them is to say they are *necessary* for, for example, life or health, which distinguishes them from the many *inessential* things in the environment. Of course, on the discrepancy definition they are not needs at all, because they are part of "the actual", not part of the gap (discrepancy) between that and the ideal. It may be useful to use a terminology from dietetics for met and unmet needs—maintenance
241

vs. incremental needs. People sometimes think that it's better to focus on incremental needs because that's where the action is required; so maybe—they suppose—the discrepancy definition doesn't get us into too much trouble. But look ahead to implementation. Where will you get the resources for the necessary action? Some of them usually come from redistribution of existing resources, that is, from robbing Peter's needs to pay for Paul's, where Peter's (the maintenance needs) are just as vital as Paul's (the incremental). This leads to an absurd flip-flop in successive years. It is much better to look at all needs when doing an NA, prioritize them (using apportioning methods not grading or ranking) and then act to redistribute old and new resources.

A better definition of need, which we might call the diagnostic definition, defines need as anything essential for a satisfactory mode of existence or level of performance. The slippery term in this is of course "satisfactory" and it is context-dependent; satisfactory diets in a nation gripped by famine may be considerably nearer the starvation level than those regarded as satisfactory in rich country during a time of plenty. That context-dependence is part of the essentially pragmatic component in NA—it is a prioritizing and pragmatic concept. Needs slide along the middle range of the spectrum from disaster to utopia as resources become available. They never cover the ends of the spectrum—no riches, however great, legitimate the claim that everyone needs all possible luxuries. But, equally, they never lose their connection to the quality.

The next major ambiguity or trap in the concept of need relates to the distinction between what we can call performance needs and treatment needs. When we say that children need to be able to read, we are talking about a needed level of performance. When we say they need classes in reading, or instruction in the phonics approach to reading, we are talking about a needed treatment. We often talk in a way that suggests the two are on a par, but in fact the gap between them is vast and can only be bridged by an evaluation of the alternative possible treatments that might yield the allegedly needed performance. Children need to be able to converse—but it does not follow they need classes in talking, since they pick it up without any. Even if it can be shown that they do need the "treatment" of reading classes, that's a long way from the conclusion that any particular approach to reading instruction is needed. The essential points are that the kind of NA with which one should begin evaluations is *performance* NA; and that *treatment* needs claims essentially require *both* a performance NA *and* a full-scale evaluation of the relative merits of the best candidates in the treatment stakes. Conceptual problems not discussed here include the problem of whether there are needs for what isn't feasible, the distinction between acquired needs (alcohol) and essential needs (food), and the ranking or apportioning of physical needs, affective needs, recreational needs, and aesthetic needs.

The crucial perspective to retain on NA is that it is a process for discovering *facts* about the functions or dysfunctions of organisms or systems; it's not an opinion survey or a wishing trip. It is a fact about children, in our environment, that they need vitamin C and basic literacy skills, whether or not they think so or their parents think so (or for that matter whether witch doctors or nutritionists or reading specialists think so). What makes it a fact is that the withdrawal of, or failure to provide these things, results in serious malfunction, by any reasonable standards of functioning. Thus models for NA must be models for truth-finding, not for achieving political agreement. That they are all too often of the latter kind reflects the tendency of those who design them to think that value-judgments are not part of the domain of truth. For NA *are* value-judgments just as surely as they are matters of fact; indeed, they are the key value-judgments in many evaluations, the root source of the values that eventually make the conclusion an evaluative one rather than a purely descriptive one.

Performance NAs are evaluative because they require the identification of the *essential*, the *important*, that which avoids *bad* results. Of course, these are often relatively uncontroversial value-judgments. Evaluations build on NAs as theories build on observations; it's not that observations are infallible, only that they're *less* fallible than theoretical speculation.

The general level of thought about NA is poor. Definitions that fail every test are common, for example, "A need is the value-judgment that *some group has a problem that can be solved*", a quote from *Need Analysis* by Jack McKillip (Sage, 1987). Needs are not restricted to groups; nor to problems; nor to conditions that are solvable, nor is it useful to build the term 'value-judgment' into the definition because it suggests a false contrast. The monograph based on this definition is, not surprisingly, only tangentially relevant to NA. More serious work has been done in philosophy, most notably in Garrett Thomson's *Needs* (Routledge & Kegan Paul, 1987). It is unfortunate that McKillip and other educational researchers have not read Thomson, nor Thomson any of the educational research where needs assessement has been so widely used.

NEUTRAL Not supporting any of the disputing factions, that is, a *political* category. No more likely to be right than they are; more likely to be ignorant; not always more likely to be objective. Hence, to be used with care, not as the always-ideal choice for judges, juries, evaluators, and so on. Absence of bias on an issue or in an area is not absence of

243

convictions in that area, hence neutrality is not objectivity. Nonevaluative *language* is also said to be neutral; but it is no more objective than evaluative language, for example, "We have just received a visit from extra-terrestrial beings" may be far more tendentious than "He's a murderer"; or vice versa.

NEW RHETORIC See **Rhetoric, New.**

NIH While these are the initials of the National Institutes of Health, they have another significance in evaluation, government, and industrial management—they stand for the dread Not Invented Here syndrome, which has probably undone more good work than most wars. An example: one of the largest school districts in the country ran a 'horserace' to find out which of several contenders was the best reading program to use. A clear winner on cost-effectiveness emerged, very close to being an outright winner, and a mile ahead on cost. Four years later, almost no one in the district office had heard of it. Explanation: a new superintendent came in and followed the 'NIH rule', namely don't use stuff you didn't introduce, because you won't get any credit for it if it works, though you'll wear the blame if it doesn't. Bring in your own candidate; you can always find some teachers who'll say it's marvelous, and you can easily avoid it being evaluated in any serious way. School boards don't know enough or aren't tough enough to insist on credentials for programs that are going to replace existing programs; they are easily persuaded that "we need a change" by evidence that there are some seriously dissatisfied customers for the present program, and some experts think there's better stuff around. That's true of everything; all that matters is what wins a fair race, not whether it has fleas. (Why hadn't anyone in the district office even *heard* of it? Because NIH applies to personnel, too; they were all creatures of the new regime.) There's more to NIH than credit, however; there's also **Power.**

NORMAL DISTRIBUTION (Stat.) Not the way things are normally distributed, though some are, but an ideal distribution that results in the familiar bell-shaped curve (which, for example, is perfectly symmetrical though few real distributions are). A large part of inferential statistics rests on the assumption that the population from which we are sampling is (more or less) normally distributed, with regard to the variables of interest, and is invalid if this assumption is grossly violated as it quite often is. Height and eye color are often given as examples of variables that are normally distributed but neither is a well-supported example. (The term "Gaussian distribution" is sometimes and much less confusingly used for this distribution.)

NORMATIVE A technical term in the social sciences that has come to mean roughly the same as "evaluative". It may have come to have

244

that meaning because the only factual basis that the self-styled "empiricists" could see for evaluative language was as a way to express deviation from an empirical norm (for example, a performance norm). Hence to say a performance was "excellent" was to say it was a standard deviation or two above the norm (or average or mean.) This superficial analysis led to such practices as grading on the curve, which involves the confusion of "better" with "good". The analysis is superficial because—among other reasons—it fails to account for the meaning of "above" in "above the norm". This is of course an evaluative term that is not reducible to statistics—or, if so reducible, is only reducible in an unspecified and much more sophisticated way which would then show the original reduction to be superficial. Thus <u>describing distributions</u> is norm-related but not evaluative; <u>ranking</u> is norm-related *and* evaluative; the language of <u>grading</u> is not (directly) norm-related but involves stronger evaluative analysis, such as justifying the conclusion that one performance is excellent, another unacceptable. The use of the term "normative" confounds these.

The usual contrast of "normative" with "descriptive" would also make no sense on the analysis just given, since that analysis is supposed to give a descriptive meaning to "normative". In fact, "normative" *does* contrast with descriptive in the usual social scientists' usage, because they ignore the analysis and use "normative" to mean "evaluative" (that is, the 'norms' refer to standards of merit or worth that almost nobody may achieve, hence are not 'normal'). But then, of course, the term "normative" (in that sense) is entirely unnecessary—one should use "evaluative" instead, and "normative" becomes just a monument to bad analysis and a love of jargon. Like the equally confused use of the term "**value-judgment**" to mean "expression of taste or mere preference", the term "normative" sacrifices a useful term to a false god. "Normative" should simply mean "directly referring to norms, whether they are descriptive or evaluative" and thus should cover "unusually tall", "atypical", "different", and so on (which refer to descriptive norms), as well as the language of ranking, like "unusually good", and "worst of all" (which are evaluative), but should *not* refer to grading language such as "worthless" or "perfect".

But do not grading terms refer to standards, that is, norms of *value*—and hence qualify as normative? Not unless you get careless about the difference between norms and standards. Grades refer to *standards of value* but not to norms—of value or anything else. Most standards are descriptive standards: "His eyes are blue" refers to standards of color; "He's 6 foot 3 inches" refers to standards of length. But those are the paradigms of *descriptive* language, so the problem

245

with saying that referring to standards indicates the use of normative language is that it destroys the distinction between descriptive and normative. "Prescriptive" is a somewhat better term to use, instead of normative, as a contrast with "descriptive", but not a very good one, since it only refers to recommendations or rules, not to all evaluative language.

The suggestion that we abandon the use of the term "normative" to mean "evaluative" leaves the other scientific sense of the term intact. For example, it preserves the useful distinction, defined below, between **norm-referenced** and **criterion-referenced** tests

NORM-REFERENCED TESTS These are typically constructed so as to yield a measure of *relative* performance of the individual (or group) by comparison with the performance of other individuals (or groups) taking the same test, for example, in terms of percentile **ranking** (cf. **criterion-referenced tests**). That means throwing out items that (nearly) all testees get right (or wrong)—these are referred to as having a near-zero 'discrimination index'—because such items do not "spread" the testee population, that is, help in ranking. What's left may or may not give a very reliable indication of, for example, reading ability as such (by contrast with *better* reading ability). Norm-referenced tests are not ideal as a *sole* basis for something like state assessment, since they make discriminating or competing more important than (or the only meaning of) achieving and severely weaken the test as an indicator of mastery (or excellence or weakness), which you should also know about. The best compromise is a criterion-referenced test on which the norms are also provided, where the **criteria** are independently documented needs.

Test experts were slow to realize the defects in norm-referenced tests; one still finds remarks in 1983 publications like this: "A test with a zero discrimination index would not reveal anything about the examinees" or "Without [discrimination] tests would be useless." Well, a zero discrimination test could reveal that the examinees were all functionally literate (or illiterate), which may be more important than revealing that they can be spread on some subscale of a literacy test after you've thrown out the items with zero discrimination, the ones that validate the test as a test of literacy. (The quotes are from p. 14 of *Test Item Bias* by Steven J. Osterlind [Sage, 1990].)

NULL HYPOTHESIS The hypothesis that the results of an experiment are due to chance. Statistics only tells us about the null hypothesis; it is experimental design that provides the basis for inferences to the truth of the scientific hypothesis of interest. The "significance levels" referred to in experimental design and interpretation are the chances that the null hypothesis is correct. Hence, when results "reach

246

the .01 level of significance", that means there's only one chance in a hundred that they would be due to chance. It does *not* mean that there's a 99 percent chance that *our* hypothesis is correct; because, of course, there may be other explanations of the result that we haven't thought of. See **Hypothesis testing.**

NUMERICAL WEIGHT AND SUM A way of handling the **synthesis** problem, described under **Weight and sum.** It is probably the most widely used methods and appears commonsensical. It is in fact fallacious and an alternative, less elegant, but valid approach is the **qualitative weight and sum** approach. NWS is sometimes called the **linear combination approach,** but that description ignores the possiblility of cutoffs on each scale, an essential feature in many practical contexts.

NUT (as in "making the nut") Management consultant jargon for the basic cost of running the business for the year. After "making the nut" one may become a little choosier about which jobs to take on, and what rates to set.

O

OBJECTIVE Unbiased or unprejudiced. "Unprejudiced" literally means not prejudged, and that etymology often misleads people into thinking that anyone who comes into a discussion with strong views about an issue can't be unprejudiced. The key question is whether the views are justified. The fact that we all have strong views about the sexual abuse of small children and the importance of education does not show prejudice, only rationality. Cf. **Neutral, Bias, Subjectivity, Perspectival evaluation, Objectives.**

OBJECTIVES The technical sense of this term refers to a fairly specific description of an intended outcome; the more general description, under which this and possibly other objectives are subsumed, is referred to as a goal. Bloom provided a major service to evaluation of educational and many other programs and curricula with the Taxonomy of cognitive objectives. It needs some supplementation—see **Paracognitive**—but was remarkably robust under thousands of critical reviews.

OBJECTIVE TESTS A term widely used by psychologists to refer to multiple-choice tests, a usage that displays the primitive nature of psychology's conception of objectivity. Obviously, a test is not made objective by eliminating the subjective element involved in grading essay answers; one source of error is reduced, but another is increased, since multiple-choice items can often be correctly answered by someone with no knowledge of the subject matter, an 'achievement' that is always difficult and usually impossible with essay items. Again, the subjectivity in the scoring key is often as great as that in the process of essay marking and less desirable because there is no chance that the errors will be demonstrated by a good essay, although item-analysis, in the rare cases where it is done, can have a similar effect.

OBSERVATION The process or product of direct sensory inspection, frequently involving trained observers. The line between observation and its normal antonym "interpretation" is not sharp and is in any case context-dependent, that is, what counts as an observation in one context ("Chang Lee just did a very well-executed dive") will count as an interpretation in another (where the diving judge's score is appealed). That happens to be an evaluative interpretation, but it might

248

just as well be causal (e.g., "The defender accidentally diverted the ball into his own goal."). Just as it is very difficult to get trainees in evaluation—even those with considerable scientific training—to write nonevaluative descriptions of something that is to be evaluated, so it is difficult to get observers to report only what's there rather than their inferences from it. The use of checklists and training can produce great increases in reliability and validity in observers; observation is thus a rather sophisticated process and not to be equated with the amateur's perceptions or reports on them. It should be clear from the above that there are contexts in which observers, especially trained observers, can correctly report their observations in evaluative terms. Another example, where no special training is involved, is reporting scores at a rifle range.

OED The usual library contains this definitive multivolume Oxford English Dictionary, but that edition is now very out of date, and only the new one, available for a thousand dollars in hard copy or on a CD-ROM disk in 1991, is authoritative, and then only for British English. The old OED is still useful for work on the etymology of many terms, and it is there we find, for example, that "evaluator" is a very recent term.

OPPORTUNITY COST Opportunity cost is the value that one gives up by selecting one of several mutually exclusive alternatives. It is one of the more recondite dimensions of **cost**, and is calculated during serious **cost analysis**. The same concept applies to investing money and to investing any other resource such as time or ego. Calculating opportunity costs is sometimes easy, but sometimes a very complex and technically demanding matter—for example, when dealing with investment portfolios—and the results are often very enlightening. The fact that there is usually an infinity of alternatives to any action, all of which are given up, does not entail that opportunity costs are infinite, because they are either taken to be the value of the most valuable forsaken alternative or the disjunction of the value of the alternatives. Nevertheless, calculating the opportunity cost of something often involves calculating a great many costs of alternatives. (This situation exactly parallels the situation in looking for critical competitors in evaluation.) As with all cost analysis, costs to all (significantly) impacted populations need to be calculated if one is to talk about 'the cost' of something, meaning the total cost picture.

At the practical level, opportunity cost analysis pays off quickly. If one asks a group of school administrators to work out the costs of adding an advanced computer course in a high school, they will work diligently over the cost of buying machines, training faculty, and so on, but will essentially never think of the *opportunity* cost to the *stu-*

dent: the amount of learning that will be lost in order to take this course, given the fixed length of the school day. Yet this is a major factor in determining feasibility. See **Cost, Critical competitor, Profit.**

OPTIMIZATION The decision strategy according to which one should select the alternative with the maximum expectancy (the expectancy of an outcome is the product of the probability of the payoff occurring by the value of the payoff). Optimization is always the correct strategy *if* the analysis is done correctly, for example, by including the utility of risk or gambling, the cost of anxieties raised and time spent on calculating strategies, and the cost of information that could be obtained by exploration or inquiry and could, with some probability, bear on the best mainstream strategy. (Search often has large costs, as does costing search.) Only computers could handle the full spread of calculations involved in this—even if they could get the relevant data—especially when there is a high "need for speed", for example, in weapon systems control.

Descriptively, people often operate on other strategies—for example, **satisficing, minimax, maximax**. These are approximations to optimization in certain limiting cases. Given costs of search and analysis, they may make more sense in particular contexts—but that can only be proved by looking at a full analysis. And, of course, people use their *estimates* of the utility of the alternatives, not necessarily the true utility of those alternatives to them. Furthermore, some of them—that is, of us—simply choose without explicit thought, or based on irrational thought, some or much of the time. Evaluation should be primarily concerned with identifying correct choices, not predicting actual choices (the task of the psychologist, economist, sociologist, and so on). Professionals in decision theory often confuse **prescriptive theories** with **descriptive** ones, complaining that optimizing is a naive or rationalistic analysis. It is only naive if you take it to be a descriptive account—and then only because the people it is describing are naive.

OUTCOME Outcomes are usually the post-treatment effects; but there are often effects during treatment, for example, enjoyment of a teaching style, which we sometimes (casually) call process. In general, we should try to distinguish: immediate outcomes, end of treatment outcomes, and long-term outcomes to be discovered in follow-ups. It is hard to get funding for the latter, although they are often much the most important, as may be the case with Headstart.

Quite different outcomes may occur to different groups of impactees or "true consumers", just as costs differ from group to group. (Costs are not completely distinct from outcomes, for example, staff exhaustion is a cost and an outcome of a demanding program [a **recoil**

250

effect]). Outcomes may be factual and evaluative (reduction of murder rate) or factual and not evaluative (reduction of morbidity) in which case they have to be coupled to needs assessment results to get into an evaluative conclusion! See also **Effect.**

OUTCOME EVALUATION Evaluations that focus on **outcomes,** rather than **process** or input, are often called **payoff evaluations.** In general, evaluations should look at both outcomes and process, if possible, as indeed they should look at anything else that is relevant, for example, comparisons.

OVERLEARNING Overlearning is learning past the point of 100% recall, and is aimed at generating long-term retention. To avoid boredom on the part of the learner, and for other reasons, the best way to do this is through reintroducing the concept (or whatever else is being learned) in a variety of different contexts. One reason that long-term studies—or the follow-up phase of an evaluation—often reveal grave deterioration of learning is that people are careless about the distinction between learning to criterion at t_1 (the end of the instruction period) and learning to criterion at t_2 (the time when the knowledge is needed, possibly years later).

OVERPOWERING A phenomenon in evaluation analogous to robustness in experimental design. It occurs when considerable differences in the values of different consumers, and in the performances of the leading competitors, are swamped by the superiority of the combined score of one competitor. See **Logic of evaluation.**

P

PAD, PADDING When a bidder goes up with a budget for a proposal, there has to be some allowance in it for unforeseen eventualities—at least if it is to be done according to sound business practices. This is often referred to as "the pad", and the practice of doing this is the *legitimate* version of "padding the budget". Padding the budget is also used as a term to refer to illegitimate additions to the budget (often treated as if they are excessive profits); but it must be realized that the pad is the only recourse that the contractor has for handling the obvious unreliabilities in predicting the ease of implementing some complicated testing program, the ease of designing a questionnaire that will get past the questionnaire review panels, or the payroll while a lawsuit is settled. See **Cost plus.**

PANELS The use of groups to do evaluation (e.g., of candidates, policies, or research proposals) is a complex subject that has been little studied. Anecdotal reports suggest that the following variations lead to very different results; some project managers feel they can control outcomes by an appropriate choice of procedure. (i) The evaluators may be asked to rate independently prior to discussion, to discuss and then rate independently, or prepare (read, or interview) separately, and then discuss to generate a group rating. (ii) The evaluators may discuss and agree on a common scoring system in advance or 'play it by ear'. (iii) They may agree in advance—or be told—how their ratings are to be combined; see, for example, **compensatory, multiple-hurdle, multiple-cutoff.** (iv) They may be 'calibrated' or calibrate themselves on a set of hypothetical or archival examples, which they discuss before turning to the real ones.

PARACOGNITIVE Part of this area borders on the affective domain, and is often but incorrectly included with it. It does include a number of perceptual, analytical, characterological, and judgmental skills that are not normally included in taxonomies of cognitive skills but that have massive, learned, cognitive (not always propositional) content, often of great importance in practice and education. It includes: the intellectual dimension of empathic insight (as evidenced in understanding questions from others, role-playing, acting, and so on); objectivity, rationality, reasonableness, or "good judgment" moral sensitivity; the ability to provide near-perfect translations; skilled reading of body

252

language and speech cues; clinical diagnosis skills; sophisticated pattern recognition (e.g., of fossil types or bird species).

PARADIGM An extremely general conception of or model for a discipline or subdiscipline, which may be very influential in shaping its development, for example "the classical social science paradigm in evaluation". Popularized in this sense by Kuhn, who (at least sometimes) got caught in the tempting but illicit fallacy of supposing that the power of paradigms includes defining truth. They define prima facie truth, but that's a long way from being the same; eventually, paradigms are rejected as too far from reality and they are always governed by that possibility. That error suffuses the most recent discussion of paradigms in evaluation, *The Paradigm Dialog*, a collection edited by Egon Guba (Sage, 1990); the essay by Denis Phillips is a notable exception. See **Relativism**. On paradigms for evaluation, see **Models**, and **Transdisciplinary model**.

PARALLEL DESIGNS (in evaluation) Those in which two or more evaluation teams or evaluators proceed independently (not necessarily concurrently). They are of great importance because: (i) of the light they shed on the largely unknown extent of intervaluator agreement; (ii) such a process increases the care with which each team proceeds; and (iii) the reconciliation process (**synthesis**) often leads to a deeper analysis than is achieved by the evaluators independently. For these reasons, it is usually better and frequently feasible to spend a given evaluation budget on two smaller teams, each getting half as much as one well-funded team. But program managers dislike this idea just *because* the teams may disagree—their real virtue! See **Parallel panels**.

PARALLEL FORMS Versions of a test that have been tested for equal difficulty and validity.

PARALLEL PANELS In proposal review, for example, it is important to run independent concurrent panels in order to get some idea of the reliability of the ratings they are producing. On the few occasions this has been done (at OE and NSF, for example), the results have been extremely disquieting, with large differences showing up. Given that unreliability guarantees both invalidity and injustice, one would expect a federal science foundation to have enough commitment to validity and justice to do routine checks of this kind, but they usually cry poormouth instead of looking for ways to get validity within the same budget. One might suspect that the real reason is not wanting to undermine faith in the system and in particular, not wanting to see the fact exposed that they have been running a poor system for a long time. In any case, dispensing funds invalidly and unfairly is not justified by saying it would cost slightly more to do it reasonably well,

253

even if it were true, since the payoffs would also be higher (from the definition of "doing it" and "reasonably well"), and justice is supposed to be worth a little. See also **Meta-evaluation** and **Self-reference.**

PARAMETERS (of an evaluation) See **Evaluation parameters.**

PARETO OPTIMAL A tough criterion for changes in, for example, an organization, society, or program; it requires that changes be made only if nobody suffers and somebody benefits. A crucial advanatage of this criterion is that it appears to avoid the problem of justifying so-called "interpersonal comparisons of utility", that is, of showing that the losses some sustain as a result of a change are less important than the gains made by others. Improving welfare conditions by raising taxes is *not* Pareto optimal, obviously. But selecting between alternative pareto optimal changes *still* involves relative hardship and benefit considerations. A major weakness in Rawls's theory of justice is the restriction to Pareto optimality. By moving to **prima facie** equality, one can develop justifications for interpersonal differences in utility.

PARETO PRINCIPLE A management maxim possibly more illuminating than the Peter Principle and **Parkinson's Law,** it is sometimes described as the 80/20 rule, or the "principle of the vital few and the trivial many", and asserts that about 80% of significant achievement (for example, at a meeting) is done by about 20% of those present; 80% of the sales come from 20% of the salespeople; 80% of the payoff from a task list can be achieved from 20% of the tasks, and so on. Worth remembering because it's sometimes true, and often surprising. For one evaluation version, see **General positive bias.**

PARKINSON'S LAW "Work (and budgets, timelines and staff size) expands to fill the space, time, and funds available." It was a considerable insight about large organizations, now part of the folk wisdom of modern management. The fact that bids on RFPs come in close to the estimated limit may not illustrate this, only that the work could be done at various levels of thoroughness or that RFP writers are remarkably good prognosticators.

PATH ANALYSIS A procedure for analyzing sets of mathematical relationships that can shed some light on the relative importance of the variables. It may even place some constraints on their causal relationship. It cannot definitely identify any one or group of them as a cause.

PAYBACK (PERIOD) A term from fiscal evaluation that refers to the time before the initial cost is recovered; the recovery cash flows should of course be **time-discounted.** Payback analysis is what shows that buying a $2,000 scanner-plus-OCR package to convert printed material to word processor files may be sensible even if the price will

254

probably drop to $1,200 in a year. If the payback period is, say, 15 months (typical of many carefully chosen installations), you will in fact lose several hundred dollars by waiting for the price to drop.

PAYOFF EVALUATION Evaluation focused on results: the method of choice apart from the fact that it involves extra costs, delay, and intervening loss of control or responsibility compared to **process evaluation**. Essentially similar to **outcome evaluation**.

PEER REVIEW Evaluation, usually of proposals or college faculty, done by a panel of judges with qualifications approximating those of the author or candidate. The traditional approach but extremely shaky. Matched panels produce different results; fatigue and learning and **halo effects** are widespread; **secret-contract bias** or fear of reprisals often corrupt it completely, and so on. The process can be greatly improved, but there's little interest in doing so, possibly because it's often serving as a legitimating or **symbolic** kind of evaluation, not a truth-seeking one. Possibly, too, the reluctance is mainly due to ignorance of the social cost of errors, plus nervousness about the time-costs of panelists. See **Calibration, Personnel evaluation.**

PERCENTILE (Stat.) If you arrange a large group in the order of their scores on a test, and divide them into 100 equal-sized groups, beginning with those who have the lowest score, the first such group is said to consist of those in the 1st percentile (that is, they have scores worse than 99% of the group), and so on to the top group, which should be called the 100th percentile: for boring technical reasons the actual procedure used only distinguishes 99 groups, so the best one can do is get into the 99th percentile. With smaller numbers or for cruder estimates, the total group is divided into ten *deciles*; similarly for four *quartiles*, and so on.

PERFECTIONISM Marks's Principle states: "The price of perfection is prohibitive". Never get letters or papers retyped when fully legible corrections can be made by hand; there aren't enough trees, days, or dollars for that. Legal documents and typographical works of art like the Dove Bible may be exceptions, but the Declaration of Independence has two insertions by the scribe so there's a precedent in a legal case (cited by Bliss.) These reflections are a great source of consolation to authors of reference works—but not to their readers.

PERFORMANCE ASSESSMENT (a.k.a. **PERFORMANCE-BASED EVALUATION**) These terms currently refer to one of the swings of the pendulum on the **hard** vs. **soft** measurement scale. (The **behavioral objectives** movement was another in the same direction.) The intent is often to get away from excessive reliance on highly fallible judgment by going to the readily observable and away from high-inference observation or highly indirect inference. The problem is that

255

the hard-nosed measures are usually somewhat oversimplified, and people eventually tire of getting no reading on the missing elements. Most recently, the performance assessment movement is trying to get away from paper-and-pencil testing by using global ratings of behavior, with the usual increase of cost and loss of reliability and validity. It seems likely that both approaches should be included on those occasions when the high price of human judgment is feasible. Even in hard-nosed fields like **computer product evaluation**, the best testing organizations introduce global ratings of the stability and quality commitment of the manufacturer in addition to all the benchmarks. The Japanese sword evaluators, who may have been the first professional evaluators and who rated blades in performance terms, based on trials in lopping limbs off live prisoners from the local jail, *also* watched every step of the swordsmith's work. See also **Competency-based, Process evaluation**.

PERFORMANCE CONTRACTING The system of hiring and paying someone to deliver (e.g., educational) services by results. They might be paid in terms of the number of students times the number of grade equivalents their scores are raised. Widely tried in the 1960s, now rare. The usual story is that it didn't work or worked only by the contractor's staff cheating ("teaching to the test"). The actual situation was that the best contractors did a consistently superior job, but the *pooled* results of all contractors were not significant. As with most innovations, the lack of sophistication of the educational decision-makers plus political pressure on the agencies (teachers unions didn't like having their people replaced by the nonunion hired guns) led to the approach being given up. Instead, we should have refined the process by hiring the better contractors, from which we might have gone on to still better teaching methods for everyone. See **regression to the mean** for an example of the need for some sophistication in setting the terms of the contract.

PERFORMANCE EVALUATION The evaluation of a particular achievement, in the form of output or process: examples include a student's performance on a test (or across a term) and a gymnast's routine on a particular apparatus such as the uneven parallel bars (or in a single competition, or across a season). Performance evaluation is sometimes but not helpfully subsumed under **product evaluation**. It is important to distinguish between performance evaluation and **personnel evaluation**, even when personnel evaluation will almost entirely consist in the integration of many performance evaluations. The evaluees should not feel that a poor individual performance will be treated as grounds for condemning them as a person; they must approach the performance, along with the evaluator, and learn from its

256

evaluation what there is to learn—and go on from there. In general, the options of **formative** and **summative, global** and **analytical,** and so on, apply as to other forms of evaluation. This approach is part of the 'climate of the classroom' and is noticeably different from one culture to another.

Performance evaluation is of historical interest because for many years in the twentieth century the term "evaluation" in the title of academic books referred only to student evaluation, and in particular only to the evaluation of student work done on tests. The interpretation of test results, whether for an individual student, a class, a school, or a district, has become a complex and sophisticated field of expertise. We have now developed subspecialties such as composition evaluation, where the original situation of disastrously low interrater reliability has been transformed, mainly by the work of Paul Diederich, into one where anyone willing to follow some simple procedures can ensure high validity.for summative evaluation. The use of simple sets of dimensions for analytical evaluation of compositions, listed on a stamp—spelling, punctuation, grammar, expression, organization, argumentation, originality, research—can produce large improvements over free-form commentary in formative evaluation. Similar locally specific checklists can do the same for other types of performance. Athletic performances are often easy to evaluate **globally** because they use some simple outcome measure, such as time taken to run a marathon; **analytically,** they are often broken down into temporal phases of the performance, but **dimensions** such as style vs. stamina vs. strategy are often useful. Gymnastic performances, as those in dancing or skating, are often scored analytically on several dimensions—each rated judgmentally—such as style, originality, difficulty, and accuracy of execution.

PERSONNEL EVALUATION Personnel evaluation has been late arriving at the New Era program evaluation party. It has generated some interesting research and some major practical (and ethical/legal) improvements over common sense practice in procedures such as interviewing. For a long time, and still today, program evaluation proceeded as if it did not have to look at personnel policy or performance in the programs under evaluation—even the 1989 edition of Rossi and Freeman, the leading program evaluation text, does not mention the term "personnel" in its index. But seriously unethical personnel procedures surely wipe out any merit in a program, and inefficient ones, like incompetent personnel, should be a cause for evaluative comment.

Typically, personnel evaluation involves an assessment of job-related skills in one or more of five ways: (i) judgmental observation of

257

job performance by untrained but well-situated observers, for example co-workers or students; (ii) judgmental observation by supposedly skilled and certainly more experienced observers, such as supervisors, personnel managers, or consultants; (iii) direct measurement of job performance parameters, on the job, by calibrated instruments (human or, usually, other); (iv) observation, measurement, or evaluation of performance on job *simulations*; and/or (v) the same, but on paper-and-pencil *tests* that examine job-connected knowledge, skills, or attitudes. These results, typically on several scales, must be (a) validated—that is, related to an analysis of job requirements or performance; and (b) weighted and integrated in some justifiable way. Doing (a) and (b) is usually far more difficult than doing the basic performance rating, but they are usually underemphasized (spectacularly so in the evaluation of teachers).

Personnel evaluation is more difficult than, for example, **product evaluation**, for a number of reasons. (On the other hand, it is less complex than **program evaluation**.) Products can be and generally are evaluated by brand and model name because of the relatively high degree of similarity between two different items off the same production line; one can hardly do this with all graduates of the same teacher training institution. Moreover, personnel evaluation is subject to complex legal constraints and two types of ethical constraint. The first type involves process restrictions to avoid, for example, invasion of privacy; the second involves the ethical dimension of performance on the part of the personnel being scored. The importance of that dimension will vary depending upon the amount of authority and interpersonal contact of the individual being evaluated, but people with professional training in a graduate social science course are usually not well prepared for developing instruments for measuring or rating it. That leads to ignoring it, a major flaw which in personnel evaluation which is part of the reason for the recent spate of exposures of unethical practices in the armed forces, the legislatures, and business. (The other part is management not caring about the ethical dimension as much as the profit or status payoffs.)

There are a number of other methodological traps in personnel evaluation that invalidate part or all of the common approaches. For example, many systems fail because they are incapable in practice of generating negative ratings, no matter how bad the performance. This is usually due to *either* the failure to provide appropriate levels of anonymity for the raters (or security for the files), consistent with relevant legislation, *or* a general fear of bad-mouthing others because it is seen as involving the sin referred to in "judge not that ye be not judged", or by the term "disloyalty". This is a solvable problem but
258

one that requires sustained and ingenious attention (see **secret-con-tract bias**.) Another mistake is to use **job analysis** (a descriptive approach) as a basis for criteria in the evaluation, since the job practice observed may not include important but rarely exercised duties, or may be in violation of the explicit or implicit contract.

Another common mistake is to put **'style** variables' into evaluation forms or reports. This is often done even when there is no solid evidence that a particular style is superior to others, for example with respect to the so-called 'democratic' or delegatory style of management. But even when style variables have been validated as **indicators** of superior performance, they typically cannot be used in personnel evaluation because the correlations between their presence and good performance are merely statistical and are thus as illegitimate in the evaluation of individuals as skin color, which also correlates statistically with various desirable and/or undesirable characteristics. "Guilt by association" is as inappropriate when the association is via a common style as when it is via a common friend, race, or religion. (See **Style research**.)

A fourth fallacy is heavy dependence upon **MBO** (Management by Objectives) techniques. These are extremely limited, for example because they ignore taking advantage of targets of opportunity or ignore good fire-fighting skills, and they are too easily manipulated. (See **Goal-free evaluation, Research-based personnel evaluation**.)

Much personnel research ignores the vast differences in the way in which performances on different dimensions, or the opinions of different judges, are combined (a special case of the **synthesis** process in evaluation). Even where some acknowledgment is made of the distinction between **multiple-cutoff** and **compensatory** approaches, the difference between different versions of each of these is rarely checked, although it can make a huge difference to results; and the possible difference between what is said to be the combinatorial procedure and what is actually done is rarely checked.

One of the most serious problems is confusion of **worth** with **merit** considerations. Bringing in grant money, for example, is still treated as if it was a 'good thing' in the context of faculty evaluation, without the slightest effort at evaluation. In fact it's usually a serious drain on institutional resources since the overhead rate is usually less than the overhead cost, and the diversion of talent from teaching or from sorely needed research toward commercially/governmentally fundable research is a loss. Other worth considerations are underrated; the most obvious is versatility, which can save the employer a fortune when there's a shift of consumer interests, but is usually selected *against* by the specialists who do most of the de facto hiring and

259

view interest in other fields as a sign of lack of commitment to their own, instead of looking at track record. Other worth entries are imagination or originality in *institutional* matters, good evaluation skills in the same arena, and flexibility.

In the view of some respected management experts, notably Drucker and Deming, the standard approach to personnel management, which includes regular evaluation of individuals, is fundamentally mistaken. They prefer evaluation of group performance and developing a sense of loyalty to the group, as is common in Japan. Both ways can work in some environments, both should be known to managers; neither are unconditionally superior.

It should be noted that the evaluation of students is an important case of personnel evaluation, one that is frequently thought to be covered by the high level of sophistication we have developed with the evaluation of student work—a type of **performance** evaluation. In fact, evaluating a student—for example, when it is done by an admissions officer for higher education, or by an employment officer for an organization hiring summer workers—takes into account not only the academic work record but also attitudes, outside interests, family background, and so on. The validity level of the usual procedures for doing this, even at the leading institutions of higher education, is still poor, although slightly better than their procedures for faculty evaluation.

A major recent effort at improvement is the publication of the *Standards for Evaluating Personnel*, a set of metacriteria developed by representatives of a large group of professional associations, chaired and edited by Dan Stufflebeam. The standards are listed and illustrated under four general headings: propriety, utility, feasibility, and accuracy. See also **Fitting the lock to the key.**

PERSON-YEARS See **Level of Effort.**

PERSPECTIVAL EVALUATION This approach to or part of an evaluation requires the evaluator to create and preferably role-play various conceptualizations of the program or product being evaluated, representing the point of view of various stakeholders or judges—and *new perspectives*. These perspectives affect every aspect of the evaluation, including cost analysis and final conclusions. Of course, where possible, the evaluators should enlist help from members of the different groups impacted; but more is required when it comes to a new perspective, which Kuhn rightly stresses as the creative act associated with a new paradigm and for which there are no identifiable advocates. The evaluator should be trained in seeing these, and ever-watchful for them. A perspective is more than just an interpretation, it is a complete point of view, somewhere along the

260

spectrum that begins with an analogy, runs on through a perception toward a gestalt and a paradigm. (The epistemological importance of this originates, as Kuhn acknowledges, in Wittgenstein's discussions of 'seeing as'.) Sometimes it's important to understand them even if they are provably inappropriate. Simple examples of new perspectives generate novel critical competitors. They are common in the product field, where efforts are made to sell new products as if they were something revolutionary. The trick there is to see how they are just a fancied up version of an old acquaintance, or how they could be matched by a combination of existing products—the so-called Personal Information Managers are an example of this. More serious examples are seeing birth control as racist; seeing the draft as a tax on the young; seeing excise taxes as disguised subsidies; seeing the attack on the marijuana trade as a major cause of alcoholism.

Advocate-adversary is a special case of perspectival evaluation, with a methodology provided; consumer-based or manager-based evaluations are other special perspectives. As in architecture, multiple perspectives are often required in order to see something in full depth. This approach is different from illuminative, responsive, and other New Wave approaches, in its commitment to the view that there is an objective reality *of which* the perspectives are merely views, each one *inadequate* by itself. The defensible version of the naturalistic approach stresses this; the flawed version favors the "each perspective is equally legitimate" approach, which is false if the perspective is claimed to be *the* reality and not *just* one aspect of it. Perspectives are sometimes usable as dimensions in one variety of analytic evaluation. See also Layering.

PERT, PERT CHART PERT stands for Program Evaluation Review Technique, a graphical management tool. It comprises a special type of flow charting in which tasks are shown as blocks above a horizontal axis representing time; the blocks typically show the resources required for the task and the start/finish times. They are connected by lines that indicate causal dependency. One of its most interesting features is the identification of the critical path, the single line from one end of the project to the other that connects those blocks with no 'slack time', that is, with no room to take longer than scheduled without pushing the project's completion date past that scheduled. In some versions, completion times (and perhaps outputs at those points) are shown at three levels, namely the latest feasible, the earliest feasible, and the most probable. This provides a good approach to contingency planning, in the hands of a skilled manager. As with all these devices, they can become a pointless exercise if not closely tied to reality, and the tie to reality can't be read off the chart.

Computer programs make PERT charting much easier and are available on micros, starting at a few hundred dollars. See **Project management.**

PHENOMENONOLOGY OF EVALUATION An aspect or neighbor of the relatively unexplored domain of the **psychology of evaluation.** Apart from the anecdotal business of how it feels to evaluate and be evaluated, from which some insights could well be obtained into better (that is, more effective, more humane, more responsible) methods of doing and presenting evaluation, there are certain highly functional aspects of the experience that deserve more attention. Refocusing is one of these; another concerns the intimate interplay between the creative, critical, and data-gathering aspect of evaluation; a third concerns the role of empathy in the evaluator's mentation, actually and ideally. On the dysfunctional side, consideration of the phenomenology uncovers some interesting reasons why evaluations are less frequently used than they should be: for example, there are the perceptions that taking account of evaluations (other than one's own) amounts to (i) conceding lack of competence, or (ii) conceding power to the evaluator.

One interesting phenomenon is the reluctance—sometimes the refusal—of an evaluee to read an evaluation of themselves, even if they know it to be almost entirely favorable. The extent and explanation of this phenomenon is unknown, but it is of some significance in certain systems of personnel evaluation—for example, in the usual system for the evaluation of teachers at the college level—that assume these evaluations are a route to improvement. This phenomenon may be related to, but is not the same as psychological denial; nor is it quite the same as embarrassment or shyness; in some cases, it may be due to extreme sensitivity to even the possibility of slight criticism. See also **Goal-free evaluation.**

PHILANTHROPIC FOUNDATIONS (evaluation for) Evaluation has had a very checkered career in private foundations. At its best, no one does it better; all too often, it is done casually or not at all. Some of the reasons for the latter situation are different from those that lead to poor evaluation in the private sector or in governmental organizations. At least one of the reasons is clearly benevolent—the foundation wants recipients to feel free of the bureaucratic hassles that often surround evaluation, divert energy from productive effort, and involve skills and hence costs not directly relevant to the project or program goals. There is no doubt some truth to this—certainly recipients report that it has this effect. But the same effect can be obtained without the substantial loss of benefits, using best evaluation practice. Other reasons for superficial evaluation are common elsewhere, such as donors

262

or staff not wanting to hear bad news, and an attitude that finds its reward mainly in the glad cries of fortunate applicants.

Foundations need to do evaluation because they have contractual or fairness obligations to donors, recipients and potential recipients, impactees, taxpayers, and the law; and because they should care about doing as much good as possible with the resources they have available. They should do evaluation, not only of recipient projects, but of their own processes, especially their **selection** of projects and staff (especially evaluation staff), and their strategies. Strategy issues that need evaluation—not necessarily professional evaluation—include translation of donors' wishes into area and process paramaters; **resource** assessment; **needs assessment** within that area; the **apportionment** profile across the area; their publicity, both for public relations and for generating applications (this is marketing, although philanthropoids do not like the name); the extent of their nondollar assistance to applicants and recipients (managerial or evaluability consulting, for example); the extent of **proactivity** (suggestion or creation of projects when applications seem inadequate); the conflict of interest problem for the board; staff - support for board; the evaluation of projects for funding; and selection of staff.

Evaluation of funded projects—often the only type of evaluation that foundations think of when they are talking about evaluation—has three major categories of benefit. These are: (i) help for the recipients in achieving their goals (indirectly, of course, this helps the foundation meet its goals); (ii) ensuring accountability to donors' wishes and the legal constraints; (iii) improving cost-effectiveness (by learning what works and does not work, for immediate and further support decisions). The first of these focuses on ensuring that—and helping—the projects do ongoing formative evaluation, so as to provide early warning of trouble, and suggestions for fixes. The second is traditional monitoring plus summative project evaluation. The third focuses on—although it is not restricted to—something which it is rarely appropriate to demand from recipients but is most important for foundations, namely the generalizability of an approach, of the materials and training procedures produced, the insights developed, and so on. It is a special kind of applied research, particularly appropriate for foundation staff; but they will sometimes need to call on program theory experts and remediators and should not assume that evaluators *per se* will be able to provide all the help they need on this point.

The **Big footprint approach** is a graphical metaphor developed to help foundations and their grantees develop a common language for talking about project effects and their assessment. Foundation staff sometimes think it's too outcome focussed, but that's a false dichotomy; if the process is the payoff, its footprint can be measured quite easily.

PLACEBO EFFECT   An effect due to the *delivery context* of a treatment as opposed to the *delivered content*. In medicine, the placebo is a dummy pill, given to the control group in exactly the same way that the test drug (or more generally, the experimental treatment) is given to the experimental group, that is, with the nurses, the doctors, and the patients in ignorance as to whether the pill given to a particular individual is a placebo or not. (This is not a valid design *for identifying placebo effect*, but it's a considerable improvement over giving no placebo to the control group.) There is some evidence that the benefits do not depend on a belief that the placebo *is* an effective drug; but they probably depend on the belief that it *may* be effective. Placebo effect is probably therefore related to some other effects of belief, especially **enthusiasm effect**. In many cases—for example, faith-healing—belief in the power of the placebo occurs and is sometimes accompanied by a very large placebo effect. In the converse case, illustrated by bone-pointing, curses, and spells, (and perhaps some TV commercials) the effect is adverse—here called a negative placebo effect.

"Bedside manner" is a common vehicle for and beneficiary from the placebo effect. It is estimated that prior to the sulfa drugs, 90% of all therapeutic results were due to the placebo effect, so it's unfortunate that bedside manner gets little play in medical practice and training. Until 1948, when the term was accepted, placebo effect got little research effort and the results of what was done were not accepted for publication. This was presumably because of the status-need—to distinguish medicine from faith-healing. Legitimation of placebo research was therefore greatly facilitated by the use of the Latin name, which gave it medical respectability. Psychotherapy has been said to be *entirely* placebo effect (Frank); a design to investigate this view presents interesting challenges.

In education and other human service areas, the placebo effect is often confused with the **Hawthorne effect**, the effect on an individual's behavior of the knowledge that the behavior is being studied. The two may well account for much of the success of innovations. This is genuine success, but it cannot be ascribed to the snake-oil itself. If it is, we may draw false conclusions about what will happen to patients taking the treatment without the presence of the enthusiasts—and enthusiasm does fade. Hence evaluations must include some hands-off testing, in which the evaluand has to fly on its own, and even then, it is

264

highly desirable if this is done at some temporal as well as spatial remove. It should also be kept in mind that the effect may be negative.

PLANNING (evaluation in) It is essential to get evaluation started before a program starts, both to get baseline data, and to evaluate the program plan, at least for **evaluability.** See **Preformative evaluation.** If your role is predefined as that of the program evaluator, formative or summative, you won't be seen as having any right to input about the program plan, which was decided on prior to funding, and long before you were identified as evaluator. This is a mistake, because you should be able to bring some important benefits to refining the plan. Alternatively, planners should have considerable evaluation training, if they are not going to call in an evaluatore early, because one way or another, half the mistakes are made before the program begins (or the RFP—which incorporates a program plan—is published). Of course, one mistake is to design a program which is essentially unevaluable, given the particular constraints of resources and context. This is not just a nuisance for you, it is a guarantee that the program managers will never know if the program owrked. But there are many other contributions the evaluation viewpoint can make, such as looking more closely at cost analysis of alternative procedures which seem equivalent to the program's authors.

PLANS (evaluation of) See **Proposal evaluation.**

PLAYERS Everyone involved in any way with an evaluand; notably, all **stakeholders** as well as **providers, supporters,** and **recipients.**

POINT CONSTANCY REQUIREMENT (PCR) The requirement on numerical scoring, for example, of tests, that a point should reflect the same amount of merit, however it is earned (that is, regardless of the item and regardless of the number of points already acquired on a particular item). It is connected with the definition of an interval scale. If PCR is violated, additivity fails, that is, some total performance X will be awarded more points than performance Y although it is in fact inferior. PCR is a very severe requirement and rarely checked at all, hence *one should normally give a global grade as well as a score* on tests in order to provide some protection against PCR failure. The keys to PCR are the **rubric** in essay/simulation scoring and item-matching on multiple-choice tests.

POINT OF ENTRY There are two point of entry problems in evaluation. The first is the client's point of entry problem and it concerns the question of when an evaluator should be brought in to look at a project; the second is the (formative) evaluator's point of entry problem, the problem of where in the time flux of decisions the evaluator should start evaluating the options that were or will be available, that is, where to start defining **critical competitors.** (Both relate to the notion of "policy space", discussed in Berk and Rossi's *Thinking About Program Evaluation*, Sage, 1990.)

The client's problem is a serious one. Project directors and program managers often feel that bringing in an external evaluator at the very beginning of a project is likely to produce a chilling effect and that the staff should have a chance to 'run with the ball' in the way they think is most likely to be productive for at least some time without critical scrutiny, admonitions about measurability of results, and so on. Evaluators often do exert a chilling effect. Sometimes they could have avoided it; sometimes not. **Goal-free evaluation** is one way to avoid it although not possible in the planning phase. It's possible on a small project to have an evaluator in for at least one series of discussions during the planning phase, maybe get by without one for a while after that, then bring one or more back in after things begin to take shape and perhaps dispense with most of them again for a second period of 'unfettered creativity'. However, there are many evaluators who have exerted a constantly stimulating and helpful effect on projects, in spite of being on board all the time. They need strength of character as well as external evaluation help to avoid the bias of co-option (going native).

The client's problem has another side, which affects the evaluator: has the evaluator been brought in early enough to do a sound evaluation of the kind that the client needs? The evaluator is often brought in too late to be able to determine baseline performance and too late to set up control groups, and is hence unable to determine either gains or causation. These problems arise with projects that were not designed with **evaluability** in mind. On a *big* project there's really no alternative to an in-house early-on-board evaluation staff.

The evaluator's point of entry problem is less obvious. It is the question of what to consider "fixed", and hence what to consider as pointless second-guessing in doing a *formative* evaluation. Suppose that one is brought in very late in a project. For formative evaluation purposes, there's really no point in second-guessing the early decisions about the shape of the project, because they're now (usually) irreversible. (For summative evaluation, it *will* be necessary to second-guess those, which means that the point of entry of the summative evaluator is always back at the moment when the project design was being determined, a point that commonly antedates the allocation of funds to the project.) The formative evaluator, however, should in fact not be restricted to looking at the set of choice points that are seen by the project staff as downstream from the point when the evaluator is called in. For the formative evaluator, the correct point of entry for evaluation purposes is the *last irreversible decision*. Even though the

266

staff hasn't thought of the possibility of reversing some earlier decisions, the formative evaluator must look into such possibilities and the cost/value of reversals.

POLICY ANALYSIS (POLICY STUDIES) The evaluation of policies, plans, sometimes proposals and possibilities; a 'normative' (better, prescriptive) science or transdiscipline like decision theory or game theory, and closely related in its emergence and methodology to evaluation. Martin Trow, a leading figure in the field, sees it as having emerged in the mid-70s from strands that included operations research, microeconomics, organizational theory, public administration, social psychology, and an increasing interest in the role of law in public policy. It is likely that one should add the emergence of program evaluation to this list. Carol Weiss and Stuart Nagel have been outstanding linkers between the two fields since before policy studies crystallized, and the AERA journal *Educational Evaluation and Policy Analysis* has been a bridging journal, only lately moving rather heavily to the policy side.

In terms of the Key evaluation checklist, a good policy analysis usually covers every step, including Recommendations, and adds nothing different except perhaps a shorter time in which to get an answer. Indeed, while the Inspectors General made a radical departure from the academic model of multiyear evaluations to insist on multimonth evaluations, the policy analyst is not uncommonly required to do multiday evaluations. There are policy studies whithatch are not tied directly to recommendations, as in retrospective ones, and mainline evaluators are sometimes called on to evaluate alternative policies, so the fields are not easily distinguishable. Nevertheless, the modal task of the policy analyst is somewhat different from that of the evaluator—it is scenario evaluation, that is, evaluation of alternative possible futures, each corresponding to a different policy. Done well, it will exhibit certain features which are quite rare in evaluation, for example, (i) heavy analysis of the ways in which a policy covers common emergencies—strikes, power failures, civil disturbance—rather than elaborating on an ideal, and (ii) focus on the way in which the policy will be self-modifying in the light of experience, including partial failure—this aspect will include some kind of evaluation system.

The policy analyst has a schizophrenic role somewhat familiar to evaluators: on the one hand, trying to provide reasonably valid research summaries to the decision-maker who is trying to make sensible recommendations before the special interest groups divide up the pie; and on the other trying to convey to the academic researcher that action often requires answers that won't meet all the standards for publication. A competent evaluator will similarly recognize the frequent necessity for fast answers and look more carefully at providing better databases of information and better damage control measures, instead of sounding like the Voice of the Ivory Tower. The main employers of policy analysts are schools of public policy, some federal agencies, and the scores of 'think-tanks' concentrated in Washington. See also **Inspection, Inspector General, Evaluation training, ELMR.**

POLITICS OF EVALUATION Depending on one's role and the day of the week, one is likely to think of politics as *dirty* politics—an intrusion into scientific evaluation—or as part of the ambient *reality* that evaluators were for a long time careless about treating as a relevant consideration. (Carol Weiss called them to order.) If one has a favorable attitude toward politics, or uses the term without pejorative connotations, one will include virtually all program background and contextual factors in the political dimension of program evaluation and demand that it be taken into account in the design. The jaundiced view simply defines it as the set of pressures that are not related to the truth or merits of the case; and the jaundiced viewers remind us that evaluators are not, by mission or training, well qualified to be political analysts, and should be very cautious about venturing into the territory of **recommendations** whose feasibility will be highly dependent on political factors. (Of course, this is quite different from holding back on *conclusions*.)

The politics of competency-based testing as a requirement for graduating seniors is a good example, and most of the same points apply to competency-testing of teachers. The situation in many states is that it has become "politically necessary" to institute such requirements, now or in the near future, although the way in which they have been instituted virtually destroys all the reasons for the requirements. That is: the requirement for graduating from the twelfth grade is "basic skills" at the seventh or eighth or fifth grade level depending on the state, a paltry standard; they require no demonstration of *other* skills; they usually do not require any demonstration of *application* skills on the basics; the exams are set up to allow multiple retakes of exactly the same test or on a very few versions of it (hence there is no proof that the *skill* is present); teachers have access to and teach to the test; other subjects are completely dropped from the 11th and 12th grade curriculum to make room for yet more repetitive teaching of drill-level basics, regardless of the effects on better students who are left languishing for years, and so on. A strong case can be made that *this* version of MCT does more harm than good, though a serious version would certainly contribute toward truth-in-packaging of the diploma. This is politics without payoff, cynical because the politicians believe they can get the credit for the move without it
268

having any actual value. That it works is due to the lack of critical skills in the citizenry, media, and legislatures. (See also **Pseudo-evaluation.**)

But on other occasions, the "politics" is what got equity into personnel evaluation, and racism (more or less) out of the curriculum materials. Then again, it also keeps serious moral education out of the public schools, and serious sex education out of many, a terrible handicap for the student and the society. Better education for the citizen about—and in—evaluation, may be the best route to improvement, short of a political leader with the charisma to persuade us of anything and the brains to persuade us to improve our critical thinking.

POLLUTION (of test scores) The result of practices aimed at increasing test scores without increasing the skills they test; a threat to validity, and hence to the public's perception of the educational achievements of their own children and the nation's. The common versions of these practices are widespread in the U.S. and the correct term for most of them is 'cheating'; the fact that it's mainly the teachers and administrators who engage in these practices, rather than the students, is hardly grounds for euphemism. Three major causes are: (i) **teaching to the test**; (ii) sending weaker students home or on a field trip, or encouraging them to stay home, on the day the test is taken; (iii) giving hints or answers, allowing extra time or cribbing, or changing the response sheets. Some aspects of the first of these, namely teaching basic test-taking skills and getting students hyped up for the test, are not unethical but can lead to seriously wrong interpretation of the results, especially if not practiced uniformly. Messick's work on **validity** is the key basis for discussion of this issue. Ref: "Raising Standardized Achievement Test Scores and the Origins of Test Score Pollution", Haladyna et al., *Educational Researcher*, June-July, 1991.

POPULATION (Stat.) The group of entities from which a sample is drawn or about which a conclusion is stated. The term was extended from its original reference to people to cover things (for example, objects on the production line, which is the population sampled for quality control studies). A less obvious extension is to circumstances (a field trial samples the population of circumstances under which a product might be used); there are still fancier extensions in statistical theory to possible measurements and configurations, and so on.

PORTRAYAL Semitechnical term for an evaluation-by-(rich)-description, perhaps using pictures, quotes, photographs, poetry, or anecdotes as well as observations. See **Responsibility evaluation, Naturalistic evaluation.**

POSITIVISM A doctrine in the philosophy of science due to Auguste Comte. It became famous mainly through the influence of a supposed variant, logical positivism, which grew out of scientists' negative reactions to the impenetrable jungles of German metaphysics in the early decades of the twentieth century. The Vienna Circle, the key group of logical positivists, eschewed all statements not directly verifiable by observation, including not only ethics but history and much physical theory. The position mellowed into the neopositivist position, which dominated philosophy of science at mid-century (Nagel, Hempel, the later Reichenbach and Carnap, Feigl, and others). Positivism was one of the sources of intellectual support for the doctrine of value-free science, which retarded the emergence of evaluation as a discipline and the use of the social sciences to serve the needs of humanity. It was not the direct source of that doctrine (Max Weber was its spiritual father) and probably not a sufficient condition for its occurrence. Recently, positivism has become a whipping boy for various new movements in social science methodology and philosophy of science, including those favoring qualitative evaluation approaches, and in the process the term has been caricatured to the point where the term "positivism" is used for what is properly called empiricism. On the way to that caricature, neopositivism is lumped in with positivism—about the equivalent of calling all Democrats Communists—and even postpositivism gets the same treatment, although the latter position handles essentially all the objections to positivism and neopositivism and in the process removes itself still further from the original position. Attacks on positivism today are not beating a dead horse, they are beating an eohippus.

POSTTEST The measurement made after the "treatment", in order to identify absolute or relative gains (depending on whether the comparison is with pretest scores or with simultaneous comparison group scores).

POWER 1. Of a test, design, analysis. An important technical concept involved in the evaluation of experimental designs and methods of statistical analysis; related to efficiency. The more powerful the test, the stronger the conclusions it will support. It is in tension with other desiderata such as small sample size, as is common with evaluative criteria.

2. In the psychology and politics of evaluation. (i) Knowledge is power, the saying goes, and although it's a more popular saying among knowledge producers than among anti-intellectual heads of state, it's an insight in many contexts. For some people, accepting evaluations from another person, certainly if they come from outside the circle of friends and family, is making a concession of need to

270

aliens, and/or creating a debt—both of which they resist strongly. Better our own power than better power from an outsider. It follows that use of evaluation findings will be much greater if the prospective user can be made a co-investigator from the beginning. That creates the dilemma in program evaluation of whether to sacrifice independence to get utilization. The soft models do it; the hard models refuse it, making it the responsibility of the prospective user to give up a stupid attitude in order to get better information. The tension between the two alternatives would be considerably reduced if **evaluation education** were a significant part of the school curriculum. (ii) Forget the arty-crafty talk about knowledge being power, let's talk *real power*. Real power is being in a position where you can hand out the contracts, sign off on the expense vouchers, hire your cousin as groundskeeper. Real power is given away if you get in the habit of following the advice of evaluators; who is going to wine and dine you if the vendors think you simply pick the best reading program from the results of field tests? And who is going to *credit your judgment* if they know you make your decisions by reading *Consumer Reports* (or the equivalent in your field)? Giving away a chance to have your judgment rated high is giving away power. See NIH (Not Invented Here). Administrators often trot out a metatheory rationalization (especially when talking to other administrators) about evaluators 'infringing on the decision-maker's territory'. This is absurd, literally speaking; but it's an insight, psychodynamically speaking, and a sinister one. If consumers and stakeholders (e.g., shareholders) fail to understand this and take explicit countermeasures, they will find their interests sold out. What countermeasures? Insistence on seeing reports from external evaluators and a statement of reasons for disregarding their recommendations whenever they are disregarded. The limiting type of case is illustrated by the **Dreyfus case**, which illustrates another aspect of power—power is not having to say you're sorry.

POWER TEST The contrast is with a speeded test, where a substantial number of testees do not finish the test. In a power test, at least 95% will finish, because speed of completion is not a part of what the test is designed to measure. This term is rarely encountered now, partly because the other meaning (the power *of* tests) gets in the way.

PPBS Program Planning and Budgeting System. The management tool developed by MacNamara and others at Ford Motor Company and taken to the Pentagon when MacNamara became Secretary of Defense; thereafter widely adopted in other federal and state agencies. Principal advantage and feature: identifying costs by *program* and not by conventional categories such as payroll, inventory, and so on. It facilitates rational planning with regard to program continuance, increased support, and so on. There are two problems: first, it's too often (virtually always) instituted as a mere change in bookkeeping procedures, without a program *evaluation* component worth the name, so the payoffs are masked or don't occur. Second, it's often very expensive to implement and unreliable in distribution of overhead, and it never seems to occur to anyone to evaluate the problem and cost of shifting to PPBS before doing it, a typical example of missing the point of the whole enterprise. Cf. **Meta-evaluation, Mission budgeting.**

PRACTICE EFFECT The *specific* form of practice effect refers to the fact that taking a second test with the same or closely similar items in it will result in improvement in performance even if no additional instruction or (other) learning has occurred between the two tests. After all, one has done all the "organizing of one's thoughts" before the second test. There is a *general* practice effect, which is particularly important with respect to individuals who have not had much—or much recent—experience with test-taking; this practice effect simply refers to improving one's test-taking skills through practice, for example, one's ability to control the time spent on each question, to understand the way in which various types of multiple-choice questions work, and so on. The more **speeded** the test is, the more serious the practice effect is likely to be. The use of control groups will enable one to estimate the size of the practice effect, but if that's not possible, the use of a posttest-only design for *some* of the experimental group will do very nicely instead, since the difference between the two subgroups on the posttest will give an indication of the practice effect, which one then subtracts from the gains of the posttest-only group to get a measure of the gains due to the treatment.

PREDICTIVE VALIDITY See **Construct validity.**

PREFORMATIVE (evaluation) Evaluation activities in the planning phase of a program; typically involve gathering baseline data, improving evaluability, designing the evaluation, improving the planned program, and so on. It's better to divide these activities between two categories: (I) formative evaluation of the plan (or **RFP**), and (II) preparation for evaluation of the program. See **Planning, Evaluation.**

PREORDINATE EVALUATION See **Responsive evaluation,** which is partly defined as being the opposite of preordinate evaluation.

PRESCRIPTIVE Laying down what *should* be done as opposed to what *is* being done (descriptive). Strictly speaking, prescriptive is not the same as **evaluative,** the general class of claims that identify things as good, better or best; roughly speaking, it is a subspecies referring to actions, recommendations, and decisions. (You can determine the best or worst composition among the English class' assignments without concluding anything about what ought to be done by you or its author.) In the limiting case where we are creating the rules, the prescriptions completely determine what is right or meritorious, for example, when developing a scoring system for a new game or grading recommendations for math achievement levels (e.g., ""Proficient" means 80% or better on these items"). Hence, the fact/value distinction is not the same as the descriptive/prescriptive distinction; but this is less harmful a confusion than the one involved in using the term "**normative**" to cover evaluative language (since that term suggests that the meaning of evaluative language is connected with norms of actual behavior). The main problem for those beginning to work on prescriptive studies is to get used to the major imprecisions that are an essential part of the work; when proposing what should be done, we are into the area of judgment and should not be concerned about 20% differences between the recommendations from different sources, whereas this would be unthinkable for normative studies

Policy studies are supposedly the area that focuses exclusively on prescriptive conclusions, although in fact they do a great deal of ordinary evaluation as well; the difference is simply that they always go on to the recommendations, whereas evaluations may not. Huey-Tseh Chen rightly points out that there can be prescriptive *theories* about, for example, social programs, by contrast with the usual descriptive ones. He gives rational decision theory as one example: p. 8 of "Issues in Constructing Program Theory", in *Advances in Program Theory*, L. Bickman, ed. (Jossey-Bass, 1990).

PRESS RELEASES The rules are: (i) Don't bother to hand (or send) out the technical version, even as a supplement; (ii) Don't bother to hand out a *summary* of the technical document; (iii) Don't bother to hand out a statement that says favorable things and then qualifies them—either the qualification or the favorable comment will be dropped; and (iv) Issue only a basic description of the program itself plus a single overview claim, for example, "Results do not as yet show any advantages or disadvantages from this approach, because it's much too early to tell. We hope to have a definite conclusion in N months". (That's an interim release; in a final release you drop the second sentence.)

PRETEST Pretests are normally said to be of two kinds or to serve two purposes; diagnostic and baseline. In a diagnostic pretest, the pedagogical function (it could be a test of health, etc. but we focus here on the educational case) is to identify the presence or absence of prerequisite skills or the places where remedial instruction should be provided. These tests will typically not resemble posttests. In baseline

273

pretesting, on the other hand, we are trying to determine what the level of knowledge (etc.) is, on the criterion or payoff dimensions, and hence it should be matched exactly, for difficulty, with the posttest. Instructors often think that using this kind of pretest will have bad results, because students will have a "failure experience". Properly managed—perhaps using **matrix sampling**—the reverse is the case. The pretest gives an unambiguous and preview of the kind of work that will be expected, which is highly desirable in itself. If it is—as it should be—gone over carefully in class, one has provided students with an operational definition of the required standards for passing. Furthermore, one has created a quite useful climate for interesting the students in early discussions, by giving them a chance to try to solve the problems with their native wit, and then showing how the content of the course helps them to do better. In many subjects, though not all, this constitutes a very desirable proof of the importance of the course. And one often discovers that some or all students are not as ignorant about the subject matter of the course as one had supposed, in which case very useful changes can be made in content, or "challenging out" can be allowed, with a reduction in costs to the student and possibly to the instructor.

Of course, treating the pretest as defining the early course content is likely to qualify as **teaching to the test** if one uses many of the items from the pretest in the posttest. But there are even times when this is entirely appropriate; and in general it is very sensible to pull items for the posttest out of a pool that includes the items from the pretest, so that at least some of them will be retested. This encourages learning the material covered in the pretest, which should certainly *not* be excluded from the course just because it has already been tested. Instructors who begin to give pretests also begin to adjust their teaching in a more flexible way to the requirements of a specific class, instead of using exactly the same material repeatedly. Thus the use of a pretest is an excellent example of the integration of evaluation into teaching, *and* a case of evaluation procedures paying off through side-effects as well as through direct effects. Direct effects of evaluation of course include the discovery that students have or have not mastered the material and are or are not able to learn certain types of material from the test, notes, and lectures provided in this course.

PRICE The money cost that is charged by vendor to consumer or client for a product or service. It is usually a small part of total cost and often more than true worth—sometimes much less. Of course, *list* price isn't the same as *street* price or *best* price, and it takes some minor skill to know how to get the best price, for example, bargaining skill in some situations. We are often misled by price, largely because

274

we are not taught much about cost analysis and partly because we're often not in a position to get the data on true cost. Legislation requiring refrigerator manufacturers to post estimates of lifetime cost on their appliances does something to counter these two deficiencies in the resources of the consumer. In its absence, the manufacturer can increase interior space and reduce manufacturing cost by reducing the amount or quality of insulation, which makes the product more attractive to both parties, if the buyer is an innocent. The buyer then pays for the manufacturer's shoddy work, and for his or her own ignorance—very heavily (perhaps twice the cost of the product). Of course, lifetime cost also involves reliability, cost of service, and cost of power.

PRIMA FACIE The key modifier in drawing evaluative conclusions; it means "on the face of it" or "presumably" or, more precisely, "strong enough to *establish* the conclusion *unless rebutted*". Scientists often think—and have been encouraged in this by philosophers of science such as Popper—that we can never prove any empirical claims in science. We can't prove them beyond the *possibility* of error, but we can prove them *beyond reasonable doubt* by establishing a series of prima facie inferences that point to them, combined with assiduous search for rebutting considerations. If the search is assiduous enough (e.g., it survives serious scrutiny by the disciplinary specialists) and the rebutting examples or counterexplanations are not found, the conclusions must be accepted (for the time being).

Small dictionaries give an alleged common parlance usage which is obsolescent, meaning merely "apparently" or "face valid". The slightly different legal meaning, provided in larger dictionaries and in *Black's Law Dictionary*, has taken over in professional literature: the difference is that a prima facie case is strong enough to justify the conclusion in the absence of rebutting evidence, a much stronger form of support than just pointing toward it (see **Secondary indicator**). Probative logic is largely based on the concept of prima facie inference; see **Logic of evaluation**.

PRIMARY INDICATOR Another name for a **criterion**, which is all or part of the meaning of the concept under examination (for example, good organization of material and good punctuation are criteria of good composition performance). To be distinguished from a **secondary indicator**, which is only connected to the criteria by empirical links (for example, good performance on an appropriate multiple-choice exam is a good indicator of essay-writing ability).

PRIMARY VALUE CLAIM A claim to the effect that something has a certain value (or merit, or worth). Distinguished from reported-value claims—claims that someone, including oneself, believes

275

something to have a certain value—here called secondary value claims.

PRISONER'S DILEMMA A classic problem in game theory, with far-reaching implications for the social sciences. It concerns two prisoners who are arrested for complicity in the commission of a crime, are put in cells between which no communication is possible, and offered a deal by the district attorney. If one turns state's evidence, and the other does not, the first will be released and the second will receive ten years. If both confess, each will receive a five year sentence. If neither confess, the evidence is insufficient to convict of a major crime, and both will receive a year's sentence on a minor charge. The challenge of the example is that for each prisoner in isolation, it appears that the best strategy is confession—since this excludes the worst result. But the best result of all—when neither confess—cannot be reached by a solo reasoning effort, since confession is too risky. The importance of the example is that it models much of the crucial part of social behavior, and it has generated a large literature in the theory of games. The only solution is through prior irreversible commitment to treat the welfare of each other as comparable to their own, and this reflects the reason for ethical training of the young. In general, it's easy to show that an ethical society has better survival value than a society of rational egoists, and that provides a reason for trying to make one's own society ethical, even at the 'cost' of being made ethical oneself. Details in *Primary Philosophy* (McGraw-Hill, 1966). A good introduction to game theory which explains the importance of the Prisoner's Dilemma is *Game Theory: Concepts and Applications* by Frank Zagare (Sage, 1984).

PROACTIVE An approach to or facet of evaluation or other research that is aimed at producing direct effects on the behavior of those being evaluated or studied, instead of trying to minimize it, as in the traditional model of social science investigations. Formative evaluation is aimed at effects, often quite direct effects. It commonly involves midterm feedback reports at public meetings and these may well lead to more direct changes than the client had expected. Public introduction of a process of evaluation, even just summative evaluation, often has a content-free proactive effect on impacted programs and personnel, one which is by no means automatically good—or bad. Proactive evaluation is laden with dangers—co-option, change not based on a completed evaluation, and so on. It is not always easy to avoid, even in the summative role: for example, when investigating the merits of a critical competitor not thought of by the program staff, one can hardly avoid getting reactions to it from the prospective consumer, who may be so taken with it as to put on pressure to bring it about

276

immediately. An example of this arises when a program evaluator notices that a foundation's community development program is not receiving applications that are as good as it appears they should be. This may be due to poor advertising, poor counseling of prospective applicants, and so on, and direct study of these processes would of course be done by any evaluator. However, even if they pass muster, there may still be a failure of imagination on the part of the foundation staff and the community in generating more powerful proposals. It is difficult to prove this without a proactive effort since it is not entirely convincing to merely mention what appear to the evaluator to be better alternatives; one needs to demonstrate their feasibility by taking them around for community reactions and commitments to tangible support. Then, of course, one has really started something. It's a serious decision whether to do this; but it may be the only way to establish a criticism that is important. See also **Evaluability assessment.**

PROBATIVE LOGIC A new (informal) logic of contextual inference that particularly focusses on inference to prima facie conclusions, steps that are valid "other things being equal", and concepts like "cause" which are as context-dependent as "large" or "good" or "explanation". It uses tools such as definitions by examples and contrasts instead of classical definitions, **criteria** instead of necessary and sufficient conditions, weighing instead of deducing, heuristics for inductive inference (not 'inspired guessing'). Probative logic is intended to represent the normal logic of discourse, and to be nearer to the logic of evaluative, legal, and most scientific reasoning than any formal logics; the latter are said to be reconstructions of varying degrees of artificiality. See **Logic of evaluation.** Probative implication, as in p probatively implies q, is sometimes symbolized by "p+q" (for "p points to q") because of the resemblance to pointing toward rather than (the converse of) deriving from. Causation might analogously be symbolized by PkQ, in order to stress the notion of agency and weaken the similarity to implication. With a typewriter, one can use the colon to suggest the constraint that probative implication places on implication, and a crossbow instead of a pistol for agency, thus: p :—> q, and P –} Q.

PROCESS What happens between input and output, between start and finish. Generalized to mean any characteristics other than input or output variables. As the name of one of the checkpoints in the Key evaluation checklist, it refers to the legitimate use of *process evaluation*, as described below.

PROCESS EVALUATION Usually refers to an evaluation of the treatment (or evaluand) that focuses entirely on variables between input and output (but it may include **input** variables); can also refer to the process *component* of a full evaluation. With exceptions to be mentioned, the process-only approach is illegitimate or a second choice except where a highly reliable connection is known to exist between process variables and outcome variables *and* if no more direct and reliable approach is available. Process evaluation is rarely the approach of choice because the connections with output quantity and quality, where they do exist, are relatively weak, often transient, and likely to generalize poorly to new situations; and the output, not the process, is the reason for the program. The classic case of improper use is the evaluation of teachers by classroom observation (the usual procedure K-12). Observing the teaching process can only provide a legitimate basis for negative evaluations, never for positive ones and is hence a seriously flawed approach (see **Teacher evaluation** and **Symmetry**). The major extenuating circumstance that can be used to justify process evaluation as the sole approach is the impossibility of doing outcome evaluation, for example because a decision must be made before the outcomes can be studied, or because resources are not available for doing an outcome study (for good reasons).

In product evaluation, we often do the equivalent of process evaluation when we buy by the name of a brand or model number (the process is 'being made by General Motors according to the specifications for model N'). If this model has recently been evaluated validly and favorably, the inference is not too bad because of the relative constancy of properties in a production run. But that constancy is only relative—manufacturers constantly change suppliers of components, suffer breakdowns, use new workers, redesign to save money, and so on; and the evaluations you see are neither infallible nor exactly tailored to your needs. So the thirty-day money-back guarantee is very important; in personnel evaluation, the probationary period is essential.

However, certain aspects of process *must* be looked at *as part of any comprehensive evaluation*, not as a substitute for inspection of outcomes (and other factors); these aspects cannot be replaced by study of outcomes. They include the legality of the process, its morality, its enjoyability, the truth of any claims involved in it, its implementation of the supposed treatment, and whatever clues it can provide about causation. (These correspond to such procedures as looking at electrical safety in product evaluation.) It might be better in teaching the subject to use the term "mediated evaluation" to refer to what is described as process evaluation in the opening sentence of this entry, and allow "process evaluation" to refer to the direct (not mediated) evaluation of process variables as part of an overall evaluation that involves looking at outcomes. It is in the latter sense that the term is

278

used in the **Key evaluation checklist**. The irony of the usual process of teacher evaluation is that the aspects of teaching process that can legitimately be looked at are usually ignored. These include accuracy and completeness of content (of presented material and answers to questions); test construction, use and marking; quality and timeliness of feedback to students; attendance/punctuality; and the scrupulous avoidance of bias.

Although it is illicit to use style variables in evaluating programs, as in evaluating personnel, there is an area between style and absolute considerations such as ethicality and legality where one may draw evaluative conclusions when observing process, at least in *formative* program evaluation. This is the area of evaluating functional components of the process. Some examples include: communications (internal and external), interface (for consumers and stakeholders), the formative evaluation system of the program, flexibility, infrastructure effectiveness, and arrangements for implementing what is learnt from feedback. Some examples of indicators that suggest a need for improvement under these headings: the program's receptionists are rude to most of a random selection of callers; the telephonists are incompetent; the senior staff is unhelpful to evaluators called in by the program to improve it; workers are ignorant about the reasons for procedures that are intrusive into their work patterns; the quality control system lacks the power to call a halt to the process when it discerns an emergency. Good evaluation should turn up and report on such matters, while witholding any overall evaluation until responses from program management have been heard. This kind of finding is less decisive than clear cases of discrimination since the latter violate absolute standards, but provide strong prima facie evidence of poor process.

Process checks include an even wider variety of considerations: when evaluating a certain type of scholarly article, one process indicator is the adequacy of the literature search; often, checking for sexist language is also relevant, as it is to curriculum or instructor evaluation; so is checking on the ethicality of testing procedures; on the accuracy of warranty claims; and on the validity of instruments used. A somewhat different type of indicator is provided by patterns that may be clues to causal connections (see **Modus operandi method**). Thus some of these process checks lead to changes in the basic description of the evaluand; some to changes in outcomes or costs; some finish up as ethical conclusions about the process that do not have to relate to the needs assessment in order to graduate into the final report. See also **Description**.

PRODUCT Interpreted very broadly, for example, may be used to

279

refer to students, and so on, as the "product" of a training program; a pedagogical *process* might be the *product* of a research and development effort.

PRODUCT EVALUATION This is generally taken to mean the evaluation of functional artefacts, but it can also be taken to include the evaluation of output from students, such as essays. (The latter would normally be classified in this work as **performance evaluation**.) First, some general remarks about the field, then some comments on the new area of computer product evaluation. Product evaluation is the best-developed and oldest field within evaluation. *Consumer Reports* used to be an almost flawless paradigm although it has deteriorated significantly in recent years, partly because it refuses to treat its own methodology as something it should be discussing, justifying, and refining—a form of behavior that must make Stuart Chase, the philosopher who co-founded it, turn in his grave. It has also greatly expanded in several respects, namely its range of interests beyond domestic product evaluation, its advertising of its own products in its own products, and its income—but not (significantly) the number of pages in the *Reports*, the number of tests, or the sophistication of the tests (see **Sensory evaluation**). On home computers it has always done a second-rate job; on cars, it is useful because its buys its own and the raters aren't part of the magazine subculture (for example, it picked up the serious fault in the BMW 320i, missed by the road testers for the pro-BMW enthusiast magazines) but it's weak on many items (e.g., instrumentation); it has stopped doing reviews in several areas—an example is mail-order, low-cost, high-durability clothing—because its needs assessment is primitive. (As this went to press, a survey of jeans appeared in the July, 1991, issue.) The **needs assessment** is mainly based on an overlong, poorly designed survey, as if **fault tree analysis, matrix sampling**, and **Delphi** techniques had never been invented. Product evaluation has become simply one competitor for its corporate attention, and it still hires only engineers for that. It appears never to contribute to the professional discussions in the literature, never funds research RFPs, and is reluctant or refuses to correct its own more serious errors in print. See also **Shared bias**.

The soft spots in *Consumer Reports* are only partly taken up by improvements in the number and quality (of the best) special-interest consumer magazines. In the car field, *Car & Driver* is now probably the best, ahead of the old front runner, *Road & Track*, and closely matched by a new and good general entry, *Automobile*. These are supplemented by some adequate entries in the four-wheel and other specialty areas. Other general entries such as *Motor Trend* are well back in the pack, but some aspects of other magazines' efforts are still valuable, for example *Popular Mechanics'* surveys of owners and listing of costs of parts. The weaknesses of enthusiast magazines in the auto field include: subculture bias (which becomes apparent when one sees the same cars reviewed in English, German, French or Italian automobile magazines); aestheticism; the use of cars supplied by the manufacturers; the near-fatal failure to be systematic (for example, there is no effort to *always* cover headlight power, wiper effectiveness, appropriateness for large, small, or older people—and one might forgive the absence of coverage of performance in snow or icy conditions on the short term tests, but not on the year-long ones). The availability and quality of product evaluation in other areas has ebbed and flowed—high fidelity, short-wave radio, photography, boating, bicycles, motorcycles, home improvement, tools, gardening, and fishing gear magazines—but their best efforts have steadily improved, notably because of the increasing recognition of the importance of comparisons and long-term tests.

In all these cases, however, the fallacies of **technicism** and of **irrelevant expertise** are serious threats to validity. They can be partly balanced by careful use of reputable owner surveys such as those from J. D. Power, but it's hard to get access to these and the way the auto companies report them has often involved complete misrepresentation (for example: "Buick is in the Top Ten"; yes, with *one* model, while their others are *near the bottom*). And the owner surveys have their own biases—the new luxury cars on the block may rate better than old stand-bys because owners don't want to admit taking the risk in vain.

The big new entry has been the microcomputer magazines (and newsletters), and they have made some significant contributions, albeit contributions whose value is largely restricted to the specialized field. A leader has clearly emerged—*PC Magazine* (whose stablemate *MacUser* is now catching up—but there are more than a dozen that should be read to get some serious depth to the evaluation of particular products (about 3000 pages a month). Methodologically speaking, the most interesting may be *Software Digest,* which was founded to provide a 'pure testing' approach, that is, one which minimized the amount of subjective judgment *in a particular case.* It has partly succeeded in this, but of course judgment still comes in at the points where you decide what to measure, how to measure it, and how to weight it in the move to the bottom line. With respect to this role of judgment, they are less forthcoming and less impressive; hence some of their overall conclusions have been shaky.

What has emerged from all this are some very useful checklists, at two levels: the general one (Ease of Learning, Ease of Use, Speed,

Power, Safety, Support, with some very careful explication of what all of these involve) and the specific ones, for example, for word processors (130+ features) or laptop computers (180 features). Along with these, there has been a gradual refinement in measurement techniques, ranging from lab procedures up to the definition of benchmarks (standardized tasks for timing/speed measurement). Benchmarking has moved from <u>theory-based</u> to <u>practice-based</u>, as the computer science emphasis has been displaced by a consumer viewpoint. (A theory-based benchmark is designed to test a dimension of theoretical interest, for example, internal (bus) throughput; a practice-based benchmark tests speed on a common task, for example, recalculating a large spreadsheet.) Some efforts have been made to make a science out of interface design and its evaluation, but intense discussion of this by many of the key players across the years (particularly on the WELL, an electronic bulletin board) has made clear that there has been little progress.

One of the major limitations in automobile evaluation was overcome by moving to follow-ups in the form of long-term road tests, usually for a year. This is still missing with computer product evaluation, and there is a serious discrepancy between the early reviews, and the truth as it emerges later, usually in the form of throwaway remarks by columnists or on the (electronic) bulletin boards which make it clear that experience has led to major revisions in opinion by the cognoscenti. There is also a seriously inappropriate limitation on the length of reviews of complex programs like the word processing programs; an effort to redress this was made in *University MicroNews*, xvi, 1989, where reviews of over 10,000 words were published, but doing so is commercially unfeasible.

For some discussion of techniques, see **Qualitative weight and sum.** Today, it would be foolish not to use a spreadsheet for product evaluation, particularly one with outlining capability (Excel 3.0 was the first of these). Refs: "Product Evaluation" in *New Techniques for Evaluation*, N. Smith, ed. (Sage, 1981); and, for a discussion of the many serious sources of bias still present in the field, "The Evaluation of Hardware and Software" in a special edition of the journal *Studies in Educational Evaluation*, on the evaluation of educational technology, edited by Aliza Duby (Tel Aviv University, 1990).

PROFESSIONAL IMPERATIVE The obligation of a professional to evaluation of oneself and one's programs; for the evaluator, it is the obligation to **meta-evaluation.** See **Professionalism.**

PROFESSIONALISM The 'professional imperative' is the obligation of professionals to maintain a high degree of competence in his or her field of expertise, from which it follows they must cooperate with *and if necessary arrange for* regular external evaluation of themselves and any programs for which they are responsible. The imperative derives from the nature of professionalism and the implied social contract of the professional. There are three linked contrasts built into the meaning of "professional". In one dimension "professional" means "highly skilled" and the contrast is with "amateur", meaning not full-time and so, by inference, less-than-highly competent; in a second, "professional" means "someone who works for pay" and the contrast is with "amateur", meaning unpaid; in a third sense, "professional" is contrasted with "production-line worker" and in this key sense, professional work is characterized by three features: (i) a high degree of required expertise, requiring considerable training and talent; (ii) the need to work without minute-to-minute supervision; (iii) work on which the lives or welfare of citizens or their children depend. (There is also a purely snobbish use of the term, according to which doctors are, and good auto mechanics are not, professionals; it has no foundation in logic, since lives depend on the expertise of both, high competence in either area requires about the same amount of talent and training, and both commonly work unsupervised.) It is these three factors that generate the connection between professionalism and evaluation, in conjunction with two incontestable observations.

The first is that no one is a good judge of their own performance, and the second is that the expertise with which a professional enters a profession is no guarantee of an indefinitely continued level of high competence. Five reasons for this are: (i) the subject matter of almost all professional fields is steadily—sometimes swiftly—changing; (ii) the methodology of almost all professional fields—which is often different from the subject matter (in teaching, it's the pedagogy as opposed to the content)—also changes steadily; (iii) job responsibilities are frequently changed for good reasons, so that new areas have to be covered; (iv) rigidification of thought in those not regularly challenged by their peers or critics undermines initial competency, often quite quickly; and (v) aging and other debilitating conditions lead to brain deterioration, often by midcareer.

Hence the moral obligation of professionals to society and to their clients entails that continuing competence be checked. This requires that they must be evaluated in some way that involves judges other than themselves, preferably judges that are not close colleagues (see **Enemies list, Accreditation**). Professionals should be able to recognize good and bad approaches to such evaluation, cooperating with good ones—not just legitimating them but facilitating them— and improving bad ones. This ability is not a common part of professional training, but it may be the most important part, from

283

society's point of view.

Codes of professional ethics for evaluators across the board do not exist, but for those engaged in personnel and product evaluation, the *Standards* in each field provide good guidance; additionally, the APA's code for psychologists covers much of the territory.

Professionalism in a wider sense is often taken to include other matters, such as concern for professional ethics, help for beginners, and help for professional associations. See **Valuephobia**.

PROFIT This term from fiscal evaluation has unfortunate connotations to the uninformed. The gravity of the misconception becomes clear when a nonprofit organization starts doing serious budgeting and discovers that it has to introduce something that it can scarcely call profit, but which does the same job of funding a prudent reserve, new programs, buildings, and so on. (It often calls it "contribution to margin", instead.) The task of defining profit is essentially a philosophical one. The technical language is not helpful: "gross profit" is the margin of receipts over the costs of materials and production. That means it has to cover all overhead (e.g., rent and administrative salaries, since these are not counted as part of the 'costs of production'), amortization of debt, and insurance. So there may be no net profit at all, although the business is, in the technical sense, highly profitable.

Ignoring that definition, and treating profit as meaning net profit, as common sense would, we still have serious problems about the cost of the money capital and the time invested when both are furnished by a proprietor/manager or by donors. Is a proprietor making a profit if this means his time is being paid for at the rate of $5 per hour when s/he could make $35 per hour in salary? If ROI on the capital investment is 3% in a market that pays 10% on certificates of deposit, is the investor "making a profit"? Using **opportunity cost** analysis, the answer is No; but the Internal Revenue Service says Yes. That's all very well for them, but it will mislead employees considering a strike. On the other hand, would a company that is making no net profit but paying its CEO $2.5 million per annum, as Apple Computer does, be entitled to argue against the strikers that it's not profitable?

If the buildings (or equipment) have been amortized completely, or were donated, can one deduct a slice of the eventually necessary replacement cost down-payment before one can talk about a profit? Should *some* recompense for risk (or prior losses) on the part of the investors be allowed before we get to "profits"? If not, we'll never get investors; if so, the unions argue that the capitalists are bloodsuckers and the workers should be getting that money. **Cost analysis**/fiscal evaluation looks precise because it's quantitative, like statistics, but

284

eventually the conceptual/practical problems have to be faced and most current definitions will give you absurd consequences, for example, "the business is (net) profitable, but I can't afford to keep it going".

PROGNOSIS Another of the tasks, like **remediation**, that clients sometimes expect evaluators to perform, but for which they have little relevant training.

PROGRAM The general effort that marshals staff and **projects** toward some (often poorly) defined and funded goals.

PROGRAM EVALUATION The largest area of evaluation to which a self-conscious specialty has been devoted, although **product evaluation** may be the largest area of practice. Program evaluation has a long history as a practice, but only became a recognized specialty in the 1960s. Earlier and notable efforts at the practice, in the U.S., include Rice's monumental Philadelphia study of the spelling bee approach in 1897, and Tyler's groundbreaking conceptualizations in the 1930s and 1940s. Much of this book refers to issues in program evaluation, and the **Key evaluation checklist** outlines one approach. The three most active subareas are education, health, and 'criminal justice' (the jargon term for law enforcement activities). These now have much too little to do with each other and are suffering from the isolation.

PROGRAMMED TEXT One in which the material is broken down into small components ("frames"), ranging in length from one sentence to several paragraphs, within which some questions are asked about the material, usually by leaving a blank that the reader has to fill in with the correct word, possibly from a set of options provided. This *interactive* feature was widely proclaimed to have great virtue in itself. It had none, *unless* very thorough R&D effort was also employed in the process of formulating the exact content and sequence of the frames and choices provided. Since the typographic format does not reveal the extent of the field-testing and rewriting (and hence conceals the total absence of it), worthless programmed texts quickly swamped the market (late 1950s) and showed that Gresham's Law is not dead. As usual, the consumers were mostly too naive to require performance data, and the general conclusion was that programmed texts were "just another fad". In fact, the best ones were extremely powerful teaching tools, *were* in fact "teacher-proof" (a phrase that did not endear them to one group of consumers), and some are still doing well (Sullivan/BRL reading materials, for example). A valiant effort was made by a committee under Art Lumsdaine to set up standards, but the failure of virtually all professional training programs for educators to teach their graduates serious evaluation

285

skills meant there was no audience for standards. The new **Evaluation Standards** from the Stufflebeam group appear to be doing better, perhaps because of mandated evaluation.

Programmed texts are relevant to evaluators in several ways. (i) They illustrate the extent to which fashion still has more effect on adoption than good evidence. (ii) They provide a very tough critical competitor for almost any text or training program, especially those with high novelty appeal, such as computer-assisted packages. (iii) They should be the method of choice for training evaluators.

PROGRAM THEORY A theory about the way that a program brings about its effects (descriptive program theories) or about ways in which it could bring about improved effects, or the same effects in an improved way (normative program theories; their importance has been stressed by Huey-Tseh Chen in *Theory-Driven Evaluations* [Sage, 1990]). Although payoffs in program theory territory will often occur and should be looked for and reported on, they are not the business of the evaluator and making them part of that business will deflect resources, effort, and intellectual focus from evaluation, which is hard enough as it is. They are the standard business of scientists or engineers of a traditional kind. In the case of normative theories about social programs, they *should* be, although they have not been, the concern of mainline social scientists. (Engineers and physicians have never had any problem about normative theorizing.) While requiring input to either kind of theory is a mistake, requiring some knowledge of the linkages in the field of the evaluand—although few of them would qualify as theories—is desirable and often essential for good program evaluation. For example, the investigator will certainly need to know about such matters as, who is the manager of which component of the project? To identify **critical competitors** and good curriculum content the **general purpose evaluator** will also need advice from those familiar with the field. Almost all that is needed is knowledge of causal connections, which is subtheoretical. The risk is requiring too much and the breakaway to the Inspector General approach to evaluation in the federal agencies is an example of the consequences of getting evaluation off its essential task. Foundations and agencies need to call on remediation or program theory experts to do some of the things they currently require of evaluators. See **Checklist approach**

PROJECT Projects are time-bounded efforts, often within a program.

PROJECTIVE TESTS These are tests with no *intrinsically* right answer where the responses are interpreted, impressionistically or scientifically, by the tester, for example, a clinical or industrial psychologist. The Rorschach inkblot test is a classic example, where the subject is asked to say what s/he sees in the inkblot. The idea behind projec-
286

tive tests was that they would be useful diagnostic tools, and it seems quite possible that there are clinicians who do make good diagnoses from projective tests. However, the literature on the **validity** of Rorschach interpretations, that is, those that can be expressed verbally as unambiguous rules for interpretation, does not establish substantial validity. The same is unfortunately true of many other projective tests, which fail to show even test-retest reliability, let alone interjudge reliability (assuming that shared bias is ruled out by the experimental design), let alone predictive validity. Of course, they're a lot of fun, and very attractive to **valuephobes**—both testers and testees—just because there are no right answers. Where the interpretation is empirically validated, as on the MMPI, there are problems about using them to support decisions affecting the welfare of the testee; see **Personnel evaluation**. But they still have a useful clinical role as a source of suggestions for direct confirmation.

PROJECT MANAGEMENT No one running evaluation projects should try to do it without project management software, since in the course of learning to use it you learn most of what you need to know about the subject, and you will need the skill. The easiest program to learn of worthwhile power, if you can get at a Macintosh, is MacProject II. Another important option on the Mac is Key Plan, which has a built-in outliner. The heavy-duty program on the Mac is Micro Planner Plus. On the PC, Time Line is the program of choice, but not easy to use. You can get the hang of something like MacProject by walking through the on-screen tutorial in half an hour or so, and you will then be able to benefit substantially. Further benefits come from further learning, but that can be done while still benefitting from the early learning. Note that if you are doing program evaluation, you should be looking at management process in the project or program under review, and you should be looking at whether and how they use project management software, so you should know something about it for that purpose. Of course, there are many other skills involved in project management, but they are well covered in the usual management texts; it's worth looking at the Great Mavericks, Drucker and Deming, in particular, if only to see that there's no One True Path.

PROPOSAL EVALUATION 1. In the generic sense, this refers to the evaluation of systematic suggestions often submitted in the form of plans. Where these concern public policy, most of the matter falls under **policy studies**. In the defense arena, it is sometimes referred to as 'scenario analysis' out of which we get 'worst-case analysis'. In business, where we may be dealing with a marketing proposal or a buyout proposal, the matter is largely one for highly technical financial

287

analysis, for example, involving discounted cash flow and risk weighting. In technology studies, whether as an academic discipline or as a tool for government agencies, the appropriate approach is technology assessment.

2. In a special sense of great importance to planners and evaluators, the term refers to the evaluation of proposals submitted for funding, typically to a foundation or government agency. This is one of the long-standing evaluation procedures that is badly in need of study and reform, like accreditation. There are now many vested interests resisting this, for example, the agency is often disinclined to have anyone discover that they have been proceeding incompetently for years (make that decades). Many smart and experienced program officers know a number of ways to manipulate review panels and procedures; and, across agencies, a few of them have even run comparative trials of different ways to do proposal evaluation. It's a disgrace that a series of task forces has never been set up to benefit from their expertise and to run further experiments. Some of the lore suggests that it's much better to insist that panelists develop and submit actual recommendations before meeting to discuss; when this is not done, the power talkers at the meeting have vastly more influence (when you've put on the record your considered opinion, you're more inclined to defend it than avoid clashing with the power talker). See **Two-tier.**

PROTOCOL See Evaluation ethics and etiquette.

PROVIDERS The people who deliver the services provided by a program; the personnel who interface with **recipients.** (Sometimes extended to include **supporters.**)

PSEUDO-EVALUATION The cover without the content. Pseudo-evaluation is not only mendacious—or, on the charitable view, grossly incompetent—but often very expensive (in consequential costs which usually far outweigh the savings in direct costs), and symptomatic of deeper and worthless values. Of course, it's common in advertising, where phony *Consumer Report*-like analyses are often printed. But it goes much deeper, as the following example shows.

In 1990, the U.S. Congress sanctioned giving the Malcolm Baldrige National Quality Award for excellence in industry to Cadillac. Presumably this was meant to boost respect for the quality of U.S. products (and hence sales), but it was simply and disgracefully a case of Congress being sucked into flackery. Evidence of superior performance or quality by Cadillac—whose slogan "The Standard of the World" once meant something —can't be found in any serious analysis of the statistics from owner surveys, or in a decade of road tests. The very week of the award, it happened that the subject of the road test report on PBS television was a current Cadillac. The image that remains in memory is some footage showing the passenger grab handle coming off in the tester's hand, a serious safety flaw. (The example is not atypical. The car in question was a factory car, lent to PBS for testing purposes, hence it was probably specially 'prepped'; and it, like the other Cadillacs roadtested in 1990, had many substantial faults of assembly as well as design.) It's true that Cadillac is making serious *efforts* to improve a sorry record, but Ford has done that before ("Quality is Job No. 1") and so has Chrysler, as Iaccoca keeps reminding us. The results in none of these cases, despite their claims to the contrary, have been comparability with the leading imports. Awards should surely be for significant *achievement*, not for efforts. Early roadtests of the 1992 Cadillac Seville suggest that the design department has at last done something worthwhile, but only time will tell whether it's just a pretty face—in any case its engine is makeshift, already scheduled for replacement during 1992. Maybe by late 1993 there would have been enough evidence to justify an award. That's only common sense, not some academic standard for serious evaluation.

'Awards for excellence' like this only show the pervasiveness of the disregard for or ignorance about serious evaluation, a consequence of which is the underemphasis on quality control (and designing for quality), that led to the 'Detroit disaster'. It is that same weakness in Congress' evaluation system that leads to the abuse of awards for excellence in the interest of trying to save the remnants of a heavily protected industry. Since an award based on pseudo-evaluation is likely to contribute to (relative) complacency at Cadillac Division of GM, pseudo-evaluation is not just misleading advertising and misrepresentation, it is often the cause of further deterioration. The fact that there are many large U.S. firms with well-deserved reputations for quality—for example WordPerfect Corporation—suggests the conclusion that this award was motivated by the wish to assist the U.S. automobile industry. So does the fact that in the quarter during which it got this award, GM declared the largest quarterly loss in the history of industry (2 billion dollars). It was particularly ironic that the award to Cadillac occurred in the year that two imported luxury cars, at the same price as Cadillac, *and in their first year of production*, went straight to the top of all the reasonably valid award lists for quality and performance.

This example can be duplicated throughout modern life and in greater depth in the auto industry. Even some consumer magazines, whose product tests are, taken as a whole, the bastion of serious evaluation in that domain, give awards which are, to put it kindly, not the

289

result of serious evaluation. The *Motor Trend* Car of the Year award is an example (in 1991 it went to the throwback Chevrolet Caprice, a two-ton car with a small and awkward-to-load trunk, a noisy 35-year-old engine, squeaks, a poor ride, and a design that results in the driver having a poor view of the corners of the car—a traffic hazard). See also **Harvard fallacy, Ritualistic evaluation, Rationalization evaluation.**

PSEUDONEGATIVE EFFECT An outcome or datum that appears to show that an evaluand is having exactly the wrong kind of effect, whereas in fact it is not. Four paradigm examples are: the Suicide Prevention Bureau whose creating is immediately followed by an increase in the rate of reported suicides; the school intercultural program that results in a sharp rise in interracial violence; the college faculty teaching improvement service whose clients score worse than nonclients; the drug education (or sex education) program that leads to "experimentation", that is, increased use. The negative effects in each of these cases are distractors, and the correct conclusion is favorable.)

PSEUDOPOSITIVE EFFECT Typically, an outcome that is consistent with the goals of the program, but in circumstances where *either* goals *or* this way of achieving the goals is in fact harmful *or* side-effects of an overwhelming and harmful kind have been overlooked. Classic case: "drug education" programs that aim to and get enrollees off marijuana and result in getting them on regular cigarettes or alcohol, thereby trading some reduction in (mostly artificial) crimes for far more deaths from lung cancer, cirrhosis of the liver, and drunken driving. (A typical example of ignoring opportunity costs and side-effects, that is, bad **goal-based evaluation.**)

PSYCHOLOGICAL EVALUATION or **PSYCHOTHERAPEUTIC EVALUATION** Particular examples of practical evaluation, in this case of subjects or patients. The first is often primarily taxonomical, the second often primarily predictive. The usual standards of validity apply, but are rarely checked; the few studies suggest that even the reliability is very low, and what there is may be largely due to shared bias. The term "assessment" is often used here instead of evaluation.

PSYCHOLOGY OF EVALUATION A little-explored domain which naturally divides into four parts—the psychology of (i) the evaluator, (ii) the evaluee, (iii) the client, and (iv) the audiences for the evaluation. The first part involves issues like the **therapeutic model,** and the second part involves phenomena like **evaluation anxiety** and **value-phobia.**

Evaluation is risky business—for the evaluator as well as the evaluee—and the causes of this are largely psychological. Evaluation

290

threatens us where we live by raising the possibility of criticism of ourselves—or of our work, which we often see as an extension of ourselves—and, more mundanely, it may raise a threat to our job. Those possibilities are enough to raise anxiety in entirely sensible people, but psychologically mature students or professionals learn to deal with it because they are committed to the overriding importance of the feedback, for example, because of the 'professional imperative' (discussed under **professionalism**). The immature or unbalanced individual or the pseudo-professional, on the other hand, reacts with an inappropriate level of anxiety, fear, hostility, and anger, often leading to incapacitating affect, unprofessional countermeasures, bizarre rationalizations like the doctrine of value-free science, or self-serving policies of incestuous evaluation. Here we see the signs of phobia. On the other side, of course, *doing* evaluation may represent an unhealthy lust for power rather than just the search for knowledge or the desire to provide a service to consumers and future consumers, service providers, citizens, and other legitimate audiences. Then there are the phenomena of the **Dreyfus case**, regularly replayed by the senior bureaucrats in police forces and governments. See also **Consonance/Dissonance, Initiation-Justification bias**.

There has been a great deal of research on decision making, and the extent to which decision-makers—the program evaluator's modal client—deviate from rational choice procedures; a useful overview is in *Decision Research: A Field Guide*, Carroll and Johnson (Sage, 1990). Evaluators in turn have extensively discussed **implementation**, especially the lack of it. However, to get the matter in perspective, one needs to look at the extent to which everyday consumer behavior is consistent with the rational model of getting and then implementing evaluation results known to *or accessible to* the consumer. Everyone knows about impulse buying, and we can require better of senior managers, but there are deeper problems. Many people clearly associate turning to—or accepting advice from—an external source of evaluation with loss of self-esteem and/or loss of power. (Knowledge *is* a form of power, so these reactions are not without a base; but they are often excessive.) Evaluators should probably be addressing these phenomena more directly in doing client needs assessment, as should professional training programs—and psychological research. See also **Phenomenology of evaluation, Refocusing**.

PSYCHOMOTOR SKILLS (Bloom) Learned muscular skills. The distinction from **cognitive** and **affective** is not always sharp, for example, typing looks psychomotor but is highly cognitive as well.

PYGMALION EFFECT An effect of expectations on human subjects, named after the legend in which a statue was brought to life by belief in its life. Usually associated with the self-fulfillling effect of teachers' beliefs about the ability of individual students on the performance of those students. Widely regarded as more powerful than it is, since the evidence in the study that made it famous was seriously flawed.

Q

QUALITATIVE EVALUATION The part of evaluation that can't be usefully reduced to quantitative measures. A substantial part of good evaluation (of personnel and products as well as programs) is wholly or chiefly qualitative, meaning that description and interpretation make up all or most of it. But the term is sometimes used to mean "nonexperimental evaluation" or "evaluation not using the *standard* quantitative methods of the social sciences", and this has confused the issue, because there is a major tradition and component in evaluation that fits the just-quoted descriptions but that involves some quantitative techniques, for example, content analysis, the auditing tradition in accounting, and the cost analysis component that should be found in most evaluations. What has been happening is a gradual convergence of the accountants *and* the qualitative social scientists toward the use of each others' methods *and* the use of some qualitative techniques from humanistic disciplines and previously low-status social sciences (for example, hermeneutics and ethnography). Serious evaluation requires all this and more, and the dichotomy between qualitative and quantitative has to be defined clearly and seen in perspective or it is more confusing than enlightening.

In the works of some of those identified with qualitative evaluation—for example, Guba, Lincoln, and Patton—the suggestion is made that the key feature of qualitative evaluation is that "the researcher is the instrument". However, that's long been a feature of the work of clinician-statisticians from the empiricist school, Meehl being the paradigm case. Qualitative evaluation is not a 'thing in itself' but rather a complement to quantitative methods, to be combined with them when and to the extent appropriate. See the next entry and also Naturalistic evaluation, Evaluation-specific methodology.

QUALITATIVE WEIGHT AND SUM A method of evaluation that uses only a grading scale for weighting the importance of dimensions of merit and for rating the performance of each evaluand on each dimension. QWS is designed to avoid the fallacies of the usual numerical weight and sum approach (NWS), which uses an interval or ratio scoring scale for weights and usually for performances as well. (Numerical weights are appropriate if used for empirically based curve-fitting, an approach which requires an independently measured criterion variable, but we here deal with the more general case of prescriptive weighting, where the criterion is to be defined by the user.) QWS includes the option of setting minima on any or all **autonomous** dimensions.

The procedure involves assigning one of five weights to each feature or dimension of performance: Essential (symbol, E); Very Valuable (symbol, * = star); Valuable (symbol, # = 'double plus'); Marginally Valuable (symbol, + = plus); Zero (symbol, 0). After dropping all candidates lacking any E feature (this is often attached to a certain level of performance on a dimension rather than being an all-or-none attribute), and all criteria with a 0 weight, one then treats the weight of a dimension as *setting the maximum utility that can be awarded to the actual performance of a candidate* (the 'line of credit' approach). For example, on a dimension weighted double plus, candidates can get a 0, +, or # for their performance. The rationale for this approach is that validity in allocating utility points is hard to justify beyond this very modest level—in fact, some research suggests that even a single category may be enough. But if one feels differently, one can allocate an accent (represented by the single quote, ', to indicate 'something more' than the utility symbol to which it is attached, giving six operating levels after the E and 0 filters are applied. Note that a particular dimension may rate an E for scores up to a cutting point, and then a single plus for performance above that in a certain range, a double plus for performance in the range above that, etc. Note also: (i) There is no necessity to specify ranges for each utility level; some may be skipped. (ii) There are some cases where the increasing score is not monotonically related to utility—excess is a flaw—an example being lightness of weight in a laptop computer. (iii) Where there is some doubt about the reliability of the performance estimate, and hence the utility awarded, put parentheses around the symbol allocated. (iv) The above procedure generates a *ranking*, but there would normally be a final *grading* step in which a decision is made as to which, if any, of the leading candidates are good enough to buy/hire/etc. One could in principle specify this in terms of a minimum number of stars, or stars and double plusses; or do it on a case-specific basis after the ranking process. With **disjunctive** testing, the rule might be "Any plus (or double plus) means a pass". In general methodological terms, this is just a matter of applying a cutoff to the total score as well as to each subscore.

After performance research is completed, **synthesis** is done by summing *within each category*, resulting in three totals for each evaluand (stars, double plusses, and plusses, with or without accents). The 'decision algorithm' is iterative—and is not always decisive. It only al-
294

lows you to use the *ranking* of these three weights. For example, you can be sure that a product with three stars is worth more than one with three double plusses (or fewer), but you can't be sure that it is worth more than one with four double plusses, without further consideration. You *can* be sure that if you get a winner on this restrictive basis (as is common), it *is* the winner, subject to checking on any symbols in parentheses, if they would make a crucial difference. If you do not get an immediate winner, you will have cut the list considerably, and a reconsideration of the weights plus a retesting, where there is any problem with test reliability—should get you to the last two, although you can work with a short list of three (less well), and with four (still less well). Then you move to dropping out any common features and their associated symbols, which simplifies the residual comparison, and doing case-specific balancing (that is, reweighting in the light of the specific performances being compared.) Some details are in "Evaluation: Logic's Last Frontier?"; *Critical Reasoning in Contemporary Culture*, Richard A. Talaska, ed. (SUNY Press, 1991).

In the personnel evaluation literature, the technical details are provided of the linear regression approach to selecting candidates for success in a job where previous records are available to generate numerical weights and a clear criterion variable can be identified. Mehrens provides full references in the article cited under **Synthesis**. Note, however, that there are hidden problems with the criterion variable usually employed (later job ratings), for example that it mistakenly omits considerations of **worth** or that it is based on ratings by a number of different judges whose consistency has not been tested. Moreover, since this approach treats all criteria used as **compensatory**, it requires separate treatment of **standalone** cutoffs; nor will it work with nonmonotonic and nonlinear relations, which are quite common (example given above).

QUALITY ASSURANCE, QUALITY CONTROL A type of evaluative monitoring, originating in the manufacturing and engineering areas, but now also used to refer to evaluative monitoring in the software and human services delivery area. This kind of evaluation is usually internal and formative; it is run by the staff responsible for the product, or by their supervisors or a special team, and is aimed at feedback to the project managers. But it should be the kind of formative that is essentially 'early-warning summative', because one is supposed to be ensuring that the product, when it reaches the consumer, will be highly satisfactory from the consumer's point of view. In the manufacturing area, quality control is often too much like program monitoring, which is checking on whether the project is on target—a form of **goal-based evaluation**. It may even be called 'zero defect'

295

quality control, and still refer only to the absence of engineer- or chemist-defined defects when the real error lies in equating those definitions to consumer-relevant defects—the fallacy of **technicism**. So it is extremely important that quality control include more than this, namely some 'hands-off' field testing coupled to very high quality analysis of the results. Only through such an approach can we find out whether the faults that we look for in the quality control process cover all the serious problem areas. One can read a complete book by one of the quality management gurus—for example, John Oakland's *Total Quality Management* (Butterworth-Heinemann, 1989)—and see no mention of this point. The focus is on statistical process control and quality-oriented management processes; but none of this is worth much unless it's tied into serious field external evaluation. See **Beta test, Focus group.**

QUALITY CIRCLES Deming's much-discussed contribution to production management techniques, rejected in the U.S. but enthusiastically accepted by post-war Japanese industry. The key idea is to use workers from the production line for quality control and process improvement instead of leaving those functions to the engineers, with or without field trials—**beta tests**—that are usually badly run. Engineers spend much of their time taking part in the quality circle meetings instead of in offices. Effects appear to be marked on morale as well as quality control. Note that the spin-off from this has to be re-engineering for quality production, not just correction of assembly line errors. The transfer back from Japan to Detroit often assumed that the error was a worker error instead of a design error, namely, designing in a way that made the assembly tasks too hard for the time allowable and the skills or equipment available. Only the incorporation of this broader perspective provides a **balance of power**, and hence active participation by the workers, who are the key information source— and only that combination yields the huge quality improvements that still separate the best Japanese from the best Detroit products. The U.S. wisdom is often expressed as "If it ain't broke, don't fix it"; the philosophy of *kaisin* might be expressed as "If it isn't perfect, improve it"; more specifically, "If it isn't perfect when it comes off the end of the production line, redesign it till it is".

QUANTITATIVE (evaluation) Usually refers to an approach involving a heavy use of numerical measurement and data analysis methodology from social science or (rarely) from accounting. Cf. **Qualitative.**

QUANTUM OF EFFORT The term contrasts with **level of effort**, and refers to the minimum amount of energy from a staff member that makes a significant difference to a project or program. While it is true that there are notable exceptions to any rule of thumb here, experienced program officers often say that 10% or 15% of a person's time is below the quantum of effort, and there are grave doubts about 20%—and some of them don't like 25%. When hiring evaluators, the key decision by the client is what level of personnel they want on call at any time, by contrast with who they would like to get advice from within, say, a week or two. It's very often essential to have someone on call who can make and is competent to make the major decisions, because they often have to made very quickly—for example, a new form is turned down in the review process, but was due to be used next week; it must be redone immediately without leaving a disastrous loophole in the data-gathering effort. See **Window dressing.**

QUARTILE (Stat.) See **Percentile.**

QUASI-EXPERIMENTAL DESIGN (Term due to Donald Campbell) When we cannot actually do a *random allocation* of subjects to the control and experimental groups; or cannot arrange that all subjects receive the treatment at the same time, we settle as next best for quasi-experimental design, where we try to simulate a **true experimental** design. This involves carefully picking someone or a group to serve as the 'control group' (that is, those who did not in fact get the primary treatment) that very closely matches the experimental person/group. Then we study what happens to—and perhaps test—our 'experimental' and 'control' groups just as if we had set them up randomly. Of course, the catch is that the reasons (causes) why the experimental group did in fact get the treatment may be because they are different in some way that explains the difference in the outcomes (if there is such a difference), whereas we—not having been able to detect that difference—will think the difference in outcome is due to the difference in the treatment. For example, smokers may, it has been argued, have a higher tendency to lung irritability, an irritation that they find is somewhat reduced in the short run by smoking; and it may be this irritability, not smoking, that yields the higher incidence of lung cancer. Only a "true experiment" could exclude this possibility, but that would probably run into moral problems. However, the weight and web of the quasi-experiments in cancer research have virtually excluded this possibility. The quasi-experimental design was a brilliant invention, brilliantly developed and defended by Campbell, Stanley and Cook across the period 1957–1979. Serious evaluations should try for it whenever true experiments are impossible. The definitive review of the literature and present status of the quasi-experiment is Tom Cook's essay in *Evaluation and Education: At Quarter Century,* McLaughlin and Phillips, eds. (NSSE/University of Chicago, 1991). See also **Ex post facto.**

QUEMAC Acronym for an approach to meta-evaluation introduced by Bob Gowin, a philosopher of education at Cornell, that is distinctive in its emphasis on unquestioned assumptions in the design. (Questions, Unquestioned Assumptions, Evaluations, Methods, Answers, Concepts.)

QUESTIONNAIRES The basic instrument for surveys and structured interviews. Design of *good* questionnaires is far more difficult than most people realize; and getting the kind of response rate on which policy can be built—in the 80% and often the 90% range—is still more difficult, although it is certainly possible and regularly achieved by the best people in the business. (i) Questionnaires are usually too long for the job to be done, often by a factor of three or five. This not only reduces response rate but also validity (because it encourages stereotyped, omitted, or superficial responses). (ii) They must be pilot-tested, preferably with subjects who free-associate as they fill it in (to an observer or a tape-recorder, either better than requiring them to make notes). (iii) Usually a second pilot-test still uncovers problems, especially of ambiguity. (iv) High response requires multiple follow-ups, including mail and phone. (v) Likert scales ("Agree strongly... Disagree strongly") are sometimes valuable, but sometimes just an attempt to avoid calling for an evaluative response ("Excellent... Worthless"), which is what you need. (vi) Response scales with an even number of points may not avoid fence-sitting—they may convert it into pseudo-effects. (vii) If you get the ratings clustering near the top of the scale, use one of the solutions mentioned under **Ceiling effect**. See also **Rating Scales, Symmetry.**

R

RANDOM A 'primitive' concept of statistics and probability, that is, one that cannot be defined in terms of any other without circularity. Texts often define a random sample from a population as one picked in a way that gives every individual in the population an equal probability of being chosen; but one can't define "equal probability" without reference to randomness or a cognate. It is not surprising that the first three "tables of random numbers" turned out to have been doctored by their authors. Although allegedly generated (in completely different ways) by mechanical and mathematical procedures that met the definition just given, they were doctored into nonrandomness, for example, because pages or columns which held a substantial preponderance of a particular digit or a deficit of one particular digit-pair were deleted, whereas of course such pages *must* occur at approximately their expected frequency in any large set of random numbers. The authors deleted these pages because they had a certain type of use in mind—using the tables as a source for relatively short lists of numbers to be used in psychological experiments. For this use, they were quite right. However, what this shows is that there is no absolute definition of randomness so a table of random numbers cannot be used as a source of random numbers that will be random for every particular purpose. The best definition is relativistic and pragmatic. A choice of an element of a set (numbers, and so on.) is *random with regard to the variable X* if it is not significantly affected by variables that significantly affect X. Hence a die or cut of cards or turn of the roulette wheel is random with regard to the interests of the players if the number that comes up is caused to do so by variables that are not under the influence of factors correlated with the player's interests. Tables of random numbers are random only with respect to certain kinds of bias (which one should state) and certain ranges of sample size.

RANKING, RANK-ORDERING Placing individuals in an order, usually of merit, on the basis of their relative performance on (typically) a test or measurement or observation. Full ranking does not allow ties that is, two or more individuals with the same rank ("equal third"), partial ranking does. In limit cases where there are large numbers of ties and a small number of distinct groups, a partial ranking—even a full ranking, in a still smaller number of cases—can

299

be inferred from a **grading**, but the reverse inference is never possible. See also **Symbolism**.

RATING Usually the same as **grading**.

RATING SCALES Devices for standardizing responses to requests for (typically evaluative) judgments. There has been some attempt in the research literature to identify the ideal number of points on a rating scale. An even number counteracts the tendency of some raters to use the midpoint for almost everything by forcing them to jump one way or the other; on the other hand, it does this by eliminating what is sometimes the only correct response and the result may be to produce an artificial bias. Scales with more than 10 points generally prove confusing and drop the raters' reliability; with 3 or less (Pass/Not Pass is a two-point scale), too much information is thrown away. Five- and (especially) seven-point scales usually work well. It should be noted that the A-F scale is semantically asymmetrical when used with the usual **anchor points**. (i.e., it will not give a normal distribution [in the technical sense] of grades for a population in which talent *is* normally distributed). See **Symmetry**. With + and - and fence-sitting (**banding**) supplements (A+, A, A-, AB, B+, B, B-, BC..), it runs to 19 points and with the double modifiers (++ and —), it has 29 points, far beyond the accuracy of any **global** grading. Note that the translation of letter grades into numbers for purposes of computing a grade-point average involves false assumptions about the equality of the intervals (of merit) between the grades and the location of the zero point. Sometimes the size of the error is serious. See also **Questionnaire, Point constancy requirement**.

RATIONALITY It is fashionable to follow Herb Simon, or to think that one is following him, in talking about 'the naive assumption of rationality' that is said to have been built into early and some current work on policy studies, implementation, and evaluation. In fact, the *comment* is naive; most of the studies were attempts to identify best practice, not actual practice. Recommendations aren't meant to be descriptions. Nevertheless, the most useful recommendations keep in mind the limits of the possible, and certainly are invalidated if too complex to explain to those who must implement them. See **Optimization, Prescriptive**.

RATIONALIZATION Pseudo-justifications, usually provided ex post facto. See **Consonance**.

RATIONALIZATION EVALUATION An evaluation is sometimes performed in order to provide a rationalization for a predetermined or at least prefavored decision. This is much easier than it might appear, and a good many managers know very well how do do it. If they want a program shot down, they hire a gunslinger; if they want one

300

praised or protected, they hire a sweetheart. Every now and again evaluators are brought in by clients who have got them into the wrong category and the early discussions are likely to be embarrassing, annoying, or amusing, depending upon how badly you needed the job. (Suchman's "whitewash" was an example.)

RAW SCORES The actual score on a test, before it is converted to percentiles, grade equivalents, and so on.

R&D Research and Development; the basic cyclic (iterative) process of invention and improvement, for example, of educational materials or consumer products: research, design, make, prepare for run, pilot run, evaluate results, design improvements, run improved version, and so on. This is technology's method, by contrast with the exploratory and hypothesis-testing process in science. See **Formative evaluation, Focus groups, Beta test.**

RDD&E Research, Development, Diffusion (or Dissemination), and Evaluation. A more elaborate acronym for the development process usually described as R&D, where formative evaluation is included in Development.

REACTIVE EFFECT (or EVALUATION) A phenomenon due to ('an artefact of') the measurement or evaluation procedure used: one species of evaluation or investigation artefact. With respect to evaluation, it has two subspecies: content effects and process effects. Evaluation-content reactions include cases of formative evaluation where a criticism in an evaluation is taken to heart by the evaluee and leads to improvement, which then renders the recommendation irrelevant because of the changes it has itself induced. Thus the measurement not only affects what is measured but invalidates the measurement's accuracy if reported without correction for the change (but see **Self-refuting evaluation**). Evaluation-process reactions include cases where the mere occurrence (or even the prospect) of the evaluation materially affects the behavior of the evaluee(s) so that the assessment to be made will not be typical of the program in its preevaluation states, as when the principal walks into the classroom and the teacher is instantly 'on best behavior'. Note that in the limit, working conditions that include a standard process of evaluation may affect the quality of work just because of that fact, not because of any particular evaluation episode.

Although reactive *measurements* have not previously been subdivided into content-dependent and content-independent, the distinction does apply there and not just to evaluations, but it is, by and large, less crucial in that context. In both cases, unobtrusive approaches may be appropriate to avoid process-reactivity; but on the other hand, openness may be required on ethical grounds. The openness may be with respect to content or with respect to process or both. (See **Reasons for evaluation.**)

Examples of reactive effects include the effect of (for example) female interviewers on male interviewees, the learning effect from doing the early questions in a test on performance on the later items, the **John Henry effect**, and the **Hawthorne effect**. Non-example: the Uncertainty Principle, contrary to the usual view (the uncertainty is part of the nature of particles, only incidentally a limitation of measurement). See also **Self-fulfillling evaluation.**

The most serious cases of reactive evaluation are analogous to iatrogenic (doctor-caused) disorders in medicine. An example is neurotic **evaluation anxiety** when caused by excessive or inappropriate evaluation; it may lead to very serious penalties for sufferers. Another family of examples involves cases where the evaluation tail wags the program dog, something which is always a sign of bad management or bad evaluation, depending on who is responsible for the bad results.

REASONS FOR EVALUATION Two common practical reasons are to improve something (**formative evaluation**) and to make various practical decisions about something (**summative evaluation**), such as whether to buy it, allow it to be sold, export it to other sites, fund it, and so on. The fact that these reasons are both tied to action reflects a common feature of evaluation, but not a universal one. People read road tests of Ferraris with much interest, rarely because they are going to make any decision about whether to lay out $170,000 for a cheap one. Pure interest in the merits of something is a perfectly good and common reason for summative evaluation, and this includes evaluation for research. Lincoln's evaluation of the five generals from which he chose Ulysses S. Grant is summative evaluation of the usual applied kind (**decision-oriented**); a contemporary historian's evaluation of them is also summative evaluation (**conclusion-oriented**). The two are different only in role (and the improved data base), not intrinsically.

There are also what might be called content-independent or process reasons for doing evaluation or having it done, for example, as part of a serious commitment to **accountability**, as a **rationalization** or excuse (for a hatchet job or for funding a favorite), to increase motivation (to get others—or oneself—to work more carefully or harder), to deflect the hostility that will be generated toward an administrator who has already and with good reasons identified the cause of a serious problem, for public relations purposes, to show who's boss, and for reasons of fairness. In the rationalization case, the *general* nature of the evaluation's content must be known or arranged in advance, for example, by hiring a known "killer" or "sweetheart". A **ritual** evaluation is done only because it is required or as a gesture to reinforce some social pattern. Other reasons, not wholly independent of the above, are for advocacy, justice, political advantage, power display, and postponement—that is, to gain time (Suchman).

In the light of this plethora, it is naive to think something has 'gone wrong' if an evaluation's recommendations are not implemented. However, if you don't feel you should be doing evaluations unless they will be implemented, you should take care to look into the context of the contract or request. In any case, it should be clear that it's a mistake to use implementation as a criterion of merit of an evaluation. See **Reactive effect, Functional analysis, Implementation, Meta-evaluation,** and, for particular reasons for one type of evaluation, **Testing.**

RECIPIENTS Recipients or users are the immediate consumers (intended or unintended). They interface directly with the providers or product; other consumers are affected indirectly (via so-called 'ripple effects'). Students at a university or clients in a clinic are recipients of the services provided. (There is some overlap between these terms and "consumer" and "stakeholder" and "audience". It is not essential they be sharply distinguished, only that all be checked.) See **Consumer, Recoil effects.**

RECOIL EFFECTS When a hunter shoots a deer, s/he sometimes bruises a shoulder. Programs affect their staff as well as the clientele. These effects are usually though not always of secondary importance (abortion clinics are sometimes proposed as counterexamples) compared to what happens to the deer or the clientele, but must be included in program evaluation. The staff is **impacted,** although they are not recipients of the services or products involved.

RECOMMENDATIONS Recommendations go beyond plain evaluative conclusions. There is only a trivial sense in which an evaluation always involves an implicit recommendation—that the evaluand be viewed/treated in the way appropriate to the value it was determined to have by the evaluation. (That sense is trivial since it converts all factual claims to recommendations—the recommendations that you should believe what they assert.) In the nontrivial sense, where "recommendation" is taken to mean "suggestions for specific appropriate actions" (for example, remedial actions), evaluations may yield none, even if every effort is made to generate them—and such efforts are frequently extremely costly. This does not mean that the evaluation is in any way incorrect or inappropriately limited; only that one hoped-for outcome has not materialized. Doctors who determine that you are suffering from an incurable disease are not shown to be guilty of misdiagnosis (that is, of having wrongly evaluated your condition) just because they can't come up with a cure. In medical and product evaluation it is obvious that remediation recommendations are not always possible even when evaluation is possible, but because the logic has not been well thought out it is widely supposed to be a sign of bad design or an absence of common humanity when personnel or program evaluations do not lead to remedial recommendations.

Sometimes evaluations are even said to be at fault when they do not lead to guaranteed-to-be-successful recommendations, and this has virtually been written into some teacher contracts. There are some people who are irremediably unable to perform a given complex task, for example, teaching in a 'war zone' school. No foreseeable amounts of progress in science or the arts of pedagogy is likely to alter that qualitative fact, though it may alter the percentage of people that can be trained up to acceptable performance levels. It is a very grave error in evaluation design and professionalism to guarantee the production of remedial suggestions—just as it is foolish for a scientist to guarantee to discover **explanations** as a result of investigation into a certain phenomenon. Doing so may multiply the cost of the investigation and the chance of failure many times and move the focus to something completely different from evaluation, thereby risking the validity or utility of the evaluation. Most evaluations **spin off** a few useful recommendations without much extra effort; these come from an analytic approach involving a good analysis of the function of the components. The main obstacle to doing more than this is that successful prescription requires not only substantial local knowledge but very special skills, skills which may still be very limited in their chance of success. A roadtester is not a mechanical engineer, a program evaluator is not a management troubleshooter, though both often suffer from delusions of grandeur in this respect. Push them too hard and you get bad recommendations—or a rash of "Recommendation: Needs Further Study". See also **Process evaluation**.

REDUNDANCY Duplicate or multiple sources for data or judgments. Redundancy has costs, but a good deal of it is necessary in most practical evaluation contexts (for the same reasons there are for getting a second opinion in medical practice), especially for personnel evaluation. The term "triangulation" is often used to indicate that a triple 'take' is highly appropriate. This is especially true where it allows one to use an indicator that is not nearly strong enough to stand on its own. In assessing the value of someone's research, for example, it is only defensible to use **citation index** data *if* one uses two other indicators (for example, number of publications, quality of journals/-publishers, reviews in professional journals) that can carry almost all the weight by themselves. See also **Parallel designs.**

REFOCUSING   In many complex evaluations—particularly of products, personnel, or programs —there comes a moment when it is almost essential to 'start all over', not with respect to redoing the fact-finding—except perhaps in minor respects—but with respect to reconceptualizing the data and, perhaps, redirecting the inquiry. (The new start is from a much more enlightened point of view than the one just reached, so what has gone before is not wasted effort.) Evaluation is in any case an iterative process, requiring one to reconsider a number of factors after one has looked more carefully at other factors. Refocusing is more than this. At a certain stage, one runs into a terminal 'failure of fit' of the tentative picture (interpretation, focus) formed during earlier cycles. This will involve some of the following: making a major change in the weights you have allocated to different dimensions of performance; making a change in the list of or definition of the criteria; making a change in the performance scores as a new consideration emerges; making a change in the critical competitors. Since refocusing sometimes reverses itself, it's essential not to discard or overwrite earlier efforts. This is one reason why the use of microcomputers is almost indispensable; you can simply save the series of refocused analyses under slightly modified filenames, and get back to them later if you need to do so. Changing the weights may itself mean bringing back into contention candidates that had previously been excluded entirely; or it may occur because you've realized that the standards you're setting rule out all contenders—one of the cases where you'll be glad that you've still got a record of the performance of the rejects. Once you've done a few evaluations using big matrixes of performance and weights on a spreadsheet—after reading this—you cannot fail to recognize the refocusing phenomenon. See also **Psychology of evaluation, Illuminative evaluation, Responsive evaluation.**

REGRESSION TO THE MEAN   You may have a run of luck in roulette, but it won't last; your success ratio will regress (drop back) to the mean. When a group of subjects is selected for remedial work on the basis of low test scores, some of them will have scored low only through "bad luck", that is, the sampling of their skills yielded by (the items on) this test is in fact not typical. If they go through the training and are retested, they will score better simply because any second test would (almost certainly) result in their displaying their skills more impressively. This phenomenon gives an automatic but phony boost to the achievements of "performance contractors" if they are paid on

305

the basis of improvement by the low-scorers. If they had to improve the score of a *random* sample of students, regression *down* to the mean would offset the regression *up* to the mean we have just discussed. But they are normally called in to help the students who "need it most"—according to test results—and that group will include a number who do *not* need help. (It will also *exclude* some who *do*.) Multiple or longer tests or the addition of teacher (expert judge) evaluations reduce this source of error. Regression to the mean is one of the consequences of the errors in any real measurement procedure. The same cause is important in many other situations; for example, when teachers who fail a competency test in their knowledge of subject matter or pedagogy, are allowed to retake, some of them will pass simply because they get lucky with the items on the second occasion, not because they have improved and are now competent. (Correspondingly, some who failed the first time were just unlucky with the particular test and always were competent, despite the appearance to the contrary.) The size of this error is usually not great for a test of any length, so it is only testees close to the margin who are misclassified.

REINVENTING THE WHEEL Evaluation is still operating in an extremely inefficient way, with its separate fields busily duplicating prior work. Even within a subfield like educational program evaluation we find that a new political interest in year-round schooling generates expensive evaluation studies without looking at previous studies of the same thing; similarly with studies of models for school evaluation; similarly with approaches to student assessment and program **assessment**. This is partly a consequence of the long period when evaluations and their methodology were treated as if they have no general significance and hence not accepted for publication, an attitude that kept them out of the database of research articles. It's partly because of the NIH syndrome, and it's partly because evaluation is a transdiscipline without a core discipline headquarters that could call for and support the development of an evaluation database. In recent years, the situation has been somewhat improved by the increased number of journals publishing reports of evaluations with some general interest, but setting up a standalone evaluation database still offers an easy way to reduce evaluation costs to governments. One of the responsibilities of field-based evaluation centers, as they continue to emerge, should be maintenance of a competent database of abstracts. (See **ELMR** for one example.)

RELATIVISM/SUBJECTIVISM The view that there is no objective truth (epistemological relativism) or, more narrowly, that there is no objective merit or value of things (evaluative relativism). On this view the scientist—or the evaluator, in the narrower form—can only identify various perspectives or perceptions, and selection of one of these is essentially arbitrary, determined by aesthetic, psychological, or political considerations rather than scientific ones. The contrary point of view would naturally be referred to as absolutism or objectivism; in one technical sense used in philosophy the opposite of subjectivism is called realism. The doctrine of relativism is fallacious, since *epistemological relativism is a self-refuting doctrine*. That is, if relativism is true, then "relativism is true" is no more true than "relativism is false", so relativism can't be true in the sense which means it isn't false, and there isn't any other sense of "true" in the English language. So relativism can hardly represent an insight, since insights are claimed to be more true than their denials. People often adopt relativism as a result of the discovery that scientific theories sometimes turn out to be wrong. One might as well believe that drivers are would-be suicides on the grounds that 125 are killed every day in the U.S. alone.

Evaluative relativism is usually a simple overgeneralization from the trite observation that tastes differ. The fact that tastes differ does not support the view that truth differs, and truth about the merit of things is one kind of truth. It's hardly a 'matter of taste' when a competent instructor determines that a student has turned in a good performance in a mathematics test.

A corollary of importance for evaluation practice is this: in a situation where a number of different evaluative views, approaches, methodologies, or perspectives on a particular program (for example) are about equally plausible, it does *not* follow that choosing any one of them is defensible. All that follows is that reporting *all* of them, *and* the statement that all of them are equally defensible, would constitute a defensible evaluation. The moment one sees that alternative views are equally well justified, although they yield incompatible results, one has seen that no one of these can be thought of as sound in itself, *just because* the assertion of any one of them implies the denial of the others, and that denial is, in such a case, illegitimate. Hence the assertion of any one of them by itself is illegitimate.

If, on the other hand, the different positions are *not* incompatible, then they must still be given in order to present a *comprehensive* picture of whatever is being evaluated. In neither case, then, is giving a single one of these perspectives defensible. In short, the great difficulties of establishing one evaluative conclusion by comparison with others cannot be avoided by arbitrarily picking one from several equally likely ones, and appealing to relativism. The only choices are to prove the superiority of one, *or* provide all as **perspectives**. That term, correctly used, implies the existence of a reality which is only partly revealed in each view.

Doing this converts incompatible reports into complementary ones, that is, it converts relativism into objectivism. Merely giving several apparently incompatible accounts in an evaluation is incompetent; showing how they can be reconciled, that is, seen *as* perspectives, is also required. (Or else a proof that one of them is right.) The presupposition that there is a single reality (in the usual sense) is not an arbitrary one, any more than the assumption that the future will be rather like the past is arbitrary; these are the best-established of all truths about the world. Determinism was equally well established and we have only had to qualify it slightly because of the Uncertainty Principle. We have not yet encountered good reasons for qualifying the assumptions of realism and induction (the technical names for the two views previously mentioned).

At the practical end of these considerations, it must be recognized that even evaluations ultimately based on 'mere preferences' may still be completely objective and completely transcend the preferences on which they are based. One must distinguish sharply between the fact that the ultimate basis of merit in such cases is mere preference, on which the subject *is* the ultimate source of authority, and the fallacy of supposing that the subject must therefore be the ultimate source of authority about the *merits* of whatever is being evaluated. Even in the domain of pure taste, the subject may simply not have researched the range of options properly, or may have been unduly influenced by labels and advertising or by recommendations from friends, so the evaluator may be able to identify critical competitors that outperform the subject's favorite candidate, *in terms of the subject's own taste.* And of course identifying Best Buys for an individual involves a second dimension (cost) that the evaluator is often able to determine and combine more reliably than the amateur.

Areas where the only basis for superiority is unidimensional, instantaneous, and entirely taste-dependent are essentially preevaluative areas, since it's not superiority but mere preference that is involved. The only conclusions that are possible are statements of liking or preference, not even statements about 'best for me'. If we move the least step away from such areas, then we find the subject beginning to make errors of synthesis in putting together two or three dimension of preference (halo or sequencing effects, for example) or in extrapolating to continued liking or superiority in a broader group than those directly sampled. These are errors that an evaluator can reduce or eliminate by appropriate experimental design, often leading to a conclusion quite different from that which the subject had formed.

One step further away, and we find the possibility of the subjects making first-level errors of judgment, for example, about what they need (or even what they want) by contrast with what they like, and these can certainly be reduced or eliminated by appropriate evaluation design. In the general case of the evaluation of consumer goods we can prove a stronger conclusion, which counts even more heavily against relativism. One can often identify the best product in a given category with complete objectivity, despite a substantial range of different interests and preferences at the basic level by members of the relevant consumer group. This is simply a question of whether the interproduct variations in performance outweigh the interconsumer variations in preference. Enormous variations in preference may be completely blotted out by the tremendous superiority of a single product over another if it scores so much on several dimensions that are accorded significant value by all the relevant consumers, that even the outlandish tastes (weightings) of some of the consumers with respect to some of the other dimensions cannot elevate any of the competitive products to the same level of total score, even for those with the atypical tastes. Thus huge interpersonal differences in *all the relevant* preferences do *not* demonstrate the relativism of *evaluations* which depend on them. See **Perspectival evaluation, Sensory evaluation.**

RELATIVISTIC EVALUATION Evaluation done relative to some set of values which is not endorsed by the evaluator: "second-hand" evaluation. It yields what are here called secondary value conclusions. The contrast is with direct evaluation, which yields primary value claims.

RELIABILITY (1. in statistics; 2. in common parlance; 3. of evaluations) 1. Reliability in the technical sense is the consistency of the readings from a scientific instrument or human judge. If a thermometer always says 90° C when placed in boiling distilled water at sea-level, it is "100 percent test-retest reliable" though inaccurate. It is useful to distinguish test-retest reliability from 'interjudge' reliability (which would be exhibited if several thermometers gave the same reading). There are many psychological tests that are test-retest reliable but not interjudge (that is, inter-test-administrator) reliable: the reverse is less common.

2. In the everyday sense, reliability includes the requirement covered by the technical term **validity**; we'd say that a thermometer that reads 90°C when it should read 100°C wasn't very reliable, just as we'd also say the same thing if it gave variable readings in boiling water at the same ambient pressure. This confusing situation could easily have been avoided by using the term "consistency" (or "stability") instead of introducing a technical use of "reliability" but that was in the

days when jargon was thought to be a sign of scientific sophistication. As it is, reliability is a necessary but not a sufficient condition for validity, hence often worth checking first since in its absence validity can't be there. Careful study of what counts as a 're-test' or 'judging the same thing' shows that in fact even reliability in the technical sense involves validity, although this is not commonly noticed. (Otherwise, we'd fault a thermometer for showing a different reading when the water in test bath had cooled off between tests.)

3. The reliability of evaluations is a largely unknown quantity. In the technical sense, meaning consistency, an estimate is easily obtained by running replications of evaluations; either serially or in parallel. The few data on these—for example, in school accreditation (one experiment), panel evaluation of proposals (a few informal experiments), or classroom evaluation of teachers (many experiments)—make clear that reliability, once you factor out spurious effects such as shared bias, is not high. The use of **calibration** exercises, **checklists**, and **training of evaluators** can improve this enormously in the course of improving validity. Paul Diederich showed how to do this with the evaluation of composition instruction, and that paradigm should generalize.

REMEDIATION The process of improvement or, derivatively, a recommendation for a course of action or treatment that will result in improvement; often resulting from **formative evaluation**. Such recommendations can spring spontaneously out of **analytical** formative evaluation, but they often require specific local 'therapeutic' expertise—they are **prescriptions**, in one sense of that term. The term "prescription" in medicine has the same meaning—it refers to a recommendation for remedial action—and medical prescription often requires much more extensive expertise than the mere identification of a serious illness in, for example, a pet or child. Evaluators are prone to regard themselves as competent to suggest remediation regimens, just because they are good evaluators in a field, but the two things are essentially different, although there are individuals with the qualifications to do both. Expert drug evaluators at the FDA are not in any position to suggest to pharmaceutical chemists how to improve a product that turns out to have unacceptable side-effects. Formative evaluation's contribution to improvement is to be the essential prerequisite to—and, later, a check on the success of—remediation. Analytic formative evaluation usually does more; it localizes the problem, and in some cases it *may* also come up with specific suggestions. But making that part of the goal of the evaluator or the expectations from one, tends to corrupt or condemn the evaluation as an evaluation. See also **Recommendation**.

REPEATED DESIGN An approach to validity studies in which an experimental or evaluation design problem is re-solved, for example, by another investigator, and the two designs compared. Ideally, the second investigator is ignorant of the first solution but some benefit accrues even in the absence of this condition partly because the second designer may more easily notice errors when the design has been set out explicitly. And competition provides—for some investigators—a stronger stimulus for a better solution than the bare problem.

REPLICATION An unfortunately uncommon phenomenon in the applied human studies fields, contrary to the usual reports, mainly because researchers do not take the notion of serious checking on implementation (e.g., through the use of an 'index of implementation') as an automatic requirement on any supposed replication. Even the methodology for replication is poorly thought out: for example, deciding on the amount of variation from the characteristics of the original subjects that is allowable under the heading of replication before getting into the area of generalization; whether the subjects have the same information about the nature of the experimental treatment or intervention; whether the replicator should have any detailed knowledge of the results at the primary site. Such knowledge is seriously biasing—even though it significantly simplifies the preparations for ranges of measurement, and so on. It is probably quite important to arrange at least some replications where the (for example) program to be replicated is simply described in treatment terms, perhaps with the remark that it has shown "significant positive *or* negative results" at the primary site.

REPORT, REPORTING The process of communicating results to the client and audiences. It may be best done orally rather than in writing, or (more commonly) by using both modalities; across time rather than at one time; using completely different versions for different audiences or just one version. This is one of several areas in evaluation where creativity and originality are really important, as well as knowledge about **diffusion** and **dissemination**. Reports should be designed on the basis of some serious thinking or research about audience needs as well as client needs. Multiple versions may use different media as well as different vocabularies. Reports are products and should be looked at in terms of the KEC—field-testing them is by no means inappropriate. Who has time and resources for all this? It depends on the size of the project and whether you are really interested in **utilization** of the evaluation. Would you write it in Greek? No, so should you *assume* that you are *not* writing it in the *equivalent* of Greek, as far as your audiences are concerned? While comprehensibility is a necessary condition for accessibility, there are

311

other dimensions, such as the dissemination procedures (should an account be published as well as delivered, and to whom?) and *radical* format issues (should pocketable versions be printed, or disk versions; should it go up on an electronic bulletin board?). See also **Layering, Data visualization.**

RESEARCH The general field of disciplined investigation, covering the humanities, the sciences, jurisprudence, evaluation, and so on. Evaluation research is one part of this. Various attempts to distinguish research from evaluation are discussed under **Generalizability, Evaluation research,** and **Conclusion-oriented research,** for example.

RESEARCH-BASED PERSONNEL EVALUATION (RBPE) Any approach to personnel evaluation that uses 'empirically-validated' indicators as criteria of merit, even if it also uses other, clearly valid, criteria of merit (such as competence/excellence in performance of duties). The use of tests other than good simulations of typical job situations is in general invalid regardless of the size of the correlation between scores on the tests and subsequent success in the job. Research on the accuracy of predictions from simulation tests is useful in improving or rejecting the tests, but the *basis* for the use of data from such tests is not the research but the fact that the tests are of job-like performance.

The arguments for rejecting RBPE are not just ethical and (sometimes) legal but also scientific. Much of what is held to be 'scientific' personnel practice is rendered invalid by these arguments, although their use can be justified when better alternatives are not feasible, for example, for national emergencies such as processing draftees. (Even then, arrangements for reversal of errors must be included.) No such exceptions apply in the normal course of personnel evaluation. The use of any such indicators, correlated or not, contaminates the evaluation procedure, rendering it invalid, and it seems certain that RBPE procedures will eventually fail in court hearings. The definitive legal analysis, as of mid-1991, is in "Legal Issues Concerning Teacher Evaluation" by Michael Rebell, in *The New Handbook of Teacher Evaluation,* edited by Jason Millman and Linda Darling-Hammond (Sage, 1990).

These 'research-based' indicators are called secondary indicators, or **style indicators,** and their use is a scientifically unacceptable substitute for the use of primary indicators or **criteria,** which are specific duties of the job. Gender is a marvelously well-substantiated indicator for a negative diagnosis of breast cancer in a male patient, but it is improper medical practice to use it instead of doing a biopsy. Thus, while it is immoral and illegal to use gender, race, and religion as a basis for job selection (and so on), it is also unscientific because it violates the 'strong requirement of total evidence'—essentially, that one

312

must *get and use* all reasonably accessible evidence when assessing probabilities or people. (This requirement is also entailed by the Federal Rules of Evidence, 1989.) Hence, in normal circumstances, there is only one personnel action that can be validly based on the use of secondary indicators—the dismissal of the user.

This severe view is not yet widely shared, and the reader will find the arguments on both sides presented in the anthology *Research-Based Teacher Evaluation* (Kluwer, 1990). An important special case of RBPE is listed in the next entry. See also **Personnel evaluation.**

RESEARCH-BASED TEACHER EVALUATION (RBTE) A special case of the preceding entry, of particular interest because many states have recently and expensively 'upgraded' their teacher evaluation systems in the direction of increased use of research-based indicators which are supposedly correlated with superior teaching style. There are strong reasons for doubting whether the correlational research that allegedly validates the indicators is **externally valid** in the first place, but even if it is, inferences from it must be discarded and replaced by inferences from evidence about performance on primary indicators—that is, those validated by their listing in 'the duties of the job'. For example, substantial use of questioning is an alleged secondary indicator of teaching success (that is, it is said to correlate with successful teaching); it cannot be used in teacher evaluation. Knowing the subject to the appropriate level, on the other hand, is a primary indicator (it is a duty of the teacher); it can be used. Note that you can't get the duties of the teacher from job descriptions. They only list the duties that differentiate that job from other teachers' jobs (e.g., teaching 12th-grade physics); what is shared, the generic duties of the teacher, is never listed. The reference cited above will lead the reader to some duties lists. See also **Duties-based teacher evaluation, Job analysis.**

RESEARCH INTEGRATION, RESEARCH SYNTHESIS See **Meta-analysis.**

RESOURCES See **Strengths assessment.**

RESPONSE SET Tendency to respond in a particular way, regardless of the merits of the particular case. Some respondents tend to rate everything very high on a scale of merit, others rate everything low, and yet others put everything in the middle. One can't argue out of context that such patterns are incorrect; there are plenty of situations in which those are exactly the correct responses on that instrument. When we're talking about response set, however, we usually mean the cases where rigid response patterns emerge from general habits and not from well thought-out consistency.

RESPONSIBILITY EVALUATION Evaluation that includes the

313

identification of person(s) responsible for outcomes, and/or the degree of responsibility, and hence usually the degree of culpability or merit. It involves one kind of **analytical evaluation**—analyzing and evaluating the reasons for actions. Responsibility presupposes causality as a necessary but not a sufficient condition; you can't be responsible for what you cannot influence. Culpability presupposes responsibility but involves further conditions from ethics (e.g., that the effects of one's actions were morally wrong). Social scientists, like most people not trained in the law or casuistry are often confused about such issues, arguing, for example, that certain evaluations shouldn't be done (or published) because "the results may be abused". The abuse is culpable; but so is *failure* to publish professional-quality work of prima facie intellectual interest or social value. A continuing example, which marked the emergence of the severe current problem: research on racial IQ differences is currently precensored by many, probably most social science journals, following the furor over the Jensen case. The reasons for this include fear of reprisal and fear that the findings will be 'abused', but the latter fear is often based on thinking that the findings have much more significance in appraising people than in fact they do have (see **Research-based personnel evaluation**). Instead of supporting censorship, researchers in a free society should commit themselves to standing against the abuse of research and researchers and realize that they are abusing the process of free research by supporting censorship. (It is sad to hear them argue that such research should not be published anyway because it really is of no legitimate interest—a criterion which would empty most journals overnight.) See "The Values of the Academy (Moral Issues for American Education and Educational Research Arising from the Jensen Case)", in *Review of Educational Research*, Vol. 40, No. 4, October, 1970.

A different kind of example involves administrators tolerating incompetent teachers in a school district because the alternative of attempting dismissal involves effort, is unpopular with the union, and is usually unsuccessful. The administrator's responsibility is to the pupils who are sacrificed at the rate of 30 per annum per bad teacher (in elementary school) and to the taxpayer; that responsibility is so serious that you (the superintendent or the board) have to try for removal because (i) you *may* succeed, (ii) the effects may be *on balance* good—for example, there may be a gain in overall motivation even if you lose the case, and (iii) you may learn how to do it better next time. (The fact is that well-prepared cases almost always succeed.) Hence, in evaluating these administrators or these school districts, one must draw highly adverse conclusions, just because the 'arguments for the defense' are invalid.

314

The evaluation of schools should (normally) only be done in terms of the variables over which the school has control. In the short run and often in the long run, this does *not* include scores on standardized tests, although it may bring in *changes* in those scores (See SEP). Evaluations themselves should not in general be evaluated in terms of results, because the evaluator is not responsible for utilization; but rather in terms of the results *if appropriately* used—and in terms of design for client's needs. Ref. on responsibility: *Primary Philosophy* (McGraw-Hill, 1966).

A crucial component of responsibility evaluation involves recognizing the responsibility we all have for accepting the views of our peers *even when they have never been challenged.* **Valuephobia** is often a group reaction; the doctrine of **value-free science** was and is largely a group belief. Neither would receive much support if explicitly addressed and discussed, but they are palliative of our anxieties to such a degree that we have managed to suppress most explicit discussion. (The same is now occurring with various politically sensitive beliefs on the campus.) Challenging beliefs you have not heard challenged requires some skill in **critical thinking,** which is one of the reasons for substantial opposition to serious critical thinking instruction—and for including that skill in the essential repertoire of **evaluation skills.**

RESPONSIVE EVALUATION Bob Stake's current approach, which he contrasts with "preordinate" evaluation, where there is a predetermined evaluation design. In responsive evaluation, one picks up whatever turns up and deals with it as seems appropriate, in the light of the past and unfolding interests of the various audiences *and* program staff. The emphasis is on rich description, personal experiences, not testing or experimental design—and not remediation. The risk is of course a lack of structure or of valid proof, but the trade-off is the avoidance of the main risk of a preordinate evaluation—a rigid investigation that misses significant occurrences, and narrow outcomes of little interest to the audiences. The chain of thought that led Stake to this position is reminiscent of the background which led Sartre to existentialism and others to situational ethics. It is well described in his paper in *Evaluation and Education: At Quarter Century* (NSSE/- University of Chicago, 1991). The main problem with the whole school of responsive-like evaluation approaches (e.g., illuminative, transactional) is that they are more interested in the process of evaluation than in the informational outcomes. This leads them to be considerate of program staff and to some extent recipients but inconsiderate of the needs of funders, legislators, parents (where the program is educational), taxpayers and planners. That seems to be shirking their responsibilities to discharge the most important social role of the professional evaluator. See Evaluation, Evaluation-specific methodology, Naturalistic evaluation, Perspectival evaluation, Relativism, Valuephobia.

RETURN ON INVESTMENT (ROI) One of the measures of merit or worth in fiscal evaluation; usually quoted as a per annum percentage rate.

REVOLUTIONS, EVALUATION OF Revolutions, whether political or technological, involve two methodological problems for evaluation: one for prospective evaluation, one for retrospective evaluation. The prospective evaluation involves determining whether a revolution would be worthwhile; here the relevant question is whether the (presumed) future benefits multiplied by the chance of success outweigh the penalties of failure multiplied by the chance of failure *plus* the cost of getting from here to there. In looking at the history of industrial strikes (which are mini-revolutions), it's clear that the chances of success and failure are rarely calculated with any care, and the benefit/cost perspective is usually limited to that of the strikers. For retrospective evaluation, since history is written by the victors, there is commonly a problem from consonance/dissonance distortion, that is, a change of values that magnifies the benefits and diminishes the value of the alternatives not chosen; not many people think hard about whether Lincoln really should have started a terrible war to prevent some states from seceding, though we're happy to condemn anyone else who looks as if they are trying to prevent some of *their* states from seceding. (More in "The Evaluation of Revolutions", in *Revolutions, Systems, and Theories*, ed. Robert G. Muehlmann, published by D. Reidel, 1979.) All of this applies quite directly and interestingly to the more mundane but more common—and just as perplexing—problem of when to update software. (Discussed in "Changing Horses in Midstream", *University MicroNews xvi*, Edgepress,1990.)

RFP Request for proposal. The standard advertised announcement calling for proposals and associated bids for a particular **scope of work**, including evaluations. Note that the RFP is sometimes as much in need of serious evaluation as the project for which it seeks evaluation; for example, it sometimes includes a complete evaluation design, and it is rare for something this complex to be flawless. Even if consultants have been used as well as internal staff to review the RFP, designs for large scale evaluations are still a cutting edge affair, and probably need review by a wide range of the best methodologists in the business. Failure to do this where necessary, and failure to do at least consultant review in other cases, leads to an immense amount of wasted time and money. Hood and Hemphill use the term "front-end evaluation" for evaluation of the concept or model built into the RFP. See **Preformative, RFQ, Two-tier.**

RFQ Request for quotation or request for qualifications. An alternative to the RFP requiring less work by the bidders. Sometimes an RFQ is in an announcement of an upcoming contract in which interested candidates are asked to express their interest and specify relevant qualifications, without having to submit a plan of work. Apart from reducing the amount of wasted time otherwise spent on plans by unsuccessful bidders this tends to keep things within what is sometimes seen as 'the old boys' network'. On the whole, it seems better to use a **two-tier** RFP or a partial RFP followed by interviews. The first-tier or partial RFP can present some typical problems that will form part of the full task, in order to identify bidders who have the relevant experience and/or bright new approaches.

RHETORIC, THE NEW The title of a book by C. Perelman and L. Olbrechts-Tyteca (Notre Dame, 1969), which attempted to develop a new logic of persuasion, reviving the spirit of pre-Ramist efforts. (Since Ramus [1572], the view of rhetoric as the art of empty and illogical persuasion has been dominant; the very concept of "logical analysis" as separate from rhetoric is Ramist.) This area is of the greatest importance to evaluation methodology as Ernest House has stressed (e.g., in *Evaluating with Validity*, Sage, 1989), because of the extent to which evaluations have—whether intentionally or not—the function of persuasion and not just reporting. The New Rhetoric emerged from the context of studying legal reasoning where the same situation obtains and was poorly recognized; it is suggestive work but not completely persuasive. The same push for reappraisal and new models of reasoning has occurred in logic (see *Informal Logic*, eds. Blair and Johnson [Edgepress, 1980]), and in the social sciences with the move toward naturalistic methodology. It is all part of a backlash against neopositivist philosophy of science and the worship of the Newtonian/mathematical model of science. Evaluation's fate clearly lies with the new movements.

RIGHT-TO-KNOW The legal domain of impacted populations' access to information; much increased under the Carter presidency in the U.S., for example through "open file" legislation. Decreased in Reagan-Bush period.

RIPPLE EFFECTS Sometimes called secondary effects. These are effects caused by the direct effects of the evaluand on the **recipients** *or* on the **providers** (the primary effects). Sometimes it's hard to decide how to divide the effects up on this basis—for example, a school band program produces effects on the band members and on those who hear its music. Effects on the second group are caused by those on the first group, but one might nevertheless include them as recipients. See also **Trickle effects** and **Side-effects**.

RISK ASSESSMENT Currently used as the name for some aspects of technology assessment, notably the analysis of possible outcomes from a proposed intervention, and their probabilities. There are some models for combining the probabilities and values/disvalues of the outcomes that have been used as guides for decision making, and they are sometimes applied in efforts at risk assessment. The classic **optimizing** approach is the most common of these and involves calculating the product of the probability of each outcome by its **utility** to give what is termed its expectancy. These expectancies are compared for each option, and the largest one is said to be the best choice. This approach converts the two dimensions of risk and utility into the one (of expectancy) and then uses ranking on the one dimension as the (derived) indicator or index of merit.

This approach is conventionally said to have certain weaknesses. For example, it appears to ignore the variable value of risk itself to different individuals; the gambler likes it, many others seek to minimize it. However, one can easily include a "utility of risk" variable. Sometimes expectancy analysis is criticized on the ground that "people don't think that way", a confusion of **descriptive** with **prescriptive**, that is, evaluative investigation. The discussion of **minimax** or **satisficing** strategies, for example, is often introduced as a step toward "a more sophisticated analysis of decision making". Minimax and satisficing are simply *less* sophisticated methods of making decisions, though they may be more common, and hence appropriate objects for study and naming by descriptive scientists. They are also easy-to-use strategies that will work reasonably well in a limited set of circumstances. The first problem is to identify that set, and the second is to determine when it applies to a real-world decision problem.

"Risk management" is a topic that has begun to appear with increasing frequency in planning and management training curricula. One reason that evaluations are not implemented is because the evaluator has failed to see that risks (which involve costs as well as probabilities) have a different significance for implementers by contrast with consumers. Elderly male-dominated legislatures making laws to control young women's access to gynecological advice and procedures provide one well-known example; heads of state deciding on war, when they believe themselves immune to any risk of death or injury, is another.

The converse example occurs when a program or policy (etc.) that should be implemented, in terms of its probable benefit to the consumers, is one which carries a high risk for the implementers because

318

their reward schedule is radically different from that of the consumer, often as a result of bad planning and management at a higher level. Two important examples are the classification of documents as top secret, and the hiring of personnel about whom there is a breath of suspicion. In each situation, the implementer gets penalized by review panels exercising 100 percent hindsight after a disaster if there was the least trace of a negative indicator, and in neither case is there ever a reward for taking a reasonable risk—in fact, there's never a review panel to look at the big winners. Consequently, the public's utilities are not optimized and are often reversed.

The present political-plus-media environment in the U.S. may be one in which the risk/cost configuration for the road to the presidency (or the legislature) is so different from that required to do the job right as to guarantee the election of incompetent incumbents who made great candidates.

RITUALISTIC or SYMBOLIC EVALUATION One of the reasons for doing evaluation that has nothing to do with the content of the evaluation (and hence is unlike **formative** and **summative**—or **rationalization**—evaluation) is the ritual function, that is, the doing of an evaluation because it is required or expected, although nobody has the faintest intention of either doing it well or taking any serious account of what it says. Evaluators are quite often called in to situations like this, and sometimes the situation is not even recognized as a case of ritual evaluation by the client. Evaluation in the vocational and bilingual education areas has a long record of being mostly ritualistic; and evaluations of preservice training in the self-satisfied professions like medicine and the law are sometimes of about the same quality. This is particularly unfortunate in the case of medicine, since some of the best evaluation anywhere is done in medicine and the area is of such importance to all of us that ignoring the brilliant work done by, for example, Christine McGuire working on the evaluation of student achievements in medicine, is highly unprofessional. It is an important part of the preliminary discussions with the client, in serious evaluation, to get clear exactly what kind of implementation is planned, under various hypotheses about what the content of the evaluation report might be; unless, of course, you have time to spare, need the money, and are not misleading any remote audiences. The third condition essentially never applies. See also **Motivational evaluation, Reactive effect.**

ROBUSTNESS 1. (Stat.) Statistical tests and techniques depend to varying degrees on assumptions about the population of origin. The *less* they depend on such assumptions, the *more* robust they are. For example, the *t*-test assumes normality, whereas nonparametric ("distribution-free") statistics are often considerably more robust. One might translate "robust" as "stable under variations of conditions and assumptions".

2. The concept is also applicable to and most important in the evaluation of experimental designs and in meta-evaluations. Designs should be set up to give *definite* answers to *as many as possible* of the *most important* questions—no matter how the data turn out. This is a quite different matter from their cost-effectiveness, power, or elegance (the latter is a limit case as efficiency or power blend into aesthetics). Evaluations should be set up so as to "go for the jugular", that is, so as to *first* get an adequately reliable answer to the key evaluative question(s), *later* adding the trimmings *if* nothing goes wrong with Part One. This affects budget, staff, and time-line planning. And it has a cost, as does robustness in statistics; for example, robust approaches will not be maximally elegant or cost-effective if everything goes right. But meta-evaluation will normally show that something close to a minimax approach is called for, which means robust evaluation. See **Fire at the horses first, Salience scoring.**

ROLE (of evaluator) The evaluator plays more roles than Olivier, or should. Major ones include **arbitrator**, attorney-surrogate, **change agent**, coauthor, confessor, educator, entrepreneur, investigator, judge, jury, manager, public relations agent, scapegoat, theoretician, "the enemy", **therapist**, and trouble-shooter. Conclusion: try for versatility, recognize your limitations, and form talented teams.

RORSCHACH EFFECT An extremely complex evaluation, if not carefully and rationally synthesized into an summary report, provides a confusing mass of positive and negative comments, and an unskilled and/or somewhat biased client can easily project onto ("see in", rationalize from) such a backdrop whatever perception s/he originally had. The name derives from the most famous projective test, the Rorschach inkblot test, and the fact that it is of somewhat dubious validity makes the label apt. Generally speaking, if this effect occurs it is the fault of the evaluator, for one of two possible reasons. First, it's usually important to directly address major possible interpretations that one is rejecting, and discussions with the client should have uncovered any strong sets toward a particular kind of interpretation. Second, in the case of what are here called **unconsummated evaluations**, the evaluator has failed to assist the client with the synthesis step and is essentially asking for projective results. See **Reporting** and **Layering.**

RUBRIC Scoring *or* grading *or* (conceivably) ranking guide for a test. The term acquired this use in the field of evaluation of student compositions and usually refers to a key for grading them or other essay answers. Evaluators of educational institutions should expect to find that the faculty uses rubrics and is familiar with the basic literature about rubrics whether they use or reject the use of essay tests. See Point constancy requirement. Ref. *The Evaluation of Composition Instruction*, 2nd. edition (Teachers College Press, 1989).

S

SALIENCE SCORING The practice of requesting respondents (for example when rating proposals) to use only those scales or check only those descriptors that, they felt, significantly (alternatively, strongly) influenced them. It focuses attention on the most important features of whatever is being rated (avoids dilution), and it greatly reduces processing time.

SATISFICING Herbert Simon's term for a common management policy of picking something acceptable rather than the "best choice" (optimizing). See **Risk assessment**.

SAWTOOTH GRAPHS These are useful for displaying overlapping normative data, for example when the suggested cutting scores for grades overlap substantially (as in the 1991 NAEP mathematics standards exercise). The proposed medians are drawn in, and the range of variation is indicated by constructing triangles with their bases on the median line, pointing above it and below it, and sized so that the distance between their apexes represents the range. A unique advantage is that these can be interspersed with the triangles on another baseline, without the triangles being superimposed; the effect is like that of the clenched teeth of a shark or two interlocking saw blades.

SCALES See **Measurement**.

SCALING This term has now acquired a use outside the measurement area; it has come to refer to the problems attendant on increasing the scale of a project or program or approach. While we are all familiar with the concept of economies of scale, we have also become increasingly sensitive to the deterioration attendant on scaling—the equivalent of the failure of reciprocity in the technology of emulsions. The most famous attack on the assumption that there is a linear relation between staff size and outcomes was centered around "the mythical man-month"; one of the most important applications occurs in computer programming, where it is sometimes referred to as the Microsoft Principle—"If one programmer takes six months to do a job, six programmers take sixteen months", or words to that effect. (The name comes from comparing Microsoft Word with Xywrite or Nisus; in each case, the product of the mighty Empire's lost the first round and could at best be said to have deadheated in the second round.) Ref: Karl Weick "Small Wins: Redefining the Scale of Social

322

Problems", *American Psychologist, 39*, pp. 40–49, 1984, has laid some groundwork for a strategy that allows for the difficulty of scaling. (Thanks to Paul Hood for the reference to Weick.)

SCHOOL EVALUATION PROFILE (SEP) An instrument for evaluating the performance of schools (and hence districts, principals, and so on), which uses only those variables that are under the control of parties to the educational undertaking. SEP was invented to provide a fair basis for evaluation of the schools in the San Francisco unified school district when it was taken over by the State of California. It consisted of several scales, performance on which was graphed to give an instantly readable profile. The scales included: Administrator Knowledge and Skills, Administrator Performance, Teaching Staff K&S, Teaching Staff Performance, Student Performance, Parental Support, District Support (and optionally State Support). A set of questions was tied to each scale, and an evaluation team was (generically) identified to get answers to the questions and integrate them into a grade on each scale. (Scores on state assessment were only used as background descriptive data.) See **Responsibility evaluation.**

SCOPE OF WORK This is the part of an RFP or a proposal that describes exactly what is to be done, at the level of description which refers to the activities as they might be seen by a visitor without special methodological skills or insight, rather than to their goals, achievements, process or purpose. In point of fact, scope of work statements tend to drift off into descriptions that are somewhat less than observationally testable. The scope of work statement is an important part of making accountability possible on a contract, and is therefore an important part of the specifications in an RFP or a proposal.

SCORING (a.k.a. marking) An evaluation procedure that consists of assigning numbers to an evaluand (usually a performance) in order to represent merit. The points are usually supposed to be of equal value. Sometimes numbers are used as grades without commitment to this **point constancy requirement**, but this is misleading—letters should be used instead, and the attempt to convert them to numbers—for example, to calculate GPAs—should be protested unless point constancy holds at least to an approximation that will not yield significant errors of interpretation. Usually tests should be impressionistically graded as well as scored, both to get the **cutting scores** and to provide insurance against deviations from point constancy. Scoring not only requires point constancy but also serious consideration of the definition of a zero score: No answer? Hopelessly bad answer? Both? ("Both" is a hopelessly bad answer.) In 'constrained scoring' a further requirement is imposed, for example that the total scores of all N evaluands should

323

add up to f(N) (e.g., should add up to N/2). This is one way to control overrating problems. See also **Raw scores, Questionnaires, Grading, Ranking, Anchoring.**

SECONDARY ANALYSIS Reassessment of an experiment or investigation, by reanalysis of the same data and/or reconsideration of the interpretation. Gathering new data would normally constitute **replication**; but there are intermediate cases. Sometimes used to refer to reviews of large numbers of studies: See **Meta-analysis, Secondary evaluation.**

SECONDARY EVALUATION (Cook) Reanalysis of original *evaluation* data—or original plus new data—to produce a new evaluation of a particular project (or other evaluand). The Russell Sage Foundation commissioned a series of books in which famous evaluations were treated in this way, beginning with Tom Cook's secondary evaluation of Sesame Street. Extremely important because: (i) it gives potential clients some basis for estimating the competence of evaluators (in the case just cited, the estimate would be fairly low); and (ii) it gives evaluators the chance to identify and learn from their mistakes. Evaluations were for too long forced into fugitive document status and hence did not receive the benefit of later discussion in "the literature" as would a research report published in a journal. (A similar problem applies to classified material.) Cf. **Meta-evaluation.**

SECONDARY INDICATOR One that is only connected with the **criterion** variable(s) by way of empirically or theoretically determined correlations. The make of a car is a secondary indicator of merit, if you know the results of road tests and long-term testing; the reliability of a car, by contrast, is a criterion of merit, sometimes referred to as a **primary indicator** of merit. In product evaluation, the use of secondary indicators is often justified, although less than ideal; but in personnel evaluation, it is essentially never justified (because one can get evidence about performance on primary indicators). See **Research-based personnel evaluation.**

SECONDARY VALUE CLAIM A claim that someone, or a group, values something to a stated extent (perhaps by comparison with certain other things). The contrast is with **primary value claims**, which are claims that an *evaluand* has (as a matter of fact) a certain value to a certain extent, perhaps to certain groups. Secondary value claims are verifiable, even when made by the person to whom they refer, since they can always be lies, and often self-deceptions. But the process of verifying them is just the process of verifying that the person *does* value something—believes that something is valuable to them—not that it *is valuable* to them (or *is good* for them, or *is worthwhile* for them, and so on). The two claims only coalesce in the case of 'mere' matters

324

of taste, that is, matters of taste where other considerations must be weighted, such as health, logic, or the law.

SECRET-CONTRACT BIAS In proposal, personnel, and particularly institutional evaluation, raters are often too lenient because they know that the roles of rater and ratee will be reversed on another occasion and they think or guess that everyone will realize that, and act accordingly, in the hope that "if you scratch my back I'll scratch yours". Many major institutions have had to abandon merit promotions or pay because they can't get peer evaluation to work, either because of poor security and fear of reprisal, or because of secret-contract bias. The second consideration is an example of the unprofessional conduct too common of the professions—substituting self-protection (of course rationalized as 'loyalty') for the protection of the client. (i) A good counterbalance is to rate everyone heavily on the long-term validity of their ratings. (ii) An easier control to instigate and use immediately is the use of an external personnel evaluator. (iii) A major improvement is possible without either of the best approaches, just by making the ratings **analytical** instead of **global**, writing clear standards (**anchors**), running raters through a few practice examples (**calibration**), and having the process supervised. See **Accreditation**.

SELECTION A key decision at which one variety of **personnel evaluation** is aimed. Conceptually it is sometimes useful to think of it as an attempt to predict the first on-job appraisal. This is not quite accurate, because the first appraisal may be poorly done, and one may be including considerations of **worth** as well as **merit**, and worth is a pay off for the organization that may not show up in individual appraisals. (For example, minority appointments outside the sales department may increase federal contracts.) The selection process is one where the cost-effectiveness of good evaluation procedures is extremely high, because of the size of the long-term investment, the bonuses from exceptionally successful selection, and the high costs of errors. It is not done in a way that is commensurate with these considerations (which have been worked out in some detail in the literature). For example, the leading component in most selection procedures is **interviewing**, which is, on the average, one of the worst evaluation procedures in any field. See also **Fire at the horses first** and **Synthesis**. Ref: "The Selection of Teachers", in *Handbook of Teacher Evaluation: Elementary & Secondary Personnel*, Second Edition, ed. J. Millman and L. Darling-Hammond (Sage, 1990).

SELECTION (or SELECTIVITY) BIAS Arises in program evaluation when selection of control or experimental group members is influenced by an unnoticed connection with desirable outcomes. Irrelevant to studies with random assignment. If differential attrition occurs, as between experimental and control group, the possibility of selectivity bias reemerges even in randomized design. See "Issues in the Analysis of Selectivity Bias", Barnow et al., *Evaluation Studies Review Annual*, Vol. 5 (Sage, 1980).

SELF-EFFACING EFFECT   An effect in which the visible benefits of a program are 'washed out' *as a result of certain phenomena which the program itself causes.* This does not mean the benefits are eliminated; it simply means that they are made much harder to see, and in particular that they tend not to show up in comparisons with other communities not receiving the support from the program under review. This loss of contrast is the reason for talking about a 'washout' and 'self effacing'; self-effacing people are not the same as ineffective people, although they both typically have a low profile.

The paradigm case of the Self-Effacing Effect was the Federal Government's ESAA program of a few years back. Large sums of money were provided to school districts, on two conditions. First, that the money was spent on projects or materials chosen from a list provided; second, that they identified a control school in the district which would not receive any of the 'treatment' (money to be spent on items from the approved shopping list). What happened in fact was that the superintendents often diverted *other* (discretionary) monies to the control school to compensate them for being deprived of the program money, and these monies were spent, typically, in ways not obviously different from the ways in which they were spent by the experimental schools. The bottom line was that no consistent and significant difference showed up between control and experimental schools. The good news is that this doesn't mean that there wasn't a benefit all round. The bad news is that in this situation when your control groups have been washed out, it's hard to prove that there was or was not a benefit. Of course, one might argue on a priori grounds that more money means more benefits, but charitable foundations and governments—and particularly their critics—are rightly suspicious of the claim that throwing money at a problem is going to be effective, let alone cost-effective. Thus, giving the money led to action which made it very difficult to detect the effects of giving the money. This is a special case of *compensatory giving by a source other than the original donor.*

Causal coupling that generates the self-effacing effect occurs under three general headings. (i) Deliberate compensation by the same source. Foundations engaged in support of particular communities will often make contributions to other, similar, communities 'to make up for' the fact they were not part of the program. Of course, these are the communities one would be using for comparisons, so the effect is masked. (ii) Deliberate compensation by another source. Another foundation or source may respond favorably to a plea from an applicant, Y, that they have the same needs as X but are not being helped by the source which has chosen to support X. Or, as in the ESAA case, the *recipient* may pass along some of the money or other monies to Y. (iii) Automatic compensation. In many states, the distribution of resources for certain programs is tied to indexes of need. These will (one hopes) be affected in the area being directly helped by the intervention under evaluation, and hence it will get less state resources, and potential comparison areas will get more, again effacing the trace of the intervention—although the intervention will in fact have produced benefits, these will not be salient.

There are ways around these problems, for example via: (i) the use of carefully selected multiple comparisons, where the redundancy covers one against the occurrence of some self-effacing interventions; (ii) the **modus operandi method**; (iii) the use of longitudinal controls (interrupted time series, etc.) One problem with the last approach is that any judges used to identify differences are likely to be aware of the presence of the treatment in one rather than another area.

SELF-EVALUATION In discussions about personnel evaluation, the suggestion is often heard that self-evaluations should be given some weight in the process, at least in the evaluation of professionals. It is essential to realize that in one sense this is completely fallacious, in another, very important; the two senses are not normally distinguished. Since professionals should have considerable skill in self-evaluation (the **professional imperative**), their efforts in this direction should be examined in the course of evaluating them. These are examined for their quality as work products—and because they may provide a basis for correcting evaluator errors, both in the self-assessment and in the evaluator's rating. But they cannot be given weight in themselves, that is, as if they were co-evaluator reports, since to do so creates a reason for inflation of the self-rating, that is, for falsifying them, and hence for invalidating them and the overall evaluation. See **Administrator evaluation**. Self-evaluation for the evaluator is of course a particularly serious obligation—'evaluation begins at home'.

SELF-FULFILLING EVALUATION A **reactive evaluation** that brings about its own truth and would not be true without being announced or published. The causal mechanism involved ranges from a felt need to make a favorable claim true (perhaps because one authored it), through cases of evaluands being so distressed by a negative evaluation as to bring about its truth, to cases of performative utterances where the utterance is the award of which it speaks. See also **Self-refuting evaluation**.

327

SELF-REFERENCE Sociology is a directly self-referent science, since the sociology of science and hence of sociology is part of it; the same is generally true of the social sciences, critical thinking, and philosophy. Pure mathematics (like astronomy and geology) is not a self-referent discipline, since its subject matter does not include the process of (or people when) doing mathematics (and so on). Physics is at best halfway to being self-referent. The discipline of evaluation, and in many cases its practice, is of its nature self-referent; but egocentrism, paranoia, and **valuephobia** represent powerful obstacles in the way of evaluating evaluation. Organizations have a prurient attraction for the obscene rationalization used in the **Dreyfus case**, where the French Army argued that its error in sending an innocent man to Devil's Island should not be acknowledged since that would weaken the public's confidence in the Army and hence weaken France. This would be a far more serious outcome, they suggested, than the incarceration of one innocent man. This disease afflicts organizations besides the armed services, especially those to whom we entrust justice—the police, the courts, the bar associations and the CIA; organized medicine, to which we entrust our health; agencies like the National Academy of Sciences or the National Science Foundation—on whom we rely for the evaluation of much research; and even Consumers Union, our leading source for product evaluation, appears not to be immune. (Teachers, including professors, are also notably unenthusiastic about it.) But all should be doing and—in the case of the institutions—publishing self-evaluations, as a professional, ethical, and scientific obligation. See **Evaluation** and **Evaluation imperative**.

SELF-REFUTING EVALUATION An evaluation whose publication brings about its falsification. Loosely speaking, one might say that many critical formative evaluations are quickly rebutted by changing the program to make the criticism no longer true. (Strictly, speaking, of course, one should attach a time variable to the evaluation; then the evaluation at t_0 is not invalidated by changes made at t_1, only by a re-publication of the same evaluation report if made, inconceivably, at t_2.) The evaluative claim that a student or a program manager is incorrigibly lazy will sometimes, however, be self-refuting in a stronger sense, that is, true unless published, false if published. There is a range of other cases of **reactive** evaluation which are close to being self-refuting; highly favorable evaluations sometimes reduce incentive so that the best intern ceases to be the best intern just because s/he was so identified. There are also **self-fulfilling evaluations**.

SEMI-INTERQUARTILE RANGE (Stat.) In testing, half the interval between the score that marks the top score of the lowest or first quartile (that is, of the lowest quarter of the group being studied, after they

328

have been ranked according to the variable of interest, for example, test scores), and the score that marks the top of the third quartile. This is a useful measure of the range of a variable in a population, especially when it is not 'normally' distributed (where the **standard deviation** would usually be used). It amounts to averaging the intervals between the median and the individuals who are halfway out to the ends of the distribution, one in each direction. Thus it is not affected by oddities occurring at the extreme ends of the distribution, its main advantage over the standard deviation, an advantage that it retains even in the case of a normal population.

SENSORY EVALUATION The methodology exhibited in sophisticated versions of blind wine-tasting. The better restaurant reviews, or the Consumers Union reports on bottled water, pancake mixes, and many other products, remind us of the important difference between dismissing something as a 'mere matter of taste' and doing sensory evaluation. The aim is of course not to *eliminate* dependence on preference but to improve the validity of the evaluative conclusions, for example, by reducing the effect of distractors (such as labels), using multiple independent raters and standardized sets of criteria. However, the conventional approach—for example, the one used by Consumers Union—still involves two problems that rule it out as the state-of-the-art for obtaining objective ratings of merit. In wine tasting, for example, suppose that the testers know how to recognize French sauternes—not an evaluative skill—and have (consciously or unconsciously) what may be the purely biased view that French wines are superior. Then, even in blind taste-testing, they might grade the California/Australian/German wines on their similarity to the French wines, which they rate as the best. Such a result therefore shows—as far as one could tell—nothing about true superiority, only about the pervasiveness of prejudice. (See **Technicism**.) The second problem is one of a family of problems that relate to the **irrelevance of expert judges**. It is the problem of changes in taste with experience. The professional taster, of wine or tea or restaurant meals, may be a poor guide to follow, for most of their audience, since their taste may have become jaded to the point where it is very different from that of the vast majority of consumers. In short, they are not experts in the relevant sense. They may or may not be experts in a significant sense—they may be able to analyze a taste or meal into components better than the beginner, and they may be able to provide a historical or comparative perspective of some value. (The proper word for them is 'connoisseur'.) But they are no guide to *merit*, since there is no basis for the view that their taste is *superior* to that of the novice. Even if the novice, later in life, will drift toward the standards the expert has

329

now—unlikely, because few novices imbibe that much good wine—they're not at that point now, and now is when they need advice.

It's fairly easy to remedy the error of using irrelevant experts for sensory evaluation, by using a panel of novice tasters instead. One problem is that their taste standards may drift under the unusual level of exposure, but this can be handled by using shifts. Another solution is to attempt calibration of the experts, so that one can convert their readings into novice readings, or find some who can role-play novices with some reliability.

SERVICE (evaluation of) See **Evaluation of service.**

SERVICE EVALUATION The evaluation of services, usually best treated as a combination of evaluation of the program and of the personnel. Ref. *Service Evaluation*, Vol. 1, no. 1, Fall 1982, Center for the Study of Services, Suite 406, 1518 K St., NW, Washington, DC20005.

SEQUENCING EFFECT The influence of the order of items (or tests, etc.) upon responses. A test's validity may be compromised when items are removed, for example, for racial bias, since the item might have preconditioned the respondent (in a way that has nothing to do with its bias) so as to give a different and more accurate response to the next (or any later) question, an example of sequencing effect.

SES Socio-Economic Status.

SHARED BIAS The principal problem with using experts' opinions as the basis for evaluation is that the agreement between them (if any) may be due to common error (known as shared bias). Obvious and serious examples occur in peer review of research proposals, where the panelists often reflect current fads in the field to the detriment of brilliant innovators (as many Nobelists report about their early attempts to get funding), and in **accreditation** (where the shared bias is due to a shared **conflict of interest**). The best antidote is often the use of some intellectually—not just institutionally—external judges (for example, radical critics of the field), plus a follow-up procedure for cases of disagreement, for example, the **wild card procedure.** Shared bias is the main reason why interjudge or intertest consistency, that is, **reliability** in the technical sense, is no substitute for **validity.** A typical example occurs in accreditation, where the driver education department (e.g., of a high school) is checked out by the 'driver ed' person on the visiting team. There is little solace to be found in the discovery that: (i) the visitor likes the department and does not recommend its abolition—although there are very serious reasons for dropping such departments when money is tight, for example, they do not reduce accidents; (ii) a second visiting panel agrees with the first one's judgment on driver ed (because *its* judgment was provided by one more member of the same self-serving group). This also

330

happens to involve conflict of interest, whereas medical fads (pneumothorax in its heyday, for example) often do not. See **Bias control**.

SIDE-EFFECTS Side-effects are the (good and bad) effects of a program or product (etc.) other than those for which it was implemented or purchased. Sometimes the term refers to effects that were expected and might even have been desired but are not part of the goals of the program, such as employment of staff. Typically, they have not been expected, predicted, or anticipated (a minor point). They may, however, be far more important than the intended effects, for example, in drug side-effects. In the KEC a distinction is made between (i) side-effects and (ii) unintended effects on nontarget populations that are in fact impacted, that is, side-*populations*, but both are often called side-effects. Side-effects identification presents a methodological problem in that evaluators are usually cued to find the intended effects (**goal-based evaluation**) and their clients are usually much more interested in progress toward the intended effects. The inevitable result of this combination of 'sets' is that the search for side-effects is often perfunctory; **goal-free evaluation** is a deliberate attempt to improve side-effect detection, and has in fact often been successful in doing so. The most important general side-effect of *evaluation*, by contrast with side-effects of a program, should be increased use of evaluation where it can be useful, and some skills in how to do it. So the evaluator should always think of being a role model and a teacher, not just a critic and remediator.

SIGMA (Stat.) Greek symbol used in lower case as name for standard deviation, in upper case to refer to the summation operator.

SIGNIFICANCE (of evaluation findings) The bottom line: the overall conclusion of an evaluation, when all relevant considerations have been synthesized, should express the evaluative significance of the evaluand. There are many kinds of significance, relating to types of consideration: for example, personal, political, social, literary, scientific, educational, professional, and intellectual. **Statistical significance**, when relevant at all, is just one of several conditions for any real significance when a certain type of quantitative data is involved, although in the social sciences it has frequently been treated as if it is the scientific surrogate for the common notions. (See **Fallacy of statistical surrogation**.) Since significance can readily be achieved by means of *qualitative* research, statistical significance is not a necessary condition for real significance; and since statistical significance can easily be achieved by minute differences that persist in very large experimental and control groups, it is not a sufficient condition for real significance (which almost always requires substantial effect size).

The absolute size of the gains attributed to the program or product being evaluated must be of substantial intrinsic value—for example, because they make a worthwhile contribution toward meeting the needs of the recipients/consumers.

To determine significance, the main 'wrap-up' or 'bottom line' checkpoint on the KEC, the evaluator must integrate the data corresponding to each of the prior checkpoints. Overall significance represents the total **synthesis** of all you have learned about the merit or worth of the evaluand—for example, a program.

Note that there is another meaning of "significance", as in "the significance of that action", important in other methodological contexts, where it is almost equivalent to "meaning".

SIMULATIONS Re-creations of, especially, typical job situations to provide a realistic test of aptitudes or abilities; analogously for program and product evaluation. See **Clinical performance evaluation, Personnel evaluation.**

SMILES TEST (of a program) People like it. Sometimes acceptable, but usually an example of substituting wants for needs.

SOCIAL INDICATOR See **Indicator.**

SOCIAL SCIENCE MODEL (of evaluation) The view that evaluation is an application of standard social science methodology. One look at the usual social scientist's effort at—or omission of—ethical analysis or **needs assessment** when doing an evaluation is enough to make clear why this view is implausible. The relation of the social science model of program evaluation to the **transdisciplinary model** of evaluation is like that between surveying and trigonometry: the latter is substantially more general than the former, applies to several other application areas (such as navigation), and solves some problems encountered by the former, but it does not replace the practical skills involved in the former. See **Evaluation.**

SOCIAL SIGNIFICANCE See **Significance.**

SOFT (approaches to evaluation). Indicators are the use of heavy evaluator interaction with program staff, **implementation** data, the **smiles test**, or substituting 'rich description' for critical analysis. See **Hard.**

SOLE SOURCE "Sole-sourcing" a contract—asking a single vendor to bid on it, or simply to do it—is an alternative to "putting it out to bid" via publishing an RFP. Sole sourcing is open to the abuse that the contract officer from the agency may let contracts to his or her buddies without regard to whether the price is excessive or the quality unsatisfactory; on the other hand, it is very much faster, it costs less if you take account of the time for preparing RFPs and proposals in cases where a very large number of these would be written for a very complex RFP, and it is sometimes mandatory when it is provable that the skills and/or resources required are available from only one contractor within the necessary time-frame. Simple controls can prevent the kind of abuse mentioned; for example, one can sole source to two different vendors for the same contract and require them to work independently, to preserve the competitive element and improve validity.

SOLICITED (research) Specific research, often specified down to the level of the research design; aimed to get some particular information developed. The contrast is with field-initiated research, which is intended to support a general area of research effort.

SPECIALIST EVALUATOR The contrast is with the GP, the **general purpose evaluator**. See **Local expert**.

SPEEDED (tests) Also called timed tests; those tests with a time limit (the time taken by each individual who finishes early is usually not recorded). These are often better instruments for evaluation or prediction than the same test would be with no time limit—usually because the criterion behavior involves doing something under time pressure, but sometimes, as in IQ tests, just as a matter of empirical fact. A test is sometimes defined as speeded if less than 75 percent finish in time.

SPILLOVER (effects) See **Trickle effects**.

SPONSOR (of an evaluation) Whoever or whatever funds or arranges funding or facilitates release of personnel and space: may or may not be the "instigator" of the KEC. Cf. **Client**.

SPREADSHEET (in evaluation) The electronic spreadsheet provides a useful and in many respects unmatchable tool for dealing with complex evaluations in the usual categories (product, policy, program, personnel). While the 3D spreadsheets, notably IMPROV on the NeXT computer, and Boeing Calc on minicomputers, are substantially better (but also harder to learn), the standard high-end programs on the micros are very useful, particularly Excel 3.0 because of its outliner feature. There will probably be a good 3D micro spreadsheet before Excel 4.0 comes out, and this should be considered; meanwhile, one can use a set of 2D layouts as a substitute. A word processor *with a table facility* can also be used, as can a database; but neither would rate better than half as good as a high-end spreadsheet.

The general approach is to get the criteria or dimensions of meritorious performance listed as row headings, and the candidates as column headings. Spreadsheets like Excel 3.0, which have built-in outliner capability are particularly useful for collapsing to a level of main headings in order to preserve perspective (very important in cases like the evaluation of laptop computers or high schools, where 200+ criteria are involved). The first column after the row headings is

333

reserved for weightings of importance and the remaining cells in the main display are filled with performance measures or ratings. While the layout can obviously be used for numerical weight and sum approaches, the validity problem makes it desirable to go to a qualitative weight and sum approach. The raw performance data is hidden one layer down in a 3D spreadsheet, or in a parallel spreadsheet when one lacks 3D capacity, but it can also be written into same cell with some care to segregate it from the normalized data or rating, perhaps with a double slash. Sources can be attached to each cell reporting raw performance data, as an electronic 'post-it note' on most spreadsheets; these can be displayed or concealed at the tap of a keystroke. Footnotes can also be attached, for special comments. In the cost analysis part of the work, the built-in repertoire of formulas that come with every spreadsheet are incomparably useful, yielding instant conversion to net present value, annualized equivalents of capital costs, post-tax cost, and so on.

Subtotals of performance scores for each candidate for each group of criteria can be automatically calculated in either the numerical or the qualitative model, in order to facilitate weighting checks; and the grand totals are of course used to determine an overall winner. Other macros can be written to facilitate microanalysis, to check for interactions, and so on. One of the most important benefits from using an electronic spreadsheet relates to a relatively newly remarked phenomenon, the 'refocusing' step. The computer allows you to save early versions of your analyses with trivial ease, instead of overwriting them or discarding them; this turns out to be extremely valuable because you will often find yourself driven back to a point where you must use some of the earlier version, and can avoid recalculating it by simply reopening 'draft 6', then doing a cut and paste operation on the part you need from it.

STABILITY A term sometimes used to refer to test-retest reliability, but more usefully restricted to the variables measured.

STAKEHOLDER (in a program) One who has substantial ego, credibility, power, futures, or other capital invested in the program, and thus can be held to be to some degree at risk with it. This includes program staff and many who are not actively involved in the day-to-day operations—for example, inventors or instigators or supporters of the program. Opponents are also, in a sense, stakeholders—like those who sell stock short or bet on a competing horse. Stakeholders may not even be aware that they are stakeholders (e.g., investors holding South African stock through a mutual fund, or those, such as environmental activist groups, who have an interest even if they have never heard of the program). Recipients are only stakeholders in an indirect

334

sense and are normally dealt with separately. Taxpayers are not significant stakeholders in most programs, since their stake in any particular program is usually small. For ethical reasons they still have to be considered because a policy of ignoring such small interests would, if generalized, lead to the absurd conclusion that taxpayers have no interest in the whole set of tax-funded programs.

STANDALONE Evaluation criteria are said to be standalone (or autonomous) if scores on them—at least, scores up to some point—cannot be obtained by using over-minimum scores on other criteria. (The contrast is with **compensatory** criteria.) The usual situation is one in which there is an 'absolute' minimum on the (standalone) criterion, identifying performance levels that have to be met for the evaluand to be acceptable, regardless of how well it does on other criteria of merit. Performance *beyond* those minima is, typically, tradeable (that is, compensatory). Even a criterion such as ethicality, which is standalone up to the point of the ethically obligatory, allows trading in the realm of supererogation. See also **Qualitative weight and sum, Multiple-hurdle.**

STANDARD The performance level associated with a particular rating or grade on a given criterion or dimension of achievements. For example, 80 percent success may be the standard for passing the written portion (dimension) of the driver's license test. A **cutting score** defines a standard, but standards can also be given in nonquantitative grading contexts, for example by requiring a B average in graduate school, or by providing exemplars, as in global grading of composition samples. Standards are prescriptive and hence are always normative in one sense (e.g., 'absolute' standards, such as "A for Excellent") and sometimes also in the other ("An A is given to the top 20%"). See also **Banding, Grading on the curve.**

STANDARD DEVIATION (Stat.) A technical measure of dispersion; in a normal distribution, about two-thirds of the population lies within one standard deviation of the mean, median, or mode (which are the same in this case.) The SD is simply the mean of the squares of the deviations, that is, of the distances from the mean.

STANDARD ERROR OF MEASUREMENT (Stat.) There are several alternative definitions of this term, all of which attempt to give a precise meaning to the notion of the intrinsic inaccuracy of an instrument, typically a test.

STANDARDIZED TEST Standardized tests are ones with standardized instructions for administration, use, scoring, and interpretation, with standard printed forms and content, often with standardized statistical properties, which have been validated on a large sample of a defined population. They are *usually* **norm-referenced**, at the

335

moment, but the terms are not synonymous since a **criterion-referenced** test can also be standardized. Having the norms (etc.) on a test does mean it's standardized in one respect, but it does not mean it's *just* a norm-referenced test in the technical sense; it may (also) be criterion referenced, which implies a different technical approach to its construction and not just a different purpose.

STANDARD SCORE Originally, scores defined as the deviations from the mean, divided by the standard deviation ("effect size" is an example.) More casually, various linear transformations of the above (e.g., z scores) aimed to avoid negative scores.

STANINES (or stanine scores) If you are perverse enough to divide a distribution into nine equal parts instead of ten (see **decile**), they are called stanines and the cutting scores that demarcate them are called stanine scores. They are numbered from the bottom up. See also **Percentiles.**

STATISTICAL SIGNIFICANCE When the difference between two results—usually the results of the control group and the experimental group—is determined to be "statistically significant", the evaluator can conclude that the difference is (probably) not due to chance. The level of significance, in this sense, determines the degree of certainty or confidence with which we can rule out chance (that is, rule out the "null hypothesis"). Unfortunately, if very large samples are used, even tiny differences become statistically significant although they may have no social, educational, or other value at all (the Sesame Street evaluation was an example of this). Omega statistics provide a partial correction. The literature on the "significance test controversy" shows why quantitative approaches presuppose qualitative ones and is indeed an example of the evaluation of quantitative measures.

There are also many occasions when results are highly and objectively significant but no statistical measure can be applied, since statistical significance cannot even be calculated except in terms of some stated hypothesis, while much evaluation—even quantitative evaluation—uses other paradigms than the classical **hypothesis-testing** approach. The significance of an intervention may be considerable even if it had no effects in the intended directions, which might be cognitive or health gains; it may have employed many people, raised general awareness of problems, or produced other gains. The absence of *overall* significance effects may also be due to the dilution of good effects in a pool of poor programs producing no effects: one cannot infer from an overall null to individual nulls. For this reason, 'lumping designs' are often less desirable than 'splitting designs' in which separate studies are made of many sites or subtreatments (see **Replication, Meta-analysis**). Omega statistics and Glass' "standardized

336

effect size" are attempts to produce measures that more nearly reflect true significance than does the p level of the absolute size of the results. See also **Raw scores, Significance, Interocular difference**.

STATISTICAL SURROGATION, FALLACY OF (a.k.a. Fallacy of Statistical Substitution) The fallacy of substituting a statistical concept for a preexisting methodological concept. A quantitative version of older fallacies such as stereotyping by treating the average member of a group as typical of all members of that group. The classic example, representing a mistake rarely made today, is the substitution of correlations for causation. Referring to factors from factor analysis as explanatory is a more serious and common instance of the fallacy, as is the supposition that two tests whose results correlate highly are 'measuring the same thing'. Scientifically speaking, the most damaging examples of this fallacy are the confusion of **statistical significance** with real significance and of test **reliability** with real reliability. Socially, the worst example would probably be the use of correlates of success as **criteria of merit** in **personnel evaluation**. See also **Incestuous validation**. Ref: "Fallacies of Statistical Substitution", in *Argumentation*, John Woods, ed., (D. Reidel, 1988)

STEM The text of a multiple-choice test item that precedes the listing of the possible responses.

STRATEGY (in the evaluation process) Also called "decision function" or "response rule". A set of guidelines for choices that may be predetermined, or conditional upon the outcomes of early choices, or even purely exploratory—that is, preliminary to main choices. See **Optimization**. The evaluation of strategies is of course part of game theory. For an example of particular interest for evaluation, see **Prisoner's dilemma**.

STRATIFICATION A sample is said to be stratified if it has been deliberately chosen so as to include an appropriate number of entities from each of several population subgroups that are of interest or with respect to which the variables under investigation may operate differently. For example, one usually stratifies the sample of students in K-12 educational evaluations with regard to gender, aiming at 50 percent males and 50 percent females. If one selects a random sample of females to make up half of the experimental and half of the control group and a random sample of males for the other half, then one has a "stratified random sample". If you stratify on too many variables you many not be able to make a random choice of subjects in a particular stratum—there may be too few eligible candidates. If one stratifies on very few or no variables, one has to use larger random samples to compensate. Stratification is only justified with regard to variables that probably interact with the treatment variable, and it only increases efficiency, not validity, unless you do it in addition to using large numbers, that is, abandon the efficiency gains it makes possible. In fact, it runs some risk of reducing validity because you may *not* cover the key variable (through ignorance) and your reduced sample size may not take care of it.

STRENGTHS ASSESSMENT Looking at the resources available for a program or project, including time, talent, funds, and space (see Costs for a full list). This process defines the "range of the possible" and hence is important in both **needs assessment** and in the identification of **critical competitors**, as well as in making **remediation** suggestions and doing **responsibility evaluation**.

STUDENT EVALUATION May mean (i) the evaluation *of* students, usually by their instructors; (ii) evaluation *by* students, usually of their instructors (the filled-in instruments are often referred to as "student ratings"); (iii) the evaluation of student *work*, that is, **performance evaluation**. Sense (i) is a species of personnel evaluation, but it is usually and mistakenly confused sense (iii), student performance or student work evaluation. In that sense, it has the distinction of being the original meaning of the term "evaluation" in the applied social sciences—books with the unqualified term "evaluation" in their title have been, for more than half a century, almost exclusively concerned with the evaluation of students (actually, students' work, usually on tests). Today, this is properly seen as one small part of educational evaluation, and as an even smaller part of evaluation as a whole. And we are now more careful to distinguish between the evaluation of students (**personnel evaluation**) and the evaluation of student work (**performance evaluation**).

In sense (ii), we find another curious situation, since student evaluation of teaching is almost never used in K–12, but constitutes almost all the evaluation of teaching that takes place at the postsecondary level. This difference is a purely cultural phenomenon, not being connected with validity in any known or likely way. Students are the only eyewitnesses to much that is relevant to teacher evaluation (e.g., favoritism, tardiness) and qualify as expert witnesses on other such matters (e.g., comprehensibility and legibility of presentations), and they will produce very good ratings if the form used is well designed and the context prepares and supports them in the evaluator role. If the form slips—and most do—into asking about style or subject matter expertise, it lays itself open to dismissal by those seeking an excuse to dismiss it. See **Teacher evaluation**.

STYLE-FREE EVALUATION An approach to **personnel evaluation** that eschews reference to **style indicators** (e.g., management or teaching style). Arguably the only legitimate approach. See **Research-**

based personnel evaluation for the style-based alternative.

STYLE INDICATOR In the sense used in personnel evaluation, a style indicator is any characteristic that describes the *way* in which something is done without reference to its success or failure, merit or worth. For example, speakers may be verbose or laconic (a matter of style); but to say that they are effective is to evaluate them. Teachers may employ Socratic or didactic styles; but to say that they are well prepared is not a comment on their teaching style, but on their merit as a teacher. In general, style variables describe ways of getting the job done, by contrast with evidence that the job is being done. See **Personnel evaluation.**

STYLE RESEARCH Investigations of two kinds: *either* descriptive investigations of the stylistic characteristics of, for example, people in certain professions such as teaching or managing, *or* investigations of the correlations between certain style characteristics and successful outcomes. The second kind of investigation has been thought to be of great importance to **personnel evaluation,** since discoveries of substantial correlations would allow certain types of evaluation to be performed on a process basis (e.g., by classroom observation) that currently can only be done legitimately by looking at outcomes (student learning and attitude to learning). However, that turns out to be an invalid approach to personnel evaluation. It still may be useful in product evaluation. The former kind of investigation—a typical example is studying the frequency with which teachers utter questions by comparison with declarative sentences or commands—is pure research, and extremely hard to justify as of either intellectual or social interest unless the second kind of connection can be made. In general, style research has come up with disappointingly few winners, if one applies serious standards of validity. (Active Learning Time, a.k.a. time on task, is probably the most important and possibly the only exception.) No doubt the interactions between the personality, the style, the age and type of recipient, and the subject matter prevent any simple general results; but the poor results of research on interactions suggests that the interactions are so strong as to obliterate even very limited recommendations. We must instead fall back to treating positive results as *possible strategies (or remedies),* not *indicators of probable merit.* See also **Style-free evaluation.**

SUBJECTIVE, SUBJECTIVITY See **Relativism.**

SUCCESS Goal-achievement of known, defensible, but not necessarily optimal goals. An evaluative term, but not one of the most important because the value is so dependent on the value of the goals. Cf. **Merit, Worth.**

SUMMARY The gentle art of summary, or précis, is a major item in the repertoire of the evaluator who wishes his or her reports to be read and understood. The more senior the decision-maker, the shorter the summary has to be—if it is to be useful. No report that takes more than ten minutes to read or present is worth much to *most* senior decision-makers in *most* situations. If it strikes a chord, then time for asking questions or reading appendixes will be found. This is not a plea for good 'executive summaries'; the need for them goes without saying (but see **Layering**). This is a prescriptive view about the *whole report*. Nor is this a sign that TV has corrupted us into consumers of 'newsbytes'. Napoleon was in the same situation as a consumer of information, and evaluators who do good needs assessments on their clients when designing reports will start treating summaries as an art form. It is a high art, which few schools now teach, and few people can do well. Ask three people to reduce a 12,000 word report which they have just read to: (i) 1,000 words, (ii) 100 words, and (iii) 25 words. The differences in quality are likely to amaze you; but improvement is rapidly acquired with (evaluated) practice.

SUMMATIVE EVALUATION Summative evaluation of a program (or other evaluand) is conducted *after* completion of the program (for ongoing programs, that means after stabilization) and *for* the benefit of some *external* audience or decision-maker (for example, funding agency, oversight office, historian, or future possible users), though it may be *done* by either **internal** or **external** evaluators or a mixture. The decisions it services are most often decisions between these options: export (generalize), increase site support, continue site support, continue with conditions (probationary status), continue with modifications, discontinue. For reasons of credibility, summative evaluation is much more likely to involve external evaluators than is a formative evaluation. It should not be confused with o u tcome evaluation, which is simply an evaluation *focused on* outcomes rather than on process—which could be either formative or summative. (This confusion occurs in the introduction to the ERS *Evaluation Standards*, 1980 Field Edition). It should also not be confused with global (holistic) evaluation—summative evaluation may be global *or* analytical. Where a summative evaluation is done of a program that has stabilized but is still running, the aim is the same: to report *on* it, not to report *to* it. Cf. **formative evaluation**.

SUNSET LEGISLATION Legal commitment to automatic close-out of a program after a fixed period unless it is specifically refunded. An intelligent recognition of the importance of shifting the burden of proof, and thus related to **zero-based budgeting**.

SUPERCOGNITIVE The domain of performance on cognitive or information/communication skills that is at the upper limit of normal

levels—for example, speed reading, speed reasoning, lightning calculating, almost-eidetic memory, speed speak or fastalk, trilinguality,
stenotyping, shorthand. Cf. **Hypercognitive.**

SUPPORT STAFF Any program staff other than the **providers** are
said to be support staff or supporting the program or to be 'part of the
infrastructure' of the program. Other supporters include those know-
ingly providing financial or other, 'in kind' support.

SURVEY METHODS (in evaluation) See **Evaluation-specific
methodology.**

SYMBOLIC EVALUATION Another term for **Ritualistic evaluation.**

SYMBOLS (for evaluative predicates and relations) The almost universal symbols for **grades** are the letters A–F, idiosyncratic in that the
mnemonic F for Fail usually replaces the sequential E; in some regions, the E is used instead. (A recent new area of use is in symboliz-
ing quality of credit risk in the multitier interest rate system for automobile loans.) They are often supplemented by a + or a –, sometimes
with exclusions: for example, A+ is sometimes not allowed as an academic grade (because it involves a numerical equivalent of more than
4 points on what is supposed to be a scale with 4 points as the maximum). More rarely there is some use of a supplementary ++, etc., or a
'straddle grade' like AB to indicate borderline performance (see
Banding). The conversion of these qualitative grades to numerical
equivalents usually does violence to them, distorting their intended
significance; for example, most instructors do not intend to suggest
that width of the B band is the same as that of the D band, the latter
normally being used to indicate a straddle between C and F. (Even
more distortion is involved in 'grading on the curve'.) An alternative
set of symbols is suggested for the **Qualitative weight and sum** procedure, where the anchor points have a different meaning. See also
Rating scales.

It is useful to have a set of symbols for ranking, and it is here suggested that for this purpose the usual >, <, =, be embellished by the
addition of a dot in the jaws of the 'greater/less than' operators, and
between or ahead of the horizontal bars of the equals sign. Thus, "A ∙>
B", for example, means "A is better than B". The main evaluation operators— ranking, grading, scoring, and apportioning—can be symbolized by their intial letters. Thus, "G(essays) + S(MCI)" is a procedural rule for generating subevaluations on a set of final exams (MCI
stands for 'multiple-choice items').

SYMMETRY (of evaluative indicators) It is a common error to suppose (or unwittingly to arrange) that the converse or absence of an
indicator of merit is an indicator of demerit. This is illustrated by the
assumption that items in evaluative questionnaires can be rewritten

341

positively or negatively to suit the configural requirements of foiling stereotyped responses. But "Frequently lies" is a strong indicator of demerit, while "Does not frequently lie" is not even a weak indicator of (salient) merit. (Salient merit, that is, commendable behavior, is what one rewards, not "being better than the worst one could possibly be".) The preceding is an epistemological point about symmetry (related to the virtue/supererogation distinction in ethics). There are also methodological asymmetries; for example, it is often thought that asking students to fill in student rating forms that list a larger number of possible faults than virtues is a bias. At some primitive level of thought, that's appealing; but if you realize that there are an infinity of wrong answers to any simple math problem, and only one right answer, you may begin to rethink the assumption. For formative purposes, one tries to list all the matters about which legitimate complaints are made in the pilot, free-response questionnaire. Each of them is an opportunity to improve. If there are more of them than there are of laudatory epithets, nothing follows about bias. "Outstanding" or "Superb" covers the absence of many faults.

SYNTHESIS (of research studies) The integration of multiple research studies into an overall picture. This is a field that has recently received considerable attention. These "reviews of the literature" are not only evaluations in themselves, with—it turns out—some quite complex methodology and viable alternatives involved on the way to a bottom line; but they are also a key element in the evaluator's repertoire since they provide the basis for identifying, for example, critical competitors and possible side-effects. See **Meta-analysis**.

SYNTHESIS (in evaluation) 1. The process of combining a set of ratings or performances on several dimensions or components into an overall rating. Rules used for this are sometimes referred to as 'decision functions', 'composition models', or 'combinatorial algorithms'; one much-researched version of the approach is referred to as the 'statistical approach'). Quite commonly, it is done by judgment (the 'clinical approach'), often impressionistically and unreliably. Since **evaluation**, of its nature, must involve *some* combinatorial step—combining facts with standards of value—it is easy to see how the concept of 'value-judgment' came to be seen as the essential element in evaluation. However, that essential integration may have already occurred in getting to the subevaluations, and does not show that evaluations always require a final synthesis step. Nor does it show that the necessary judgments are essentially subjective in the sense of arbitrary or unreliable, let alone invalid. Counterexamples come from medical diagnosis, the diamond grading process, real estate assessment, timber cruising, in the courts, or at sheep dog trials.

Many terms are or can be used instead of "synthesis", including the following (ones preferred by a survey of graduate student are in italics): aggregating, amalgamating, blending, bonding, coalescing, *combination*, combining, compiling, composition, compounding, compressing, concatenating, conjoining, consolidating, focusing, fusing, incorporating, integrating, *integration*, interlacing, joining/junction, judging/judgment, merge/merging, pulling together, *reduction*, synthesing/*synthesis*, uniting/union. There are problems about any choice, but the number of options suggests the importance of the concept in our intellectual processes.

The combinatorial process is usually necessary and defensible but it is sometimes inappropriate—for example, when it requires a decision on relative weighting that may be impossible for the evaluator, or will cause unnecessary pain. On such occasions the appropriate procedure is just to give the ratings or performances on the separate dimensions and explain why no more is possible. In all other cases, doing only that is only doing a partial evaluation, referred to here as an **unconsummated** or **fragmentary** evaluation (e.g., a components-only evaluation). The failure to take the last hurdle is sometimes due to **valuephobia**, since it may avoid the necessity for an evaluative conclusion at all. More often, it is due to poor analysis of the function of evaluation; for example, it is often said that **formative** evaluation of teachers does not require an overall evaluation, only a profile report. This is seriously wrong and may lead to extremely misleading feedback to the teachers. One must tell them 'what it all adds up to', not just give them the bits and pieces. Otherwise they may read into the subevaluations what they want to see there ("nobody's perfect") and not realize that they are in serious trouble. Note that the synthesis process is frequently involved even in assembling data on subdimensions to obtain a global description on that dimension; and of course, it is always involved in obtaining dimensional or component subevaluations. Hence synthesis is not always avoided by avoiding the final use of it.

It is desirable, in evaluation reports, to give an explicit statement and justification of the synthesis procedure, and provide evidence that it was in fact the one used, since the effort to do this will often lead to the recognition of: (i) arbitrary assumptions; (ii) inconsistent applications of the supposed standards; or (iii) inconsistencies between rhetoric and practice. In the evaluation of faculty, for example, the de facto weighting of research vs. teaching is often nearer to 5:1 in institutions whose rhetoric claims parity, and it may vary widely between departments or between successive chairs in the same department. The synthesis of student course work into a letter grade is often cited as an example of indefensible practice; this belief led several colleges in the 1960s to submit 'evaluative essays' about each student applying to graduate school (e.g., St. John's and UC/Santa Cruz). Generally, this meant that the admissions committee at the college to which application was made had to do the conversion to grades; in short, it passed the buck for the synthesis to people who didn't know the student. Student grades are perfectly defensible summative evaluations, though certainly inadequate for formative feedback to the student.

"Synthesis by salience summary" illustrates another trap; a teacher is rated on 35 scales by students and the printout only shows cases of statistically significant departures of the ratings from the norms. Evaluation is done by looking at the number of cases of significant departures from the mean. This may seem plausible at first sight; but (i) the dimensions have not been independently validated (and are not independent); (ii) many of them are style characteristics that shouldn't be there at all; and (iii) it involves the confusion of **ranking** with **grading**.

The importance of synthesis is illustrated by a psychiatrist on the staff of the University of Minnesota who became legendary for requesting a grant so that a graduate student could "pull his research results together"; his "research results" being a complete set of taped recordings of five years of therapy covering several dozen subjects. Evaluators who are tempted to "turn the facts over to the decision-makers, and let *them* make the value-judgments" should remember that evaluations are interpretations that require *all* the professional skills in the repertoire; a scientist's role does not end with observation or, usually, measurement. (See **Summary.**)

Various procedures have been advocated for the combinatorial step. Numerical **weight and sum** synthesis is a linear approach and sometimes works acceptably well. Frequently we need to add minima to some of the dimensions—modified weight and sum. Rarely, as in the evaluation of backgammon board positions or evaluating patients on the MMPI, we need nonlinear synthesis rules. More often, we need to avoid the strong assumptions—for example, about utility distributions—on which weight and sum approaches are based, and use a **qualitative weight and sum** model. The social science effort in this area has centered around 'multiattribute utility analysis', though it is rarely applied within evaluation (it is not even mentioned in any of the leading texts). It involves some unrealistic assumptions and some logically unsound ones, but is suggestive in several ways. Some worked examples are provided in *Need Analysis* by McKillip, Sage, 1987.

344

In personnel evaluation, a vocabulary has been developed for the leading alternatives in synthesizing ratings on different tests or by different interviewers: see **Multiple-cutoff** (a.k.a. conjunctive model) and **Compensatory**. An useful overview is provided by Mehrens in his chapter "Combining Evaluation Data from Multiple Sources" in *The New Handbook of Teacher Evaluation*, Millman and Darling-Hammond, eds., (Sage, 1990). However, all but one of these approaches are limited special cases of the models referred to in the preceding paragraph; the exception is the "disjunctive model" which refers to cases where there are a number of ways to pass a test—for example, retakes or several interviewers— and passing any one of them is acceptable.

Synthesis is perhaps the key cognitive skill in evaluation: it covers everything invoked by the phrase "balanced judgment" as well as apples and oranges difficulties. Its cousins appear in the core of all intellectual activity; in science, not only in theorizing and identifying the presence of a theoretical construct from the data but in research synthesis. In evaluation, the wish to avoid it manifests itself in **laissez-faire** evaluation's extreme forms of the **naturalistic approach**. Balking at the final synthesis is often (not always) due to balking at the value-judgment itself and a symptom of **valuephobia**.

2. Synthesis may also refer to the process of reconciling multiple independent evaluations of the same evaluand. In this sense, it is a much abused and little studied process of great importance. For example, if drafts of the independent evaluations have to be submitted to a committee chair or client prior to the group synthesis session, the final results are very different from those where this requirement is not imposed (because of the increased need to fight for an already "public" conclusion in which your ego is invested). See **Parallel panels, Convergence group, Meta-analysis**.

3. Synthesis is sometimes involved in defining a criterion variable, where there are a number of criteria to be combined. Again, the process has been not been subject to a great deal of serious analysis, given its importance. See **Qualitative weight and sum, Logic of evaluation**.

SYSTEMS ANALYSIS The term is generally used interchangeably with "systems approach" and "system theory". This approach places the product or program being evaluated into the context of some total system. Systems analysis includes an investigation of how the components of the program/product being evaluated interact and how the environment (system) in which the program/product exists affects it. The "total system" is not clearly defined, varying from a particular institution to the universe at large, hence the approach tends to be more an orientation than an exact formula, and the results of its use range

345

from the abysmally trivial to considerable insights.

T

TA Technology Assessment. An evaluation, particularly with respect to probable impact, of (usually new) technologies. Discussed in more detail under **Technology assessment** below.

TARGET POPULATION The intended recipients or consumers. Cf. **Impacted population.**

TAXONOMIES Classifications—for example, Bloom's taxonomies of educational objectives. A huge literature has grown up around these taxonomies, which are somewhat simplistic in their assumptions and excessively complex in their ramifications, but provide a useful start for many evaluation designs. The unit in a taxonomy—a single category—is known as a taxon.

TEACHER EVALUATION Faculty in a school or college are not always teachers (sometimes they are researchers and sometimes athletic directors), and not all those who teach are on the faculty (for example, some administrators and all counselors and nurses). Those labeled "teachers" are normally staff who teach but usually have other duties. "Teacher evaluation" thus requires more than merely evaluating their teaching and a great deal more than evaluating what they do in a classroom. As a first step, it requires identifying their other duties, setting minimum levels of acceptable performance on them, and weighting them relative to teaching. The evaluation of teaching itself requires evidence about: (i) the quality of what is taught (its correctness, currency, and comprehensiveness); (ii) the amount that is learned; and (iii) the professionality and ethicality of the teaching process. The ethics refers to, for example, justice in grading, and the avoidance of teaching to the test, racism, favoritism, and cruelty in contacts with students and colleagues. Professionality refers to the possession and use of appropriate skills and attitudes in, for example, maintaining discipline, the construction of test items, helping beginning teachers, and improving one's own skills—even one's spelling skills, since one has to write on a chalkboard and report card. (More details in **Duty-based teacher evaluation.**)

There are two mild surprises in this. First, professionality does not include most of what goes into "methods" courses, because little of it has been validated. (The time would have been better spent trying to increase the teachers' competence in the subject matter, or in testing or instructional materials design). Second, professionality not only includes the obligation to undertake workshops or courses (or special reading programs) on new materials, developments in the subject areas, and approaches to teaching, but the obligation to steady self-evaluation, for example, via using student questionnaires or gain scores. Whenever possible, consideration in the evaluation of teachers should be given to the amount of learning—and enthusiasm for learning and inquiry—that they impart to *comparable* classes, using *identical* tests, which have been *scrupulously administered, blind-graded* and *just-created* (that is, made up by random sampling from a large item pool with external validation). They should never be evaluated on the performance of their students when entry and support levels and **teaching to the test** are not controlled. Ref. *The New Handbook of Faculty Evaluation*, edited by Jay Millman and Linda Darling-Hammond (Sage, 1990). See also **Synthesis**.

It is a sign of the state of the schools—and of educational personnel evaluation—that teachers are normally evaluated by someone making a few visits to their classroom. Such an approach is completely invalid, for at least half a dozen independently fatal reasons. (i) Since a teacher teaches around a thousand class sessions in a year, and since the way things go in the class often varies considerably across the year—and sometimes from day to day—a sample size of less than .5 percent is completely inadequate. (ii) Since any visitor affects the behavior of the teacher and the students to an unknown extent, the sample is not only too small, it is nonrandom. (In districts where the visit has to be preannounced, it is even more atypical.) (iii) Since in most cases the principal or another administrator to whom the teacher is known in other contexts does all or part of the evaluation, matters of personal liking or disliking are sure to come in; the use of a team is not a reliable way to avoid this. (iv) Since administrators came up through the ranks of teachers, they are likely to have strong preferences for the style of teaching that worked for them; but that is simply 'style bias', since there are many very different styles that work well. The use of checklists that allow reference only to 'research-based' styles does not improve the situation (see **Research-based teacher evaluation**). (v) Since administrators know little about the subject matter dealt with by many secondary teachers, they are unable to pass judgment on an essential element in teaching—the quality of the content. (vi) Whatever happens in the classroom—grotesque incompetence apart—the merit of a teacher depends heavily on the way they handle the rest of their duties, to which no attention is usually paid. (vii) Any process that gives inconsistent results as between judges cannot give valid results,

348

and the evidence available on intervisitor consistency strongly suggests that it is very low on all variables not excluded by the considerations already mentioned (when **shared bias** is excluded).

There are some valid criteria that can be observed in a classroom visit. They include some that, if consistently present, would be enough to justify dismissal (gross abuse of students, massive ignorance of subject matter, complete inability to maintain order). But they do not include enough to give a rating of competent or better, because so much of a teacher's duties cannot be seen in the classroom and because the sample is inadequate and of unknown representativeness. Even to see, and correctly weight, the positive and negative indicators that are visible requires the most rigorous training—not currently available anywhere—because there are so many irrelevant phenomena present to contaminate the observations.

The enforced methodology of structured classroom observation systems introduces other gross errors. For example, in one of the most sophisticated systems running today, a teacher is failed if s/he does not ask or ask for questions in the portion of a single class that is observed, whether or not doing so is appropriate at that particular point in the course. At best, this is a serious case of distortion of teaching to fit the evaluation; at worst, it represents completely inappropriate worship of style in place of success.

Teachers receive negligible preparation on a number of matters that are close to the heart of their duties, such as how to construct valid tests, how to grade tests, how teachers should and should not be evaluated, how to remediate weaknesses and develop systematically, how to think critically and teach critical thinking, how to proofread, and so on. It follows that the evaluation of teachers often has strong implications for the training of teachers. We have not yet begun systematic development of this connection.

There are about dozen usefully distinguishable models of teacher evaluation in current use or with impressive backing, and there are many places (e.g., Holland) which do none at all. The current swing of the pendulum in teacher evaluation, as in student evaluation, is toward using procedures that are: more global (by contrast with 'checklist approaches'—here meaning checklists of observable classroom micro-behaviors); involve more high-inference conclusions by observers (typically experienced teachers); focus on teachers' thinking as much as on their observable behavior; and are more closely tied to development than to 'judgment' (here used to mean mere rating of merit). There are some good reasons for trying to move in these directions, but of course, the problem is to retain reasonable standards of validity, reliability, fairness, and cost-feasibility. None of the attempts to date show the slightest sign of succeeding in this, in fact, rather the reverse. For example, some currently favored evaluation models show strong signs of over-intellectualizing the process—e.g., by stressing reflective teaching—which may penalize 'natural teachers' (these models are, on the other hand, quite good for preservice training). Other show signs of being more subject to bias than the checklist approaches—for example, the assessment center approach, where everything hinges on the view of 'expert judges'. For another approach, see **Duties-based teacher evaluation**. See also **Personnel evaluation, Style research, Research-based teacher evaluation.**

TEACHING TO THE TEST 1. The original sense of the phrase refers to the practice of teaching just or mostly those skills or facts that will be tested. This is usually based on prior knowledge of, or inference as to, the test content. In the exceptional case where the test is fully comprehensive this is no crime—for example, if it tests knowledge of the "times tables" by calling for all of them. But most tests only sample a domain of behavior and are used to generalize from performance on that sample to overall performance in the domain in normal circumstances, and that generalization will be invalid when teaching to the test has occurred—so teaching to the test is fraudulent.

2. In an extended sense, the term also covers: (i) teaching test-taking skills; (ii) providing special motivation or incentives for test performance; (iii) using materials specially developed to increase test performance without (as far as we know) increasing mastery of the domain of skills or knowledge the test is designed to test (this includes adjusting the curriculum to match the particular test). The first two of these activities are not necessarily fraudulent but are likely to lead to mistaken inferences by parents and community about the significance of the results; see **Pollution.**

A serious weakness of teacher-constructed tests is that they create the same situation ex post facto: see **Testing to the teaching.**

TECHNICISM The valuing of pragmatically meaningless technical specifications. An error that occurs in the process of, or subsequent to, replacing subjective judgments by measurements, usually done in the interest of increasing objectivity. It is the problem of treating the measurements as significant in themselves in a range of the variable which has no direct value to the user. Example: in the high-fidelity audio field, a widely adopted ideal for equipment is for it to have a flat response from 20Hz to 20,000Hz. ("Flat" meaning plus or minus one to three decibels, depending on how pure the purist is.) Now, essentially all of the people who can afford the very expensive equipment required to meet this standard are of mature years, and it's almost certain that their hearing tops out below 10,000Hz. Hence a good deal of what they're valuing is meaningless to them—and very expensive. Other examples include valuing a top speed over 160 mph in a car and camera-lens resolution in binocular optics.

In a straightforward sense this shows bad judgment or, more exactly, **inappropriate values**, and it's smart to avoid getting into this trap. However, there is another way of looking at it, by subsuming it under the heading of connoisseur's criteria. From this point of view, a technophile can't be said to be *wrong* to value an artefact for one of its powers—for example, wristwatch accuracy within a millisecond a month—even if he or she will never benefit from it). The best compromise is to warn people well in advance of this risk, avoid misleading them in the evaluations, and offer attractive alternatives (since people often fall back into technicism). The problem is that the experts who do the evaluations frequently succumb to technicism themselves and become evangelists for it. See **Fallacy of irrelevant expertise**. Of course, some technicist values can be faulted, at least in principle, on ethical grounds. For example, valuing the blown Corvette ZR-1 because it will do more than 200 mph will surely be said by some to exhibit socially undesirable values. In any case, developing extremely expensive tastes is, for most of us, a self-frustrating solution to the problem of defining the good life. See **Connoisseurship model**.

TECHNOLOGY Technology has four aspects of particular relevance to evaluation. (i) At its best, evaluation in the R&D process used in technology attains a very high standard from which all evaluators can learn; but it is also interesting that even leading companies—for example, from the automobile and computer industries—often exemplify worst practice. The first of these phenomena comes from **product evaluation**, but bears on all evaluation; the second bears crucially on **utilization**. (ii) Good examples of R&D in the history of technology illustrate what is missing from many efforts at major social change, where the idea is still pervasive that the great problems in the health care, criminal justice, or education sectors can be fixed by someone with a bright idea and an inspirational speaking style. Evaluators called in to evaluate such 'restructuring' efforts need to remember that social engineering is more rather than less complicated than product development, and should therefore demand more rather than less of the combination that characterizes technology breakthroughs: thorough background research, planning that covers all worst-case scenarios, *many* cycles of field-testing, *tough* evaluation, *multiple* solutions, direct attack on the problems of **scaling**, and serious cost-analysis. At the moment, our political machinery, with its short attention span, media focus, 'cult of personality approach', is too close to controlling the social change process, and too far from the reality of what it takes to do it well. Changing that situation is an educational process to which evaluators have to contribute by hanging tough with the evaluations, instead of looking for future contracts by giving encouraging reports, the usual source of **general positive bias,** which undercuts efforts to learn from our mistakes.

(iii) The third reason for evaluators to look at technology is in order to do, speak to, and learn from, a new kind of evaluation there which has only become significant quite recently—a substantial extension of product evaluation. This is **technology assessment** (TA), outlined in the next entry. (iv) The fourth interesting feature of technology is its importance for understanding the role of metatheory in the development of a discipline, a matter of immediate concern for evaluation. Technology is a not-quite discipline, a melange of studies and crafts, a classic example of the disasters that befall a would-be discipline without a halfway sensible metatheory. The first sign of this is the extraordinary situation about the meaning of the term "technology" itself. As with the term "evaluation", the most bizarre suggestions abound, reflecting total confusion about the nature of the subject. While technologists in *specific* fields have sensible enough implicit notions, they have not expanded them into any logically acceptable *general* position. This metatheoretic vacuum has been largely filled by obscurantist metaphysics about the nature of technology, written by people with little understanding of—and strong feelings against—the enterprise. Since it is impossible to talk about TA—or about any of the other features of technology of interest to the evaluator—without a reasonably clear notion of the limits of the field, a sketch of a more realistic account is provided here.

"Technology" is a double-aspect term—just like "research", "science", "methodology", or "evaluation"—in that it refers to a process and also to the product of that process. In the case of technology, the product is the set of human artefacts (the inanimate objects we create) and the process is whatever it takes to make them. What it takes to *use* them is not technology but technique (a.k.a. skill or art). Technology usually is the technology of a particular culture at a particular time in history (as in "Mayan technology") but sometimes it refers to a particular family of artefacts (as in "magneto-optical storage technology today").

The extraordinary situation about the definition of technology is that: (i) the rather obvious definition just given—reflecting the implicit use of most technologists, archaeologists, and anthropologists—cannot be matched in any reference work; (ii) one of the multivolume encyclopedias of technology provides no definition at all although its selection of articles reveals an implicit and absurdly narrow

352

definition; (iii) several other encyclopedias, histories, and dictionaries of technology use definitions of the generic term that are clearly incorrect (e.g., they omit low technology and/or recreational and/or art technology); and (iv) the definitions that are provided are all different from this one, and *also* different from each other. Common errors are to identify technology with: heavy industry technology; with the use of machines; with all practical problem-solving techniques; with applied science; with all of a society's survival techniques; or to include the techniques for the *use* of artefacts in technology, instead of just the techniques for the *production* of those artefacts.

This confusion is a sign of a field without a plausible metatheory. Given the size of the enterprise, some explanation of its absence is required and it must surely be due to an unholy alliance of two complementary metatheories, both of them implicit and simplistic. One is shared by many technologists, who see their domain as the domain of the practical, and hence opposed to the theoretical or philosophical. Hence, the very idea of something like a philosophy of technology is seen as alien in spirit to technology itself. (While one sometimes finds a similar attitude in scientists' view of philosophy of science, it is less widespread there, since both see themselves as contributors to the domain of abstract thought.) One might as well argue that members of the orchestra should foreswear the study of musicology. The other half of the alliance is the implicit metatheory of scientists who often perceive and represent technology as largely the same as the manual arts; in fact, technology goes as far beyond the manual arts as science goes beyond the skills of lab technicians.

For reasons set out in the introduction to this volume, the lack of a metatheory is always expensive and here the bill starts with loss of tangible support and status. Science has stolen much of the funding and prestige that belong to technology, mainly because scientists are more articulate about their own metatheory, which, not surprisingly, rates science as the master and technology as the slave. That view is in fact less plausible than its opposite. However, although technology is the older and more important of the two, its relationship to science is better seen as that of an older sibling. Another cost of the metatheory-poverty of technology, as with evaluation, is retardation in the development of its specific applications, for example computer science and engineering. Both have been left without a serious account of themselves, apart from a limited philosophical interest in the issue of computer simulation of human behavior.

Modern explicit metatheories for technology started with the Marxian view of craft as the foundation on which science was built, a

353

view which has more to recommend it than its opposite, but not enough to survive detailed historical analysis. The two powerful camps today come from two other sources, although each has flaws of comparable seriousness. The first source was a group of Continental metaphysicians like Heidegger and Habermas whose writings are notably obscure and seem only vaguely related to technology as the practitioner understands it; but the clouds are occasionally rent by a stroke of lightning, illuminating one or another interesting feature. The second source was scientists who saw technology as an intellectually low-status spinoff from science (philosophers have largely shared this disdain).

The quality of the European metaphysics is hard to determine precisely, partly because the term "technology" in English does not have an appropriate translation in most other languages. Combined with the confusion about the definition of the term in English, the result has been translations which wrongly suggest that these writers were simply talking about what English-speakers (other than philosophers) mean by technology. However, reasonably bilingual authors have developed the original themes and they have become the dominant view in philosophy of technology. These approaches tend to be short of *serious* discussions of the methodology of technology (see R&D), technology assessment, the difficult questions about the boundaries of technology (especially the question of the status of natural and artificial languages), and the virtues of technology.

Given that much of the general philosophical metatheory is critical of technology it is not surprising that the more friendly metatheory coming from science—the view of technology as applied science—has received so much support, even from technologists. But the usual version of this is paternalistic, logically and historically unsound, and mainly an excuse for exploitation of the public recognition of the importance of technology. The highly articulate Big Science establishment naturally favors this 'science-driven' metatheory because it implies that the way to improve technology is to put money into science. Given that there is almost no overlap of goals or essential skills between science and technology, the science-driven metatheory is simply a fantasy reminiscent of the popular defense of Latin in the curriculum of the 1930s on the grounds that it improved critical thinking. It may be worse: it encourages the false view that students need to succeed in the 'math/science track' to enter for a serious career in technology. Bright students who find advanced math and science boringly abstract then suppose they cannot become serious technologists, a major loss of talent for technology.

A reasonable metatheory for technology should accommodate at

354

least the following considerations: (i) technology aims to invent and improve material products, whereas science attempts to describe, explain and predict natural and social phenomena; (ii) the methodology of technology is R&D, while that of science is perhaps something like the hypothetico-deductive method, but certainly not R&D; (iii) serious technology is about a million years old, while science has been around less than half of one percent of that time; (iv) many and perhaps most great technologists in recorded history have had little or no scientific expertise; (v) even in the highest of high-tech areas today, such as the computer field, many and perhaps most of the major contributions come from people without any scientific background; (vi) it's probably still more usual for technology to spin off branches of science than the reverse—it is certainly common; (vii) almost all sciences in history and today are completely dependent on the technology of instruments, while the reverse is not the case; and (viii) civilization is possible without science but it is not possible without technology. Note the significance of these points for science curriculum evaluation, and for any overall curriculum evaluation, given that the latter usually omits any treatment of technology except by courtesy of the science teacher—having the fox mind the chickens—or as manual arts—treating the chickens as fertilizer-producers.

Two authors who transcend the simplistic metatheories are Kelvin Willoughby, whose *Technology Choice* (Westview, 1990) makes a serious contribution to the study of technology, especially 'appropriate technology'; and Don Ihde who wrote strongly on what he called the "The Historical-Ontological Priority of Technology over Science", in *Philosophy and Technology*, Durban and Rapp, eds. (Reidel, 1983), and has recently put forward some other important views in *Instrumental Realism* (Indiana, 1991). The key journal will probably be the new *Technology Studies*.

TECHNOLOGY ASSESSMENT (TA) A burgeoning field of evaluation that aims to assess the total impact of a technology—typically a new technology. Often done in the public interest, but equally important as a guide to commercial development or part of history. The first two applications involve a hybrid between futurism and systems analysis and, not surprisingly, they are done at every level from extremely superficial to brilliant. OTA, the U.S. Congress' Office of Technology Assessment, usually scores well above the middle of the possible range. The average quality level of TA even in the technical press is in need of substantial improvement: the widespread prediction that cassette recorders would displace books was clearly fallacious even at the time, if one did any systematic analysis. One good feature of the futurism part of TA, methodologically speaking, might seem to be that in the long run we'll know who was right; but so much of the analysis is expressed in terms of *potential* that refutation is hard. For example, one is now tempted to predict that handheld battery-run OCR scanners with voice input/output and a built-in printer will virtually eliminate the necessity for instruction in reading skills by the year 2000. In the example just given, the words "eliminate the necessity" ensure that the claim will not be falsified by the nonoccurrence of the phenomenon described. The attached checklist is somewhat more comprehensive than anything in the literature at the moment; many of the checkpoints are enlarged on elsewhere in this book, for example, in the KEC.

1. NAME, AIM, AND NATURE OF THE TECHNOLOGY Corresponds to the Description checkpoint in the KEC; it is *much* harder to get or construct an unbiased account than beginners can believe.

2. PERFORMANCE TESTING

• Testing includes testing the ergonomics (human interface) for ease of learning/use, safety, and so on—and any other features of design that are not tested under other headings. Thus, the aesthetics of the design should be market tested where there are signs of strongly favorable/unfavorable reactions since this will affect use and sales.

• Testing includes testing all 'features and flaws', whether or not they relate to the intended use of the product; babies don't read instruction manuals or warning signs. And it includes finding nonapparent features and flaws from studies of use.

3. IMPACTED POPULATION Who will be (or was) affected, directly or indirectly?

4. COST ANALYSIS For each subgroup of the impacted population. Must include nonmoney as well as money costs, for example, health costs, quality of life and worklife costs (e.g., noise level), legal and ethical costs, that is, all negative results of getting *and sustaining* the technology. TA is notable for its concern with environmental impact, for example, effects on scarce resources, pollution, effects of the infrastructure (e.g., the roads not the mining operation itself), loss of jobs especially for particular groups (minorities, women, mothers, and so on), effects on private sector, on centralization of power and habitation—all of this in the immediate and long run, including probable spinoffs (note the **futurism** component).

5. BENEFIT ANALYSIS The other side of the costs coin. Note societal payoffs like creation of jobs (for starting as well as from the results of the technology), contributions to knowledge or to the progress of technology, empowerment, reduction of excessive urbanization,

356

and ethical benefits such as improvements in human rights; again, immediate and long run, and spinoffs .

6. COMPARISONS What are the alternatives? How do they score? This is the time to remember the lessons of appropriate technology. Heliographs are often better than telegraphs, but they get forgotten in the march of progress, simplistically conceived.

7. MARKET IMPACT Here one needs to distinguish several types of market: the 'natural market' (as with the apocryphal better mousetrap—the market finds the product) vs. the artificial market (cosmetics) vs. the assisted market (information without the hard sell, for example, family planning, but possibly with some effort to link populations for whom there is no net payoff separately, but which would benefit collectively, for example, videodisk in schools). Again, look for short and long term results from the technology and *from probable spinoffs.*

8. OVERALL EVALUATION Combines the above and relates to relevant issues, usually whether to support with investment of scarce resources, facilitation, and so on, or whether to move for a ban or tax. Usually requires more of a cost-benefit than a straight cost-effectiveness analysis. (A concise example, referring only to leading elements, occurs in the comments on the book-disk in the preface to this book.)

9. RECOMMENDATIONS If local and political knowledge is good enough; not always possible, even when a comprehensive TA is done, because, for example, one may not be able to tell what the capital market's response will be to a new offering.

NOTE: The scope of TA is obviously affected by the definition of "technology" used, and the term is notorious for absurd definitions or, as in the case of one multivolume encyclopedia of technology, the absence of definition.

TERROR An effect frequently induced by goal-free evaluation (sometimes by the *thought* of it) in most of the cast of evaluation actors—evaluators, program managers, evaluees. The "terror test" is the use of this awful threat to weed out the incompetent. Since everyone uses goal-free evaluation whenever they buy anything for themselves, it is not a good sign of their concern for consumers that they think it inappropriate for program evaluation.

TEST ANXIETY A species of **evaluation anxiety.** Tests can lose *or gain* validity when the subjects are more anxious than they would be in the criterion situation, or when the tests cover a domain poorly matched to the test's alleged domain; but they are better than most observers, including the classroom teacher, in many cases. The problem is not that the teacher doesn't know more about the student; it's simply that the reports from different teachers do not agree well and

357

are usually more ambiguous to many audiences than test results. See Teaching to the test, Testing to the teaching.

TEST BIAS See Item bias.

TESTING Testing may be just measurement, but in many cases such as education or the job market it is simply the name for any specific and explicit effort at performance or attitude evaluation, usually of students or employees (prospective or actual). The main contrasts are with ongoing observation (supervision), and with practicing or regular work. Testing does not have to be done in any particular way; structured observation of task performance as in a swimming test can be as well done and as valid as any paper-and-pencil test. Testing is the most common procedure for determining the success of students and the effect of programs, service delivery personnel (e.g., teachers), process (e.g., curricula), environments, or the usual mix of all four. Testing became quite sophisticated long before a serious discipline of evaluation emerged—because it was seen as in the legitimate scientific tradition—but this precociousness entailed insensitivity about many fundamental issues (such as validity, bias, grading on the curve, and objectivity) and about the use of tests in, for example, personnel evaluation, even about the implicit evaluative component.

It is common for teachers to complain about testing, especially external testing, as an intrusion into or a parasite on teaching, a kind of bureaucratically imposed burden. On the contrary, valid testing *including external testing* is an integral part of any serious approach to teaching, since it represents: (i) the only way for teachers to find out whether their teaching is successful, and for which students in what respects it needs improvement; (ii) the only way for students, parents, and counselors to find out how well the student is managing in a given area of the curriculum; (iii) the only way for the school administration to find out whether it is running a successful school; (iv) one of the best ways for future employers or educational institutions to find out which applicants have mastered which needed subjects; (v) one of the best ways to show students exactly what the goals of the course are; (vi) a good way to get students involved in serious discussion of topics (via discussion of their efforts in a pretest or midterm); and (vii) one way for prospective parents to check on the success of a teacher.

An antitesting attitude in a teacher is about as sensible as an antitesting attitude in someone hired to write a computer program. Without testing, not only are we acting as if we had the right to be unaccountable, but we are building our self-esteem on sand. To accept that basis for self-esteem shows it to be worthless.

Since resentment is most often incurred by external tests in education, it is worth remembering that they originated as a device to avoid racism (Disraeli brought them in because widespread anti-Semitism in the English universities and public schools was excluding many of the best students) and they continue to serve that purpose well. They also avoid other serious biases of teacher-made tests (e.g., **teaching to the test**).

TESTING TO THE TEACHING The error of designing tests to measure just what was actually taught instead of testing learning in the domain about which conclusions will be or need to be drawn; the most common error of teacher-made tests. Tests of a reading program that only use words actually covered in class will give a false (overoptimistic) picture of general reading skills. Valid tests draw samples from the whole domain that was supposed to be covered and about which conclusions will be drawn, whether it is medieval philosophy (as described in the course catalog) or ninth-grade algebra as described in the state curriculum. It is almost impossible for the teacher of a course to construct tests that avoid this source of invalidity, because they are too concerned with constructing tests that will be fair to the students (and, perhaps, that will make themselves look good). So they only include material that they covered. But tests have other functions, typically, and one of them is to determine the extent to which defined domains have been mastered. Sometimes that is of paramount importance (as with basic skills and where a course is one in a series of prerequisites) and sometimes it is of very little importance, for example, in a Selected Problems course. In such cases, the principal criterion of validity is matching the de facto course coverage. As with "**teaching to the test**", testing to the teaching will not be improper in these cases where the test covers the whole domain.

Testing to the teaching is usually defended in terms of a metatheory proposition that seems unchallengeable: "It wouldn't be fair to test the students on material haven't covered." The mistake is to think that fairness overrides all other functions of testing. The fairness part can be covered in externally-set tests by suggesting that students indicate what questions were not covered in the course. See **Homeopathic fallacy**.

Is the argument here based on the view that goal-based evaluation is sometimes the best way? No; it's based on the view that contracts are an obligation and that the academic needs of students are often not best defined by instructors of particular courses.

TEST WISE Said of a subject who has acquired substantial skills in test-taking—for example, learning to say "False" on all items that say "always" or "never", or—to give a more sophisticated example— learning not to guess on items one hasn't time to think out if a "correction for guessing" is being used, but to do so if it is not.

THEORY, THEORIES General accounts of a field of phenomena, generating at least explanations and sometimes also predictions and generalizations; often but not necessarily involving theoretical entities that are not directly observable. A luxury for the evaluator, since they are not even essential for **explanations**, and explanations are not essential for 99% of all evaluations. It is a gross though frequent blunder to suppose that "one needs a theory of learning in order to evaluate teaching". One does not need to know anything at all about electronics to evaluate electronic typewriters, even formatively, and having such knowledge often *adversely* affects a summative evaluation.

The most interesting thing about theories for the evaluator is the evaluation of theories. There is not even the semblance of an algorithm for this most crucial of all scientific activities. We can identify criteria—as long as we are avoid the mistake of thinking that criteria are necessary conditions or that they have to be operationally defined. Leading criteria include explanatory power, predictive power and accuracy, economy of assumptions, fertility of implications, cross-field support (e.g., by analogy), and simplicity of claims. See also **Checklist, Conceptual scheme, Evaluation theories,** and **Program theories.**

THERAPEUTIC ROLE OR MODEL (of evaluation or of the evaluator) The very nature of the evaluator's situation creates pressures that sometimes molds it into a therapist-patient or group therapy role—or something analogous to it—and there are some evaluators who favor emphasis on this role. This is particularly but not only true with regard to external evaluation. First, there often is—in such a case—the client's feeling of having exhausted his or her own resources, needing help badly, perhaps desperately. Second, there is the attentive, inquiring, nonjudgmental (at first) role of the evaluator in developing background and a sense of the problem. Third, there is often growing anxiety about the perceived threat of the evaluation outcomes to self-esteem and anxiety about continued loss of functionality in some vital areas (see **evaluation anxiety**). Fourth, an initial aura of expertise and esoterica surrounds the external expert, supported by the technical jargon and mysterious rites prescribed by the good doctor in the continuing process of the evaluation. Since it's arguable that there is little more to psychotherapy than this package, an amalgam that is enough to generate at least the placebo effect, the analogy is clear—and should be disturbing. On the other hand, evaluators cannot allow themselves to be too concerned by this, to the point of removing oneself from contact with the client, since it is after all the case that one wants to help the client, and not by use of surgery or

360

pharmacology; in some sense, one *is* dispensing psychological remediation. Contact with evaluees is another matter; in **goal-free evaluation**, it does not occur, and this is one way to reduce anxiety, suitable to some evaluees but the reverse of what others prefer. Where it does occur, in much formative evaluation, for example, the therapist role again emerges, especially if there is any sign of **valuephobia**.

If the success of an evaluation is due to placebo or Hawthorne effects there is a risk of evanescence, and the evaluator who fades back into the hills after the farewell dinner with an ecstatic client should come back or sneak back for a look a year later if s/he wants to get a good idea of whether any recommendations were: (i) immediate solutions to the problems; (ii) adopted; (iii) supported; (iv) worked in the long run. Hence follow-up studies, sadly lacking in psychotherapy research (or innovative evaluation) and often devastating when done, are just as important in meta-evaluation—and a modest level of follow-up should be seen as part of the professional obligation of the evaluator.

TIME COSTS It is essential to distinguish between two types of time cost, and cover both when doing **cost analysis**. In commonsense terms they correspond roughly to what we call time and timeliness, but one sometimes encounters the distinction being made in terms of "absolute time vs. relative time" or "calendar time vs. clock time". For example, if the only time you can get your car tested for emissions compliance is next Monday, and this fits badly with your schedule, there is a time(liness) cost which is quite different from the cost of the time the actual test will take. A common example in evaluation is the difference between the time cost—to an administrator and her or his staff—of bringing in an evaluator, and the time(liness) cost of a tardy report.

TIME DISCOUNTING A term from fiscal evaluation that refers to the systematic process of discounting future benefits—for example, income—due to the fact that they *are* in the future and hence (regardless of the *risk*, an essentially independent source of value reduction for merely probable future benefits) *lose the earnings* that those monies would yield if in hand now, in the interval before they will in fact materialize. Time discounting can be done with reference to any past or future moment, but is usually done by calculating everything in terms of true present value.

TIME MANAGEMENT An aspect of management consulting with which the general practitioner evaluator should be familiar; it ranges from the trivial to the highly valuable. Psychologists from William James to B. F. Skinner are among those who have made valuable contributions to it and it *can* yield very substantial output gains at very small cost both for the evaluator and for clients or evaluees. Few of the later suggestions are as good as James' recommendation that one list today's tasks with the least enjoyable at the top and start there, perhaps since that gives you the largest reduction of guilt and increases the attraction of the remaining list. Ref: James McCay, *The Management of Time* (Prentice Hall, 1986) or Jeffrey Mayer, *If you haven't got the time to do it right, when will you find the time to do it over?* (Simon & Schuster, 1990), a book with a better title than content, but still of some value.

TIME SERIES See **Interrupted time series.**

TRAINING OF EVALUATORS General purpose evaluators, like philosophers, and unlike virtually every other kind of professional, should be regarded as having an obligation to know as much as possible about as much as possible. While it is feasible and indeed quite common for evaluators to specialize either in particular methodologies or in particular subject matter areas, the weaknesses due to this are usually rather obvious in their work. It is probably a consequence of the relative youth of evaluation as a discipline that the search for illuminating analogies from other disciplines is still so productive; but the other reason for versatility will always be with us, namely that it enables one to do better as an evaluator in a wider range of subject matter areas. Columbia University used to have a requirement that students could not be accepted for the doctorate in philosophy unless they had a Master's degree in another subject, and an analogous requirement might be desirable in evaluation. However, it is commonly asserted that the preliminary degree should involve heavy training in statistics, tests, and measurement. The problem with that requirement is that it leads to a strong bias in the eventual practice of the professional. While skill in the quantitative methodologies is highly desirable, it should not be set as a *preliminary* to evaluation training; the reverse sequence may be preferable, with some alternatives allowed. Training in logic and applied ethics would have an equal claim to primacy and would be more relevant to the increasingly common use of qualitative methods in evaluation.

A simple formula for becoming a good evaluator is to start by learning how to do everything that is required by the **Key evaluation checklist.** Although the formula is simple, the task is not. Nevertheless, it may be better to specify the core of evaluation training in this way rather than by listing supposed prerequisite competencies. People get to be good evaluators by many routes, and the field would probably benefit by increasing the number of routes rather than by limiting the access routes. Perhaps the only essential prerequisite is a commitment to evaluation that is strong enough to survive a thorough exposure to what it involves, and how hard it is—on the evaluator as well as the evaluee. See **Evaluation skills**.

There are evaluation specialties of particular importance and long tradition—for example, the evaluation of student work, which academic researchers and the great testing companies have brought to a high art without getting involved in much of the general field of evaluation. However, we are increasingly finding that study of the general theory of evaluation is paying off for these specialties. A good recent example is Messick's foundational work on **bias** and there is an increasing interest in expanding beyond the realm of multiple-choice exams for reasons which come in part from general evaluation theory. See **Multiple-rating item**.

TRAIT-TREATMENT INTERCONNECTION A less widely-used term for aptitude-treatment interaction, though it is actually a more accurate term.

TRANSACTIONAL EVALUATION (Rippey) Focuses on the process of program improvement, for example by encouraging anonymous feedback from those that a change would affect and then a group process to resolve differences. Though a potentially useful *implementation* methodology in many cases, transactional evaluation does not help much with many dimensions of systematic evaluation such as cost analysis or control of evaluator bias due to the intimate social interaction involved in the transactional approach. **Illuminative evaluation, naturalistic evaluation,** and **responsive evaluation** are fellow-travelers on the **qualitative evaluation** ship. See also **Summative evaluation**.

TRANSCOGNITIVE The domain consisting of **Supercognitive** and **Hypercognitive**.

TRANSDISCIPLINARY MODEL OF EVALUATION The conception of evaluation as a **transdiscipline** is developed in the introduction to this work, especially in the section on The Country of the Mind, but the transdisciplinary *model* or *view* of evaluation—perhaps as near as it is possible to come to a paradigm for evaluation—involves more than the transdisciplinary *element*. That describes one function of evaluation; its nature is more complex. In the first place, unlike other transdisciplines or at least to a much greater extent, it is extraordinarily multidisciplinary (see **Evaluation**). Secondly, and distinctly, it is multi*role*; that is, the evaluator typically has to perform in a number of very different ways, some of which are normally the province of another profession. The most common of these are the research role (which combines an investigative phase with an analytic one and perhaps a theorizing one), the instructional role, the therapeutic role, the public relations role, the support staff

363

role, the entrepreneurial role and the managerial role; but it is also common for the job to require playing the role of arbitrator, scapegoat, trouble-shooter, inventor, conscience, jury, judge, or attorney. Third, evaluation is a practical activity in a much stronger sense than, for example, applied mathematics. This fact shows up in, for example, the attempts to distinguish it from 'real' research. While that restriction is too severe, the service function *is* crucial—most evaluators have *clients* not just readers and there are many differences between these, not least the legal ones. The day may come when there are evaluators who restrict themselves to evaluation theory, but they would not then represent the whole of evaluation. Fourth, evaluation is omnipresent in the thinking and making processes. Nothing else is like that except logic and perhaps observation, and neither makes any sense as a model for evaluation—the one too abstract, the other too unitary. So evaluation has a nature, a flavor, a gestalt of its own. It is idiosyncratic and complex to the extent that it requires a special kind of paradigm—and perhaps the ubiquity and versatility of electricity provide as good a match as any.

TRANSDISCIPLINE Transdisciplines such as statistics, logic, or evaluation, are disciplines whose subject matter is the study and improvement of certain tools for other disciplines. That study generates some general methodology, epistemology, and ontology relating to these tools, much of it interwoven with one or more metatheories. Transdisciplines often have several semiautonomous fields of study connected with them (for example, biostatistics, formal logic). One contrast is with <u>interdisciplines</u>, which focus on an area where several disciplines overlap—medical ethics or ergonomics, for example. "<u>Multidisciplinary</u>", although often used as a synonym for "interdisciplinary" usually refers to activities that use the *methods* of several disciplines on a problem without as strong a suggestion that the subject matter constitutes an autonomous discipline located adjacent to their fiefdoms.

TREATMENT A term generalized from medical research to cover whatever it is that we're investigating; in particular whatever is being applied or supplied to, or done by, the experimental group that is intended to distinguish them from the comparison group(s). Using a particular brand of toothpaste or toothbrush or reading an advertisement or textbook or going to school are all examples of treatments. "Evaluand" covers these, but also products, plans, people, and so on.

TRIANGULATION Originally the procedure used by navigators and surveyors to locate ("fix") a point on a grid. In evaluation, or scientific research in general, it refers to the attempt to get a fix on a phenomenon or measurement (and, derivatively, an interpretation)

364

by approaching it via several—quite often, more than three—independent routes. For example, if you want to ascertain the extent of sex stereotyping in a company, you will interview at several levels, you will examine training manuals and interoffice memos, you will observe personnel interviews and files, you will analyze job/sex/-qualification matches, job descriptions, advertising, placement of ads, internal support systems, and so on. In short, you avoid dependence on the validity of any one source by the process of triangulation. Note that this is quite different from looking at multiple traits/-dimensions/qualities to synthesize them into an overall evaluative conclusion. Triangulation provides 'redundant' (really, confirmatory) measurement; it does not involve the conflation of ontologically different qualities into estimates of merit (worth, value, and so on.) Patton usefully distinguishes four types of triangulation: multiple methods, multiple sources within one method, multiple analysts, and multiple theories or perspectives.

TRICKLE (OR TRICKLE-DOWN) EFFECTS Indirect or delayed effects; "spillover" and "ripple effects" are rough synonyms; "cascade effects" usually refers to effects that are in a causal sequence starting with the original effect, rather than just delayed.

TROUBLE SHOOTING The process of identifying and, often, fixing defects, originally in machinery and consumer products, now used for programs and projects. Note that it (logically) can't begin until trouble has occurred and been noticed, and hence evaluation has occurred. Hence trouble shooting is a different process from **evaluation**; it begins with **diagnosis**, and includes **remediation**.

TRUE CONSUMER Someone who, directly or indirectly, intentionally or unintentionally, receives the services (etc.) provided by the evaluand. It is sometimes appropriate to segregate the service providers although they are also part of the **impacted population**. Usually a very different group from the target population (intended recipients).

TRUE EXPERIMENT A "true experiment" or "true experimental design" is one in which the subjects are matched in pairs or by groups as closely as possible and one from each pair, or one group, is *randomly assigned* to the control group while the other becomes part of the experimental group. The looser-and-larger-numbers version skips the matching step and just assigns subjects randomly to each group. This was the ideal design in the eyes of those working on the task of evaluating social interventions—notably Suchman and Campbell—in the late 1960s, and they only settled for **quasi-experimental designs** because they thought true experiments were rarely possible. It is a hard approach to implement on a large scale—because the real world tends to leak around the edges of the partition between the control and experimental group—and fell from grace for some years. More recently, however, many large-scale real-world true experiments have been done. Since every other approach is open to more serious sources of error, the fact that the alternatives are often easier to implement is not decisive. More effort should probably be spent on hybrid designs, in which small experiments where good control is possible are combined with looser designs for the total group. Boruch spells out one version of this possibility in an excellent overview in *Evaluation and Education: At Quarter Century*, (University of Chicago, 1991). Cf. Ex post facto design, Stratification, Quasi-experimental design.

TWO-TIER SYSTEM (Also called Multitier System, and Hierarchical system) A system of evaluation, sometimes used in proposal evaluation (but also with considerable potential in personnel evaluation) where an attempt is made to reduce the total social cost of the ordinary RFP system by requiring two rounds of competition. The first round, the only one RFP'd, involves stringent length restrictions on the proposal, which is supposed to indicate just the general approach and, for example, personnel available. These brief sketches are then reviewed by panels that can move through them very fast, and a small number of promising ones are identified. Grants are (sometimes) made to the authors of this "short list" of bidders to cover their costs in developing full proposals. The small number of full proposals is then reviewed by the same or a smaller group of reviewers or reviewing panels—a second tier of the review system. The mathematics of this varies from case to case, but it's worth looking at an example. Suppose we simply put out the usual kind of RFP for evaluation of the educational benefits from college science teaching laboratories (vs. computer simulations of labs vs. the same time spent on increased text treatment of experiments and lab techniques). We might get back 600 or 1,200 proposals, averaging perhaps 50 or 60 pages in length. For convenience, let's say they average 50 pages and we get 1,000 of them, not uncommon. That's 50,000 pages of proposals to be read, and 50,000 pages of proposals to be written. Even if reviewers can "read" 200 pages an hour, and even if we only have three people reading each proposal, we're still looking at 750 hours of proposal reading, which means about 100 person-days of reading, that is, a panel of 12 working for eight days, two panels of 12 working four days, or ten panels of 10 working for one day. One problem is expense, another is that you can't get good reviewers for four days; the multiple panels require more agency personnel to staff and then have to face the serious problem of interpanel differences.

Now if we go to a two-tier system, we can place an upper limit of, say, five pages on the first proposal and, although we may get a few more, that's a benefit since it means that we'll get some entries who don't have the time or resources required to submit massive proposals. So we might start with 1,200 five-pagers, which is 6,000 pages, and we've immediately got a reduction of 88 percent in the amount of reading that's done, with the result that a single panel can reasonably manage it. Then there will be perhaps ten or twenty best proposals coming in at the 50-page length, which can be handled quite quickly, and indeed much more carefully, by the same panel, reconvened for that purpose. Notice also that the reading speed for the first tier of proposals may also be higher since all the readers have to do is to be sure they're not missing a promising proposal, rather than to rank-order for final award. And validity should be higher. Notice the triple savings that are involved: the proposers can save about 90 percent of their costs (it may not be quite so high, because shorter proposals take more than a prorated-by-page amount of resources, but it's still substantial); the agency saves a great deal of cost in paying raters or panelists and heavy staff work costs; and the reliability of the process as well as the quality of available judges goes up significantly. Hence the small subsidy for the second-tier proposal is more than justified, both fiscally and in terms of encouraging entries from people who couldn't otherwise afford it, and better entries from those that can. Moreover, it's morally dubious to issue RFPs that will cost other people vast amounts of time and paper, nearly all of it certain to be wasted.

TYPE I/TYPE II ERRORS See False positive/negative, **Hypothesis testing.**

U

UNANTICIPATED OUTCOMES Often used as a synonym for **side-effects**, but only loosely equivalent, because: outcomes may be unanticipated by inexperienced planners but are readily predictable by experienced ones; effects that are anticipated but not goals are (sometimes) still side-effects—and sometimes not (for example, having to rent offices.)

UNCERTAINTY (as in 'evaluating uncertainty') See the entry on **Risk assessment.**

UNCONSUMMATED EVALUATION One species of incomplete, partial, or **fragmentary** evaluation. It is the kind which omits an overall conclusion even when there it would be useful and is feasible. Evaluations may describe or evaluate all components or dimensions (**analytical** evaluations) but lack any overall conclusion because the evaluator thinks this absence is proper practice ("I give the clients the facts, it's up to them to apply their values.") The error in this view is explained under **synthesis.** Such evaluations are simply incomplete, and in a respect that involves omitting what is often the most important single element in an evaluation. See **Weight and sum, Rorschach effect.**

UNOBTRUSIVE MEASUREMENT The opposite of **reactive** measurement. One that produces no reactive effect; a famous example is observing the relative amount of wear on the carpet in front of interactive displays in a science museum as a measure of relative amounts of use. Sometimes unethical, and sometimes ethically preferable to obtrusive evaluation. ("Obtrusive" is not necessarily "intrusive"; it may be obvious but not disruptive.)

USE (of evaluation findings) See **Utilization.**

USER See **Recipient.**

UTILITY (Econ.) The value of something to someone or to some institution. Sometimes 'measured' in the hypothetical units of "utils". The problem of "interpersonal comparisons of utility" has traditionally been the stumbling-block of (welfare) economics (it led van Graaf to abandon the field after writing one of the most important books in it and has led to the relative neglect of the field in recent years). It is the problem of how to weight the value of something that happens to, or is allocated to, one person against the value of the same thing happen-

368

pening to another person. If there's no way to do that, there's no way to draw conclusions about the best policy for a group of people. But of course there *is* a way to make interpersonal comparisons of utility; it is done on the basis of the prima facie equality of those people's rights. This is the fundamental principle of ethics, and the economists knew very well that there was such a principle. Unfortunately, their nerve failed at the next step, which was to see that ethics is a branch of welfare economics (or vice versa, or that it is the overlap territory between policy science and welfare economics). Instead, blinded by the **value-free doctrine** about the nature of science, they threw up their hands and resigned. See **Apportionment, Cost, Ethics.**

UTILIZATION (of evaluations) Carol Weiss has suggested "use" as a substitute for "utilization"; one might also use "impact". The term "implementation" is also used as if it were synonymous, but this assumes that the proper role of evaluation is to produce **recommendations**, since only recommendations are capable of being implemented. However, many evaluations cannot and should not incorporate recommendations. Measures of evaluation use are tricky; one problem is that much influence is considerably delayed, and it's very hard to get follow-up studies funded. Another problem is with "conceptual use" as in "The ideas caught on even if the recommendations were never implemented".

Utilization has been a matter of considerable concern to evaluators for twenty years. There have been extensive studies of the extent to which evaluations are implemented. The results of these studies are fairly consistent: the *immediate* effects are usually less than one would hope, but the *long-run* effects are considerable, although quite sporadic. There is a legitimate and an illegitimate reaction to this, and many of the discussions are well into the second category. The legitimate reaction is to make sure that considerations of utilization/implementation are planned into evaluations from the first moment, just as **evaluability** should be planned into programs. If the client isn't in a position to—and motivated to—utilize the results appropriately, an ethical question arises as to whether the evaluation should be done at all. Here are a dozen procedures for improving utilization. (i) Focus the evaluation on the decisions that have to be made and on variables that the client controls; (ii) soliciting and using suggestions from the whole impacted, audience, and stakeholder population about the design; (iii) getting feedback on findings before final report is submitted (if possible); (iv) using appropriate language, length, and formats in the report(s); (v) putting representatives of the clients and the evaluees on the evaluation team or advisory panel; (vi) demonstrating that **cost-free evaluation** is possible and will be done; (vii) designing within the resource limitations; (viii) identifying and focusing on positive benefits of the evaluation if implemented; (ix) establishing a **balance of power** to reduce threat; and, most important, (x) placing a heavy emphasis on explaining/teaching about the particular and general advantages of evaluation and about the value of the findings in this case. Finally, work toward starting earlier next time; don't assume the evaluation has to be done as late as it was done this time, try to get an evaluator into the formative process and into the **preformative** as well; that's how evaluability gets in place, and the payoffs get tailored to the project's needs for payoffs.

It is not a help that most evaluators lack background in such matters as **evaluation anxiety**, a major obstacle to utilization; of equal or greater importance to utilization is the **power** connection. Many evaluators lack the PR, presentational, or personal skills that contribute to utilization; and many lack the sense that they have duties toward clients and audiences *and stakeholders/consumers* that may extend beyond handing over a piece of paper. Unless these factors have been well covered, the failure to implement is at least largely the fault of the evaluator.

Suspect reactions to low utilization include (i) viewing failure to use as prima facie evidence of unsoundness. (This is comparable to treating the competence of principals as measurable by the test scores of their pupils.) In the opposite direction, indicators of misapprehension include: (ii) lengthy complaints about—or indeed worrying about—the irrationality or irresponsibility of bureaucrats and others in not utilizing evaluation results; (iii) getting professional associations to campaign to get managers to increase utilization; and (iv) doing the *usual kind* of interviews or surveys on their reasons for not utilizing. These reactions are illegitimate because they rest on the assumption that the results *should* have been utilized, or that the interviewees will be candid about why they should not be implemented. Given the well-established mediocre quality—including marginal relevance to policy (especially by the time of submission)—of many of the most expensive and well-backed evaluations, these assumptions suggest a serious lack of evaluative skills by the people who make them. Correct procedure for studies of evaluation use should begin with a review by a tough panel of good evaluators and clients, *who were not involved* in the particular efforts whose use is under study. Berk and Rossi put the general point of view expressed here very well in *Thinking About Program Evaluation* (Sage, 1990, p. 10), but the position is rare.

Overemphasis on utilization as a criterion of successful evaluation creates a strong conflict of interest situation for evaluators, because it

370

places pressure on them to adjust the findings to what decision-makers are willing to do rather than to what they should do.

None of these cautions are meant to suggest that no one should study or attempt to increase utilization. It is a phenomenon of the greatest interest and importance, especially in government. Much can be learnt from such studies about how to improve evaluations, as well as about how to facilitate their use when their content, format, and so on, deserve it. Notable and appropriate work, focusing on the organizational learning approach, has been done by the powerful Working Group on Policy and Program Evaluation, a task force of the International Institute on Administrative Sciences; the Group currently has 28 members from 13 countries. (See the interview with the Group's chair, Ray Rist, in the February, 1991, issue of *Evaluation Practice*.) See also Implementation of evaluations, Responsibility evaluation.

V

VALIDITY The phrase "validity of a test" (or an evaluation) really refers to the validity of a claim about its use in a certain context. The claim may be built into its title ('intelligence test') or into some fairly detailed remarks in the administration or interpretation instructions. This leads to the usual definition: "A test is valid if it measures what it purports to measure", a definition which entails that if you describe a test in different ways its validity will vary. It can be **reliable** (in the technical sense, that is, consistent in the results it yields) without being valid, and it can be valid without being **credible**. But if it's valid it has to be reliable—if the thermometer is valid, it must say 100°C *whenever* placed in pure boiling water at 1 atmosphere pressure, and hence must agree with itself, that is, be reliable. There are various subspecies of validity in the test jargon (especially **face, content, concurrent, construct,** and **predictive** validity), but they represent an inflation of methodological or circumstantial differences into supposed conceptual distinctions, except perhaps "content-valid". With tests used in **personnel evaluation,** content validity *under scrutiny by expert analysts* may be the key property of tests, since we have to abandon correlational research as the fundamental validation mechanism. In this sense, however, one should perhaps regard content validity as a form of construct validity.

Serious investigation of validity will identify the appropriate emphasis for the test being studied. One should not talk about "valid in *this* sense, but not in *that*", only about "*validity* (of the appropriate type)"; validity, it has become clear (and the 1985 *Standards* assert), is a unitary concept; and, we should add, they unify around construct validity. The key reference is Messick's essay in the Third Edition of *Educational Measurement,* ed. Robert Linn, ACE/Macmillan, 1989. Dispute continues about the extent to which validity should take social and ethical consequences of testing into account, with Messick following Cronbach in arguing that this is essential. It is certainly important to ensure that we avoid *errors* in test construction and use that have adverse social consequences.

Valid evaluations are ones that take into account all relevant factors, given the whole context of the evaluation (particularly including the client's needs) and weight them appropriately in the synthesis process. One may or may not build issues of credibility and the appropriateness of the reports into the validity of the evaluation; following Messick on test validity, one would do so. (See **Meta-evaluation**).

"Validity" as used in logic refers to the property of deductive arguments that are logically impeccable, whether or not rhetorically impressive. Logicians tend to think that talking about the 'validity' of tests is a corruption of the proper usage (theirs); study of the OED shows the reverse to be the case. See **External validity**, **Generalization**.

VALUE-ADDED An approach to institutional and program evaluation which tries to avoid the **Harvard fallacy** by focusing on the extent to which the input is improved by exposure to the program, by contrast with looking at the quality of the output. There are major technical difficulties on the measurement side, but one can get useful indications from available methodology.

VALUED PERFORMANCE A term used occasionally to refer to what is here called "contextually evaluative".

VALUE-FREE DOCTRINE The belief that science, and in particular the social sciences, should not—or cannot properly—draw evaluative conclusions 'within science', that is, from premises that are either scientifically verified or definitionally true. The view is part of the **metatheory** of science, especially the social sciences, and if one (correctly) treats that as part of science, the theory is self-refuting. ("It's wrong to talk of right and wrong", cf. "Everything I say is a lie"). The doctrine is of central importance to evaluation, since if true it would invalidate almost any claims to objective evaluation within, for example, the social sciences and education. The doctrine in its modern form originated in some cautionary remarks by Weber at one of the earliest professional meetings of the emerging discipline of sociology; he warned his colleagues against rushing in to do politically sensitive studies on social institutions. Within a few years, this sensible if somewhat spineless advice had been converted into a metatheoretic dogma of implacable opposition to evaluative research, a doctrine that formed part of what was loosely called **empiricism**.

It is essential to understand that this position has nothing to do with the straw-man version of the value-free doctrine—the claim that scientists' activities and their conclusions are never affected by their personal or cultural values. No one ever believed that. Sometimes those effects are legitimate (selecting a field of study because of one's personal interests, when no ethical barrier exists), sometimes illegitimate (Lysenko, racist theories). An alternative straw-man involves identifying the value-free doctrine with the view, or as involving the view, that science has no political consequences or significance. The straw-man versions are almost always the ones attacked by those claiming to show that science isn't really value-free, notably the antipositivist and antiempiricist groups in contemporary thought—for example the **constructivists** or the 'critical theory' group.

The value-free doctrine is often mistakenly assumed to be a *consequence* of empiricism—the view that science is, or should be, based on testable factual assertions. In fact the inference from empiricism to the value-free doctrine requires the further premise that inference from facts (and definitions) to values is impossible. Scientists—and empiricists—under the influence of simplistic empiricist philosophy of science thought this further premise was obviously true (it is often assumed that the value-free doctrine is part of the empiricist position). Moreover, Hume, Moore, and others had offered simple and plausible proofs of the impossibility of deriving facts from values. They were near enough to correct in supposing that one can't *deduce* values from facts, but they were wrong in supposing that this meant one can't *reliably infer* values from facts.

The error is analogous to the error of supposing that one cannot infer conclusions about theoretical constructs from observations. It is simply the error of thinking that deductive inference exhausts the repertoire of good reasoning. In fact, inductive inference, the main tool of science, is fully up to the inference from observations to theories, or we would never be able to argue rationally for theoretical claims. (Thus Popper's simplistic attack on induction is partly responsible for the continued support of the value-free doctrine.) The way we do this is usually via eliminative inference ("inference to the best explanation"), not by Popper's alternative of 'inspiration' or 'guessing'. A similarly flexible but teachable and evaluable process— probative inference—makes it possible to infer from factual and definitional premises to evaluative conclusions. The alternative is to think that *Consumer Reports* is committing a fallacy with every recommendation, and that democracy has no objective merits.

Apart from the logical error in the proof of the value-free claim, there is refutatory evidence. Any examination shows that science is suffused with highly responsible and well-justified scientific evaluations—of research designs, of estimates, of fit, of instruments, of explanations, of research quality, of theories, and so on. (Medicine and engineering never had much self-doubt about the appropriateness of evaluative conclusions; perhaps because their self-concept was stronger than that of the social sciences.) That the value-free position was maintained at all in the face of these phenomena requires an explanation in terms of **valuephobia**. See also **Logic of evaluation, Needs assessment.**

374

VALUE-IMBUED TERM See **Contextually evaluative.**

VALUE JUDGMENT Originally, a judgment as to the merit, worth, or value of something; extended to cover all claims about value (some of which are matters of calculation or observation). This extended use stereotypes value claims, and by so doing, reinforces the mistaken view that value claims are essentially subjective. The judgment of experts is often *provably* highly reliable, and more often *provably* much better than any alternative. And the practice of even observational sciences like much of astronomy and field biology involves very extensive use of judgment. Still, it is true that judgments are less reliable than the *simplest* observations under ideal conditions, and less reliable than *simple* calculations. Since evaluation typically involves multiattribute integration, it's not surprising that judgment is often involved—through the weighting and combining of the various attributes. But the idea that value-judgments must always be arbitrary/subjective/unscientific was only built into the concept of value-judgment as the doctrine of value-free science took hold. It may be best to abandon the term "value-judgment" in order to avoid the penumbra of relativism that is now attached to it. See also **Synthesis.**

VALUEPHOBIA Irrational fear of evaluation, often manifested in unreasonably strong dislike of—or opposition to—evaluation. Not to be confused with the perfectly normal condition of dislike or anxiety about being evaluated, nor with reasoned opposition to poor evaluation procedures. Valuephobia is usually rationalized by some oxymoronic myth about the impropriety of evaluation. These have an ancient lineage: "judge not that ye be not judged" is the Biblical precursor of the **value-free doctrine,** and just as inconsistent with the practice of those proposing it (since it entails adverse judgment of those who judge). The story of the Garden of Eden is also revealing: it is the fruit of the tree of *knowledge of good and evil* that is forbidden, because such knowledge is reserved for the gods—but Adam and Eve are condemned for eating it, although they could not have distinguished right from wrong without it. In later years, the right to determine the most serious kinds of error was reserved to a priesthood rather than a deity. Valuephobia is usually strongest in its group form, where the individual impropriety of the view can be hidden behind groupthink, and disguised by a belief that is the duty of the priesthood to identify and burn the witches or heretics who challenge existing standards of value or propriety. The widespread acceptance of the doctrine of value-free science is a groupthink phenomenon, exploiting evaluation anxiety at the expense of rationality, since any scientist can see—once the point is made—the essential role that evaluation plays in every science.

Valuephobia is the extreme form of one kind of evaluation anxiety, a relatively new clinical classification. The first anthology is *The Handbook of Social and Evaluation Anxiety* edited by Harold Leitenberg (Plenum, 1990). Test anxiety and pregame anxiety are some of the best-known cases of evaluation anxiety, occasionally reaching a level of clinical significance but typically representing a reaction with survival value. The social variations of evaluation anxiety range from normal through avoidant personality disorders to the extreme of social phobia (first recognized in the official taxonomy in 1980 (DSM–III–R)). These are said to derive from "fears of rejection, humiliation, criticism, embarrassment, ridicule, failure, and abandonment" (Leitenberg, p. ix). A sign of the early state of the art is that the book's 32 contributors essentially never mention a common and expectable *defense* against evaluation anxiety—that of (antievaluator) hostility and attack—with which experienced evaluators are familiar, nor do they discuss the group version of the phenomenon, nor the fear of *formal* personnel or program evaluations. This is no doubt because the authors rarely encounter these conditions in their patients, who are typically individuals incapacitated by anxiety rather than striking back because of it. Common symptoms of the valuephobic include denial of anxiety (despite evident distress), projection of fault onto the evaluator or potential evaluator (or evaluation system), irrelevant and excessive personal attack on the evaluator, invention or adoption of bizarre rationalizations for dismissal of any possible evaluation outcome, the invocation of professionally outlandish maneuvers to foil the performance or implementation of the evaluation.

Valuephobia is common even among professionals, who have an obligation to evaluation (the **professional imperative**). It is strongly amplified as a group phenomenon, where the group may not include any individually phobic individuals, but the response of the group is phobic, is accepted by the individual members, and governs some of their behavior. This version created and maintained the myth of value-free science and is responsible for many of the more extreme attacks on properly-used testing or course grading, on program evaluation in the interest of accountability, and on the evaluation of college faculty. It is usually in this sense that references are made in the present work to responses as valuephobic—typically the individual is not phobic, but has subscribed to a group view or form of behavior that is phobic—and has the responsibility for so doing.

Etiologically, the knee-jerk defensive strategy of attacking anything that threatens is part of the basis for an aggressive reaction by a valuephobic, and unprofessional in itself. But part of valuephobia

376

goes deeper, into the reason for the unwillingness to face possibly unpleasant facts about oneself even when doing so means large long-run benefits. This phenomenon—related to "denial"—is seen in people who won't go to a doctor or dentist because they don't want to *hear* about imperfections. Valuephobia, or evaluation anxiety that falls some way short of phobia, leads to many abuses in applied evaluation systems, of which the following are to some degree notable: (i) the pathetic guarantee that a personnel evaluation process is to be instituted "only to help, not to criticize" (help cannot be justified unless there are valid reasons to think the helpees are less than perfect, that is, a basis for criticism that in the limit morally requires adverse action); (ii) the substitution of implementation **monitoring** for outcome-based program evaluations; (iii) the refusal of professional associations to use professional standards in their own **accreditation** or enforcement procedures; (iv) pathological efforts to avoid the use of the term "evaluation" in favor of some allegedly less-threatening synonym (such as "assessment"), instead of facing the professional responsibility to do and undergo evaluation; (v) excessive involvement of evaluation staff with program staff (in order "to reduce anxiety" or "to improve implementation" or "to improve relevance"), which predictably produces pablum evaluations; and (via guilt) to the absurd ratio of favorable to unfavorable program evaluations—absurd given what we find out when we do secondary evaluations or meta-evaluations. Evaluators adopting the 'soft models' of evaluation, like **transactional** and some versions of **responsive** evaluation, often congratulate themselves on avoiding phobic reactions; but the secret of this 'success' is of course the removal of threat by removal of teeth, which abandons accountability, responsibility, and a good deal of objectivity.

The clinical status of valuephobia as a U.S. cultural phenomenon is more obvious to a visitor from another country such as England, where very tough criticism in the academy is not taken personally to the degree it is here; and it is in this country that Consumers Union was listed by the Attorney General as a subversive organization and (independently) banned from advertising in newspapers. But the ubiquity of valuephobia is more important than local differences; Socrates was killed for his teaching and application of evaluative skills, and dictators today seem no less inclined to murder their critics than the Greek quasi-democracy. Humility may best be construed not as the avoidance of self-regard but as the encouragement and valuing of criticism of oneself. Such valuing should also be aimed for as the outcome of successful self-treatment for valuephobia. Of course, valuing criticism of oneself should be combined with some capacity to distinguish good from bad criticism. See **General positive bias, Edu-**

cational role, Empiricism, Kill the messenger, Dreyfus case.

VALUES (in evaluation, and in measurement) The values that make evaluations more than mere descriptions can come from a variety of sources. They may be picked up from a credible and well-tried set of standards such as professional standards. They may come from a needs assessment that might show that children become very ill without a particular dietary component (that is, they need it). Or they may come from a logical and pragmatic analysis of the function of something, which leads to conclusions such as "processing speed in a computer is a prima facie virtue" or "the duties of a house surgeon include settling staff disputes". They may even come from a study of wants *and* the absence of ethical impediments to their fulfilllment (for example, in building a better roller-coaster.) This latter kind of value is of course a descriptive value—what *do* people value—rather than the prescriptive kind that appear in the conclusions of evaluative arguments, which specify what people *should* do—sometimes even, should value. (Getting from facts of that kind to evaluative conclusions is discussed in the **Logic of evaluation** entry.) In general, the problem in evaluation is first to identify relevant values, and then to validate (some of) them; see **Illicit values, Inappropriate values**.

In each of these cases, the foundations are factual and the reasoning is logical—nothing is involved that would disgrace a scientist. But something hovers in the background that scientists are embarrassingly incompetent to handle, namely ethics. Without *doing* ethics, however, many evaluations can be validated by just checking for salient ethical considerations that *might* override the nonethical reasoning, as one checks for other sources of possible error.

The values/preferences that sometimes come into the evaluation, as a kind of data, range in visibility from obvious (the results of political ballots) to very inaccessible (attitudes toward job security, women supervisors, censorship of pornography). Most instruments for identifying the more subtle ones are of extremely dubious validity; they are best inferred from behavior. Although that inference is also difficult, at least it begins with the kind of event we are (usually) hoping to influence. Some simulations are so good that they probably elicit true values, especially if not very important ones are involved; but usually behavior in real situations should be used. See **Affect**.

The values of people that are involved with programs are not definitive of the merit of a nonrecreational program, but often form crucial input to the needs assessment, and often affect it indirectly. See Ethics.

VARIABILITY The extent to which the population is spread out over its range, as opposed to concentrated near one or a few places (or modes)—the feature that produces **dispersion.**

VIRTUAL REALITY Computer-created three-dimensional space, experienced using special goggles, headphones, and gloves which immerse the user in the sight, sound, and some aspects of the feel and control of the virtual world. The offspring of a recent marriage of computer-assisted design—Autodesk has been the icebreaker—and simulator technology, although it currently lacks the gravitational acceleration so impressive in the Disneyland spaceship trip, the Mercedes simulator at Unterturkheim, and no doubt in some Air Force training equipment. At the practical end, this makes it possible to let a client stroll and lounge around in a virtual house or office building, operate its solar controls during the simulation of seasons, and so on, and tell the architect what changes to make; a prospective purchaser 2,000 miles away could do the same with virtual versions of available houses and rental units. It allows someone to get experience driving a lunar lander or a road train (the triple trailer 70-wheeler used in the Australian outback) or driving along the main arteries of the brain or the main arms of the galaxy.

Some of its importance to evaluation lies in the opportunity to extend the range of formative feedback into the period before huge investments in construction and manufacturing occur to make real working models, samples, or pilot runs, and in the possibility of using it to create scenarios that can provide critical competitors for consumer reactions. Also important for evaluation purposes is the potential to improve data visualization and presentation substantially, by enhancing the sense of reality in reports and their attempts to convey the 'feel' of an evaluand. As we meld multimedia control technology into virtual reality, we will also be able to convey impressions of how various human candidates, programs, and products would perform on future tasks, based on the integration of performance on simulations with other testing. Some interesting ethical questions will arise.

W

WEIGHT AND SUM (or WEIGHTED-ADDITIVE) The dominant model for complex product evaluation and in particular for the the process of synthesis in evaluation. There are several variants and all can be used descriptively (e.g., to predict how decisions will be made), prescriptively, or evaluatively. We are here concerned with prescriptive uses. In the most common version, the numerical weight and sum (NWS) model, a generic form of Multi-Attribute Utility Analysis, the dimensions of merit are weighted for their relative importance (for example on a 1-3, 1-5, or 1-10 scale) and then points are awarded for the merit of each candidate's performance on each of these valued dimensions, for example, on a 1-5 or 1–100 scale. The products of the weights and the performance scores are calculated and totaled for each candidate, the best candidate being the one with the highest total. Although this is a very convenient process, sometimes approximately correct, and nearly always clarifying, there are many traps in it, some of which do not leave traces, so one can't tell when NWS is giving you the wrong answer. The most obvious problem, which is fixable, is that no set of weights can cover the situation in which a minimum performance on some of the dimensions is essential (e.g., your car must seat four 6-footers). In the NWS/M model (NWS with minima) each of these minimum requirements is checked before any other analysis begins and only the performance above the minima is weighted for the later phase.

The most intransigent problem arises from the fact that no selection of standard scales for rating weights and performance can avoid errors, because the number of criteria is not preassignable. (It typically runs from a dozen to a couple of hundred.) So, either a large number of trivia will swamp crucial factors (to a degree you did not intend) or they will have inadequate total influence, depending on how many factors there are. (Allowing a fixed number of points for the total number of weighting points, a procedure used in *Consumer Reports,* reduces but does not eliminate this problem.) A second major problem arises from interactions between factors (this is best handled by redefining factors, but it takes considerable skill to do this, and the solution is always ad hoc. Third, NWS assumes linearity of utility (points) across the range of performance variables, which is clearly

380

false. (This can be partly handled, but only partly handled, in NWS.) Fourth, although NWS allows many candidates to be compared—and this is useful as a crude first filter—in the end you have to get down to pairwise comparisons to avoid context shifts. (Some details are in *Evaluation News* Vol. 2, No. 1, February 1981, pp. 85-90).

An alternative to NWS has been proposed that handles the above problems: the **qualitative weight and sum** (QWS) approach. This relies on ordinal scaling of importance rather than interval scaling; it is more complex but not esoteric. It is briefly described in an entry under that name. A good background text for the general topic is *Decision Research: A Field Guide* by Carroll and Johnson (Sage, 1990).

WELFARE ECONOMICS The field within economics concerned with developing procedures for the rational social distribution (pricing, etc.) of valuables. It became more or less moribund because it has to, but could not, handle the problem of interpersonal comparisons of utility. There's no way to do that short of making some ethical assumptions, and according to the usual doctrine that was improper (but see Ethics, Utility, and Apportionment).

WHISTLE-BLOWERS There are whistle-blowers who turn others in to promote their own career or for revenge or reward, but there are many others in the annals of the subject who appear to have been motivated by a desire to save the lives of children or nations or to see justice done or to put a stop to corruption. Their reports of their treatment after the hearings that justified their actions and led to the punishment of the wrong-doers are remarkably uniform and extremely significant. The comments of the woman doctor who finally—after going through all the channels—blew the whistle on the attempt to conceal the harmful effects of thalidomide are typical: "When I walked along the corridors of the building," she said, "people I had known for years looked the other way so as not to meet my eyes. When I ate in the cafeteria, mine would often be the only table with empty chairs at it." Loyalty is valued over the lives of children, even loyalty to immoral liars. The test she passed—the test of whether you join the conspiracy or blow the whistle when all else fails—is one faced time and time again by every evaluator who does nontrivial work. Some of their colleagues will make it clear enough how they feel about evaluation in general ("a nonsubject", "based on simple logical errors", "a grandiose attempt to dress up personal prejudices", and so on), and about negative reports in particular. Few solo evaluators survive this pressure for long. One result is what is called here the phenomenon of **general positive bias**; another is the retreat to **pseudo-evaluation**. The best antidote is the use of teams; failing that, strong networking with other evaluators.

WHITEWASH (Suchman) See **Rationalization evaluation**.

WHOLISTIC Alternative spelling of "holistic"; see **Global.**

WHY DENY A conference with the staff of a funding agency, which unsuccessful bidders on an RFP may request and at which they are informed about the reasons why they lost out. One of the consequences of the recent move toward openness. Unfortunately the failure to use salience scoring and other systematic procedures means that reviewer and staff feedback is very difficult to interpret in a useful way.

WILD CARD PROCEDURE An approach to funding designed to handle part of the problem of shared bias in proposal evaluation (especially in the funding of research). The idea is to sequester a small amount of the support available (e.g., 2–5%) to fund ideas with large possible payoffs, even if the probability of success is judged to be small by most of the raters. This can be done in various ways—for example, by allowing everyone on the panel (assume the panel is around 4–9 people) to nominate one applicant for a wild card award, which is granted if one other person will support it (use **apportioning** if this leads to over-budget commitment). Or everyone can rate each application on a 'wild card scale' as well as on the regular scale. The aim is to avoid the present tendency toward exclusion of heresy, especially in tight funding times, given the evidence, based on long experience, that people seen as heretics often lead the way to the big breakthroughs.

WINDOW DRESSING The practice of putting big names on a proposal, though the fine print reveals they will be contributing too little time to share responsibility. Fine to put them on the advisory panel; misleading to list them as staff. See **Quantum of effort.**

WINE TASTING See **Sensory evaluation**.

WIRED A contract or an RFP is said to be "wired" if either through its design and requirements or through an informal agreement between agency staff and a particular contractor it is arranged so that it will go to that contractor. Certainly illegal, and nearly always immoral. The mere fact that the RFP—with intrinsic good reasons—predetermines the contractor, for example, because the problem can in fact only be handled by an outfit with three Cray computers, does not constitute wiring.

WORTH Usually refers to the value to an institution or collective, by contrast with intrinsic value, value by professional standards, or value to an individual consumer (**merit**). For example, when people ask "what something is worth", they are usually referring to *market value*, and market value is a function of the market's (hypothesized) behavior toward it, not of the thing's intrinsic virtues or its virtues for an identifiable individual. The worth of a professor (to an institution) is a function of variables such as the enrollment in her or his classes, grant-getting performance (but see **Personnel evaluation**), relation to the college's mission, role modeling function for prospective/actual women or minority students, prestige for the institution, *as well as* his/her professional merit. Performance at a reasonable level on the latter is a necessary but not sufficient condition for the former. Worth factors which are insufficiently valued in most personnel evaluation include versatility of two varieties—fast learning ability, and large repertoire. Both of them pay off for the institution in terms of cost-savings and flexibility under changing demand. (The research literature suggests they are also the best predictors of job success, so they might justify election to the ranks of merit qualifications, although antithetical to the usual specialist criteria.) The worth of an applicant to the college to which s/he has applied is often ignored as a criterion variable in favor of their probable success there, but it may be a superior criterion or an important supplementary one. For example, one should probably consider the importance of the contribution they might make to the school (e.g., via adding cultural diversity). Cf. **Success**.

X Y Z

ZERO-BASED BUDGETING (ZBB) A system of budgeting in which *all* expenditures have to be justified rather than *additional* expenditures (that is, variations from "level funding"). Temporarily fashionable in Washington in the1970s, its merits for summative evaluation were overwhelming; the practical difficulties are easily handled, but the political squawks from entrenched programs may be harder to manage. The original reference is to Peter Pyrrh's book of this title. See **Apportionment.**

ZONING See **Banding.**

ACRONYMS & ABBREVIATIONS

AA Audit Agency—a division of federal departments that reports directly to the Secretary and does initial audits (cf. **GAO**) that amount to evaluations of programs and contracts, including evaluational ones. Has moved from CPA orientation to much broader approach and often does very competent work (though spread a little thin); still doesn't look at, for example, validity of test instruments used. Cf. **OIG**.

AAHE American Association of Higher Education

AI Artificial intelligence (the field of research not the use of jargon)

ABT Properly, Abt Associates. Large shop with strong evaluation capability; headquartered at Cambridge, Massachusetts

ACT American College Testing

AEA American Evaluation Association

AERA American Educational Research Association

AID Agency for International Development

AIR American Institutes for Research, a Northern California-based contractor with some evaluation capability

ANCOVA Analysis of covariance

ANOVA Analysis of variance

ANPA American Newspaper Publisher's Association

ATI Aptitude-treatment interaction

AV Audiovisual

AVLINE Online audio-visual database maintained by the National Library of Medicine

CAI Computer-assisted instruction

CAL Computer-assisted learning; currently more fashionable than, but essentially the same as CAI

CBO Congressional Budget Office. Provides analysis and evaluation services to Congress, as GAO does for the Executive Branch.

CBT Computer-based training. CAI for rich customers—for example, banks.

CBTE, CBTT Competency-Based Teacher Education, Training

CDC Control Data Corporation; at one point, it was one of the top five computer companies, famous for its support of PLATO, the largest CAI system.

CEDR Center for Evaluation, Development and Research (at Phi Delta Kappa)

CEEB College Entrance Examination Board

CEO Chief Executive Officer; COO for Chief Operating Officer is sometimes used with much the same meaning.

CFE Cost-free evaluation

CIPP Daniel Stufflebeam and Egon Guba's model, which distinguished four types of evaluation: context, input, process, and product—all designed to delineate, obtain, and provide useful information for the decision-maker.

CIRCE Center for Instructional Research and Curriculum Evaluation, University of Illinois, Urbana, Illinois; long-time HQ for Bob Stake

CMHC Community Mental Health Center or Clinic

CMI Computer Managed Instruction; often means that the testing and record-keeping, but not the instruction, is computerized.

CN *Consultant News*, the highly independent newsletter of the management consulting field, run by talented loner Jim Kennedy

COB Close of business (end of working day; proposal deadline)

COO Chief Operating Officer

COPA Council on Post-Secondary Accreditation

CREATE The Center for Research on Educational Accountability and Teacher Evaluation. A federally funded R&D center, located at the Evaluation Center, Western Michigan University, and headed by Daniel Stufflebeam

CRT Criterion-referenced test

CSE Center for the Study of Evaluation (at UCLA)

CSMP Comprehensive School Mathematics Study Group

DBMS Database Management System. Computer software for creating databases

DBTE Duties Based Teacher Evaluation

DEd (properly **ED**) Department of Education (ex-USOE)

DOD Department of Defense

DOE Department of Energy

DRG Division of Research Grants

DRT Domain-referenced test

DSS Decision Support Systems are usually computer-based systems for applying standard decision making techniques like linear programming to, for example, the accounting and inventory problems of the executive.

EA Evaluability assessment (typically of a large program)

ED Education Department

EIR Environmental impact report

EN *Evaluation News,* the original newsletter journal of the Evaluation Network, now *Evaluation Practice,* a refereed journal.

en *evaluation notes,* a professional newsletter on evaluation methodology published by Edgepress for some time

ENet Evaluation Network, a professional association of evaluators now merged into the AEA

EPIE Education Products Information Exchange

ERIC Educational Resources Information Center; a nationwide information network with its base in Washington, DC, with subject-specialized clearinghouses at various locations in the U.S. Available as an online database.

ERS Evaluation Research Society, a professional association of evaluators, now merged into the AEA

ESEA Elementary and Secondary Education Act of 1965

ETS Educational Testing Service; headquartered in Princeton, NJ and with branches in Berkeley and Atlanta.

FDA Food and Drug Administration

FRACHE Federation of Regional Accrediting Commissions of Higher Education

FY Fiscal year

G&A General and administration (expenses, costs)

GAE Goal-achievement evaluation—basically, monitoring

GAO General Accounting Office. The principal semiexternal evaluation agency of the Federal government, now joined by the Offices of the Inspectors General

GBE Goal-based evaluation

GFE Goal-free evaluation

GIGO Garbage in, Garbage Out (from computer programming; see meta-analysis)

GP General-purpose evaluator

GPA Grade point average

GPO Government Printing Office, Washington, DC

GRE Graduate Record Examination

HEW Department of Health, Education and Welfare, subsequently divided into ED and HHS

HHS Department of Health and Human Services

IBM International Business Machines, Inc.

IG Inspector General

IOX Instructional Objectives Exchange, a major contractor

JND just noticeable difference, the 'quantum' of felt or perceived effects

K $1,000 as in "16K for evaluation"

K-12 Kindergarten through high school years (cf. **preK–18**)

K-6 The domain of elementary education

KEC The Key evaluation checklist

KISS Keep It Simple, Stupid

LEA Local education authority (for example, a school district)

LSAT Law School Admission Test

MAS Management Advisory Services; term usually refers to subsidiaries of the Big 8 accounting firms

MBO Management by objectives

MCI Multiple-choice item

MCT Minimum competency testing

MIS Management Information System; often an office (empire) in a large company that is responsible for the computer system. On the small scale, a computerized database combining fiscal, inventory, and performance data.

MMPI Minnesota Multiphasic Personality Inventory; one of the most widely-used of the empirically validated clinical tests.

MOM Modus operandi method

MRI Multiple-rating item

NAEP National Assessment of Educational Progress

NCATE National Council for Accreditation of Teacher Education

NCES National Center for Educational Statistics

NCHCT National Center for Health Care Technology

NIA National Institute on Aging

NICHD National Institute of Child, Health and Human Development

NIE National Institute of Education (in ED)

NIH National Institutes of Health (includes NIMH, NIA, etc.); *or* Not Invented Here (so don't encourage its use because you won't get any credit)

NIJ National Institute of Justice

NIMH National Institute of Mental Health

NSF National Science Foundation

NSSE National Society for the Study of Education, an association and, since 1901, publisher of a yearbook series that distributes via the University of Chicago Press.

NWL Northwest Lab, Portland, Oregon. One of the federal network labs and R&D centers; in early years had much the strongest evaluation tradition (Worthen, Saunders, Smith)

OCR Optical character recognition. A software program that converts input from a scanner into a character stream

OE Office of Education

OERI Office of Educational Research and Improvement, U.S. Department of Education

OHDS Office of Human Development Services

OIG Offices of the Inspectors General; an office which is to be found in 67 or more federal agencies, and whose responsibilities are similar to those of program evaluator. These offices report to the Congress as well as the agency and typically the program.

OJT On-job training

OMB Office of Management and Budget

ONR Office of Naval Research; sponsor of, for example, the first *Encyclopedia of Educational Evaluation*

OPB Office of Planning and Budgeting

OTA Office of Technology Assessment of the U.S. Congress

P&E Planning and Evaluation; a division of HEW/HHS, including regional offices, where it reports directly to Regional Directors. In ED, currently called OPB

PBTE Performance based teacher education

PDK Phi Delta Kappa, the influential and quality-oriented educational honorary society that publishes *The Kappan*

PEC Product evaluation checklist

PERT Program Evaluation and Review Technique

PHS Public Health Service

PLATO The largest CAI project ever; the original headquarters were at the University of Illinois/Champaign. Mostly NSF funded in development phase, then CDC-controlled.

PPBS Program Planning and Budgeting System

PreK–18 From pre-kindergarten through the doctorate; the whole range of education

PSI Personalized System of Instruction (a.k.a. The Keller Plan)

PT Programmed text

RAND Santa Monica-based contract research and evaluation and policy analysis outfit. Originally, a U.S. Air-Force 'creature' (civilian subsidiary), set up because they couldn't get enough specialized talent from within the ranks—the name came from Research ANd Development. Now an independent nonprofit, though still does some work for USAF.

RBTE Research-based teacher evaluation

RFP Request for proposal

RN Registered nurse

SAT Scholastic Aptitude Test. Widely used for collect admissions.

SDC Systems Development Corporation in Santa Monica; another large shop like RAND with substantial evaluation capability.

SEA State education authority

SEP School Evaluation Profile, invented to provide a graphic representation of school health as seven bars on a bar chart

SES Socio-economic status

SMERC San Mateo Educational Resources Center—an information center that housed numerous collections of educational materials to meet the information needs of educators in several states surrounding California. Most collections are "in-house" but SMERC also has access to ERIC files. SMERC is located in Redwood City, California, and was notable for some years as a center for educational courseware evaluation.

SMSG School Mathematics Study Group. One of the earliest and most prolific of the federal curriculum reform efforts.

SRI Originally Stanford Research Institute; in Menlo Park, California; once part-owned by Stanford University, now autonomous. Large shop which does some evaluation.

TA Technology assessment; or, technical assistance

TAT Thematic Apperception Test

TCITY Twin Cities Institute for Talented Youth. Site of the first advocate-adversary evaluation (Stake and Denny)

USAF United States Air Force. Heavy (and pretty competent) R&D commitment, like the Navy, and unlike the Army.

USDA United States Department of Agriculture

USOE United States Office of Education, now ED or DEd (Department of Education)

WICHE Western Interstate Clearinghouse on Higher Education

ABOUT THE AUTHOR

MICHAEL SCRIVEN took degrees in mathematics and mathematical logic from the University of Melbourne, obtained his doctorate in philosophy at Oxford and has taught in the US and Australia, in departments of mathematics, philosophy, history and philosophy of science, psychology, and education, including twelve years at the University of California/Berkeley. He spent shorter periods as a visiting Fellow at the Center for Advanced Study in the Behavioral Sciences (Palo Alto); the Center for Advanced Study in Theoretical Psychology (Edmonton); the Educational Testing Service (Princeton); the Center for the Study of Democratic Institutions, and as a Whitehead Fellow at Harvard University. His 280 publications are in the fields of his appointments and in technology studies, computer studies, and evaluation. He is currently professor and director of the Evaluation Institute at the Pacific Graduate School of Psychology in Palo Alto, and runs a project on teacher evaluation for the federal R&D Center on Educational Accountability at Western Michigan.